STUDIES IN BAPTIST HISTORY /

The British Nation is Our Nation:
The BACSANZ Baptist Press and the
South African War, 1899-1902

International Baptist Studies

STUDIES IN BAPTIST HISTORY AND THOUGHT

Series Editors

Curtis W. Freeman   Duke University, North Carolina, USA
Stephen R. Holmes   King's College, London, England
Elizabeth Newman   Baptist Theological Seminary at Richmond,
                         Virginia, USA
Philip E. Thompson   North American Baptist Seminary, Sioux Falls,
                         South Dakota, USA

Series Consultants

D.W. Bebbington   University of Stirling, Stirling, Scotland
Paul S. Fiddes   Regent's Park College, Oxford, England
Stanley E. Porter   McMaster Divinity College, Hamilton, Ontario,
                         Canada

The British Nation is Our Nation: The BACSANZ Baptist Press and the South African War, 1899-1902

International Baptist Studies

Gordon L. Heath

First published 2017 by Paternoster

Paternoster is an imprint of Authentic Media
PO Box 6326, Bletchley, Milton Keynes, MK1 9GG

authenticmedia.co.uk

British Library Cataloguing in Publication Data
A catalogue record for this book is available from the British Library

ISBN 978-1-84227-936-6

Printed and bound by Lightning Source

Series Preface

Baptists form one of the largest Christian communities in the world, and while they hold the historic faith in common with other mainstream Christian traditions, they nevertheless have important insights which they can offer to the worldwide church. Studies in Baptist History and Thought will be one means towards this end. It is an international series of academic studies which includes original monographs, revised dissertations, collections of essays and conference papers, and aims to cover any aspect of Baptist history and thought. While not all the authors are themselves Baptists, they nevertheless share an interest in relating Baptist history and thought to the other branches of the Christian church and to the wider life of the world.

  The series includes studies in various aspects of Baptist history from the seventeenth century down to the present day, including biographical works, and Baptist thought is understood as covering the subject-matter of theology (including interdisciplinary studies embracing biblical studies, philosophy, sociology, practical theology, liturgy and women's studies). The diverse streams of Baptist life throughout the world are all within the scope of these volumes.

  The series editors and consultants believe that the academic disciplines of history and theology are of vital importance to the spiritual vitality of the churches of the Baptist faith and order. The series sets out to discuss, examine and explore the many dimensions of their tradition and so to contribute to their on-going intellectual vigour.

  A brief word of explanation is due for the series identifier on the front cover. The fountains, taken from heraldry, represent the Baptist distinctive of believer's baptism and, at the same time, the source of the water of life. There are three of them because they symbolize the Trinitarian basis of Baptist life and faith. Those who are redeemed by the Lamb, the book of Revelation reminds us, will be led to 'fountains of living waters' (Rev. 7.17).

My Baptist grandfather Leslie, from whom I received my middle name, was born in England at the zenith of the British Empire. The prospect of a better future motivated him to leave the metropole and migrate to the periphery — the Dominion of Canada. I dedicate this book to him.

Contents

Acknowledgements

This project began with a serendipitous discovery in the Canadian Baptist Archives (Hamilton, Canada). As I was browsing the shelves I found that the archives had in its collection a number of decades of the *South African Baptist*, with a complete run from the South African War years. Up to that point I had focused solely on Canadian Protestants and the war, but reading the response of Baptists in the *South African Baptist* got me thinking beyond the borders of Canada and across the oceans to how denominations in different parts of the empire experienced the conflict. Soon after my discovery I applied for a Lilly Research Grant for travel to Britain and Australia to gain access to other Baptist papers. The staff at Lilly provided the funds to travel during my research leave from McMaster Divinity College. I am thankful to both organizations for making the financing and time for research possible.

Funding for a number of conference presentations of my research findings was provided by grants. Both the Social Sciences and Humanities Research Council (SSHRC) and McMaster Arts Research Board provided travel grants, and for those I am thankful.

This work has drawn from a number of different archives. Matt Lowe and Adam McCulloch at the Canadian Baptist Archives have provided important assistance. Pat Townsend at the Baptist archives at Acadia (Wolfville, Canada) has also been a much-appreciated source of expertise and aid. The archivists at the Baptist archives at Regent's Park College (Oxford, UK), Baptist Union of Victoria archives at Whitley College (Melbourne, Australia), and the New South Wales archives at Morling College (Sydney, Australia) were very flexible and helpful when I swooped in and needed to get research done in a hurry (or when I emailed later for material I had missed). Emily Burgoyne at Regent's Park deserves special mention for her quick and helpful responses to my requests. A particular word of thanks to Ken Manley for his assistance and hospitality during my trip to Australia - travel to a country on the other side of the world is certainly easier when one has a friendly contact who models professional and Christian collegiality. It was a pleasure to meet Robert (Bob) Linder at Morling College: this cross-border friendship has blossomed into the development of joint research projects.

Acknowledgements

David Parker (*Queensland Baptist*) and Martin Sutherland (*New Zealand Baptist*) were kind enough to send me digital copies of Baptist newspapers that I would have otherwise been unable to access.

Thanks to James Robertson (now Dr. Robertson) and Sid Sudiacal, two TAs who have worked on sources and the manuscript. They have patiently endured my idiosyncrasies.

Many scholars have provided input into the project in various ways - a reminder to me of the influence a guild can have on one's development and production as a scholar. The following people have been particularly helpful in providing hospitality, direction, encouragement, overall critical comments and/or input in the formation of specific chapters: David Bebbington, Anthony Cross, Ian Randall, John Briggs, Paul Fiddes, Laurie Guy, Ken Manley, Carman Miller, Robert Linder, Stuart Piggin, and Marita Munro.

I appreciate the staff at Paternoster responding so professionally and favorably to my initial inquiries regarding publication of the manuscript. Every interaction since that time has been helpful, courteous, and formative for the development of the book.

Finally, I would like to thank my wife Virginia, and children Joshua and Natasha, for support throughout a project that frequently took me away from home (and kept me distracted many days when I was at home). Their support was critical to the completion of this project.

Introduction

"The sympathy for the Boers because of their alleged religious character, which has existed in some quarters is really without foundation. They are not the religious people some suppose them.... War with them will be greatly regretted, because it would be at great cost of life and treasure, but the course of the Boers may make war inevitable." *Religious Intelligencer*, 2 August 1899, 4.

"War is barbarous, un-Christian, an appeal to brute force, and the 'sum of all the villanies.' We can only determine whether of the two who make the quarrel is the stronger. In this instance, if a remedy – which we deny – war would be more than the evil to be remedied. But, come what may, the benediction will be with those who seek after the things which make for peace. 'Blessed are the peacemakers, for they shall be called the sons of God.'" "Why Not Arbitrate?" *Baptist Times and Freeman*, 15 September 1899, 609.

Before the apocalyptic Great War (1914-1918) devastated a generation and eclipsed any previous war's significance, the South African War (1899-1902)[1] had been the major war of recent memory. At the turn of the century reports of diplomacy, intrigue, heroism, and far-flung imperial battles captured the imagination and fuelled the passions of supporters as well as critics of empire. Newspapers struggled to keep up with the "huge appetite" for war news.[2] The new technology of undersea cables allowed war correspondents to give relatively immediate first-hand accounts of their observations. Jingoistic newspapers contributed to the imperial zeal that reached a feverish pitch during the "longest, costliest, bloodiest and most humiliating war fought by Britain between 1815-1914,"[3] and the war dominated the domestic politics and foreign policy of the British, Australian, Canadian, South African and New Zealand (BACSANZ)[4] governments at the turn of the century.

Throughout the summer of 1899 tensions had risen between Britain and the two Boer republics. Newspaper reports from British authorities and eyewitnesses in Africa indicated that war seemed probable. BACSANZ Baptist papers provided details and commentary on the looming crisis, and the range of commentary often reflected wider societal unease – especially in Britain – over the

---

[1] Also called the Boer War, Anglo-Boer War, or the Second Anglo-Boer War (the First Anglo-Boer War was 1880-1881). Afrikaans call the war *Vrijheidsoorlog* ("freedom wars").
[2] Denis Judd and Keith Surridge, *The Boer War* (London: John Murray, 2002), 251.
[3] Iain R. Smith, "The Boer War," *History Today* 34 (May 1984): 47.
[4] BACSANZ will be used to shorten the cumbersome listing of Britain, Australia, Canada, South Africa and New Zealand.

justice of the imperial cause. There were expressions of sympathy for the cause of the British or the plight of the Boers, and articles condemning all sides.

Canadian Baptists in Ontario and Quebec read about the looming war in the *Canadian Baptist*. British and Canadian war preparations were briefly outlined, and when war seemed inevitable, the front-page editorial lamented what might have been.[5] The editorial decried the emigration of millions of English, Scot and Irish to the United States instead of to South Africa where they could have offset the numerous and potentially disloyal Boer inhabitants within British territory. However, despite failures of British emigration policy, and the obvious war preparations on both sides, a "slight chance" for peace was still considered a possibility due to the efforts of a those in England working for peace. The *Religious Intelligencer* of New Brunswick also monitored the brewing crisis in South Africa. Like its Baptist counterpart in central Canada, the *Intelligencer* defended the British cause, and clearly and passionately placed the blame for the conflict on the Boers:

> The sympathy for the Boers because of their alleged religious character, which has existed in some quarters is really without foundation. They are not the religious people some suppose them. It is shown that they left the Cape because they would not acquiesce in the abolition of slavery. They slaughtered the Zulus of Natal, and as they crossed Vaal they actually exterminated the natives. Their brethren accepted British civilization. The Orange Free State has no difficulty and gets along well with the British. But when an obstinate people stand directly in the way of civilization, plunder the miners and refuse every offer for fair treatment, they can have very little sympathy. The Boers are plundering and oppressing the miners because they happen to be in territory they claim, over which Great Britain, however, claims suzerainty. War with them will be greatly regretted, because it would be at great cost of life and treasure, but the course of the Boers may make war inevitable.[6]

The *Messenger and Visitor*, another Maritime Baptist publication, also closely followed the course of events in South Africa and reported regularly on the growing crisis throughout the summer and early fall.[7] The publication expressed some sympathy for the Boers and their conflict with Britain;[8] however, by October, when war seemed to be inevitable, the editorial position of the

---

[5] *Canadian Baptist*, 5 October 1899, 638; *Canadian Baptist*, 12 October 1899, 639.

[6] *Religious Intelligencer*, 2 August 1899, 4.

[7] See "The Transvaal," *Messenger and Visitor*, 26 July 1899, 1; "The Transvaal Resolution," *Messenger and Visitor*, 9 August 1899, 1; "A Firm Position," *Messenger and Visitor*, 9 August 1899, 1; "The Transvaal Situation," *Messenger and Visitor*, 16 August 1899, 1; "President Kruger," *Messenger and Visitor*, 23 August 1899, 1; "South Africa," *Messenger and Visitor*, 27 September 1899, 1; "The Orange Free State," *Messenger and Visitor*, 4 October 1899, 1; "Johannesburg," *Messenger and Visitor*, 4 October 1899, 1.

[8] See Barry Moody, "Boers and Baptists: Maritime Canadians View the War in South Africa," unpublished paper. This sympathy can most readily be seen in its editorial "Inglorious War," *Messenger and Visitor*, 6 September 1899, 1.

Messenger and Visitor was that the Boers had conducted their negotiations in a "shifty and impractical" way.[9] Consequently, while its conduct was not impeccable, Great Britain was considered "not to blame" for the tensions.[10]

In the weeks before the war, the *New Zealand Baptist* included commentary on the uncertainty surrounding South Africa. The tenor of the paper was that Britain had done all it could to settle the dispute peacefully, and had, as a result, "cast the onus of responsibility upon her opponent."[11]

In Australia, the *Queensland Baptist* made no mention of the rising tensions, but the *Southern Baptist* weighed in on the crisis.[12] Commentary in June noted that war was imminent, Kruger's "infatuated policy" was to blame, and that God's intervention was necessary to prevent "a calamity" in South Africa.[13] Hope was expressed in early August that the difficulties could be settled without bloodshed, and the presence and conduct of President Kruger at the recent Baptist meetings in Pretoria provided a positive impression of a man who appeared to be a "God-fearing" Christian.[14] There was even sympathy expressed for Kruger and the Boers due to the "dark scheming of wealthy men" on the British side who were after, among other things, gold.[15] As expectations for a peaceful resolution faded, there was no sign of jingoism in the paper. In fact, war was deemed to be a "dreadful remedy" and "dire arbiter,"[16] a horrible work that needed to be avoided,[17] and both sides were culpable:

> War may have begun in Africa before this appears in print. We hope not, but at the present both parties seem ready to rush into the conflict. It is a sad affair, and we fail to see what honour England can gain when it is all over. Kruger is a professed, we hope a true, Christian, though somewhat of a fanatic. He is in the wrong, but is there no way of putting him right expect by the slaughter of men? As for the eagerness of Australians to join the English ranks, we wish they were as ready to go into Africa with the gospel.[18]

Sympathy was especially expressed towards their "brethren" in South Africa who would experience the horrors of the war with consequences "too shocking to contemplate."[19]

---

[9] "The Transvaal Bluff," *Messenger and Visitor*, 11 October 1899, 1.

[10] "The Transvaal Bluff," *Messenger and Visitor*, 11 October 1899, 1.

[11] "Let Loose the Dogs of War." *New Zealand Baptist*, October 1899, 153.

[12] No extant copies of the 1899 *Baptist* could be found, so it remains to be seen whether or not it provided commentary on pre-war tensions.

[13] "A Boer War," *Southern Baptist*, 29 June 1899, 134.

[14] "The Transvaal Difficulty," *Southern Baptist*, 3 August 1899, 157.

[15] "The Transvaal Difficulty," *Southern Baptist*, 3 August 1899, 157; "The Difficulties Connected," *Southern Baptist*, 17 August 1899, 170.

[16] "As We Write," *Southern Baptist*, 12 October 1899, 218.

[17] "Our Two Eyes and Our Two Ears," *Southern Baptist*, 28 September 1899, 205.

[18] "We May Have Begun," *Southern Baptist*, 12 October 1899, 217. An earlier edition blamed the war on "Boer stupidity." See "The Transvaal," *Southern Baptist*, 2 September 1899, 206.

[19] "Our Intensest [sic] Sympathies," *Southern Baptist*, 12 October 1899, 217.

The British *Baptist Times and Freeman* was even less supportive of Britain's cause, reflecting the opposition to the war among British nonconformists. An article in July by John Clifford provided a scathing critique of the pro-war position.[20] Speaking for what he called the "Nonconformist conscience," Clifford threatened the government with opposition to a declaration of war that would make an "exceedingly uncomfortable time for the Government." He claimed that there were three parties that promoted the war, the "lust for revenge party" (to redress the embarrassing defeat of Majuba[21]), the "party of gold" (to drain the Transvaal of its wealth) and the "jingoistic party" (to grow the empire). The alleged cause for war – the franchise for the Outlanders – was, for Clifford, nothing but a hypocritical farce because women in Britain did not have the vote and the House of Lords ruled without being elected. By comparison, he considered the Outlander's "grievances [to be] a mere flea-bite" to the British having to bear with "the obstinacy and stupidity of the House of Lords." In the weeks that followed, the paper provided details of the ongoing negotiations, never diverting from its position that peace was desirable and the pressures of the jingoes were to be resisted.[22] It printed a resolution of the Welsh Baptist Union that called upon the powers to settle their dispute by diplomacy or arbitration,[23] and when war seemed imminent it encouraged arbitration and opposed war as a means to settle the dispute. It read:

> War is barbarous, un-Christian, an appeal to brute force, and the "sum of all the villanies." We can only determine whether of the two who make the quarrel is the stronger. In this instance, if a remedy – which we deny – war would be more than the evil to be remedied. But, come what may, the benediction will be with those who seek after the things which make for peace. "Blessed are the peacemakers, for they shall be called the sons of God."[24]

---

[20] John Clifford, "The Transvaal Crisis," *Baptist Times and Freeman*, 14 July 1899, 469-470.

[21] Majuba was a humiliating defeat inflicted on the British by the Boers in the First Boer War, 1881.

[22] "Good News from the Transvaal," *Baptist Times and Freeman*, 21 July 1899, 481; F.A.J., "Empire and Fame," *Baptist Times and Freeman*, 28 July 1899, 506; "Parliament and the Transvaal Crisis," *Baptist Times and Freeman*, 4 August 1899, 513; "The Transvaal Troubles," *Baptist Times and Freeman*, 4 August 1899, 518; "Britishers and Boers," *Baptist Times and Freeman*, 18 August 1899, 558; "Complication," *Baptist Times and Freeman*, 18 August 1899, 558; "The Transvaal Crisis," *Baptist Times and Freeman*, 1 September 1899, 577; Thomas Comber, "The Transvaal Crisis," *Baptist Times and Freeman*, 1 September 1899, 590; "Mr. Asquith on the Transvaal Crisis," *Baptist Times and Freeman*, 8 September 1899, 593; "Mr. John Morley's Watchword – 'Patience'," *Baptist Times and Freeman*, 8 September 1899, 593; "Peace!" *Baptist Times and Freeman*, 22 September 1899, 637.

[23] "The Transvaal Crisis," *Baptist Times and Freeman*, 8 September 1899, 598.

[24] "Why Not Arbitrate?" *Baptist Times and Freeman*, 15 September 1899, 609.

At this early stage of the conflict, the British *Baptist Times and Freeman's* stance against the war was already radically different from most of its colonial counterparts.

The state of affairs of Baptists in South Africa was unique because they were in the very theatre of the potential conflict. What made their circumstances even more exceptional was the fact that their May 1899 Assembly meeting had taken place in the heart of Boer territory before tensions had begun to escalate. Their meeting was held in Pretoria in the Transvaal, and President Kruger had actually addressed their meeting.[25] The cordial feelings expressed at that assembly had raised hopes as to the possibility of long-term peace between the Boers and the British: "there can be no doubt that such an event was important: it goes far to alleviate the misunderstandings and to strengthen all the harmonizing influences that may exist between the people, [sic] of South Africa."[26] But over the summer months it became clear that the trajectory was not towards a peaceful settlement of differences. The September issue noted the uncertainty surrounding the political situation, and declared that the paper would avoid the partisan approach of other papers and do what Christians needed to do it times of crisis – pray and trust in God's providence: "We follow the policy that is always open to Christian men, without compromising patriotism, in every crisis of our imperial relations with others – to sue Heaven for peace, and pray against war with all our might....We are in the hands of that All-Wise will and power at all times."[27] Besides a brief mention of Chamberlain's view of the strategic importance of South Africa, and the printing of Kipling's "The White Man's Burden," there were no references to rising tensions in the October issue.[28]

The hopes for peace were shattered by the Boer's pre-emptive strike, and on 11 October 1899 the British empire was officially at war in South Africa against the Transvaal Republic and the Orange Free State. Once war was declared, the Baptist press in four continents provided regular coverage of the war. The Australian *Southern Baptist* followed the conflict with intense interest. Despite acknowledging the abilities of their "strong and brave" adversary, the paper made it clear where its sympathies lay.[29] In articles such as "What the Boer War is About," readers were presented with arguments that defended the justice of the imperial cause.[30] Another Australian paper, the *Queensland Baptist*, was initially hesitant to pronounce on the justice of the cause, but after a few months of war declared that when the "calls for assistance [from Britain] comes, there must be no

---

[25] "Report of the Baptist Union Congress at Pretoria," *South African Baptist*, May 1899, 150-167.
[26] "To the Work," *South African Baptist*, June 1899, 173.
[27] "Kept in Peace," *South African Baptist*, September 1899, 21-22.
[28] Rudyard Kipling, "The White Man's Burden," *South African Baptist*, October 1899, 38; "News by Mail," *South African Baptist*, October 1899, 47.
[29] "Victorian," *Southern Baptist*, 18 January 1900, 14.
[30] "What the Boer War is About," *Southern Baptist*, 18 January 1900, 15.

hesitation in responding."[31] In the days before the conflict began, the *New Zealand Baptist* declared that the British had done all that they could to avoid war. Consequently, had "Briton and Boer fought two months ago, the world would have sided in sympathy with the Boer. If now they fight, the world will regard the defeat of the South Africans as a fitting punishment for unpardonable obstinacy."[32] Not surprisingly, the *South African Baptist* lamented the devastation caused by the war. The churches had been hit hard by the war that had engulfed their region: "Our congregations have been scattered, our ministers have been driven from their homes, and probably every single Church in the country has suffered great financial loss."[33] The British *Baptist Times and Freeman* criticized the machinations of Cecil Rhodes and Joseph Chamberlain, as well as the zeal of the "jingoes," that made "peace impossible and war inevitable."[34] Nevertheless, due to humanitarian concerns, the paper wished for a speedy British victory. The *Canadian Baptist* declared that the Boers were to blame for the war, for it had been the Boer ultimatum that "cut short the negotiations for a peaceful settlement."[35]

Such commentary in the Baptist press provides evidence that late-nineteenth century BACSANZ Baptists in the metropole and peripheries enthusiastically identified with Britain and its empire, and understood their fortunes to be inextricably bound together. One New Zealand Baptist expressed well this notion when he declared: "[T]he British nation is our nation; we are a living part of that Empire, and they and we - Britain and New Zealand - must rise *or fall* together."[36] Even those who were opposed to the war were often enamored by popular notions of empire and hoped for a British victory, and, despite some misgivings and criticisms, there were shared assumptions about the imperial identity and purpose that were in a symbiotic relationship with evangelical identity and purpose. The central contention of this book is that BACSANZ Baptist imperialism in the metropole and peripheries contributed to both a global and regional identity, as well as a common purpose. That imperial identity in no way undermined denominational distinctiveness, for Baptist and imperial identity and purpose were fused. The shared imperialism of the metropole and peripheries was also contextualized and shaped by domestic factors, so much so that imperialism was a particular form of nationalism for Baptists in Canada, Australia, New Zealand and South Africa. Of particular interest in this research is how that the fusion of Baptist identity and purpose with popular imperialism

---

[31] "The Boer War," *Queensland Baptist*, November 1899, 151; "Another Contingent from Queensland," *Queensland Baptist*, January 1900, 2.
[32] "Let Loose the Dogs of War," *New Zealand Baptist*, October 1899, 154.
[33] "A Point of Honour," *South African Baptist*, 1 September 1900, 125.
[34] "The Transvaal War," *Baptist Times and Freeman*, 10 November 1899, 769.
[35] "War With the Boers," *Canadian Baptist*, 19 October 1899, 8.
[36] S.R. Ingold, "The War in South Africa: The Christian's Proper Attitude Regarding It," *New Zealand Baptist*, April 1900, 61-62.

was nurtured by the international network of Baptist newspapers. The international network of Baptist papers nurtured not only denominational fidelity but also imperial loyalties. In a very tangible way, the Baptist press within the empire played an important part in the building of a global, denominational, evangelical, and imperial identity and bond that transcended regional and national identities. At the same time, various newspapers were active in the nation-building role that attempted to shape political opinions and forge what was deemed to be an acceptable Christian nation and a patriotic commitment to their particular national or regional identity.

While the British background of most BACSANZ Baptists meant that Baptists in the peripheries shared much in common, their social location in uniquely diverse contexts in different hemispheres of the globe contributed to quite dissimilar contexts for life and ministry. The Baptist experience of winter was different in Canada from that in the South African veldt. Baptists in Britain may have travelled on the same side of the road as those in Australia, but the vast expanses of Australia differed dramatically from the confined cities and landscape of Britain. While Baptists in Canada, South Africa, New Zealand and Australia all had to deal with what to do with indigenous peoples, Baptists in Britain had no such national problem.[37] By 1899, Canadian Baptists had belonged for a quarter century to a new political identity called the Dominion of Canada, Australian Baptists in the six colonies were preparing for the new Commonwealth of Australia (formed in 1901), and New Zealand and South African Baptists were still members of British colonies. Despite these and many other differences related to the particular religious, national and geopolitical milieu of each denomination, there were elements shared by Baptists that transcended these temporal identities and realities.

A number of recent works on evangelicals have identified the commonalities of the global evangelical experience. One example is the recent multi-volume series on evangelicalism by InterVarsity Press. In the opening volume, *The Rise of Evangelicalism*, Mark Noll notes that the danger in a global history of evangelicalism is that it confuses or misses particular national histories. He goes on to say, however, that a global history of evangelicalism is still needed for at least two reasons.[38] First, a global history "recognizes the sometimes neglected historical reality that the significant evangelical movements in one place have almost always been linked to evangelical movements in other places." Second, that evangelicalism has grown far beyond the "narrow geographical confines of Britain and North America." Another example is Mark Hutchison and John Wolfe's *A Short History of Global Evangelicalism* that identifies generic and

---

[37] Pearson argues that the "presence of aboriginal peoples with distinct juridical and political statutes" was a primary difference between Britain and the colonies. See David Pearson, "Theorizing Citizenship in British Settler Societies," *Ethnic and Racial Studies* 25, no. 6 (November 2002): 989-1012.

[38] Mark Noll, *The Rise of Evangelicalism: The Age of Edward, Whitefield and the Wesleys* (Downers Grove: IVP. 2003), 22.

organic connections among the evangelical community, as well as particulari-
ties.[39] This work on BACSANZ Baptists shares the concern for a global history
and contributes to the growing research on world-wide evangelicalism, identifying universal imperial convictions as well as particularized viewpoints of
Baptists shaped by regional identity and loyalties.

This book also builds on the conclusion of David Bebbington in regards to
his observation that "[p]eople are moulded by their circumstances and consequently the Christian community is swayed by its setting."[40] Bebbington has
shown how British evangelicals often mirrored popular culture, and were very
much influenced by the "high culture" of the Enlightenment and Romanticism.
Bebbington asks: "How have cultural attitudes shaped the expression of the
Christian gospel in Britain?"[41] This research narrows the focus of his question
to that of the influence of imperialism, and expands the scope of his question
from merely examining British evangelicals to adding Canadians, Australians,
South Africans and New Zealanders. Baptists were firmly embedded within
their culture, and the displays of imperialism indicate significant support for
popular imperialism. The degree to which they supported popular expressions
of imperialism indicates an affinity with the "masses" that suggests a closing of
the gulf between evangelicals and the wider culture.[42]

Not surprisingly, there were differences among evangelicals (and between
Baptists). For instance, Sam Reimer has demonstrated that while there may be
shared assumptions and a common subculture among American and Canadian
evangelicals, significant national and regional differences remain.[43] Elizabeth
Mancke reinforces Reimer's conclusions, for she demonstrates how the impact of
local government policy on political loyalties and identity contributed to important differences between groups that had common origins.[44] This study of
Baptists and empire provides a vivid illustration of Reimer's and Mancke's
point – for BACSANZ Baptist imperialism was shaped by domestic and regional concerns. Nevertheless, despite intense regional and national pressures,
in the metropole and peripheries there were shared ideals and attitudes when it
came to Baptists and imperialism.

---

[39] Mark Hutchinson and John Wolffe, *A Short History of Global Evangelicalism* (Cambridge: Cambridge University Press, 2012)

[40] David Bebbington, "Evangelicalism and British Culture," *Perichoresis* 6, no. 2
(2008): 131.

[41] Bebbington, "Evangelicalism and British Culture," 132.

[42] Bebbington minimizes the affinity of evangelicals and popular culture, and claims that
the greatest influence on evangelicals was high culture (intellectual movements such as
the Enlightenment). See Bebbington, "Evangelicalism and British Culture," 153.

[43] Sam Reimer, *Evangelicals and the Continental Divide: The Conservative Protestant
Subculture in Canada and the United States* (Montreal: McGill-Queen's University
Press, 2003).

[44] Elizabeth Mancke, *The Fault Lines of Empire: Political Differentiation in Massachusetts and Nova Scotia, ca.1760-1830* (New York: Routledge, 2005).

As one would expect, a global history of Baptists identifies commonalities among Baptists in different nations. For instance, H. Leon McBeth noted that Baptists in different parts of the empire shared "common threads" that united their work.[45] What he had in mind was a mutual theology of Baptist distinctives (eg. believer's baptism, congregational government, religious freedom) and common struggles (eg. shortage of pastors and finances, minority status, theological battles). A number of recent global histories recognize that despite the reality of common Baptist practices that most often mark Baptist life and thought, there are often important differences. As Bill Leonard argues, "amid certain distinctives, Baptist identity is configured in a variety of ways by groups, subgroups, and individuals who claim the Baptist name."[46] While the emphasis on the unity and diversity of the global Baptist family is helpful and needed, what has been overlooked is an identification and analysis of imperialism among Baptists in the British Empire. More specifically, what McBeth or others overlook is that there was another thread that united Baptists in the various hemispheres: a commitment to the ideals and reality of imperialism. McBeth and Leonard allude to it when they lump together Baptists in Canada, Australia, New Zealand and South Africa in their analysis of Baptists in "Greater Britain." Nevertheless, the shared identity and assumptions that came with living in "Greater Britain," a distinctly imperial community, is not explored. Bebbington's recent global history of Baptists does place the global communion of Baptists in an imperial context, and suggests that Baptists within the empire were often amenable to its benefits, but his focus on imperialism is secondary.[47] Robert E. Johnson's introduction to the global Baptist community is even more explicit regarding Baptist life and growth in the British Empire, but he pays little attention to the imperial assumptions among adherents of that global community.[48]

BACSANZ Baptists had much in common as members of the British Empire. This work is a fusion of studies produced by Bebbington, Noll, Hutchinson, and Wolffe that acknowledge commonalities among the global evangelical (and Baptist) community with those such as Armitage or Douglas Cole that argue for the reality of a global imperial identity that transcended national boundaries. Reacting to Carl Berger's focus on national imperial identities, Cole sought to identify the impact of imperial identity on various parts of the empire, and argued that there was a shared global Britannic nationalism in the peripheries. His concern was that those such as Berger who focus on national identity "tend to omit the shared ideas, assumptions, and ideals that would unite certain Australians, Canadians, New Zealanders, Britons, and South Africans to the extent that they

---

[45] H. Leon McBeth, *The Baptist Heritage* (Nashville: Broadman Press, 1987), 322.
[46] Bill J. Leonard, *Baptist Ways: A History* (Valley Forge: Judson Press, 2003), xiii.
[47] David Bebbington, *Baptists Through the Centuries: A History of a Global People* (Waco: Baylor University Press, 2010), ch.13.
[48] Robert E. Johnson, *A Global Introduction to Baptist Churches* (Cambridge: Cambridge University Press, 2010).

would collectively label themselves as imperialists and jointly collaborate in the realization of common aims."[49] In a similar fashion, Terry Cook writes that for some imperialists like George R. Parkin, there was no distinct nationalism outside of the Britannic whole.[50] Taking Cole's and Cook's conclusion as a starting point, this research identifies the "shared ideas, assumptions, and ideals" among BACSANZ Baptists that reflected their imperial zeal and their common aims.

More recent scholarship has echoed Cole's and Cook's conclusions regarding the grander imperial identity within the disparate regions of the empire, but have also noted that the imperial idea in the various colonies was far from homogeneous; rather than uniform it was imagined, elastic and contested, often meaning "different things to different people."[51] There were also contextual differences shaped by geography, military strategy or domestic politics. J.G.A. Pocock emphasizes the writing of history from the periphery "with a minimum reference to 'the Commonwealth experience' and with none at all to the internal development of any other 'British' society."[52] While there is merit to the claim that each colony had its own particularized historical evolution, the difficulty with Pocock's suggestion is that Baptists in the peripheries would not have recognized any history written of their experience that did not place British identity and history at the forefront of the Baptist story. Baptists in Canada, Australia, New Zealand and South Africa understood their individual and collective history as an integral part of British history, rooted not just in patterns of migration but also in shared ideological convictions. David Armitage's *The Ideological Origins of the British Empire* is a helpful reminder of the breadth and power of those ideological convictions to unite disparate parts of the empire.[53]

It is important to observe that imperialism among Baptists in the empire was not deemed to be necessarily at odds with two important loyalties. One loyalty related to national or regional identity. Barbara R. Penny has identified the fusion of nationalism and imperialism in Australia – they were not considered to be mutually exclusive.[54] Berger's conclusions regarding imperialism in Canada are remarkably similar. He explores many facets of imperialism in Canadian culture at the turn of the century and understands the imperial impulse in Cana-

---

[49] Douglas L. Cole, "Canada's 'Nationalistic' Imperialists," *Journal of Canadian Studies* 5 (August 1970): 44-49.

[50] Terry Cook, "George R. Parkin and the Concept of Britannic Idealism," *Journal of Canadian Studies* 10 (August 1975), 15-31.

[51] Duncan Bell, *The Idea of Greater Britain: Empire and the Future of World Order, 1860-1900* (Princeton: Princeton University Press, 2007), 7. See also Hilary M. Carey, *Empires of Religion* (Houndmills: Palgrave, 2008).

[52] J.G.A. Pocock, *The Discovery of Islands: Essays in British History* (Cambridge: Cambridge University Press, 2005), 42.

[53] David Armitage, *The Ideological Origins of the British Empire* (Cambridge: Cambridge University Press, 2000).

[54] Barbara R. Penny, "Australia's Reactions to the Boer War - A Study in Colonial Imperialism," *Journal of British Studies* 7, no. 1 (November 1967): 97-130.

da during the war to be one form of Canadian nationalism. It was this type of nationalism, he argues, that explains Canada's enthusiastic participation in an imperial war.[55] The confluence of national and imperial identities will be elaborated upon below. Suffice to say that loyalty to the empire, the Union Jack, and the monarchy was not considered by those within the empire to make one disloyal to one's national or regional identity. In fact, for most, national identity could not be envisioned outside of the empire. Again, as one New Zealander stated, "[T]he British nation is our nation."[56] A second loyalty was to the evangelical distinctives of spreading the gospel and a concern for social justice. Evangelicals had been "hitching a ride for the gospel" for a number of years, taking advantage of the spread of empire when it suited their purposes.[57] BACSANZ Baptists were convinced that the missionary enterprise had benefited from the spread of European empires, and that an imperial victory in South Africa was essential if missions were to progress. Consequently, the evangelical passion for spreading the gospel was, in no small measure, a reason for supporting the empire. As for an active faith, the empire was deemed to be an agent for good, and its advance was considered to be one way to rid the world of the scourge of slavery. Consequently, national and imperial identities were, in a number of ways, fused with evangelical convictions and imperatives. Or, to use the words of Cole, the shared "Britannic nationalism" in many ways was merged with evangelical (Baptist) identity and purpose.

Of course, BACSANZ Baptists were not a monolithic movement. British Baptists were divided about the war and South African Baptists were disappointed with the lack of British Baptist support for their dire wartime situation. Support for imperialism also did not mean that the empire could not be criti-

---

[55] Carl Berger, *The Sense of Power: Studies in the Ideas of Canadian Imperialism, 1867-1914* (Toronto: University of Toronto Press, 1970). Other important authors in this category are Norman Penlington, *Canada and Imperialism, 1896* (Toronto: University of Toronto Press, 1965); Robert Page, "Canada and the Imperial Idea in the Boer War Years," *Journal of Canadian Studies* 5 (February 1970); Robert Page, *The Boer War and Canadian Imperialism* (Ottawa: The Canadian Historical Association, 1987); Robert Page, "Carl Berger and the Intellectual Origins of Canadian Imperialist Thought, 1867-1914," *Journal of Canadian Studies* 5 (August 1970): 39-43; Douglas Cole, "Canada's 'Nationalistic' Imperialists," *Journal of Canadian Studies* 5 (August 1970), 44-45; Terry Cook, "George R. Parkin and the Concept of Britannic Idealism," *Journal of Canadian Studies* 10 (August 1975), 15-31; Philip Buckner, "Whatever Happened to the British Empire?" *Journal of the Canadian Historical Association* 4 (1993): 3-32; Phillip Buckner, "Canada," in *The Impact of the South African War*, eds., David Omissi and Andrew S. Thompson (Houndmills: Palgrave: 2002).

[56] S.R. Ingold, "The War in South Africa: The Christian's Proper Attitude Regarding It," *New Zealand Baptist*, April 1900, 61-62.

[57] Stuart Piggin's phrase. See Stuart Piggin, "The American and British Contributions to Evangelicalism in Australia," in *Evangelicalism: Comparative Studies of Popular Protestantism in North America, the British Isles, and Beyond, 1700-1990*, eds., Mark Noll, David Bebbington and George Rawlyk (Oxford: Oxford University Press, 1994), 294.

cized. In fact, the imperialism of the BACSANZ Baptists often necessitated criticism of the empire, for the righteous expectations of an alleged Christian empire necessitated that domestic and imperial authorities be castigated for their ungodly conduct. British bungling on the battlefield was lamented by embarrassed and angry supporters who wished for had expected a quick British victory.

The primary focus of attention in this research is the relationship between the denominational press and popular imperialism. Noll further develops Bebbington's fourfold description of evangelical distinctives by adding genealogy to the equation.[58] This is an important addition, for the individuals, associations, books, practices, perceptions and networks of influence that he identifies as genealogy were an important part of the global evangelical (and Baptist) communion, and those connections – it will be shown – played a vital role in the formation and dissemination of popular imperialism. Both Susan O'Brien and William Brackney have identified the role of Baptist literature in the formation of an international movement. O'Brien has identified the role of publishing in the early decades of evangelicalism, and how the international publishing network united disparate parts of the movement with one another and with what they deemed to be the work of God's Spirit. She writes:

> During the headiest years of revival – 1740 to 1745 – ministers, revival activists, and the converted could all place themselves within an international movement by reading, writing, listening, and talking….there was also a lively sense, as Jonathan Edwards wrote to one of his correspondents, that 'the Church of God, in all Parts of the World, is but one. The distant members are closely united in one Glorious Head. This Union is very much her Beauty.'[59]

Brackney notes that while "unique indigenous communities and movements of Baptists grew up" in various parts of the world, there were still "clearly identifiable Baptist principles" that linked the larger Baptist community.[60] Those links were nurtured by, among other things, Baptist publications read on both sides of the Atlantic.[61] Increasingly, historians are recognizing the important role that newspapers played in the construction and sustaining of a British

---

[58] Bebbington's fourfold characteristics of Biblicism, Conversionism, Activism and Crucicentrism are the most commonly held descriptors of evangelicalism. See David Bebbington, *Evangelicalism in Modern Britain: A History from the 1730's to the 1980's* (Grand Rapids: Baker Book House, 1989), ch.1. For Noll's description, see Noll, *The Rise of Evangelicalism*, 18-21.

[59] Susan O'Brien, "Eighteenth-Century Publishing Networks in the First Years of Transatlantic Evangelicalism," in *Evangelicalism: Comparative Studies of Popular Protestantism in North America, the British Isles, and Beyond, 1700-1990*, eds., Mark Noll, David Bebbington and George Rawlyk (Oxford: Oxford University Press, 1994), 39.

[60] William H. Brackney, "Transatlantic Relationships: The Making of an International Baptist Community," in *The Gospel in the World: International Studies, Volume One*, ed., David Bebbington (Carlisle: Paternoster Press, 2002), 60.

[61] Brackney, "Transatlantic Relationships," 68-69.

Introduction

world among colonists around the globe. Carl Bridge and Kent Fedorowich write of the "plethora of networks" that acted as "cultural glue" which "held together" the British world, including religious publications and networks in their conclusions.[62] By the end of the nineteenth century, that international network of Baptist denominational papers continued to unite the movement and act as "cultural glue" for Baptists empire-wide, and with the increase in technology over the century (especially trans-continental ocean cables), communication had multiplied exponentially (as did the ability of the press to shape public opinion). Bebbington describes the impact of this technology on evangelical global contacts as revolutionary.[63] This research will demonstrate how the international network of newspapers among Baptists not only contributed to a global Baptist community, but also nurtured an ardent imperialism among that same community.

Increasingly throughout the nineteenth century newspapers became a forum for the expression of public opinion.[64] The role of newspapers in the shaping of public opinion is widely recognized. For instance, the "New Journalism" was linked to the New Imperialism, and John A. Hobson, one of the most prominent late-Victorian opponents of imperialism, was concerned about the power of the press in promoting imperialism.[65] John Bourinot claimed that the influence of the press played a key role in educating the "masses" about the key issues of the day.[66] Others have also noted the influence of the press in swaying wartime public opinion.[67] Paula Krebs goes so far as to argue that the press actually created the spontaneous outburst of imperial fervor during the South African War.[68] While there were limitations on what influence the press could have on its readers, the press did have the power to set agendas, mobilize, stereotype, confer status, manipulate, socialize and legitimize.[69] And that power of the press extended to the Baptist denominational newspapers. However, the ignor-

---

[62] Carl Bridge and Kent Fedorowich, "Mapping the British World," in *The British World: Diaspora, Culture and Identity*, eds., Carl Bridge and Kent Fedorowich (London: Frank Cass, 2003), 6. Also in Carl Bridge and Kent Fedorowich, "Mapping the British World," *Journal of Imperial and Commonwealth History* 31, no. 2 (2003): 6.
[63] David Bebbington, *The Dominance of Evangelicalism: The Age of Spurgeon and Moody* (Downers Grove: InterVarsity Press, 2005), 78-81.
[64] Stefanie Markovits, "Rushing Into Print: 'Participatory Journalism' during the Crimean War," *Victorian Studies* 50, no. 4 (Summer 2008): 559-586.
[65] John A. Hobson, *Imperialism: A Study* (London, 1902).
[66] John George Bourinot, *The Intellectual Development of the Canadian People: An Historical Review* (Toronto: Hunter, Rose & Company, 1881), 83.
[67] Judd and Surridge, *The Boer War*, ch.19; Peter Harrington, "Pictorial Journalism and the Boer War: The London Illustrated Weeklies" in *The Boer War: Direction, Experience and Image*, ed., John Gooch (London: Frank Cass, 2000), 224-244.
[68] Paula Krebs, *Gender, Race, and the Writing of Empire: Public Discourse and the Boer War* (Cambridge: Cambridge University Press, 1999).
[69] Paul Rutherford, *A Victorian Authority: The Daily Press in Late Nineteenth-Century Canada* (Toronto: University of Toronto Press, 1982), 7-8.

13

ing of the denominational press by many historians is surprising due to the importance of denominational newspapers in the shaping of public opinion in the late-Victorian period. In his article on the national vision of the Methodist Church in Canada, William Magney claims that "historians of national sentiment in Canada who ignore the writings of Church journals, and the declarations of the institutional churches, do so at their own peril, for they overlook one of the most fertile sources of nationalistic writings in existence."[70] Magney's observation applies equally to the various late-Victorian BACSANZ Baptist newspapers, and this research focuses on those papers and the imperialism that they promoted.

Keith Sinclair argues that "[i]t is difficult to exaggerate the importance of newspapers in stimulating national sentiment. They create a sense of community. They enable us to sense – to feel that we *know* – what other members of our community, quite unknown to us as individuals, are doing."[71] John MacKenzie has noted how in Britain there was no pressing need for government agencies to be involved in imperial propaganda, for a number of non-governmental agencies were enthusiastically doing it for them.[72] MacKenzie was not necessarily referring to Christian denominations, but the extent to which late-Victorian BACSANZ Baptist newspapers supported and promoted imperialism is one clear example of such voluntary promotion of the empire. The wartime Baptist newspapers were active in shaping their constituent's attitudes to empire, war, national identity and civic responsibility in a way not usually recognized by contemporary historians. The international network of Baptist papers also played a role in nurturing not only denominational loyalties but also imperial loyalties. This is what Simon Potter refers to as "diverse connections" and "complex webs of communication" that "forged links between each of the settler colonies."[73] Or what Tony Ballantyne refers to as "webs of empire," those "networks, connections, and webs of exchange" that directly shaped life in the peripheries.[74] In a very tangible way, the Baptist press within the empire played an important part in the building of a global denominational, evangelical and

---

[70] William H. Magney, "The Methodist Church and the National Gospel, 1884-1914," *The Bulletin* (1968): 5

[71] Keith Sinclair, *A Destiny Apart: New Zealand's Search for National Identity* (Wellington: Allen and Unwin, 1986), 138.

[72] John M. MacKenzie, *Propaganda and Empire: The Manipulation of British Public Opinion, 1880-1960* (Manchester: Manchester University Press, 1984), 2-3.

[73] Although in his analysis Potter did not mention the religious press. See Simon J. Potter, "Communication and Integration: The British and Dominions Press and the British World, c.1876-1914," *Journal of Imperial and Commonwealth History* 31, no. 2 (2003): 191. See also Simon J. Potter, "Communication and Integration: The British and Dominions Press and the British World, c.1876-1914," in *The British World: Diaspora, Culture and Identity*, eds., Carl Bridge and Kent Fedorowich (London: Frank Cass, 2003), 190-206.

[74] Tony Ballantyne, *Webs of Empire: Locating New Zealand's Colonial Past* (Wellington: Bridget Williams Books, 2012), 295.

imperial identity and bond that transcended regional and national identities. At the same time, various newspapers were active in the nation-building role that attempted to shape political opinions and forge what was deemed to be an acceptable Christian nation and a patriotic commitment to their particular national or regional identity.

Methodology

This research draws from diverse fields of research (denominational, evangelical, imperial and national), and as a result relies on a variety of different methodologies and approaches. In a number of ways, this work on Baptists and imperialism mirrors the author's previous analysis of Canadian Protestants and the South African War which drew heavily on wartime denominational publications.[75] Consequently, many of the themes outlined and assumptions held in this study will echo those of *A War with a Silver Lining*.

Troy Paddock and Glenn Wilkinson provide examples how newspapers can be treated by historians concerned with war, propaganda and popular culture.[76] The BACSANZ Baptist newspapers contained repeated references to the empire and to the war. But just how much do the official church statements, or comments by clergy, or newspaper editorials reflect the opinions of church members and the denomination at large? Paddock makes a few distinctions that are helpful. First, he differentiates between government propaganda and propaganda produced by private enterprise. What was printed in the Baptist press was private, and thus what was contained in Baptist papers was a source of popular imperial sentiment neither under the direct control of government (much to the chagrin of some in government) nor funded by government. Second, he makes a distinction between "public opinion" and "published opinion." The limitations of using denominational publications, official statements and sermons are obvious: perhaps the editor (usually a clergyman) who put together the newspaper, or clergyman who preached the sermon, held such views, but did Baptists in the pew? One needs to be careful about assuming that what was in the press was automatically held by all. Nevertheless, the sheer volume of commentary and – when it occurred – unanimity of support in the newspapers (and in official denominational statements) suggests that there was a considerable degree of support for the views expressed in print. Wilkinson notes that the late-Victorian newspapers are an exceptional source of infor-

---

[75] Gordon L. Heath, *A War with a Silver Lining: Canadian Protestant Churches and the South African War, 1899-1902* (Montreal: McGill-Queen's University Press, 2009).

[76] Troy R. E. Paddock, ed., *A Call to Arms: Propaganda, Public Opinion, and Newspapers in the Great War* (Westport: Praeger, 2004); Glenn R Wilkinson, *Depictions and Images of War in Edwardian Newspapers, 1899–1914* (New York: Palgrave Macmillan, 2003). See also Glenn R Wilkinson, "'To the Front': British Newspaper Advertising and the Boer War." in *The Boer War: Direction, Experience and Image*, ed., John Gooch (London: Frank Cass, 2000), 203-212.

mation for cultural and social historians. Because a newspaper needs to connect immediately with its readership there is a "form of two-way communication" between the paper and its readers, reflecting in its pages the immediate events and perceptions of the period. Wilkinson writes "images in newspapers had to conform to the perception of war that readers already held. In this regard, newspapers had little or no thought for posterity or future reputations of their creators, and they needed to create and foster an immediate connection with their reader audiences."[77] He goes on to say that "this makes the newspapers a form of two-way communication, with readers more than 'blank slates' awaiting to be etched with how to think about the world by the press." There are also pitfalls to using newspapers as primary sources. Peter Hennessy has notes that one of the most significant issues related to the use of newspapers as primary sources is editorial bias, and writes that the "value of any report or piece of commentary has to be judged in the light of a paper's editorial predilections as well as the writer's own bias. The fair-mindedness which ought to characterize the historian's work cannot be assumed to govern that of journalists."[78] Nevertheless, newspapers can be seen to represent the views of readers to a degree. However, whether or not and to what degree they reveal the views of the readers, a study of Baptist newspapers reveals telling aspects of the late-Victorian denominational newspaper industry in a manner similar to Jacqueline Beaumont's examination of *The Times* or Mark Hampton's of the *Manchester Guardian*.[79] Hampton argues that such a study "provides a valuable window into the theory and practice of journalism at the end of the nineteenth century" as well as a "particularly concentrated examination of ... journalistic culture"

---

[77] Wilkinson, "To the Front," 203-204. The editor of the Australian paper the *Southern Baptist* identified but lamented this tendency to give the readers what they wanted: "It is frequently said that the papers reflect the wishes of the public. The papers must supply the sensational, the humorous, the personal, because this is what the public demands. That is, instead of attempting to elevate public opinion, the Press will pander to its more ignoble tastes because of financial considerations. We believe that things are not so bad as this assumption implies. There is more fibre in our nation, more earnestness and strenuousness, than is generally recognized. The Press too often appeals to the galleries, instead of to the minds and hearts of the majority of our land." See "Do People Want It?" *Southern Baptist*, 14 May 1902, 109.

[78] Peter Hennessy, "The Press and Broadcasting," in *Contemporary History: Practice and Method*, ed., Anthony Seldon (Basil: Blackwell, 1988), 20. For another discussion of the perils and pitfalls of using newspapers for research, see Roberto Franzosi, "The Press as a Source of Socio-Historical Data: Issues in the Methodology of Data Collection from Newspapers," *Historical Methods* 20 1 (Winter 1987): 5-16.

[79] Jacqueline Beaumont, "*The Times* at War, 1899-1902," in *The South African War Reappraised*, ed., Donal Lowry (Manchester: Manchester University Press, 2000), 67-83; Mark Hampton, "The Press, Patriotism, and Public Discussion: C.P. Scott, the *Manchester Guardian*, and the Boer War, 1899-1902," *The Historical Journal*, 44, no.1 (2001): 177-197.

during a time when "intensified 'jingoistic' fervour" created tensions for papers.[80]

Historians of Christianity have begun to note the importance of the imperial and British connection to denominations in early nineteenth-century British North America.[81] Rather than placing the denominations on a trajectory towards independence from Britain, they have correctly noted that the imperial connection and identity often remained (though frequently contested, or as imagined constructions) and provided an ideological framework for their relationships with one another and their role in Canada, North America and the world. Duncan Bell in *The Idea of Greater Britain* notes that the imperial ideal in Britain and the colonies was often a constructed and imagined ideal that served different purposes in different parts of the empire for different reasons, and his observation equally applies to BACSANZ Baptist churches.[82] This imperial and British connection needs more exploration, for it provided a crucial racial and ideological backdrop for the churches' support for late-Victorian conflicts, as well as the two global conflagrations in the twentieth century. What needs to be kept in mind when exploring imperial identities and the churches is that not everyone supported imperialism. For instance, in Canada, French Catholics and English Protestants had very different conceptions of empire.[83]

The conclusions of Bebbington, Laurie Guy, Stuart Piggin, Ken Manley, and Phyllis Airhart in regards to the churches and nation-building provide a helpful template for understanding the aspirations and activities of the churches at the

---

[80] Hampton, "The Press, Patriotism, and Public Discussion," 179-180.

[81] Nancy Christie, "Introduction: Theorizing a Colonial Past: Canada as a Society of British Settlement," in *Transatlantic Subjects: Ideas, Institutions, and Social Experience in Post-Revolutionary British North America*, ed., Nancy Christie (Montreal/Kingston: McGill-Queen's University Press, 2008), 3-41; Todd Webb, "How the Canadian Methodists became British: Unity, Schism, and Transatlantic Identity, 1827-54," in *Transatlantic Subjects: Ideas, Institutions, and Social Experience in Post-Revolutionary British North America.* ed., Nancy Christie (Montreal/Kingston: McGill-Queen's University Press, 2008), 159-198;Todd Webb, "Making Neo-Britons: The Transatlantic Relationship between Wesleyan Methodists in Britain and the Canadas, 1815-1828," *British Journal of Canadian Studies* 18, no.1 (2005): 1-25; Denis McKim, "'Righteousness Exalteth a Nation': Providence, Empire, and the Forging of the Early Canadian Presbyterian Identity," *Historical Papers, CSCH,* 2008, 47-66; Todd Webb, *Transatlantic Methodists: British Wesleyanism and the Formation of an Evangelical Culture in Nineteenth-Century Ontario and Quebec* (Montreal/Kingston: McGill-Queen's University Press, 2013).

[82] Bell, *The Idea of Greater Britain.*

[83] For a study of Canadian anti-imperial sentiment, see Carman Miller, "English-Canadian Opposition to the South African War as Seen through the Press," *Canadian Historical Review* 55 (December 1974): 422-438; Karen Ostergaard, "Canadian Nationalism and Anti-Imperialism, 1896-1911," (PhD dissertation, Dalhousie University, 1976). For French-Canadian views of empire, see A.I. Silver, "Some Quebec Attitudes in an Age of Imperialism and Ideological Conflict," *Canadian Historical Review* 57 (December 1976): 441-460.

end of the nineteenth century and the first half of the twentieth century. All five note how the churches were imbued with the same national dream. At the end of the nineteenth century, and into the twentieth, denominations wielded an influence on society unlike any other institution, and they had taken upon themselves the identity of nation-builders.[84] While nation-building meant many things, at the very least it meant building a united, democratic, distinctly Christian (hopefully mainly Protestant) nation. During the South African War, commitment to nation-building meant that Baptists took it upon themselves to construct imperial and national ideals and identity through their services, sermons, organizations and literature. It also meant supporting the war effort in numerous practical ways. Heath's observations on the Canadian Protestant press as a nation and empire-building press equally apply to BACSANZ Baptist publications, for all the papers had a nation-building vision imbedded within their mandate.[85] Key social gospel studies such as that provided by Richard Allen also need to be included in the analysis of the churches, nation-building and war, for the social gospel impulse was an important part of the churches' mandate to better the nation and the world; this included going to war to bring justice to the oppressed.[86] These impulses were mirrored in BACSANZ churches.

What about some of the recent theories surrounding nation-building and imperialism? How do those theories relate to researching the churches and war? First, no single theory is completely satisfactory because no single theory can completely account for the many and complex experiences of the churches. At times, such attempts seem simplistic and mono-causal. For instance, Krebs suggests that the imperial fervor shown in England during victories over the Boers was created by the press.[87] Certainly, the secular and denominational press played an important role in the formation of imperial attitudes. However, the press was often shaped by the contributions and expectations of the contributors and subscribers in a symbiotic relationship.[88] Second, some theories seem

---

[84] David Bebbington, *The Nonconformist Conscience: Chapel and Politics, 1870-1914* (London: George Allen and Unwin, 1982); Laurie Guy, *Shaping Godzone: Public Issues and Church Voices in New Zealand, 1840-2000* (Wellington: Victoria University Press, 2011); Stuart Piggin, *Evangelical Christianity in Australia: Spirit, Word and World* (Melbourne: Oxford University Press, 1996); Ken Manley, *From Woolloomooloo to 'Eternity': A History of Australian Baptists, Vol. 1* (Milton Keynes: Paternoster, 2006); Phyllis D. Airhart, "Ordering a New Nation and Reordering Protestantism, 1867-1914", in *The Canadian Protestant Experience, 1760-1990*, ed., George A. Rawlyk (Burlington: Welch, 1990), 98-138.
[85] Gordon L. Heath, "'Forming Sound Public Opinion': The Late Victorian Canadian Protestant Press and Nation-Building," *Journal of the Canadian Church Historical Society* 48 (2006): 109-159.
[86] Richard Allen, *Religion and Social Reform in Canada, 1914-1928* (Toronto: University of Toronto Press, 1971).
[87] Krebs, *Gender, Race, and the Writing of Empire.*
[88] Gordon L. Heath, "Passion for Empire: War Poetry Published in the Canadian English Protestant Press during the South African War, 1899-1902," *Literature and Theology* 16

to impose certain motives upon the period and people being studied (Edward Said's *Orientalism* is one example – although his identification of the construction of the "Other" is helpful[89]). While certainly power is an important element of the analysis of missionary attitudes and actions, Jane Samson argues convincingly that a more nuanced approach to power and motives is called for.[90] Andrew Porter's recent work on the history of British Protestant missionaries is an example of such an approach that demonstrates how the relationship between missionaries, church and empire was more complex and ambiguous than previously thought.[91]

One particular work that is valuable when exploring the churches and nation-building is H.V. Nelles' *The Art of Nation-Building*. Nelles argues that the commemoration of Quebec's Tercentenary in 1908 was "an act of self-invention."[92] It was an opportunity where various parties remembered the past, but also negotiated to shape the future. It was a time when Canada had not yet been "made," and thus, it was an opportunity to forge bonds between French and English, elite and masses, and monarchy and people. In a similar way, through their many public services, symbols and sermons during the war BACSANZ Baptists sought to shape a yet "unmade" Canada or Australia or New Zealand. Whether it was the idea of a Christian (Protestant) Australia or New Zealand with a providential mission within the British Empire, the vision of a racially homogenous (Anglo-Saxon) nation, or the concept of a Canada radically distinct from the United States, the churches were active participants in shaping what the past had been and what the future held. They assumed that such a vision would solidify the present and future aims of the church. Related to Nelle's argument is Eric Hobsbawm and Terence Ranger's concept of invented traditions.[93] The churches were active participants in inventing traditions of what the past had been and what the future held for the colony (or nascent nation). They assumed that such traditions would solidify the present and future aims of the church.

As correctives to any claims that imperialism was somehow foisted on the masses by church leaders are Philip Buckner's essay on the Royal Tour of 1901 and Jonathan Vance's book on the memory and meaning of the First World

---

(June 2002): 127-147.

[89] Edward Said, *Orientalism* (London: Penguin Books, 1978).

[90] Jane Samson, "The Problem of Colonialism in the Western Historiography of Christian Missions," *Religious Studies and Theology* 23 (2004): 2-26.

[91] Andrew Porter, *Religion versus Empire? British Protestant Missionaries and Overseas Expansion, 1700-1914* (Manchester: Manchester University Press, 2004).

[92] H.V. Nelles, *The Art of Nation-Building: Pageantry and Spectacle at Quebec's Tercentenary* (Toronto: University of Toronto Press, 1999).

[93] Eric Hobsbawm and Terence Ranger, eds., *The Invention of Tradition* (Cambridge: Cambridge University Press, 1983).

War.[94] Buckner correctly identifies how the popular sentiment expressed towards the monarchy was not simply created by elites or even by the monarchy, but rather, was an expression of how those with a British heritage imagined their national identity. Much of the imperial sentiment expressed within the churches simply reflects the most basic reality that many in the Protestant churches had a British background, and this shaped how they imagined the nation should be. Like Buckner, Vance argues that the meaning found in the First World War in the decades that followed the war was not something that was merely constructed by elites. While Vance is referring to post-First World War memory or myth in Canada, from the very opening shots of the South African conflict there were certain "myths" surrounding the memory and meaning of the war's events, and the churches were often at the forefront of the interpretation of the war's meaning. Nevertheless, neither the churches as a whole, nor individual members, had their memory forced upon them by "elites." Church leaders may have invented traditions and memories, but both church leaders and individual members owned their understanding of the events, and also contributed to the ongoing memory and meaning of the war. Why? Because, as Vance argues for those during the First World War, those alive during the conflict found such myths provided meaning in a world filled with threats and uncertainty.

The Baptist Press

As noted above, the primary focus of this research is the imperialism within the BACSANZ Baptist publications that acted in whole or in part as newspapers. By the end of the nineteenth-century the telegraph had transformed the newspaper industry's ability to access information (and do it quickly), and like their secular counterparts, the Baptist newspapers took advantage of the available domestic and international news made available by cable and mail. The speed by which information by undersea cable could travel to the distant colonies was deemed to be a marvel. In 1803, it took ten months for news to arrive in Australia from Britain. By 1850, it only took four months. After the Suez Canal was opened, news could arrive in forty-four days. After the installation of cable in 1872, news could arrive within hours.[95] Editors counted on a wide variety of sources to fill their pages. Reprinting articles from other Baptist papers was common, as was reprinting articles from other denominational and secular pa-

---

[94] See Philip Buckner, "Casting Daylight upon Magic: Deconstructing the Royal Tour of 1901 to Canada," *Journal of Imperial and Commonwealth History* 31 (May 2003): 158-189; Jonathan Vance, *Death So Noble: Memory, Meaning, and the First World War* (Vancouver: UBC Press, 1997).

[95] K.S. Inglis, "The Imperial Connection: Telegraphic Communication between England and Australia, 1872-1902," in *Australia and Britain: Studies in a Changing Relationship*, eds., A.F. Madden and W.H. Morris-Jones (Sydney: Sydney University Press, 1980), 21-38.

pers. The reprinting of articles from other Baptist (and evangelical) papers was one way in which the press promoted and nurtured the global Baptist (and evangelical) community. Items were often anonymous, for it was common practice to print material with no author identified. Reports from missionaries and church officials from South Africa played a role similar to foreign correspondents in secular papers. Sermons from lesser and well-known preachers were published as were articles from a wide variety of sources. Some of the larger papers reprinted cable reports from London, and the London origins of most news reports played a part in the papers being decidedly pro-British in their reporting.[96] The coverage from a number of these publications was so extensive that it would have been possible to have a fairly comprehensive knowledge of world events by simply reading one's denominational newspaper (and in some cases, the weekly denominational paper was the only paper read in a home). Like their more established and wealthy secular counterparts, the larger Baptist papers also used foreign correspondents to gain eyewitness accounts of international events, but with an important difference: the foreign correspondents for the church press were sometimes missionaries, church workers and chaplains, and their eyewitness accounts were often printed and commented on.[97]

Finances were an ongoing concern for editors. In order to balance the budget, various methods were used to increase circulation.[98] The *New Zealand Baptist* even resorted to original, but hackneyed, poetry in an attempt to inspire support and the payment of overdue subscriptions.[99] Papers often had agents appointed in each local church to promote the paper and pastors were expected

---

[96] For instance, the English papers in Canada received their information about the war primarily from London-based wire services, whereas the French papers in Canada received their news primarily from Paris-based wire services. The origins of these cables influenced the reporting and thus the paper's perspective. See Page, *The Boer War and Canadian Imperialism*, 17.

[97] Not all correspondents were church-related. For instance, the *Baptist* printed an article written for the *Daily Telegraph* by its special correspondent with Australian troops in South Africa. See Frank Wilkinson, "The Army Chaplain," *Baptist*, 1 March 1901, 9-10. For a discussion of the changing role of foreign correspondents during the late Victorian period, see Stephen Badsey, "War Correspondents in the Boer War," in *The Boer War: Direction, Experience and Image*, ed., John Gooch (London: Frank Cass, 2000), 187-202.

[98] For instance, see "On the Editorial Stoep," *South African Baptist*, July 1899, 197-198; "News and Notes," *Queensland Baptist*, November 1897, 149; "To Our Readers," *Queensland Baptist*, October 1899, 127; "Our Subscribers," *Queensland Baptist*, June 1900, 71; "It Will Pay Your Church to Push 'The Baptist'," *Baptist*, 1 August 1901, 14. For information on the British Baptist press, and the need for Baptists to read and support their paper, see "A Word for Ourselves," *Baptist Times and Freeman*, 18 January 1901, 37; "Our Relation to our own Literature has often been Simply Contemptible," *Baptist Times and Freeman*, 10 May 1901, 310.

[99] "The Sorrowful Sigh of the 'New Zealand Baptist'," *New Zealand Baptist*, May 1900, 67.

to publicize the paper from the pulpit and disseminate it in his visits to parishioner's homes.[100] Denominational officials were also expected to promote the paper. The papers themselves encouraged readers to increase circulation, sometimes with fervent exhortations.[101] However, not all initiatives to increase circulation benefited the financial bottom line. During the war the *South African Baptist* was distributed free to the sailors on ships arriving in Algoa Bay for the sole purpose of evangelism.[102]

The editors provided overall direction for the paper. Most were ordained pastors.[103] As can be imagined, denominational considerations were of primary importance, and it is difficult to determine just how much freedom editors had as they went about their daily business. In the BCOQ *Baptist Yearbook* for 1900, there was a brief summary of the changes made to the way in which the office of the editor of the *Canadian Baptist* was to operate (those changes were being made while the Board of Publication looked for a new editor). In those changes, one gets an idea of the close connection between denomination and press, and a sense of how much pressure was on the editor to be faithful to the denomination and its doctrines. The report of the Publication Board of the Convention stated:

> The Board, as far back as December, 1899, came to the unanimous conclusion that we should have a managing editor who would be responsible to the Board:
>
> • For seeing that suitable editorials appeared upon subjects of interest and importance.
>
> • For keeping the tone and teaching of our paper in accord with the known views and policy of the denomination.
>
> • For preparing editorial notes on live topics, upon which the brightness and usefulness of a paper so largely depend.

---

[100] "List of Church Agents for the 'Baptist'," *Queensland Baptist*, April 1900, 56; "Agents," *New Zealand Baptist*, September 1900, 136; Church Agents for *The Baptist*," *Baptist*, 1 January 1901, 15; "An Increased Circulation," *Baptist Times and Freeman*, 21 December 1900, 1027.

[101] "Can You Help?" *Baptist Times and Freeman*, 21 December 1900, 1027.

[102] See "Our Current Funds," *South African Baptist*, October 1899, 45; "Our Current Funds," *South African Baptist*, November 1899, 65; "Our Current Funds," *South African Baptist*, October 1900, 143; "Our Current Funds," *South African Baptist*, December 1900, 162; "Our Current Funds," *South African Baptist*, January 1901, 2; "Our Current Funds," *South African Baptist*, February 1901, 15; "Our Current Funds," *South African Baptist*, April 1901, 46; "Our Current Funds," *South African Baptist*, May 1901, 53; "Our Current Funds," *South African Baptist*, August 1901, 93; "Our Current Funds," *South African Baptist*, September 1901, 105.

[103] Trinier claims that all but two editors of the *Canadian Baptist* were ordained men, and all had academic training at a "high level." Most served before or after in colleges or universities. None had any professional training in journalism before their editorial duties began. See Harold Trinier, *A Century of Service: Story of The Canadian Baptist, 1854-1954* (Toronto: Board of Publication of the Baptist Convention of Ontario and Quebec, 1958), 138. F.W. Boreham, the editor of the *New Zealand Baptist*, was also the President of the New Zealand Baptist Union.

- For the careful editing of correspondence and news.
- For making judicious selections from exchanges.
- A list of ministers and laymen might be prepared by the Board, to be revised from time to time, to whom the editor should look for supplies of articles and notes
- For an editor to conduct *The Baptist* upon this method, we want a man who is a sound Baptist and a devoted Christian, with common sense, without fads or extreme opinions, but with judgment and literary taste, and some practical experience in the conduct of a paper, and we should have associated with him an editorial committee with whom he could consult from time to time, especially as to the exclusion of communications or articles upon which he was in doubt, and who would also from time to time advise him as to the advisability of giving prominence to particular views of truth and policy
- The managing editor would be expected to come into contact with the thought of our body both by correspondence and by attendance at the important associational and denominational meetings.[104]

This concern for having a Baptist view of issues was no different than what other denominations were concerned with: the religious press was to be a voice for the parent denomination. The papers committed significant space to detailing denominational events and details of official meetings. Despite the obvious denominational affiliation and loyalties, however, they also criticized their own denomination's decisions and developments (not to mention other Protestant denominations and/or Roman Catholics). In doing so, the papers acted as a medium for constructive criticism of the denomination.

This research is based on the following Baptist newspapers. The *Baptist Times and Freeman* was the result of a merger between *The Freeman* and *Baptist Times* in February 1899. It was the weekly official organ of the Baptist Union of Great Britain and Ireland (published in London), and dealt extensively with matters related to the denomination, nation, missionary enterprise and empire.[105] It was also the largest and most comprehensive BACSANZ Baptist paper. Its coverage of international and domestic events was unmatched by other Baptist papers (although the weekly Canadian papers *Canadian Baptist*, *Religious Intelligencer*, and *Messenger and Visitor* were close).

---

[104] *BCOQ Yearbook* (Toronto, 1900), 272. In regards to this statement of editorial policy in the Baptist paper, Harold Trinier suggests that the "rumblings of the coming Fundamentalist-Modernist controversy" most likely made it necessary for the editor to be sound in doctrine, and for the Baptist Board to have more control over the contents of the denominational press. See Trinier, *A Century of Service*, 88.

[105] For commentary on the merger, see B. Evans, "The Father of 'The Freeman'," *Baptist Times and Freeman*, 5 January 1900, 12-13; *Baptist Union of Great Britain and Ireland Handbook*, (1901), 67. The paper moved to move from twenty to sixteen pages, but on larger paper. See *Baptist Times and Freeman*, 21 December 1900, 1027. The editorial office moved to London in 1901. See *Baptist Times and Freeman*, 16 July 1901, 482.

Four Canadian papers were consulted: one from western Canada, one from central Canada and two from eastern Canada (there was no national Baptist paper).[106] The *Western Baptist*, published in Vancouver, was the official organ of the British Columbia Baptist Convention. This eight-page monthly was edited by Rev. W. B. Hinson (until 1901). The *Canadian Baptist*, published in Toronto, was the official paper of the central-Canadian Baptist Convention of Ontario and Quebec. It was a weekly paper with a circulation in 1901 of over 5600.[107] The *Religious Intelligencer*, published in Fredericton, was the weekly paper of the Free Baptist denomination. The editor was the Rev. Dr. Joseph McLeod. The *Messenger and Visitor*, published in Saint John, was the weekly publication of the Baptist Convention of the Maritime Provinces. The editor was S. McC. Black.[108]

In 1895, Baptists in the states of South Australia, Victoria and Tasmania merged their papers into one bi-weekly paper entitled the *Southern Baptist* which was published in Melbourne. The Baptist Union of New South Wales published the monthly *Baptist* in Sydney[109] and Baptists in Queensland published the monthly *Queensland Baptist* in Brisbane. It was edited by Rev. W. Higlett.[110] All three of these papers were consulted. Circulation figures are difficult to attain but it seems that the *Queensland Baptist* circulation was equal to five-sixths of the membership, or around 1,575.[111] No national Australian Baptist paper came into existence until the *Australian Baptist* was started in 1913.[112] (Baptists in Australia did not organize into a national union until the formation of the Baptist Union in 1926.)

---

[106] For an annotated bibliography of late-Victorian Canadian church publications, see Heath, "Forming Sound Public Opinion."

[107] The *Baptist Yearbook* (1901) reported that the *Canadian Baptist's* subscription total was 5,666. Covering international, national, and denominational news, as well as a wide range of other human interest stories, the sixteen page paper was published in Toronto every Thursday. An editorial committee of three people were in place until the end of 1901. (C. Goodspeed, A. Blue and G.R. Roberts until December 13, 1900 and C. Goodspeed, Cline, and G.R. Roberts until December 1901.) Beginning in January, 1902, George R. Roberts became the managing editor.

[108] For a brief explanation of the paper, see "The Messenger and Visitor," *Messenger and Visitor*, 28 November 1900, 4.

[109] No extant copies of 1899 issues of the *Baptist* could be found for this research.

[110] He was replaced by Rev. W. Whale in 1901. See "Change of Editor," *Queensland Baptist*, December 1900, 159. See also "Plans for 1902," *Queensland Baptist*, December 1901, 160; "Things New and Old," *Queensland Baptist*, January 1901, 7.

[111] "Statistics," *Queensland Baptist*, October 1900, 129

[112] For a summary of Australian Baptist periodicals, see Ken Manley, *From Woolloomooloo to 'Eternity': A History of Australian Baptists, Vol. 2* (Milton Keynes: Paternoster, 2006), 776-777. For a summary of Baptist papers in New South Wales, see Alan C. Prior, *Some Fell on Good Ground: A History of the Beginnings and Development of the Baptist Church in New South Wales, Australia, 1831-1965* (Sydney: Baptist Union of New South Wales, 1966), ch.16.

The *New Zealand Baptist* was a monthly paper that traced its origins back to a Baptist paper started in 1876. After a number of name changes, it was published as the *New Zealand Baptist* by the New Zealand Baptist Union.[113] Frank W. Boreham was the editor beginning in 1899.[114] Martin Sutherland has noted how this paper played an important role in the formation and preservation of denominational identity in New Zealand.[115]

The *South African Baptist* was the official paper of the Baptist Union of South Africa. It was formed in 1894 by the Baptist Union of South Africa and was a monthly paper with a circulation of around 850.[116] The *South African Baptist* was the only Baptist paper adversely affected by the war. In the opening months of the conflict, the paper could be delivered to subscribers in battle zones.[117] In January 1900, the editor announced a cessation of production until circumstances improved.[118] By the summer of 1900, the early British defeats had been reversed with battlefield victories and advances into the heartland of the Boer republics. As a result, the paper started publication again in July 1900.

While they certainly varied in size, frequency of publication and editorial opinion, these Baptists papers shared a number of similar characteristics. They were all official organs of the denomination and were expected to speak with a distinctly Baptist voice to the issues. Funds were limited and editors were usually clergymen. They were heavily dependent on printed material from other papers as well as published reports from official news sources. Eyewitness reporting on the war often came from missionary or clergy reports from South Africa. They also shared the conviction that the press had a role to play in not only building the church, but also in shaping political convictions that would ultimately shape the nation/colony and empire.

In regards to the extent and frequency of war coverage, there was significant disparity. The resources of the papers varied considerably, and the larger week-

---

[113] McBeth, *The Baptist Heritage*, 329. On certain months the *New Zealand Baptist* included as a supplement a small paper entitled the *Missionary Messenger*, a publication of the New Zealand Baptist Missionary Society. However, a number of these supplements have not survived and few are extant.

[114] Paul Tonson, *A Handful of Grain: The Centenary History of the Baptist Union of New Zealand, Volume One – 1851-1882* (Wellington: New Zealand Baptist Historical Society), 67-68.

[115] Martin Sutherland, "The *NZ Baptist* as an Agent of Denominational Identity, 1874-1960," *Pacific Journal of Baptist Research* 3, no. 1 (April 2007): 23-39.

[116] Sydney Hudson-Reed, *Together for a Century: The History of the Baptist View of South Africa, 1877-1977* (Pietermaritzburg: South Africa Baptist Historical Society, 1977), 76. The *Southern Baptist* stated in 1899 that it issued 11,500 in the past year. See "On the Editorial Stoep," *South African Baptist*, August 1899, 7. The annual report in 1899 stated that the paper has a balanced budget, and that the editor was Rev. A. Hall. See "Report of the Baptist Union Congress at Pretoria," *South African Baptist*, May 1900, 162.

[117] "On the Editorial Stoep," *South African Baptist*, November 1899, 61.

[118] "On the Editorial Stoep," *South African Baptist*, January 1900, 96.

ly papers such as the *Baptist Times and Freeman, Canadian Baptist, Religious Intelligencer* and *Messenger and Visitor* provided substantially more wartime coverage than the bi-weekly *Southern Baptist*, or monthlies *Queensland Baptist, Baptist, New Zealand Baptist, Western Baptist* and *South African Baptist*. The weekly papers acted as newspapers, with the smaller papers providing much less reporting on events that could have been four weeks old by the date of publication. For instance, the monthly *Queensland Baptist* intentionally did not attempt to provide blow-by-blow accounts of the events in South Africa and purposefully ruled out providing a chronicle of the war,[119] whereas the various weeklies provided weekly cable reports and running commentary on the war's most recent activities. However, to a greater or lesser degree, all the papers included commentary on the war and imperial issues.

Imperial sentiment or descriptions of wartime activities was embedded in articles not necessarily published because of the war: local church reports often included information about special services related to the war's events, reprinted assembly reports contained resolutions or decisions related to the war, published financial reports detailed giving related to various causes supported by the local churches such as the Patriotic Fund, and advertising contained imperial themes. Along with these inadvertent references to empire and war, there were items published directly related to the conflict in South Africa. Editors satisfied the hunger for war news and appealed to the heightened imperial fervor with running commentary on the war as well as sermons, editorials and articles related to the great imperial issues of the day. Battles, contingent send-offs and returns, performance of local troops in South Africa (a point of pride for the colonies), chaplaincy issues, deaths of soldiers, maps, histories of South Africa, domestic political debates, and global geo-political struggles such as the Boxer Rebellion in China or America's war in the Philippines were of interest to readers and editors made sure were commented on in their papers. Sometimes, they even took issue with opponents of the war or critics of Britain's cause in South Africa, thereby acting as apologists for the cause.

Conclusion

Chapter Two examines the birth and growth of Baptists, taking note of the imperial context of their origins and subsequent spread to the nether regions of empire. The social location of each Baptist communion had a direct bearing on specific reactions. Nevertheless, shaped by over a century of British imperial success, and nurtured by waves of British immigration, British leaders, British financial support and British literature, BACSANZ Baptist identity and purpose had become fused with popular expressions of imperialism.

Chapter Three details the South African War and the general reaction of the churches in Britain, Australia, Canada, South Africa and New Zealand. As the

---

[119] "Some War Items," *Queensland Baptist*, March 1900, 29.

review of literature indicates, the war has drawn the attention of historians of various sorts and in varying degrees. Domestic debates, the evolution of national identity in the colonies, political opposition or support, popular levels of imperialism, as well the events of the actual military conflict have all been a focus of numerous historians. What has been lacking, in varying degrees, however, are the studies concerning churches and the war. No one has moved beyond probing national church bodies, failing to explore transnational contacts, especially as it relates to imperial identities. By directing sustained attention to BACSANZ Baptists, this research significantly advances the analysis of the complicity of religion and empire in the heyday of Western imperialism and wild jingoism, and provides a unique global history of Baptists seen through the lens of imperialism. As the following chapters will demonstrate, imperial commitments of BACSANZ Baptists remained a potent factor in the development of Baptist views of national and global identity, history, providence, justice, and missions.

Chapters Four and Five deal with issues related to identity, in particular national and global identity. Chapter Four demonstrates how BACSANZ Baptists were loyal citizens of the empire as well as patriotic members of their nation, dominion, federation or colony. The fusion of nationalism, imperialism and Baptist identity can be readily seen in the various Baptist paper's wartime coverage. Once war had been declared, the papers made it clear that they – and Baptists at large – were patriotic, supported the troops, and embraced the imperial cause. The nature and extent of the wartime coverage bears this out. The war engendered a great deal of public interest, and papers in general increased coverage of the war to satisfy reader's demands for war news. As the following chapter indicates, their national identity was inextricably tied to their British heritage and imperial connections. Chapter Five shows that while BACSANZ Baptists had particular national identities, they also shared a global identity, both real and imagined. BACSANZ Baptists may have been on the margins in terms of percentage of population, and even looked upon askance by the larger denominations, but the global Baptist community provided Baptists with a sense of belonging to something grander that transcended their small regional presence. They were loyal to their nation, dominion, federation or colony, but they also believed they belonged to a global community that was distinctly Baptist, British and imperial. The Baptist press played an important role in the construction of this real, yet imagined, community.

Chapters Six and Seven deal with issues related to purpose, in particular the pursuit of justice and the spread of missions. Chapter Six deals with justice. From their genesis, evangelicals displayed a passionate concern for justice, and the connection between Baptists and justice has a considerable history. By the late-nineteenth century, it was clear to BACSANZ Baptists that there was no empire as righteous as their empire. While marked by injustices, the empire was still considered to be the most benevolent and just empire on the face of the earth; where the Union Jack flew, liberty and justice reigned. For Baptists con-

cerned with the advancement of justice, there was no identity crisis in supporting the empire for the best way to spread justice was to expand the empire.
Conversely, any contraction of empire was deemed a threat to peace, justice
and the advancement of human progress. In other words, for many Baptists in
the metropole and peripheries, humanitarian concerns - which included the
promotion or defense of justice - often had an imperial solution, even if it
meant going to war. However, it is also too simplistic and simply erroneous to
assume that BACSANZ Baptists were uncritical propagandists for the empire.
Those who are uncomfortable with the language of righteousness or justice
bolstering the imperial cause need to be reminded that it was this sense of
righteousness that also made it possible to criticize imperialism. The demand
for righteousness meant that there was a continuous examination as to whether
or not the empire was living up to its high calling; prophetic denunciations and
calls for prayer and fasting followed if national or imperial sins were evident.
Another common thread running through the varied commentary on the justice
of the war was a conviction that a victory would be best for all: even if the war
was unjust in its origins, it was believed that the best outcome for all would be
a British victory. Chapter Seven deals with missions. Confident that they could
discern God's providential working in history, BACSANZ Baptists were convinced that the British Empire had been established for the advancement of,
among other things, missionary work. In their minds, there was no dissonance
between their evangelical mandate to spread the gospel and their support for the
empire. After all, the empire not only protected the missionaries but also pried
open doors for their arrival by overthrowing unjust rulers and establishing British rule amenable to Christian missions. One of the reasons for BACSANZ
Baptist support for the war effort in South Africa, then, was that a British victory would oust what they deemed to be the unjust and anti-missions Boers with
an enlightened and benevolent British rule that favored the work of missionaries. While the conflation of the empire and missions means that there were assumptions about the benevolent rule of Britain that those in the twenty-first
century find offensive, it also meant that BACSANZ Baptists believed that God
expected much from his chosen vessel. The demands of righteousness cut both
ways, and the expectations of righteousness meant that any displays of hubris,
militarism, injustice, or exploitation were to be roundly condemned. The tacit
conviction undergirding the wartime BACSANZ Baptist denunciations of militarism and the evils of empire was that God had weighed the empire and found
it wanting; thus, the early defeats. A revived and purified national vision bereft
of a jingoistic imperialism and one marked by a sober realization of God's
providential destiny for nation and empire was what the churches sought to
engender. The difficulty lay in maintaining enthusiasm for empire and its God-
given role in raising up nations while at the same time avoiding pagan corruptions of said enthusiasm. The task was daunting, but the commentary in the
BACSANZ Baptist press indicates that many were up to the challenge. Attempts to extinguish the growing militarism and shape the budding patriotism

of the new nation, dominion, federation or colony reflected the churches' conviction that they were to play a key role in the formation of the new nation. Along with reforms such as the development of temperance societies and laws related to the Lord's Day, attempts were initiated to ensure a vibrant, passionate, but also Christian expression of patriotism.

In conclusion, BACSANZ Baptist imperialism was a shared global phenomenon that transcended regional identities. It provided both a global community and regional identity for nascent, often isolated, Baptist communities in the colonies. It also was inextricably fused to Baptist evangelical identity and purpose. This shared global imperial identity and purpose was nurtured by the international network of Baptist newspapers. Nevertheless, that shared imperialism was contextualized and shaped by domestic factors so much that imperialism was a particular form of nationalism for Baptists in both the metropole and peripheries.

Chapter One

In the Footsteps of Empire:
The Birth and Growth of Baptists

"I feel from the glimpses I have already obtained of Sydney and Melbourne the greatness of your mission as Christians, as Christian preachers and as Christian churches, and the momentous influence you must exert on the development of the Empire." "The Rev. Dr. Clifford," *Queensland Baptist*, June 1897, 77.

Baptist birth in Britain was concurrent with the beginnings of what would eventually become a vast overseas empire. Over the course of the seventeenth century, Britain was successful in waging war with its chief imperial competitors (Holland, Spain, and especially France), and its territory expanded accordingly (or contracted, in the case of the United States in the eighteenth century). Initially, attempts were made by the British Crown to take advantage of the lucrative sugar trade, which meant conquest and settlement (some not successfully) in the Caribbean: Saint Lucia (1605), Grenada (1609), Saint Kitts (1624), Barbados (1627), and Nevis (1628). Colonies in North America at Jamestown (1607), Plymouth (1620), and Salem (1628) were just the start of what would become by the end of the seventeenth century the Thirteen Colonies. The origins of Baptists had nothing to do with the birth of the overseas empire, but Baptists in subsequent decades certainly benefited from its expansion. A great deal of Baptist growth around the globe – to Canada, Australia, New Zealand and South Africa in particular – followed the advances of the British Empire.[1] The imperial origins and context of those colonies must be considered when examining Baptist growth, identity and purpose, especially since the day-to-day reality of being in the empire had a direct bearing on how Baptists justified support for war. In fact, one of the most significant cultural influences on the formation of Baptist views on war has been that of empire, and one simply cannot understand Baptists and their views on war without considering their relationship with empire.[2]

Despite common ancestry, it needs to be noted that the impact of local government policy on political loyalties and identity can lead to significant differ-

---

[1] For a helpful placing of early Baptist growth in the empire, see Johnson, *A Global Introduction to Baptist Churches*, ch. 3.

[2] Gordon L. Heath, "Engaging War and Empire: 400 Years of Baptist Attitudes and Actions," in *'Step Into Your Place': The First World War and Baptist Life & Thought*, ed. Larry Kreitzer (Oxford: Regent's Park College, 2014), 158-188.

ences between groups such as Baptists that had common origins.[3] It is also important to identify the specific peculiarities of each Baptist communion under consideration. Particular political and social realities not only shaped the ways in which Baptist local church ministry unfolded, but also influenced Baptist responses to empire and war. As will be elaborated on in subsequent chapters, BACSANZ Baptist views of the war and empire were remarkably similar in a number of ways, yet the milieu in which they were forged made for important distinctions and reactions.

Britain

Early seventeenth-century England was still reeling from the impact of the Protestant Reformation that began in the previous century with the German monk and theologian Martin Luther (1483-1546). The Protestant cause in England waxed and waned under the various monarchs: advancing under Henry VIII (1491-1547) and Edward VI (1547-1553), retreating under Mary (1553-1558), and then advancing again under the settlement made by Elizabeth (1558-1603). The arrangement with Elizabeth, however, left a number of reformers discontent, for they had wanted the Church of England to go even further in the reforms and completely eliminate any vestiges of Roman Catholicism. A number of disgruntled reform movements such as the Puritans eventually separated from the state-sponsored established church. Facing persecution for their dissent, the ardent reform-minded groups had two options: flee from the continent and find settlement in the fledgling Thirteen Colonies or remain in England to face persecution for trying to bring about the rebirth of what they considered to be the true church.

The first Baptists were members of those discontented Protestants. Discussing the debates over the origins of the Baptist movement is beyond the scope of this chapter; suffice it to say here that the first Baptists were from England who separated for a number of reasons from the Church of England.[4] The first Baptists had a revolutionary (and illegal) vision for the church – a church comprised of believers only. This was similar to the Anabaptists, for they too rejected an established church and a parish system of being born and baptized into a church. It has sometimes been called a voluntary religion, for a person voluntarily seeks membership in a local church, a local church voluntarily associates with other Baptist churches, and members and churches voluntarily work together on various mission projects.[5] They believed in baptizing adults who made a profession of faith, rather than baptizing infants who could not – and only such baptized believers were to be members of the church. They also rejected the Church of England's episcopal hierarchy and ran their churches on

---

[3] Mancke, *The Fault Lines of Empire.*
[4] For a recent analysis of Separatist, Anabaptist or even much earlier origins of Baptists, see Bebbington, *Baptists Through the Centuries*, ch. 3.
[5] Brackney, *The Baptists*, 71.

a congregational model of church governance that left all decisions in the hands of each local church congregation. They were ground-breaking and outspoken advocates of religious freedom; the state was deemed to be necessary but was to have no say in the affairs of the church. More specifically, it was not to enforce orthodoxy or conformity to the Church of England and remain aloof from the local church's internal matters. An association described a group of Baptist churches in geographical proximity that chose to associate with one another and work together on common projects. A group of associations often formed a union, convention or denomination. A Baptist church did not have to join an association, but most did (and still do). They were not inherently pacifists like Mennonites or Quakers, nor did they necessarily have qualms about trying to influence the laws of the land (e.g. Sabbath laws, temperance).[6] They were also supporters of the empire.

The origins of the first Baptist churches can be traced back to John Smyth (c.1570-1612). Smyth has been called "the Baptist pathfinder" and the one who "stands at the fountainhead of consecutive Baptist history."[7] These churches are often referred to as General Baptists.[8] In 1586, Smyth entered Christ's College, Cambridge University, in order to prepare for ministry as an Anglican priest. After graduating in 1590, he was invited to stay and teach at Christ's College. He was ordained as an Anglican priest in 1594. During his time at Cambridge he was influenced by Francis Johnson, a separatist who later led a separatist congregation.[9]

At first, Smyth was a moderate Puritan, but his views quickly became more radical. In fact, he spent some time in prison for his outspoken criticisms of the established church. Like many in his day, his language was harsh. He considered many Anglican priests to be "too papist," infant baptism was equated with spiritual adultery, and he was known to rebuke prominent sinners by name from the pulpit. There is not a great deal known about Smyth between 1600 and 1606, but it is certain that he continued to publish his criticisms of the state church.[10]

---

[6] Anthony R. Cross, "Baptists, Peace, and War: The Seventeenth-Century British Foundations," in *Baptists and War: Essays on Baptists and Military Conflict, 1640s - 1990s*, eds., Gordon L. Heath and Michael A. G. Haykin (Eugene: Pickwick, 2015), 1-31.

[7] McBeth, *The Baptist Heritage*, 32.

[8] General Baptist churches held to the Arminian version of the faith (Jacobus Arminius, 1560-1609). Unlike the Calvinists, General Baptists stressed human ability to choose (or renounce) to follow Christ and that no one was predestined to hell/heaven. Particular Baptist churches held to the Calvinist version of the faith (John Calvin, 1509-1564). Unlike their Arminian and General atonement counterparts, these Baptists believed in a particular atonement – that Christ died only for the elect. They also stressed how humanity could not respond or chose, but needed God's grace and election in order to do so.

[9] In this context, a separatist was a person who wanted to separate from the Church of England.

[10] His two major works during this time were *The Bright Morning Starre* (1603) and *A Paterne of True Prayer* (1605).

In 1606, Smyth lived in Gainsborough, in the Midlands. Smyth was occasionally asked to preach in the church when the minister was away. When the church authorities heard that he was preaching they decreed that the practice must stop. This was, as one historian notes, the "final straw" that caused Smyth to finally quit the Church of England and become associated with a group of separatists in the area.[11]

The move to join a separatist church was a dangerous one. King James I threatened to force such dissenters out of the land if they did not conform to the state church. The risk of detection and persecution increased as the church in Gainsborough grew, so the church divided into two smaller groups. Smyth joined with a well-to-do layperson named Thomas Helwys to provide leadership to one of the groups. Both groups fled to Holland around the same time (1607). The Smyth-Helwys group adopted believer's baptism and became Baptists, the other group left in 1620 on board the *Mayflower* to the nascent empire in America. Smyth and Helwys (along with their followers) split over Smyth's affinity for the Mennonites. Smyth was never received into membership in the Mennonite Church (although his followers eventually would in 1615) and he died of illness on 20 August 1612 outside of any formal church.

In 1611, Helwys led his small band of followers back to Spitalfield, a section of London. This is considered to be the first Baptist Church on English soil. Once he was back in England, Helwys published his famous work *A Short Declaration of the Mystery of Iniquity* (1612), an attack on the Church of England and defence of religious liberty that drew the government's attention. He was imprisoned and died in Newgate Prison in 1616. Upon Helwys' imprisonment, the leadership of the church passed into the hands of John Murton (or Morton). Murton also died in prison (1626), but the churches continued to grow. By 1624, there were at least five General Baptist churches in England; by 1650 there were at least forty-seven.[12]

One key figure to note in regards to Particular Baptist origins is Henry Jacob (1563-1624). While Smyth was becoming radicalized at Cambridge, Jacob was developing a more moderate form of criticism at Oxford. Jacob called for reform in the Church of England but did not initially advocate separation. His relatively restrained *Reasons taken out of God's Word and the best humane Testimonies proving a necessitie of reforming our Chvrches in England* (1605) attracted the attention of the State and he was subsequently imprisoned. Upon his release, he fled to Holland like so many others. There, he served as a pastor of an independent church.

In 1616, Jacob returned to England and founded a church in the Southwark section of England. This is often called the JLJ church: its three pastors were Henry Jacob, John Lathrop, and Henry Jessey. This church would eventually give rise to the first Particular Baptist Church. In 1622, Jacob went to Virginia

---

[11] McBeth, *The Baptist Heritage*, 33.
[12] McBeth, *The Baptist Heritage*, 39.

where he later died in 1624. Other Particular Baptist churches remained in London and, by 1644, seven churches in the London area issued a joint statement of faith.

Baptist churches carried out their ministry into the seventeenth century facing significant obstacles. As W.T. Whitley states, Baptists "were at liberty to live, be governed, pay taxes, think, print, preach, worship, on very simple conditions. But every avenue to civic and national life was blocked; some low post under the guardians, a halberd in the army, or warrant in the navy, was the limit of possibility."[13] However, the fortunes of Baptists changed significantly due to the evangelical revivals that occurred under figures such as John and Charles Wesley and George Whitefield, and reported by Jonathan Edwards.[14] As a result of these mid-late eighteenth-century revivals their numbers rose substantially in Britain and America.

By the nineteenth century, Baptists had gained much in the way of enfranchisement, numbers, and organization. Baptists and other nonconformists benefited from the repeal of the Test and Corporations Acts in 1828, a law that had limited the rights of non-Anglicans. Baptist church membership in England, Wales, Scotland and Ireland (England and Wales being by far the two largest contingents) in 1900 was around 362,000 with over 6,600 church buildings.[15] Nevertheless, Baptists in Britain remained a relatively small nonconformist denomination, for in the same year Church of England membership was close to 2,100,000, Scottish Presbyterians at 1,164,000, Roman Catholics at 2,000,000, and total nonconformists (including Baptists) just over 1,800,000.[16] Baptists had initially organized by association, but larger national unions followed. Baptists formed the Baptist Missionary Society in 1792 as a means to support and carry out overseas missions work primarily in areas controlled by the British Empire. Particular Baptists formed the Baptist Union of Great Britain (England and Wales) in 1813, and in 1891 the Baptist Union was adapted to allow for both General and Particular membership. The Baptist Union of Scotland was formed in 1865. These unions joined associations in common causes and provided necessary support for the local churches.

Despite their small numbers within the larger religious landscape, Baptists were usually not an isolated sect disengaged from the wider culture – especially

---

[13] W.T. Whitley, *A History of British Baptists* (London: The Kingsgate Press, 1932), 198.

[14] Roger Hayden claims that the reporting of Edwards played a huge role in the stoking of revival fires among British Particular Baptists. He writes, "It is almost impossible to exaggerate Jonathan Edward's impact on eighteenth-century Particular Baptists." See Roger Hayden, *English Baptist History and Heritage* (Didcot: Baptist Union, 2005), 120.

[15] Robert Currie, Alan Gilbert, and Lee Horsley, *Church and Churchgoers: Patterns of Church Growth in the British Isles since 1700* (Oxford: Clarendon Press, 1977), 163, 213.

[16] Currie et al., *Church and Churchgoers*, 25.

after the repeal of the Tests and Corporation Acts opened up educational and public service opportunities. The ministry of the world-renowned late-Victorian Baptist preacher Charles Haddon Spurgeon contributed to the increased respectability of Baptists as well as global influence of Baptists in places such as Tasmania and New Zealand (where, as will be noted below, Spurgeon's son Thomas pastored a church).

The floodgates of British emigration opened after the revolutionary wars in America and France, with approximately 22.6 million people leaving the British Isles between 1815 and 1914.[17] Over half of those settlers went to the United States, with the remainder going mainly to the colonies of Canada, Australia, South Africa and New Zealand. For those not heading to the US, Canada was the "favoured destination for British migrants" until around 1870, when the opening of the Suez Canal and technological improvements in ship design and communication made travel to Australia and New Zealand more appealing.[18] Included in those waves of settlers were Baptists, and churches in the colonies were both born and bolstered by their arrival.

Canada

The pattern of Baptist settlement in what would eventually be called Canada was from east to west. New England Baptists arrived in Nova Scotia mid-eighteenth century to take over land that had been vacated by the expulsion of the French-speaking Acadians. Other Baptists continued to arrive from the Thirteen Colonies (later the United States), and churches were planted in Nova Scotia and New Brunswick. Baptists benefited from the New Light revivals under Henry Alline (1748-1784) and by the end of the eighteenth century the first Baptist association of nine churches was formed. Baptists were particularly concentrated in the Annapolis Valley and South Shore in Nova Scotia, and the St. John River Valley in New Brunswick. The ending of the American Revolutionary War in 1783 brought about a remarkable change in the religious composition of the British territory, for during and after the war over 50,000 loyalists headed north to British-held territory (both the Maritimes and Upper and Lower Canada). Within the mix of Loyalists who arrived in the frontier land of Upper and Lower Canada were Anglicans, Presbyterians, Methodists, Lutherans, Mennonites, and Quakers, but few Baptists. After the flood of Loyalists came American settlers (including Baptists) to what would eventually be called Ontario. With the aid of American missionaries and the arrival of Baptist British settlers Baptist work continued to grow slowly in Central Canada.

Maritime Baptists formed their first association in 1800, and Upper Canada followed a few years later in 1802 (some Upper and Lower-Canadian Baptist churches belonged to American associations). Unlike other Baptists in this re-

---

[17] Bridge and Fedorowich, "Mapping the British World," 4.
[18] Bridge and Fedorowich, "Mapping the British World," 4.

The British Nation is Our Nation

search, Canadian Baptists did not organize nationally in a Baptist Union. Instead, Baptists organized within regional conventions:[19] the Maritime Baptist Convention formed in 1846, the Baptist Convention of Ontario and Quebec began in 1888, and western Baptists organized later with the establishment of the Baptist Convention of Western Canada in 1907.

At the end of the nineteenth century, Canadian churches wielded a significant amount of influence in the formation of public morals, religious beliefs, and political sentiments. The Protestant churches had an influence on English Canadian society unlike any other institution. By the end of the nineteenth century, there was a broadly-based Protestant consensus to forge ahead with making the new Dominion a Christian nation.[20] In French Canada, it was the Roman Catholic Church that held power with 2,229,600 members, whereas in English Canada, the big four Protestant denominations dominated the religious landscape. Neck and neck in the race for the title of the largest Canadian Protestant denomination were the Methodists and Presbyterians. In 1901, Methodists comprised 17.1% of the population and Presbyterians accounted for 15.7%. In third place was the Anglican Church with 12.7% and Baptists a distant fourth place with 318,666 adherents that represented 5.9% of the population. Together, these four denominations comprised 51.4% of Canadians. The Roman Catholic Church made up 41.5%. The remaining less than 10% was comprised of a wider variety of smaller (mainly Protestant) groups.[21]

There was significant optimism at the turn of the century due to a booming economy, the discovery of gold in the Klondike, and the arrival of new waves of settlers. This growing sense of optimism was shared by the four major Canadian Protestant denominations and they were confident that they could overcome their obstacles and continue the transformation of Canada into a Christian nation.

---

[19] The Canadian Baptist Federation was formed in 1944, but this was an umbrella organization wherein the regional conventions remained.

[20] Airhart, "Ordering a New Nation and Reordering Protestantism," 99.

[21] In 1901, Ontario's Anglican, Baptist, Methodist and Presbyterian membership made up almost 75% of the population. 18% of Ontario's population was Roman Catholic. The Anglicans, Baptists, Methodists and Presbyterians dominated the Protestant religious landscape in Ontario, comprising over 95% of all Protestants in Ontario. See Neil Semple, *The Lord's Dominion: The History of Canadian Methodism* (Montreal: McGill-Queen's University Press, 1996), 181-182. However, in terms of percentage of population, Baptist strength was in the Maritimes, where Baptists comprised 25-35% of the population. See Brian Clarke, "English-Speaking Canada from 1854," in *A Concise History of Christianity in Canada*, eds., Terrence Murphy and Roberto Perin (Oxford: Oxford University Press, 1996), 263.

Australia

Australia was targeted for settlement by British authorities after the loss of the Revolutionary War with America. Settlement began in 1788 near Sydney Cove (narrowly beating the French who also had strategic designs on the region). Initially, the majority of those arriving were convicts, but over the following decades increasing numbers of settlers arrived (the last convict ship arrived in 1868).[22] Baptist settlers arrived in Australia from Britain in the early 1830s. The first worship service was organized in Sydney in 1831. By the mid-1830s, a number of congregations were established.[23]

Baptist growth began in New South Wales and moved westward to the other states: Tasmania, Victoria, South Australia, Queensland and Western Australia. By the end of the century, Baptists had grown to include 18,261 members, 236 churches, and 169 ordained ministers.[24] In 1891, South Australia had the highest percentage of Baptists (10 members per 1000 population), 4.5% in Victoria, 5% in Queensland, 4% in Tasmania and only 1.5% in New South Wales.[25] They were at their peak in 1901 when they comprised 2.37% of the population.[26] By comparison, Anglicans were 40%, Roman Catholics 23%, and other Christian denominations were 34%, out of a population of 3.8 million.[27]

---

[22] W.D. Borrie, "'British' Immigration to Australia," in *Australia and Britain: Studies in a Changing Relationship*, eds., A.F. Madden and W.H. Morris-Jones (Sydney: Sydney University Press, 1908), 101-116.

[23] Tony Cupit claims that the first known Baptist to arrive in Australia was a convict named Richard Boots, who arrived in 1811 to serve time at the penal colony at Sydney Cove. See Tony Cupit, "Patterns of Development among Baptists in Australia, New Zealand and Papua New Guinea in the First Fifty Years since their Respective Beginnings," in *The Gospel in the World: International Studies, Volume One*, ed. David Bebbington (Carlisle: Paternoster Press, 2002), 252. See also Ken R. Manley, "'Our own church in our own land': The Shaping of Baptist Identity in Australia," in *Baptist Identities: International Studies from the Seventeenth to the Twentieth Centuries*, eds., Ian M. Randall, Toivo Pilli and Anthony Cross (Milton Keynes: Paternoster, 2006), 284; Ken Manley and Michael Petras, *The First Australian Baptists* (Eastwood, NSW: Baptist Historical Society of NSW, 1981), 25-26; J.D. Bollen, *Australian Baptists: A Religious Minority* (London: Baptist Historical Society, 1975); Philip J. Hughes, *The Baptists in Australia* (Canberra: Australian Government Publishing Service, 1996).

[24] Church membership figures found in the 1899 *Baptist Union Handbook*, as quoted by McBeth, *The Baptist Heritage*, 327. Manley notes, however, that census figures are significantly higher than the handbook figures. For instance, the total census figure in 1901 for Baptists in all of Australia was 89,349. See Manley, *From Woolloomooloo to 'Eternity,'* 108; Hughes, *The Baptists in Australia*, ch.5.

[25] Manley, *From Woolloomooloo to 'Eternity'*, *Vol. 1*, 108.

[26] Hughes, *The Baptists in Australia*, 39; Manley, "Our own church in our own land," 282.

[27]

www.abs.gov.au/ausstats/abs@.nsf/7d12b0f6763c78caca257061001cc588/636F496B2B 943F 12CA2573D200109DA9?opendocument

While Australian Baptist churches had a "fundamental British orientation,"[28] Australian Baptist life included a significant German presence. Germans were the third largest immigrant group of European settlers (after British and Irish), and a number of them were Baptists.[29] Nevertheless, the predominantly British origins of the denomination meant that Australian Baptists had a racial and cultural orientation that expected and encouraged imperial connections with England and the empire.

Baptist associations formed within the various colonies of New South Wales, Victoria, Queensland, South Australia, Tasmania, Western Australia. The formation of the new Federation in 1901 inspired Baptists to begin to work towards a national identity. They formed a national paper *The Australian Baptist* in 1913, but it was 1926 before they formally organized on a national level with the birth of the Baptist Union of Australia.

Baptists in Australia faced a number of problems. McBeth notes that the churches suffered from the irreligion of the earliest colonists (the continent being a dumping ground and penal colony for many of Britain's worst criminals), divisions among Baptists, neglect from Baptists in Britain, dependence upon lay preachers, and an identification with the lower classes.[30] They were criticized for their Puritanism,[31] and were divided on how to go about engaging social issues and modern theologies.[32] Nevertheless, Australian Baptists sought to engage in Australian public life as well as forge a particular Australian Baptist identity.[33] Unlike Canadian Baptists who relatively ignored the formation of their Dominion of Canada on 1 July 1867 (as did most other Canadian denominations at the time[34]), Australian Baptists celebrated the birth of the Australian Commonwealth on 1 January 1901. The development of a national voice and identity, however, was limited by their minority status, reputation as wowsers,[35] and sectarian strife (like many Baptists in other countries, Australian Baptists were ardently anti-Catholic[36]). Despite such handicaps, the end of the century

---

[28] Manley, *From Woolloomooloo to 'Eternity'*, *Vol. 1*, 108-109. See also J. D. Bollen, "English-Australian Baptist Relations, 1830-1860," *Baptist Quarterly* 27, no. 7 (July 1974): 290-305.

[29] Manley, *From Woolloomooloo to 'Eternity'*, *Vol. 1*, 168-176.

[30] McBeth, *The Baptist Heritage*, 325-327. For an analysis of English Baptist neglect of Australian Baptists, see Bollen, "English-Australian Baptist Relations," 290-305.

[31] Manley, *From Woolloomooloo to 'Eternity'*, *Vol. 1*, ch.7.

[32] Manley, *From Woolloomooloo to 'Eternity'*, *Vol. 1*, ch.7.

[33] For a discussion of the development of Australian Baptist identity, see Manley, *From Woolloomooloo to 'Eternity'*, *Vol. 1*, ch.5; Manley, "Our own church in our own land."

[34] Preston Jones, "'His Dominion'?: Varieties of Protestant Commentary on the Confederation of Canada." *Fides et Historia* 32 (Summer/Fall 2000): 83-88.

[35] A derisive term for those who sought to reform the morals of others. Australian Baptists, Methodists and Presbyterians were all mocked as "wowsers." See Manley, *From Woolloomooloo to 'Eternity'*, *Vol. 1*, 353.

[36] Manley, *From Woolloomooloo to 'Eternity'*, *Vol. 1*, 200-203.

was marked by a degree of optimism as the churches looked to the new century and the possibilities before them.

New Zealand

While various European trade settlements were loosely established in New Zealand in the early nineteenth century, the threat of unruly settlers, possible French imperial encroachment, and inroads by the New Zealand Company led to British control being formalized in 1840 with the signing of the Treaty of Waitangi with the Maori. New Zealand formally became a colony of Britain in May 1841.

The first Baptist settlers began arriving in 1841, and often met for worship with other denominations due to a lack of pastors and churches.[37] The arrival of Decimus Dolamore in 1851, the first Baptist pastor in New Zealand, led to the forming of the first Baptist church in Nelson colony that same year. Baptists continued to arrive as the immigrants and churches benefited from their arrival. Baptist strength was located around Auckland and Wellington on the North Island, and Christchurch and Dunedin on the South Island.[38] However, Baptists remained a relatively small minority in the larger Christian community. Significant English settlement in the north led to Anglican strength in that region, Scottish settlement in the south meant that Presbyterianism was strongest in the south, and Catholics settled primarily on the west coast of the South Island. Those three groups – in that order – dominated the Christian landscape.

The organization of the churches began in 1873 with an association of six churches that came together to form the Canterbury Baptist Association. The Baptist Union of New Zealand, comprised of twenty two churches, was formed in 1882. while the New Zealand Baptist Missionary Society was formed in 1885. The churches were struck a blow in the 1880s when economic recession led to numerous Baptists leaving for Australia or back to Britain. The number of church attendees declined between 1882-1892.[39] While the 1890s were the "golden age" for New Zealand politics in regards to sweeping social reforms concerning land, labor and liberties, Baptists "were not much involved" in poli-

---

[37] McBeth, *The Baptist Heritage*, 328. The July 1842 special issue of the *Baptist Magazine* encouraged an entire community to emigrate to New Zealand; although no Baptist community en masse took up the offer, individual Baptists did. See Tonson, *A Handful of Grain*, 71. See also Martin Sutherland, "Baptist Expansion in Colonial New Zealand," *New Zealand Journal of Baptist Research* 9 (2004): 3-23.

[38] McBeth, *The Baptist Heritage*, 328. See also Bill Leonard, *Baptist Ways: A History* (Valley Forge: Judson Press, 2003), 298.

[39] McBeth, *The Baptist Heritage*, 332. That period has been referred to as the "Long Depression," "Long Stagnation," or the "Black Eighties." See James Belich, *Paradise Reforged: A History of the New Zealanders from the 1880s to the Year 2000* (Honolulu: University of Hawai'i Press, 2001), ch.1.

tics, for they were "numerically insignificant and were struggling to maintain their life and witness."[40]

Besides the struggle with declining numbers due to periods of emigration, Baptists in New Zealand faced similar problems that other settler Baptist communities in the white colonies faced such as lack of leaders and resources, minority status, and theological conflicts that stifled growth. The "more confined environment" in New Zealand also often "exacerbated difficulty and differences"[41] for the struggling churches.

There were thirty-five churches in 1903. Local church membership numbered 3,721 adherents and 16,035 people self-identified as Baptists during the 1903 census. However, the fortunes of Baptists began to turn with the advent of the new century. Successful evangelism and economic development led to growing optimism. Over the course of the next decade, Baptists formed twenty-two new churches, and in some cases experienced almost 50% growth.[42]

South Africa

The Baptist presence in South Africa was also a result of the expansion of the British Empire. There had been tensions between the Dutch settlers and the British authorities ever since the British annexation of the Boer territory during the Napoleonic Wars in 1806. In 1837, there began a Boer movement northward out of the reach of British rule in a migration coined the Great Trek.

The first English Baptists arrived with the earliest settlers in 1820 in the Cape Colony, and a number of German settlers in the 1850s added to the ranks of Baptists.[43] In fact, by the time the Baptist Union was formed in 1877, German Baptists slightly outnumbered the English Baptists. Baptist expansion among the Dutch settlers occurred, but was quite limited.

Baptist growth was northwards, with aims of bringing the gospel to the hinterland and "natives." Limited resources meant that the churches had to rely on the arrival of settlers for infusions of people and finances. Theological controversy—whether dealing with the debate between Calvinism and Arminianism or the question of open vs. closed communion—also hindered the church from further growth.

The formation of the Baptist Union was an important development in the life of the South African Baptists, although the number of Baptists in the newly-

---

[40] J. Ayson Clifford, *A Handful of Grain: The Centenary History of the Baptist Union of New Zealand, Volume Two – 1882-1914* (Wellington: New Zealand Baptist Historical Society), 57.

[41] Cupit, "Patterns of Development," 254.

[42] Clifford, *A Handful of Grain*, 71.

[43] This material on South Africa Baptist history taken from McBeth, *The Baptist Heritage*, 332-334; Sydney Hudson-Reed, ed., *Together for a Century: The History of the Baptist Union of South Africa, 1877-1977* (Pietermaritzburg: South African Baptist Historical Society, 1977).

formed union was modest: six churches (four English and two German). By 1894, the union had over 3,000 European members and close to two hundred African members. Although this signalled significant growth, Baptists were still in no position to compete with the demographically dominant denominations such as the Anglicans and various Reformed Dutch churches. They also failed to make a significant impact among indigenous groups whose numbers were significantly larger than all the white settlers combined.

In March 1899, the Baptist Assembly met for the first time outside of British territory. The site was Pretoria, the capital city of the Transvaal Republic. Transvaal President Kruger addressed the Assembly and, at the time, Baptists were impressed with his kind words and formal greeting. Sadly, the collegial cross-border feelings would not last long. In the following months, tensions rose as war loomed on the horizon and the very same Kruger became the per-sonification of the Boer hatred of all things British. With the outbreak of war, South African Baptists faced the devastation of war unlike their co-religionists in Britain, Canada, Australia or New Zealand. For instance, South African Baptists had to abandon the Forward Movement started in 1899 and create a War Losses Fund to respond to the devastation occasioned by the conflict. The situation of South African Baptists also attracted the attention of British Baptists. In October 1901, they formed the South African Colonial and Missionary Aid Society to help with ministers for vacant pulpits, finances for missions, and new churches. The society was quite successful in increasing the profile of South African Baptists among British Baptists, especially in the pages of the *Baptist Times and Freeman*.

Conclusion

Baptists were born in Britain in the early seventeenth century around the time of the beginnings of the British Empire in the Americas. Baptist growth in sub-sequent centuries was due to a variety of factors, including a number of interre-lated imperial and British connections. The global British imperial struggles and successes of the eighteenth and nineteenth centuries determined the desti-nation of most Baptist immigrants. From the eighteenth-century Baptist plant-ers who arrived in Nova Scotia to take over farms from the displaced Acadians to the nineteenth-century settlers who followed the flag into New Zealand after the Treaty of Waitangi, Baptists had benefited from the advances of the empire.

Ties to the empire often remained generations after the arrival of the initial settlers, and those ties were nurtured by British leaders, British financial sup-port, and British literature. The lack of educational facilities in the colonies meant that for decades the churches had to rely on imported leaders. The influ-ence of British leaders can readily be seen in such examples of the influence of Spurgeon on Tasmanian churches, the leadership of his son Thomas in New Zealand Baptist churches, or the dependence of Canadian Baptists on British leaders.[44] In the late nineteenth century, more graduates of Spurgeon's College travelled to Australia or New Zealand than to the United States of South Africa. The majority of Baptist ministers who came from Britain to Australia were also trained at Spurgeon's College.[45] Visits by prominent British Baptists were cause for rejoicing, and in such visits the imperial connection was often highlighted. For example, responding to a Queensland Baptist request to include their association in his upcoming visit to Australia, Dr. Clifford extolled the work of the Queensland Baptists for what they contributed to Australia and the empire: "I feel from the glimpses I have already obtained of Sydney and Melbourne the greatness of your mission as Christians, as Christian preachers and as Christian churches, and the momentous influence you must exert on the development of the Empire."[46] This placing of denominational work in a larger imperial context was repeated by numerous lesser-known preachers imported into the colonies from Britain over the course of the nineteenth century. Financial support was a common theme in the early decades of Baptist settlement, and during the war the calls for financial assistance from South African Baptists to their Baptist brothers and sisters in Britain were marked by a sense of urgency. The literature available to Baptists was initially all produced in Britain, but by the end of the nineteenth century Baptists in the colonies had developed their own press. Nevertheless, material from Britain was still circulated, and the Baptist press was still very much dependant on British cable news and reprinted articles and sermons from Britain. One net effect of the ongoing reliance of the Baptists in the colonies on British leaders, financial support, and literature was the continuance of British imperial connections and a sense of belonging to a larger Baptist and British family.

Once established in the colonies, Baptists continued to look forward to further waves of immigrants for reinforcements. Those immigrants transformed the identities and loyalties of the churches. For instance, the arrival of British Baptists after the War of 1812 was instrumental in transforming the Upper Canadian Baptist churches from an American orientation to a British one. Another example is how waves of British settlers in the late-nineteenth century cemented and deepened British connections to the distant islands of New Zealand.

---

[44] For a summary of the British influence among Baptists in the peripheries, see Robert S. Wilson, "British Influence in the Nineteenth Century," in *Baptists in Canada: Search for Identity Amidst Diversity*, ed., Jarold K. Zeman (Burlington: G.R. Welch, 1980), 21-43; Ken Manley, "'The Magic Name': Charles Haddon Spurgeon and the Evangelical Ethos of Australian Baptists," *Baptist Quarterly* 40, no. 3 (July 2003): 173-184; Ken Manley, "'The Magic Name': Charles Haddon Spurgeon and the Evangelical Ethos of Australian Baptists," *Baptist Quarterly* 40, no. 4 (October 2003): 215-229; Ken R. Manley, "'To the Ends of the Earth': Regent's Park College and Australian Baptists," *Baptist Quarterly* 42 (April 2007): 130-147; Bollen, "English-Australian Baptist Relations"; Piggin, "The American and British Contribution to Evangelicalism in Australia."

[45] Stuart Piggin, *Evangelical Christianity in Australia: Spirit, Word and World* (Oxford: Oxford University Press), 58.

[46] "The Rev. Dr. Clifford," *Queensland Baptist*, June 1897, 77.

Indeed, for much of the nineteenth century the predominantly British origins of new settlers meant that the familial connections to mother Britain and empire were deepened and strengthened.

The social location of each Baptist communion often had a direct bearing on specific reactions. The presence of a divided English-French Canada over the war meant that Canadian Baptists had to deal with domestic opposition to the war in a way that Baptists in the other colonies did not. Another striking example of unique circumstances having a bearing on the Baptist response to the war and empire is that of the delicate and desperate situation of Baptists in war-torn South Africa. Nevertheless, shaped by over a century of British imperial success, and nurtured by waves of British immigration, British leaders, British financial support and British literature, BACSANZ Baptist identity and purpose had become fused with imperialism. The following chapters explore how the Baptists' imperial commitments remained a potent factor in the development of views of national identity, global identity, justice and missions.

Chapter Two

The South African War

The war in South Africa was the "longest, costliest, bloodiest and most humiliating war fought by Britain between 1815-1914." Iain R. Smith, "The Boer War," *History Today* 34 (May 1984): 47.

European nations had rapidly expanded their overseas empires in the final decades of the nineteenth century and in the scramble for Africa almost the entire continent of Africa fell under the sway of a European power. Over 70 million Africans were added to the British Empire between 1882 to 1898 "at a cost of some 15p each."[1] By 1899, with an empire upon which the "sun never set," Britain was unique among the world powers and was the "world's greatest imperial power, at least in terms of territory and population."[2] This power, Byron Farwell claims, contributed to Victorian hubris, and "never before, nor since, had Britons swelled with such an intensity of imperial pride."[3]

In 1897, Britain celebrated its vast empire as well as the sixtieth anniversary of the reign of Queen Victoria. The highlight of the Jubilee celebrations was on 22 June, when the royal procession that included 50,000 troops from the various regions of the empire made its way from Buckingham Palace to St. Paul's Cathedral. The *Times* remarked: "History may be searched, and searched in vain, to discover so wonderful an exhibition of allegiance and brotherhood among so many myriads of men...The mightiest and most beneficial Empire ever known in the annals of mankind."[4] Poets, song writers, politicians, and preachers all extolled the virtues of the empire and its queen, and newspaper editors provided daily news and pictures to satisfy an almost insatiable appetite for things imperial. Despite its superpower status, however, there were gnawing doubts about Britain's ability to protect its empire. Along with the usual threats of other European imperial powers, rapid German and American economic and military growth made Britain's supremacy seem increasingly precarious. Those external threats, combined with worry over domestic social ills, eroded national

---

[1] D. M. Schreuder, *The Scramble for Southern Africa, 1877-1895: The Politics of Partition Reappraised* (Cambridge: Cambridge University Press, 1980), 2.

[2] Lawrence James, *The Rise and Fall of the British Empire* (New York: St. Martin's, 1994), 215.

[3] Byron Farwell, *The Great Anglo-Boer War* (New York: W. W. Norton, 1976), 53.

[4] As quoted in Denis Judd, *The Boer War* (London: Hart-Davis, MacGibbon, 1977), 132.

confidence, and the jingoism of the day was, in part, due to the feelings of insecurity felt by Victorians.

The most pressing problem facing the imperial authorities in 1899 was what
to do with the Transvaal Republic and the Orange Free State, the two Boer republics bordering their Cape and Natal colonies in South Africa. Ever since the
British annexation of the Boer territory during the Napoleonic Wars in 1806
there had been tensions between the Dutch settlers and the British authorities.
In 1837, there began a Boer movement northward out of the reach of British
rule in a migration coined the Great Trek. In 1852, Britain recognized the new-
ly formed Transvaal Republic in the Sand River Convention and the Orange
Free State in the Bloemfontein Convention in 1854. Peace was not to last, however, for in its desire to unite all of South Africa under the Union Jack, Britain
annexed the Transvaal in 1877. More conflict followed, with the Transvaalers
rebelling against British rule in 1880. Called the First Boer War by some, this
conflict included the Majuba Hill defeat of British troops, much celebrated by
the Boers and bemoaned by the British.[5] The Pretoria Convention in August
1881 ended the immediate hostilities. This arrangement gave the Transvaalers
complete self-government, subject to suzerainty of Queen Victoria. The Convention of London in 1884 was a revised version of the Pretoria Convention,
with one important difference; the Convention of London did not include any
reference to British suzerainty. This omission would lead to conflict in the
years to come, for its omission was interpreted differently by both the British
and the Boers.

The discovery of diamonds in 1867, and then of gold in the Transvaal in
1887, complicated the already fragile relations between Britain and the two
republics. Paul Kruger, president of the Transvaal during the South African
War, claimed that the "first and principal cause" of British aggression was the
discovery of the gold fields.[6] A related complication was the flood of foreigners
into the republic after the discovery of the gold. These Outlanders, or Uitland-
ers ("outsiders"), many of whom were British citizens, were not granted the
same rights as the Boers.

On 31 December 1895, claiming the Outlanders' grievances against the
Transvaal government as just cause, Cecil Rhodes, Prime Minister of the Cape
Colony, initiated a raid led by Dr. Leander Starr Jameson into the Transvaal
Republic with the aim of encouraging a revolt against the Transvaal authorities.
The Jameson Raid was a short-lived debacle, and the 500 or so raiders surren-
dered on 2 January 1896. One immediate result of the raid was a heightened

---

[5] For accounts of this conflict, see Joseph H. Lehmann, *The First Boer War* (London:
Jonathan Cape, 1972); Geo. R. Duxbury, *David and Goliath: The First War of Independence, 1880-1881* (South African National Museum of Military History, 1981); Oliver Ransford, *The Battle of Majuba Hill: The First Boer War* (London: John Murray,
1967).
[6] Paul Kruger, *The Memoirs of Paul Kruger* (Toronto: George A. Morang and Company
Limited, 1902), 120.

sense of distrust between the two republics and the British.[7] Despite the efforts of many to find a way around the impasse between Briton and Boer, by the summer of 1899 it appeared that another war was imminent.[8]

The Outbreak of War

The Boers invaded British territory on 11 October 1899, and Britain and its empire was officially at war.[9] The war went wrong for the British right from the start, with the Boers advancing into British territory and besieging the towns of Ladysmith, Mafeking and Kimberley. Humiliating losses on the battlefield continued into the new year. However, in the opening months of 1900 the fortunes of war turned and the British advanced into the two Republics and captured their capitals in March and June 1900. Victory was not immediately forthcoming, for the Boers shifted their strategy to a guerrilla campaign which prolonged the war for two more years at great cost.

As the war dragged on much of the initial support waned. One issue in particular that led to public outcries was the military's scorched earth policy along with that of concentration camps for Boer women and children. Emily Hobhouse's report in 1901 that detailed the horrors of the camps fuelled anti-war proponents, and led to the government launching the Fawcett Investigation (which confirmed Hobhouse's claims). The war ended on 31 May 1902 with the signing of the Treaty of Vereeniging. The two republics were absorbed into the British Empire, and the Union of South Africa was eventually formed in 1910.

The war cost Britain over 220 million pounds, and it took up to 440,000 troops to subdue the two republics. The human cost of the war was appalling: 22,000 British soldiers dead (7,800 of those killed in battle, the others died mainly of disease), between 6,000 and 7,000 Boer soldiers, and in the concentration camps comprised almost solely of Boer women and children the grim total of somewhere around 28,000 dead, along with 20,000 black Africans

---

[7] In the opinion of Winston Churchill, the Jameson Raid marked the beginning of many of Britain's woes. He said, "I date the beginning of these violent times in our country from the Jameson Raid." As quoted in Elizabeth Longford, *Jameson's Raid: The Prelude to the Boer War* (London: Grenada, 1982), 25.

[8] For summaries on the events leading up to the hostilities of 1899 see A.N. Porter, *The Origins of the South African War: Joseph Chamberlain and the Diplomacy of Imperialism, 1895-99* (Manchester: Manchester University Press, 1980); Iain R. Smith, *The Origins of the South African War, 1899-1902* (London: Longman, 1996).

[9] For accounts of the conflict in general, see Farwell, *The Great Anglo-Boer War*; Judd and Surridge, *The Boer War*; Peter Warwick, ed., *The South African War: The Anglo-Boer War 1899-1902* (Burnt Mill: Longman, 1980); Bill Nasson, *The South African War, 1899-1902* (Oxford: Oxford University Press, 1999); Greg Cuthbertson, Albert Grundlingh, and Mary-Lynn Suttie, eds., *Writing a Wider War: Rethinking Gender, Race, and Identity in the South African War, 1899-1902* (Athens: Ohio University Press, 2002).

dead.[10] As for the colonial contribution, approximately 30,000 overseas colonial troops participated in the conflict (7,368 Canadians, 16,632 Australians, 6,343 New Zealanders), while 52,000 came from Natal and Cape Colony (although a number came from the two conquered republics).[11]

Britain

The war was initially supported by a majority of Britons since British society was "imbued with a degree of nationalism and militarism."[12] However, there was a significant pro-Boer element.[13] The Khaki Election in 1900 was fought primarily over the war: the Conservative government of Prime Minister Lord Salisbury won, his cause bolstered by the recent triumphs of the British in South Africa.

Pro-Boer voices in Britain were often ridiculed and even faced mob violence. Britain's European imperial competitors privately and even publicly celebrated the bungling of the empire's armies, behaviour that provoked outrage in Britain over the perfidy of such nations. It seemed to many in Britain that other nations were plotting against them, and were even considering allying themselves with the Boers. Irish nationalists did sympathize with the Boers, people that seemed to them to be co-sufferers under imperial rule. What made it worse among British public opinion was that a number of Irish volunteered to fight with the Boers (despite the fact that significant numbers of Irish fought in the British army against the Boers).

---

[10] David Omissi and Andrew Thompson, "Introduction: Investigating the Impact of the War," in *The Impact of the South African War*, eds., David Omissi and Andrew Thompson (Houndsmill: Palgrave, 2002), 7-8.
[11] Thomas Pakenham, "The Contribution of the Colonial Forces," in *One Flag, One Queen, One Tongue: New Zealand, The British Empire and the South African War*, eds., John Crawford and Ian McGinnon (Auckland: Auckland University Press, 2003), 59.
[12] M.D. Blanch, "British Society and the War," in *The South African War: The Anglo-Boer War 1899-1902*, ed., Peter Warwick (Burnt Mill: Longman, 1980), 210-237.
[13] For instance, see Bernard Porter, *Critics of Empire: British Radicals and the Imperial Challenge*, 2nd ed. (London: I.B. Tauris, 2008); Arthur Davey, *The British Pro-Boers: 1877-1902* (Cape Town: Tafelberg Publishers Limited, 1978); Paul Laity, "The British Peace Movement and the War," in *The Impact of the South African War*, eds., David Omissi and Andrew S. Thompson (Hounds Mill: Palgrave, 2002), 138-156; Alan Jeeves, "Hobson's *The War in South Africa: A Reassessment*," in *Writing a Wider War: Rethinking Gender, Race, and Identity in the South African War, 1899-1902*, eds., Greg Cuthbertson, Albert Grundlingh and Mary-Lynn Suttie (Athens: Ohio University Press, 2002), 233-246; Bernard Porter, "The Pro-Boers in Britain," in *The South African War: The Anglo-Boer War 1899-1902*, ed., Peter Warwick (Burnt Mill: Longman, 1980), 239-257; David Nash, "Taming the God of Battles: Secular and Moral Critiques of the South African War," in *Writing a Wider War: Rethinking Gender, Race, and Identity in the South African War, 1899-1902*, eds., Greg Cuthbertson, Albert Grundlingh and Mary-Lynn Suttie (Athens: Ohio University Press, 2002), 266-286.

The churches in Britain were divided over the war. With a few notable exceptions, the Church of England was virtually unanimous in its support of the war effort, the conviction being that Britain's cause was righteous and needed to be defended.[14] The rhetoric of a number of Anglican clergymen revealed a commitment to the ideal of empire with concomitant notions of Anglo-Saxon superiority and advanced rule of justice. However, even with almost universal support for the empire and its war aims, there were prophetic critiques of the sins and hubris of the nation.[15] Unlike the Anglican experience, there were considerable ruptures among the nonconformists (denominations outside the structure and authority of the established Church of England, such as Congregationalists, Methodists, Quakers, Presbyterians and Baptists). While the roots of opposition to the war were not always religious,[16] the nonconformist conscience was "pricked" by the war.[17] A number of helpful studies have detailed those divisions, Greg Cuthbertson's being one of the most extensive.[18] He outlines how the scope of nonconformist opposition to the war is difficult to discern, how the movement failed to create a mass movement (partly due to nonconformists already being captivated with Britain's imperial project), how much of the churches' pacifism ended when the war was declared, how a great deal of

---

[14] Margaret Blunden, "The Anglican Church during the War," in *The South African War: The Anglo-Boer War, 1899-1902*, ed., Peter Warwick (London: Longman Group Limited, 1980), 279-291; Mark D. Chapman, "Theological Responses in England to the South African War, 1899-1902," *Journal for the History of Modern Theology* 16, no. 2 (December 2009): 181-196.

[15] Mark Allen, "Winchester, the Clergy and the Boer War," in *God and War: The Church of England and Armed Conflict in the Twentieth Century* (Surrey: Ashgate, 2012): 15-31. See also Mark D. Chapman, "Theological Responses in England to the South African War, 1899-1902," *Journal for the History of Modern Theology* 16, no. 2 (December 2009): 187-191.

[16] Nash, "Taming the God of Battles," 266-286.

[17] Cuthbertson's expression. See Greg Cuthbertson, "Pricking the 'Nonconformist Conscience': Religion against the South African War," in *The South African War Reappraised*, ed., Donal Lowry (Manchester: Manchester University Press, 2000), 169-187.

[18] Cuthbertson, "Pricking the Nonconformist Conscience." See also Greg C. Cuthbertson, "The Nonconformist Conscience and the South African War, 1899-1902," (DLitt dissertation, University of South Africa, 1986); Greg C. Cuthbertson, "Preaching Imperialism: Wesleyan Methodism and the War," in *The Impact of the South African* War, eds., David Omissi and Andrew S. Thompson (Houndmills: Palgrave, 2002), 157-172. See also H.H. Hewison, *Hedge of Wild Almonds: South Africa, the 'Pro-Boers' and the Quaker Conscience, 1890-1910* (London: James Curry, 1989); David Bebbington, *The Nonconformist Conscience: Chapel and Politics, 1870-1914* (London: George Allen and Unwin, 1982); Noel J. Richards, "Political Nonconformity at the Turn of the Twentieth Century," *Journal of Church and State* 17 (1975): 239-258; Robert S. Wilson, "A House Divided: British Evangelical Parliamentary Influence in the Latter Nineteenth Century, 1860-1902," (PhD dissertation, University of Guelph, 1973), 454; Stewart J. Brown, *Providence and Empire, 1815-1914* (Harlow: Pearson, 2008), 435-436; A. Wilkinson, *Dissent or Conform? War, Peace and the English Churches, 1900-1945* (London: SCM, 1986).

the nonconformist opposition was from Quakers, Primitive Methodists and Free Methodists, and how the "most articulate and persuasive" voice against the war was Rev. Dr. John Clifford, a Baptist leader of considerable reputation in and out of Baptist circles. Clifford's outspoken attacks on the acquiescence of churches to jingoistic imperialism made him a number of enemies, and while Baptists en masse did not follow his antiwar position, his influence on Baptists remained significant.]

Canada

Most of the works dealing with Canada's role in the war can generally be placed within the rubric of political histories. These works on foreign policy are helpful for their placing of Canadian attitudes and defense policy decisions in the context of imperial and international pressures and responsibilities.[19] Not necessarily fitting within the category of political histories are the numerous studies that deal with the French-English social tensions in Canada, the specific histories of Canadian military units or organizations, or the numerous biographies of veterans.[20] These works describe the imperial sentiment that was at a feverish pitch during the war, national and international pressures that helped to shape attitudes to the war, as well as the domestic problems caused by the war. A formative work in the area of Canadian imperialism is Carl Berger's *The Sense of Power*. Berger explores many facets of imperialism in Canadian culture at the turn of the century. He understands the imperial impulse in Canada during the war to be one form of Canadian nationalism. It was this type of nationalism, he argues, that explains Canada's enthusiastic participation in an imperial war.[21] Phillip Buckner's work on Canadian imperial identity explores

---

[19] See Donald C. Gordon, *The Dominion Partnership in Imperial Defence, 1870-1914* (Baltimore: The John Hopkins Press, 1965); R. A. Preston, *Canada and "Imperial Defence": A Study of the Origins of the British Commonwealth Defence Organisation, 1867-1919* (Toronto: University of Toronto Press, 1967); Ramsey Cook, Craig Brown and Carl Berger, eds., *Imperial Relations in the Age of Laurier* (Toronto: University of Toronto Press, 1969); C. P. Stacey, *Canada and the Age of Conflict, 1867-1921*, vol. 1 (Toronto: University of Toronto Press, 1992).

[20] Carman Miller, "Research Resources on Canada and the South African War." *Archivaria* (Summer 1988): 116-121.

[21] Other important authors in this category are Norman Penlington, Robert Page, Douglas Cole, Terry Cook and Phillip Buckner. Penlington in *Canada and Imperialism* claims that Canada's participation in the war can best be understood in the context of Canadian and American animosity. He argues that Canada participated in the British cause in South Africa primarily because Canada needed British support in its land claims against the United States in the Yukon and British Columbia. Page, "Canada and the Imperial Idea" and *The Boer War*, illustrates how English Canada was passionate in its support for imperialism. See also Page, "Intellectual Origins of Canadian Imperialist Thought," 39-43. Buckner echoes Page's observations on how deeply rooted imperial concerns were among Anglophone Canadians. See Buckner, "Whatever Happened to the British Empire" and "Canada."

themes such as gender, economics and technology, but not religion.[22] The most authoritative work on Canada's involvement in the war is Carman Miller's *Painting the Map Red*.[23] While it acknowledges the important role of the churches in forming attitudes towards the war and claims that they were generally supportive of the war, Miller's work focuses primarily on the experiences of the Canadian troops who went overseas to South Africa. He pays relatively little attention to the reasons for the churches' support for the war.

Historians of Christianity in Canada such as John Webster Grant, Brian Clarke and John Moir briefly identify the imperial sentiment in the churches,[24] and William H. Magney, Neil Semple and Phyllis Airhart examine the nationalistic impulse in the Methodist church before and after the turn of the century.[25] Harry Renfree makes no mention of Canadian Baptist attitudes to the war in the standard Canadian Baptist denominational history *Heritage and Horizon*.[26] However, Heath's *A War with a Silver Lining* explores the response of Canadian Anglicans, Baptists, Methodists and Presbyterians to the war.[27] Support for the war expressed in the Canadian Protestant churches was rooted in the conviction that the war had a "silver lining." A British victory, it was believed, would lead ultimately to a furthering of the churches' own aims. Central to the ministry of

---

[22] Phillip Buckner, ed., *Canada and the British Empire* (Oxford: Oxford University Press, 2008); Phillip Buckner, ed., *Canada and the End of Empire* (Vancouver: UBC Press, 2005).

[23] Carman Miller, *Painting the Map Red: Canada and the South African War, 1899-1902* (Montreal/Kingston: McGill-Queen's University Press, 1998). Another helpful book detailing Canada's participation in the war is Brian A. Reid's *Our Little Army in the Field: The Canadians in South Africa* (St. Catherines: Vanwell Publishing Limited, 1996).

[24] John Webster Grant, *The Church in the Canadian Era* (McGraw-Hill Ryerson Limited, 1972. Reprint, Vancouver: Regent College Publishing, 1988); Clarke, "English-Speaking Canada From 1854," 304-305; John Moir, *Enduring Witness: The Presbyterian Church in Canada*, 2nd ed. (Burlington: Eagle Press Printers, 1987), 185-186, 192.

[25] William H. Magney, "The Methodist Church and the National Gospel, 1884-1914." *The Bulletin* 20 (1968): 3-95; Neil Semple, *The Lord's Dominion: The History of Canadian Methodism* (Montreal: McGill-Queen's University Press, 1996), ch.8; Airhart, "Ordering a New Nation."

[26] Harry A. Renfree, *Heritage and Horizon: The Baptist Story in Canada* (Mississauga: Canadian Baptist Federation, 1988).

[27] Gordon L. Heath, *A War with a Silver Lining: Canadian Protestant Churches and the South African War, 1899-1902* (Montreal: McGill-Queen's University Press, 2009). Other articles by Heath that deal with the churches and imperialism are as follows: Gordon L. Heath, "'Were We in the Habit of Deifying Monarchs': Canadian English Protestants and the Death of Queen Victoria, 1901," *Canadian Evangelical Review* (Fall 2005–Spring 2006): 72-97; Gordon L. Heath, "'Citizens of that Mighty Empire': Imperial Sentiment among Students at Wesley College, 1897-1902," *Manitoba History* (June 2005): 15-25; Gordon L. Heath, "Sin in the Camp: The Day of Humble Supplication in the Anglican Church in Canada in the Early Months of the South African War," *Journal of the Canadian Church Historical Society* 44 (Fall 2002): 207-226; Heath, "Passion for Empire," 127-147.

the churches was a concern for justice, nation, empire and missions. The application of justice, the development of the new nation Canada, the unifying and strengthening of the empire, and the spreading of missions were shared goals. A British victory in South Africa would help to accomplish all four of those at once. Those four aims had been pursued by the churches before the war began, but the war brought them into sharper focus and provided a unique context for their expression. Underlying support for the British cause was the belief in the providential establishing of the empire for the spreading of civilization and Christianity. Consequently, concomitant with these four aims was the idea that a British victory would benefit all involved; it would be good for Canadians, good for Britons, good for the empire, good for the entire world, and even good for the Boers. How could one not support the imperial effort, it was believed, with the interests of church and missions, nation and empire, the secular and the sacred, so intertwined? It was a war with a silver lining.[28]

Australia

Australia's commitment of 16,000 soldiers was over twice the size of Canada's, an important detail when colonies vied for the glory of who was the most loyal to mother England. A number of works deal with Australia's late-Victorian foreign policy, battlefield performance, and attitudes on the homefront.[29] L.M. Field provides a helpful summary of Australia's reasons for supporting the far-flung imperial conflict, a number of them remarkably similar to the Canadian experience: insecurity due to what was deemed foreign threats and the need to

---

[28] In a number of other articles, Heath demonstrates how Baptists were zealous imperialists and nationalists (something not considered to be mutually exclusive), but at the same time critical of what they deemed to be excesses and sins of empire. See Gordon L. Heath, "When Missionaries Were Hated: An Examination of the Canadian Baptist Defense of Imperialism and Missions during the Boxer Rebellion, 1900," in *Baptists and Mission*, eds., Ian M. Randall and Anthony R. Cross (Milton Keynes: Paternoster, 2007), 261-276; Gordon L. Heath, "Traitor, Half-Breeds, Savages and Heroes: Canadian Baptist Newspapers and Constructions of Riel and the Events of 1885," in *Baptists and Public Life in Canada*, eds., Gordon L. Heath and Paul Wilson (Eugene: Pickwick, 2012), 198-217; Gordon L. Heath, "The Nile Expedition, New Imperialism and Canadian Baptists, 1884-1885," *Baptist Quarterly* 44, no. 3 (July 2011): 171-186; Gordon L. Heath, "Canadian Baptists and Late-Victorian Imperial Spirituality" *McMaster Journal of Theology and Ministry* 15 (2013-2014): 165-196.
[29] T.B. Millar, *Australia in Peace and War: External Relations 1788-1977* (Canberra: Australian National University Press, 1978); Craig Wilcox, *Australia's Boer War: The War in South Africa, 1899–1902* (Oxford: Oxford University Press, 2002); R.L. Wallace, *The Australians at the Boer War* (Canberra: Australian War Memorial and Australian Government Publishing Service, 1976); Barbara Penny, "The Australian Debate on the Boer War," *Historical Studies*, 14 (April 1971): 526-545; C.N. Connolly, "Class, Birthplace, Loyalty: Australian Attitudes to the Boer War," *Historical Studies*, 18 (1978): 210-232.

solidify British promises of aid if attacked.[30] Despite its helpful summary of the passions and commitments that led to support for the war, Field's attention to the churches and how they understood the war is limited. As for widespread and exuberant displays of imperialism, Stephen Clarke and Craig Wilcox's research indicates that such passions were not manufactured in London or by military leaders, and were very similar to passions expressed in other parts of the empire: "The view from Wollongong or Wagga Wagga was little different to that from Wellington or Winnipeg."[31] However, the church's support for such imperialism is rarely discussed.

While there may have been a "demise of the imperial ideal" since the end of the Second World War,[32] late-Victorian Australian nationalism has been portrayed as inseparable from its imperial identity. This "duality of Australian self-perception" that Gavin Souter observes in *Lion and Kangaroo* is noted (and often lamented) by those exploring the development of Australian national identity.[33] However, missing in these narratives of evolving national identities and participation in the war is a sustained focus on the churches. Michael McKernan in *Australian Churches at War* and Robert D. Linder in *The Long Tragedy* have provided this type of concentration for the First World War, but

[30] Laurie Field, *The Forgotten War: Australian Involvement in the South African Conflict of 1899-1902* (Melbourne: Melbourne University Press, 1979), 3. For further discussion of strategic similarities between Australia and Canada, see John C. Blaxland, "Strategic Cousins: Canada, Australia and their use of Expeditionary Forces from the Boer War to the War on Terror," (PhD dissertation, Royal Military College of Canada, Kingston, 2003).
[31] Quote from page 151, Craig Wilcox, "The Australian Perspective on the War," in *One Flag, One Queen, One Tongue: New Zealand, The British Empire and the South African War*, eds., John Crawford and Ian McGibbon (Auckland: Auckland University Press, 2003), 151-164. See also Stephen Clarke, "Desperately Seeking Service: The Australasian Commandments and the War," in *One Flag, One Queen, One Tongue: New Zealand, The British Empire and the South African War*, eds., John Crawford and Ian McGibbon (Auckland: Auckland University Press, 2003), 12-27.
[32] Stuart Ward, *Australia and the British Embrace: The Demise of the Imperial Ideal* (Melbourne: Melbourne University Press, 2001).
[33] Gavin Souter, *Lion and Kangaroo: The Initiation of Australia 1901-1919* (Sydney: Collins, 1976), 109. See also Neville Meaney, "Britishness and Australian Identity: The Problem of Nationalism in Australian History and Historiography", *Australian Historical Studies* 32 (2001): 76–90; Ward, *Australia and the British Embrace*; W.G. McMinn, *Nationalism and Federalism in Australia* (Oxford: Oxford University Press, 1994); Barbara R. Penny, "Australia's Reactions to the Boer War – a Study in Colonial Imperialism," *Journal of British Studies* 7, no. 1 (November 1967): 97-130; S. Alomes, *A Nation at Last? The Changing Character of Australian Nationalism, 1880-1988* (Sydney: Angus & Robertson, 1988); J. Eddy and D. Schreuder, eds., *The Rise of Colonial Nationalism* (Sydney: Allen & Unwin, 1988); L. Trainor, *Imperialism and Australian Nationalism: Manipulation, Conflict and Compromise in the Late Nineteenth Century* (Cambridge: Cambridge University Press, 1994); Neville Meaney, "Britishness and Australia: Some Reflections," in *The British World: Diaspora, Culture and Identity*, eds., Carl Bridge and Kent Fedorowich (London: Frank Cass, 2003), 121-135.

the research on the Australian churches and the South African War is limited at best.[34]

The few articles that do pay particular attention to the churches and the war note their ardent imperialism. Arthur Patrick identifies how most Australian Methodists were pro-war, ardent defenders of empire, who believed that God in his providence would ultimately bring victory to the British cause.[35] The Methodist impulse to Christianize society, he concludes, was one important reason for their support. Their zeal for the imperial cause was rooted in the widespread conviction that the spread of the empire in Africa advanced civilization to the betterment of its subjects, and especially the fact that it helped put an end to the bane of slavery. Both Brian Fletcher and Robert Withycombe make it clear that late nineteenth-century Australian Anglicans were, for the most part, committed to the ideals of the empire and Australia's active engagement and defense of the same.[36] Despite active participation in events that nurtured a nascent and growing distinctly Australian identity, the Britishness and whiteness of Australia was encouraged by church authorities. Withycombe claims that the nationalities expressed and supported by the church were "complex, actively debated, but not clearly defined." What was clear was that there were common elements in the churches' attitudes:

> They include: the British monarchy as a focus of devoted loyalty and a moral icon; the British Empire as vital to their young nation's current security, identity, and future destiny; the peculiar duties and responsibilities incumbent upon members of the British, English, or "Anglo-Saxon" race; a shared fear of imperial *hubris*; and a cultural struggle in pulpit, press, and schoolroom to represent their history in ways that would educate adults and children towards a higher moral responsibility and so fulfil visions that were both national and imperial. It soon becomes clear that both before and after 1914, Anglicans resident in Australia apparently did not easily distinguish Australian nationalism from an Anglo-Saxon imperialism (and white racism).[37]

---

[34] Michael McKernan, *Australian Churches at War: Attitudes and Activities of the Major Churches, 1914-1918* (Sydney: Catholic Theological Faculty and Australian War Memorial, 1980); Michael McKernan, *Padre: Australian Chaplains in Gallipoli and France* (Sydney: Allen & Unwin, 1986); Robert D. Linder, *The Long Tragedy: Australian Evangelical Christians and the Great War, 1914-1918* (Adelaide: Openbook Publishers, 2000). See also John A. Moses, "Australian Anglican Leaders and the Great War, 1914-1918: the 'Prussian Menace,' Conscription, and National Solidarity," *Journal of Religious History* 25, no. 3 (October 2001): 306-323.

[35] Arthur Patrick, "'A Dreadful But Absolute Necessity': The Boer War according to The Methodist," *Church Heritage* 6, no. 4 (1980): 109-121.

[36] Brian Fletcher, "Anglicanism and Nationalism in Australia, 1901-62," *Journal of Religious History* 23 (June 1999): 215-233; Robert S.M. Withycombe, "Australian Anglicans and Imperial Identity, 1900-1914," *Journal of Religious History* 25, no. 3 (October 2001): 286-305.

[37] Robert S.M. Withycombe, "Australian Anglicans and Imperial Identity, 1900-1914," *Journal of Religious History* 25, no. 3 (October 2001): 287.

These works provide much needed commentary and analysis on Anglicans (and to a lesser degree the Methodists), but much more is needed. In regards to Baptists and the war, the recent two-volume work on Australian Baptist history by Ken Manley, *From Woolloomooloo to 'Eternity'*, identifies the war and imperial context, but pays significantly more attention to the First World War.[38]

New Zealand

Coverage of New Zealand's role in the war falls primarily into two related categories: New Zealand's contribution to the war, and the development of national and imperial identities. In regards to the war and New Zealand's contribution, a number of recent works, such as John Crawford and Ian McGibbon's *One Flag, One Queen, One Tongue: New Zealand, the British Empire and the South African War*, provide an excellent contemporary analysis of many aspects of the New Zealand and the war. Both Malcolm McKinnon and Megan Hutching have demonstrated how not all New Zealanders were supporters of the war.[39] McKinnon notes that opposition to the war was based on a number of factors, such as pacifism, anti-capitalism, Gladstonian liberalism, Irish nationalism (a link was seen between the struggle for rights of Boers and the Irish in Ireland), and war weariness. Hutching shows how the National Council of Women (NCW) opposed the war due to a commitment to international arbitration as a way to settle disputes and the natural concern mothers had for their sons. Despite these dissenting voices, numerous works have demonstrated that the majority of New Zealanders endorsed the sending of ten contingents to South Africa and displayed "overwhelming" public support for the war in its early stages.[40] Ellen Ellis' conclusions suggest that even the majority of New

---

[38] Manley, *From Woolloomooloo to 'Eternity'*.

[39] Malcolm McKinnon, "Opposition to the War in New Zealand," in *One Flag, One Queen, One Tongue: New Zealand, The British Empire and the South African War*, eds., John Crawford and Ian McGibbon (Auckland: Auckland University Press, 2003), 28-45; Megan Hutching, "New Zealand Women's Opposition to the South African War," in *One Flag, One Queen, One Tongue: New Zealand, The British Empire and the South African War*, eds., John Crawford and Ian McGibbon (Auckland: Auckland University Press, 2003), 46-57.

[40] Ian McGibbon, ed., *The Oxford Companion to New Zealand Military History* (Auckland, 2000), 59. See also, D.O.W. Hall, *The New Zealanders in South Africa, 1899-1902* (Wellington: Department of Internal Affairs, 1949); Ian McGibbon, *The Path to Gallipoli, Defending New Zealand 1840-1915* (Wellington: GP Books, 1991); John Crawford with Ellen Ellis, *To Fight for the Empire: An Illustrated History of New Zealand and the South African War, 1899-1902* (Auckland: Department of Internal Affairs, 1999); Christopher Pugsley, *The ANZAC Experience: New Zealand, Australia and Empire in the First World War* (Auckland: Reed, 2004), ch.2; John Crawford and Ian McGibbon, eds., *New Zealand's Great War: New Zealand, The Allies, and the First World War* (Auckland: Exisle, 2007).

Zealand women were "an active force" supporting the war effort.[41] Works have also dealt with the actual performance of New Zealand troops in the various theatres of war (in part to rethink the popular mythology that developed around the performance of the various New Zealand contingents),[42] the impact of the war on the development of New Zealand's military and strategic orientation,[43] the composition of the contingents,[44] the overall contribution of colonial forces,[45] and the response of the Maori to the war.[46]

The development of national and imperial identities has been the second area of attention for historians concerned with the war and New Zealand. Zealous loyalty to empire was common among most New Zealanders – a devotion shared by colonialists in Canada and Australia – and this has been noted by a number of contemporary historians.[47] What that imperial commitment meant in the development and construction of a distinctly New Zealand national identity has been the focus of historians such as Keith Sinclair and James Belich. Sinclair argues that both New Zealand and Canada shared a commitment to the empire out of a fear of a larger and looming neighbor; for Canada it was the United States and for New Zealanders it was Australia. He claims there was a New Zealand nationalism, but it was slow to develop independent of imperial identity: "A new nationalism was rising strongly among New Zealand-born. This sentiment was, in the long run, bound to predominate. But earlier British and imperial attitudes persisted and, indeed, in some ways were being rein-

---

[41] Ellen Ellis, "New Zealand Women and the War," in *One Flag, One Queen, One Tongue: New Zealand, The British Empire and the South African War*, eds., John Crawford and Ian McGibbon (Auckland: Auckland University Press, 2003), 128-150.

[42] John Crawford, "The Best Mounted Troops in South Africa?" in *One Flag, One Queen, One Tongue: New Zealand, The British Empire and the South African War*, eds., John Crawford and Ian McGibbon, (Auckland: Auckland University Press, 2003), 73-99.

[43] John Crawford, "The Impact of the War on the New Zealand Military Forces and Society," in *One Flag, One Queen, One Tongue: New Zealand, The British Empire and the South African War*, eds., John Crawford and Ian McGibbon, (Auckland: Auckland University Press, 2003), 205-214.

[44] Colin McGeorge, "The Social and Geographical Composition of the New Zealand Contingents," in *One Flag, One Queen, One Tongue: New Zealand, The British Empire and the South African War*, eds., John Crawford and Ian McGibbon, (Auckland: Auckland University Press, 2003), 100-118.

[45] Pakenham, "The Contribution of the Colonial Forces," 58-72.

[46] Ashley Gould, "'Different Race, Same Queen': Maori and the War," in *One Flag, One Queen, One Tongue: New Zealand, The British Empire and the South African War*, eds., John Crawford and Ian McGibbon (Auckland: Auckland University Press, 2003), 119-127.

[47] Ian McGibbon, "The Origins of New Zealand's South African War Contribution," in *One Flag, One Queen, One Tongue: New Zealand, The British Empire and the South African War*, eds., John Crawford and Ian McGibbon (Auckland: Auckland University Press, 2003), 1-11; Crawford and Ellis, *To Fight for the Empire*.

forced [by trade and migration]."[48] Belich contextualized New Zealand identity in what he calls the "recolonialization" of New Zealand. The late-nineteenth century waves of British immigrants made for a colony that was "Better British" – an ideology that stressed the British identity of New Zealanders, and even their superiority over other colonies and even Britain itself: "Better British ideology melded an increasingly intense assertion of Britishness with a pre-existing popular self-image and an embryonic collective identity. It maintained that New Zealanders were even more loyal and closely linked to Old Britain than other neo-Britains, but also that they were in some respects superior to Old Britons."[49] The manifestations of imperial zeal need to be seen as manifestations of this British identity, and that Better Britonism lasted well into the twentieth century. As others have noted, the war did begin a trajectory towards the development of a New Zealand national identity.[50] Ballantyne's recent work on "webs of empire" reinforces this trajectory of taking seriously New Zealand's imperial past, in particular the "interactions between global forces, imperial linkages, and local developments on the ground on the New Zealand frontier."[51]

As the case in the other colonies, what has been ignored in the analyses of New Zealand and the war has been a focus on the attitudes and actions of the churches. A number of authors have noted how the churches on the whole provided "strong religious sanction for the war"[52] and "threw themselves into support for the war effort."[53] However, there has been scant attention paid to the churches and the war. Laurie Guy's analysis of Baptist pacifists does indicate that support for the war was widespread among Baptists, but his attention is focused primarily on the First World War.[54] The most extensive source for an analysis of the New Zealand churches and the war is Hugh Morrison's look at Protestant mis-

---

[48] Keith Sinclair, *A Destiny Apart: New Zealand's Search for National Identity* (Wellington: Allen and Unwin, 1986), 108.

[49] Belich, *Paradise Reforged*, 78.

[50] Crawford with Ellis, *To Fight for the Empire*, 93.

[51] Ballantyne, *Webs of Empire*, 12-13.

[52] Guy, *Shaping Godzone*, 249.

[53] Peter Lineham, "First World War Religion", in *New Zealand's Great War: New Zealand, The Allies, and the First World War*, eds., John Crawford and Ian McGibbon (Auckland: Exisle, 2007), 469. See also Hugh Laracy, "Priests, People and Patriotism: New Zealand Catholics and the War, 1914-1918", *Australian Catholic Record* 70, no. 1 (1993): 14-26.

[54] Laurie Guy, "Baptist Pacifists in New Zealand: Creating Divisions in the Fight for Peace," *Baptist Quarterly*, 40, no. 8 (October 2004): 487-499. The denominational history of New Zealand Baptists makes little mention of the war. See J. Ayson Clifford, *A Handful of Grain: A Centenary History of the Baptist Union of New Zealand, Volume Two, 1882-1914* (Wellington: New Zealand Baptist Historical Society, 1982), 68, 114-115.

sionaries and imperialism in the late-nineteenth and early twentieth century.[55] While he notes that nationhood was a contested category, he asserts the fact that "New Zealand reflected British attitudes and trends is hardly surprising given its close imperial ties in this period. At the same time New Zealand was not a carbon copy of the metropole." He also claims that "theological and philosophical thinking about missions in late-nineteenth and early-twentieth century New Zealand were not easily disentangled from language extolling the virtues of Western civilization, and more particularly those of the British Empire." Central to the churches' imperial ideology was that the providentially established empire was a means to international unity, it exhibited superior moral qualities, and it had a trusteeship for the "lesser" races. Those imperial sentiments were bolstered by the shared British cultural and familial roots of New Zealanders.

South Africa

Optimists in government and the military had been confident that colonists from the Cape Colony and Natal would not be needed to crush the Boers, and as a result the war was initially envisioned to be a war fought by the British Army against the two Boer republics. However, by the end of the war, volunteer British South African colonists joined in the fighting and even local "blacks" had been issued arms for what was supposed to have been a "white man's" war.[56] The presence of Boers in British territory (a majority in some places) meant that the British were also concerned about a pro-Boer uprising within their own colonies. The successful wartime excursions of Boer commandoes into the Cape Colony and Natal stoked these fears; if they continued, it may have led to an uprising. When the war ended, British, Canadian, Australian and New Zealand soldiers returned to lands untouched by war. However, victorious Cape Colony and Natal troops returned home to an unpromising future marked by economic uncertainty, destroyed property, and racial tensions.

Ian van der Waag notes that the war was a traumatic experience for South Africa, and that it has "always been controversial." He summarizes how past writing on the war reflected the shifting loyalties and oft-tortuous history of the racially divided nation. Even now, there is still a need for a history that avoids repeating the myths of the past.[57] As for the immediate impact of the war, Brit-

---

[55] Hugh Morrison, "'But we are Concerned with a Greater Imperium': The New Zealand Protestant Missionary Movement and the British Empire, 1870-1930," *Social Sciences and Missions* 21, no. 1 (2008): 97-127.

[56] This arming of the "blacks" was feared by the minority white British and Boers, for it was deemed that providing training and arms to such a large mass of potentially hostile people could only bode ill for the future.

[57] Ian van der Waag, "War Memories, Historical Consciousness and Nationalism: South African History Writing and the Second Anglo-Boer War, 1899-1999," in *One Flag, One Queen, One Tongue: New Zealand, The British Empire and the South African War,*

ain's stated aim of absorbing the two republics into the empire was completed with the signing of the Treaty of Vereeniging on 31 May 1902. Less than a decade later, on 31 May 1910, the Union of South Africa was formed, with the key leaders of the new Dominion being Boers. The British may have won the war, but the Boers had won the peace. Despite the war being fought, in part, to alleviate the suffering of the "blacks" under Boer rule, they were the real losers whose plight had quickly been forgotten by the British in their desire for peace and harmony in their new conquest. Apartheid would soon follow.

The opinion of South African churches about the war carried significant weight in Britain, Canada and Australia because they were what seemed to be an "independent moral endorsement of the justice of the British cause" as well as eyewitness accounts of a distant and murky conflict.[58] As a result, pro-war statements from South Africa were circulated widely outside of South Africa by apologists for the war, as were anti-war statements by those opposed to the war. Anglican opinion in South Africa mirrored that of Anglicans in Britain. The argument that the war would advance Christian missions was advocated early on by Bishop Bransby Key of St. John's Kaffraria in the eastern Cape. Key's argument (and others like them from the war region) was convincing to many, and subsequently was oft-repeated in the following years by those who supported the missionary enterprise.

The nonconformist position was not as divided as it was in Britain, indeed nonconformists in South Africa were distraught by their pro-Boer (or anti-war) co-religionists in Britain.[59] Greg Cuthbertson notes that nonconformist support can be seen in the number of ministers that volunteered to be chaplains. He also argues that the majority of nonconformists echoed the sentiments of Key who believed that a British victory would advance the cause of missions among the "natives." The most significant nonconformist opponents of the war were the Dutch Reformed churches. However, there were a few individual British ministers who openly declared their pro-Boer position – often facing the wrath of colleagues and parishioners for doing so.[60] The history of South African Baptists has been written with little or no commentary on the war.[61] In the lone

---

eds., John Crawford and Ian McGibbon (Auckland: Auckland University Press, 2003), 180-204.

[58] For the following comments on South African Anglicanism, see Blunden, "The Anglican Church during the War."

[59] For the following comments on South African nonconformity, see Cuthbertson, "Pricking the Nonconformist Conscience," 169-187.

[60] For a brief summary of South African church attitudes to imperialism and the war, see Rodney Davenport, "Settlement, Conquest and Theological Controversy: The Churches of Nineteenth-Century European Immigrants," in *Christianity in South Africa: A Political and Cultural History*, eds., Richard Elphick and Rodney Davenport (Berkeley: University of California Press, 1997), 62-64.

[61] H.J. Batts, *The History of the Baptist Church in South Africa: The Story of a 100 Years, 1820-1920* (Cape Town: T. Maskew Miller, nd); Sydney Hudson-Reed, *History of the Baptist Union of South Africa, 1877-1977* (Pietermaritzburg: S.A. Baptist Histori-

article that explores South African Baptists and the war, Frederick Hale argues that Baptists had a pre-war history of supporting the advancement of the empire if it meant that British mission work could gain a foothold in new lands.[62] Once the war had been declared, only a few Baptists differed from the shrill calls for British victory. In fact, he claims prominent Baptists assumed "pro-war stances which even some Anglican ecclesiastics in southern Africa would have rejected."

Conclusion

The war has drawn the attention of historians of various sorts and in varying degrees. Domestic debates, the evolution of national identity in the colonies, political opposition or support, popular levels of imperialism, as well the events of the actual military conflict have all garnered the attention of historians. For whatever reasons, the churches and their attitudes and reactions to the war have not had the same appeal. The most extensive research has been directed at the British, Canadian, and South African churches, while the war and the churches in Australia and New Zealand received less attention. As for a focus on Baptists, the most sustained attention has been on Canadian Baptists. No one has moved beyond probing national bodies to exploring the transnational contacts, especially as they related to imperial identities. By directing sustained attention to BACSANZ Baptists this research will significantly advance the analysis of the complicity of religion and empire in the heyday of Western imperialism and wild jingoism, as well as provide a unique global history of Baptists seen through the lens of imperialism.

---

cal Society, 1977); Sydney Hudson-Reed, *By Taking Heed...The History of Baptists in Southern Africa, 1820-1977* (Roodepoort: Baptist Publishing House, 1983).

[62] For the following comments on South African Baptists, see Frederick Hale, "Captives of British Imperialism? Southern African Baptists and the Second Anglo-Boer War, 1899-1902," *Baptist Quarterly* 34, no.1 (January 2001): 15-26. For a brief discussion of Baptist and the war, as well as the larger context of Baptists and social justice in South Africa, see Frederick Hale, "The Baptist Union of South Africa and Apartheid," *Journal of Church and State* 48 (Autumn 2006): 753-777.

Chapter Three

National Identity

"God speed Australia on her new path of progress. The old world and the new will meet on 1st January 1901. The heart of the empire will centre in Sydney for the time being, and the voice of gladness will echo around the world. It is a great occasion, calling for great thanksgiving to God and a new consecration to a life of righteousness. We may say advance Australia but remember it is on your knees."
"God Speed Australia," *Southern Baptist*, 3 January 1901, 2.

Research on Baptists has often focused on what seems to be a never-ending Baptist struggle for identity. While the minority status of Baptists in society in general, and the diversity of beliefs that often followed from congregational government, have led to varying degrees of angst regarding Baptist identity, what is apparent during the war years was that BACSANZ Baptists shared an identity as loyal citizens of the empire and were patriotic members of their nation, dominion, federation or colony. They also had no particular qualms about being involved in national affairs. Baptists were firmly against an established church and believed that the state needed to stay out of the affairs of the church. Baptists in Britain lived in the context of an established church, but they, along with other British nonconformists, made it clear that they considered a state church an unbiblical compromise. Baptists in Canada, Australia, New Zealand and South Africa also opposed a state church, and were vigilant to ensure that the Anglican Church did not become an established church nor tried to act like one. That is not to say that opposition to an established church translated into eschewing political involvement or a radical sectarian disengagement from society. On the contrary, Baptists were actively involved in politics and various social and moral reforms such as the temperance movement or imposition of Sabbath laws. In varying degrees, they were also absorbed with domestic politics and budding nationalism, and they saw themselves as partners in the nation-building enterprise.

Imperialism among BACSANZ Baptists was not deemed to be necessarily at odds with national or regional identity, for, as Carl Bridge and Kent Fedorowich argue, one could have multiple (although related) identities: "The rise of colonial national identities did not contradict or undermine imperial Britishness. One person might have a number of concurrent identities. Just as in Britain one could be a Liverpudlian, Lancastrian, Englishman and Briton, so in New Zealand one might be an Aucklander, North Islander, New Zealander and

Briton."[1] As noted in Chapter One, Barbara Penny identifies how nationalism and imperialism in Australia were not considered to be mutually exclusive.[2] Carl Berger's conclusions regarding imperialism in Canada are remarkably similar. He explores many facets of imperialism in Canadian culture at the turn of the century and understands the imperial impulse during the war to be one form of Canadian nationalism.[3] It was this type of nationalism that explains Canada's enthusiastic participation in an imperial war. The confluence of national and imperial identities among BACSANZ Baptists will be elaborated upon below; suffice to say that loyalty to the empire, the Union Jack, and the monarchy was not necessarily considered by those within the empire to make one disloyal to one's national or regional identity. In fact, for most, national identity could not be envisioned outside of the empire. It should be noted, however, that the imperial identity within the disparate regions of the empire was not always far from homogeneous; rather than uniform it was imagined, elastic and contested, often meaning "different things to different people."[4] While this was certainly the case among BACSANZ Baptists, this research notes that there were similarities among BACSANZ Baptists that reveal a remarkably similar imperialism, especially as it related to their evangelical identity and purpose.

The fusion of nationalism, imperialism and Baptist identity can readily been seen in the various Baptist papers' wartime coverage. Once war had been declared, the papers made it clear that Baptists were patriotic, supported the troops, and identified themselves as imperialists. Even the papers and individuals that were critical of the war made it clear that their patriotism and support for imperialism was not in question. The nature and extent of the wartime coverage reflects this reality. The war engendered a great deal of public interest and papers benefitted from the seemingly insatiable demand for war news. Reporting in the Baptist press followed this general pattern. For instance, in December 1899 the *Baptist Times and Freeman* started a weekly "War Jottings" section against its own earlier commitment to stay away from the activity of jingoistic papers that went into detail about the war.[5] After the capture of the two Boer republic's capitals in mid-1900, interest in the war waned, and thus coverage in the newspapers began to wane as well. Other imperial conflicts in 1900, especially in China, had also begun to eclipse the events in South Africa. Nevertheless, interest in the war remained until the peace settlement in 1902.

---

[1] Bridge and Fedorowich, "Mapping the British World," 6. Also in Bridge and Fedorowich, "Mapping the British World," 6.
[2] Penny, "Australia's Reactions to the Boer War."
[3] Berger, *The Sense of Power.*
[4] Bell, *The Idea of Greater Britain,* 7.
[5] In October, it stated that it would not be like other papers. By December, it began a war summary section that provided weekly blow-by-blow coverage of the war. See "Peace in War," *Baptist Times and Freeman,* 20 October 1899, 728; "War Jottings," *Baptist Times and Freeman,* 29 December 1899, 885. Other papers also started a weekly column.

The following analysis of BACSANZ Baptist national identity in the press re-
volves around commentary related to domestic issues and matters related to
contingents, and how that commentary indicates the fusion of nationalism, imperialism, and Baptist identity.

Britain

Nonconformists in Britain at the end of the nineteenth century were in a "confident mood."[6] British Baptists shared in the general sense of optimism among
nonconformists, an optimism rooted in growing numbers, increased influence,
and rising social status. Like other nonconformists, they were active in the political affairs of the nation, sending members to Parliament, seeking to influence laws, and urging social reforms.[7] They also were increasingly supportive
of imperialism, a conviction shared by a growing number of nonconformists.[8]
However, as the domestic reaction of Baptists to the South African War indicates, that support was not unqualified, and their growing confidence led to a
willingness to speak out against perceived injustices. Baptists were ardently
patriotic, but that patriotism did not translate into blind obedience. Like other
nonconformists, Baptists were divided over support for the war and a number
of high profile leaders were outspoken critics of it.

Weekly coverage of international affairs in the *Baptist Times and Freeman*
was extensive, with reporting on the Boxer Rebellion in China,[9] relations with
America,[10] attitudes and threats on the continent,[11] German challenges,[12] lesser

---

[6] Bebbington, *The Nonconformist Conscience*, 1.

[7] Bebbington, *The Nonconformist Conscience*; Wilson, "A House Divided."

[8] Bebbington, *The Nonconformist Conscience*, ch.6.

[9] "The Chinese Trouble," *Baptist Times and Freeman*, 22 June 1900, 497; "Chinese
Affairs," *Baptist Times and Freeman*, 22 June 1900, 497; "The Boxers," *Baptist Times
and Freeman*, 25 May 1900, 413; "Affairs in China," *Baptist Times and Freeman*, 8
June 1900, 454; "Later News from China," *Baptist Times and Freeman*, 8 June 1900,
454; "Alarming News from China," *Baptist Times and Freeman*, 15 June 1900, 473-
474; "The Coming War," *Baptist Times and Freeman*, 15 June 1900, 474; "Affairs in
China," *Baptist Times and Freeman*, 29 June 1900, 518; "The Chinese Army," *Baptist
Times and Freeman*, 29 June 1900, 518; "The Chinese Trouble," *Baptist Times and
Freeman*, 6 July 1900, 537; "Mob Rule," *Baptist Times and Freeman*, 6 July 1900, 537;
"The Chinese Crisis," *Baptist Times and Freeman*, 13 July 1900, 557; "Later Chinese
News," *Baptist Times and Freeman*, 13 July 1900, 557; "The War in China," *Baptist
Times and Freeman*, 20 July 1900, 577; "The Cry for Vengeance," *Baptist Times and
Freeman*, 20 July 1900, 584; "American Baptists in China," *Baptist Times and Free-
man*, 20 July 1900, 584; Dr. Edwards, "Protestants and Roman Catholics in China,"
Baptist Times and Freeman, 8 November 1901, 757; Martyred China Missionaries,"
Baptist Times and Freeman, 8 November 1901, 757-758; "Martyred Chinese Missionar-
ies," *Baptist Times and Freeman*, 3 January 1902, 13; "A Strange Scene at Peking,"
Baptist Times and Freeman, 17 January 1902, 37-38.

[10] "Anglo-American Alliance," *Baptist Times and Freeman*, 17 November 1899, 785;
"Cousinly Sympathy," *Baptist Times and Freeman*, 19 January 1900, 42; "Britain and
America," *Baptist Times and Freeman*, 9 February 1900, 102; "Anglo-American Rela-

imperial conflicts,[13] matters related to nations such as Bulgaria, Russia, Korea, and Japan,[14] and the reaction to Boer delegates travelling in Europe and America.[15] Its domestic coverage was also extensive, and readers could rely on regular reports related to wartime domestic activities such as budgetary matters,[16] home defence issues,[17] and parliamentary debates.[18] Baptists were encouraged to participate in politics in order to bring righteousness to bear on national and

---

tions," *Baptist Times and Freeman*, 16 March 1900, 202; "The American Presidential Election," *Baptist Times and Freeman*, 13 July 1900, 557; "The New Policy of America," *Baptist Times and Freeman*, 7 June 1901, 369.

[11] "Complications," *Baptist Times and Freeman*, 18 August 1899, 558; "Possible Mobilisation," *Baptist Times and Freeman*, 9 February 1900, 102; "The Queen," *Baptist Times and Freeman*, 16 February 1900, 122; "Our Neighbours the Powers," *Baptist Times and Freeman*, 16 February 1900, 122; "The New Armada," *Baptist Times and Freeman*, 23 March 1900, 226; "France," *Baptist Times and Freeman*, 30 March 1900, 249; "The Imperial Meeting," *Baptist Times and Freeman*, 20 April 1900, 313; "Mr. Kruger," *Baptist Times and Freeman*, 23 November 1900, 937.

[12] "The German Fleet," *Baptist Times and Freeman*, 6 April 1900, 274; "Germany and the Boers," *Baptist Times and Freeman*, 21 December 1900, 1018; "Anglo-German Relations," *Baptist Times and Freeman*, 31 January 1902, 77.

[13] "Trouble in Ashanti," *Baptist Times and Freeman*, 13 April 1900, 294; "The Golden Stool," *Baptist Times and Freeman*, 20 April 1900, 313; "Ashanti," *Baptist Times and Freeman*, 27 April 1900, 334; "Ashanti," *Baptist Times and Freeman*, 18 May 1900, 393; "The Khedive," *Baptist Times and Freeman*, 29 June 1900, 518; "Kumasai Relieved," *Baptist Times and Freeman*, 20 July 1900, 577.

[14] "Russia, Korea, and Japan," *Baptist Times and Freeman*, 25 May 1900, 414; "Bulgaria and the Powers," *Baptist Times and Freeman*, 16 March 1900, 202.

[15] "On Behalf of the Enemy," *Baptist Times and Freeman*, 11 May 1900, 373; "The Boer Delegates in America," *Baptist Times and Freeman*, 25 May 1900, 414.

[16] "Our Little War," *Baptist Times and Freeman*, 7 December 1900, 978; "Features of Parliament," *Baptist Times and Freeman*, 21 December 1900, 1026-1027; "A War Budget," *Baptist Times and Freeman*, 18 April 1902, 289.

[17] "A New Scheme of Defence," *Baptist Times and Freeman*, 18 May 1900, 393.

[18] "Parliament," *Baptist Times and Freeman*, 9 February 1900, 101; "Parliament," *Baptist Times and Freeman*, 23 February 1900, 142; "Parliament's Last Days," *Baptist Times and Freeman*, 10 August 1900, 637; "Undigested Empire," *Baptist Times and Freeman*, 10 August 1900, 638; "Lord Salisbury's Speech," *Baptist Times and Freeman*, 16 November 1900, 917; "The Policy in South Africa," *Baptist Times and Freeman*, 14 December 1900, 997; "The War Vote," *Baptist Times and Freeman*, 14 December 1900, 997; "Our War Administration," *Baptist Times and Freeman*, 15 March 1901, 165; "Lord Roseberry - Is It 'The Last Phase'?," *Baptist Times and Freeman*, 26 July 1901, 493; "The Week," *Baptist Times and Freeman*, 8 September 1899, 593; "Public Speeches," *Baptist Times and Freeman*, 26 January 1900, 61; "Parliament," *Baptist Times and Freeman*, 2 February 1900, 81; "Parliament," *Baptist Times and Freeman*, 9 February 1900, 101; "Parliament," *Baptist Times and Freeman*, 23 February 1900, 142; "The Budget," *Baptist Times and Freeman*, 9 March 1900, 181; "Parliament," *Baptist Times and Freeman*, 16 March 1900, 202.

imperial affairs.[19] The national parliamentary election in 1900 received extensive coverage, and hope was expressed for an increased number of Christians in municipal and federal positions.[20]

Despite the initial desire to stay away from reporting on actual battle-related affairs, the editor of the *Baptist Times and Freeman* eventually succumbed to market pressure and started a weekly "War Jottings" column in December 1899 providing a blow-by-blow account of events in South Africa. It was followed by a column "South African Jottings." A similar column arose to follow events in China during the Boxer Rebellion.[21] Regular coverage of the war in Africa continued into the summer of 1901when reporting waned and moved away from the front pages. It was also eclipsed for a brief time during the height of the conflict in China.[22] Nevertheless, to a greater or lesser degree coverage of the war remained throughout the entire conflict.

While the performance of British troops in the opening months of the conflict was lamented, praise was directed to leaders such as Lord Roberts and Lord Kitchener for their Christian lifestyle and battlefield prowess.[23] Articles on the return of General Buller and the surrender of Boer General Cronje also made it into the paper.[24] More common, however, were reports on the fortunes of British troops on the battlefield. The early British losses at the hands of the Boers had been embarrassing and sobering, but, once the battle turned in Britain's favour, the military advances in early 1900 received substantial cover-

---

[19] "Features of Parliament," *Baptist Times and Freeman*, 21 December 1900, 1026-1027.
[20] "The General Election," *Baptist Times and Freeman*, 30 March 1900, 249; "Roberts and Khaki," *Baptist Times and Freeman*, 8 June 1900, 454; "The General Election," *Baptist Times and Freeman*, 21 September 1900, 757; "Nonconformist Parliamentary Candidates," *Baptist Times and Freeman*, 5 October 1900, 798; "Liberalism and Imperialism," *Baptist Times and Freeman*, 23 November 1900, 937; "The General Election," *Baptist Times and Freeman*, 12 October 1900, 813; "Latest Results," *Baptist Times and Freeman*, 12 October 1900, 813; "After the Battle," *Baptist Times and Freeman*, 19 October 1900, 842-843.
[21] "War Jottings," *Baptist Times and Freeman*, 12 January 1900, 32-33; "South African Jottings," *Baptist Times and Freeman*, 13 July 1900, 558; "The Situation in China," *Baptist Times and Freeman*, 27 July 1900, 612.
[22] The paper reported that all interest had shifted to the events in China. See "Transvaal War," *Baptist Times and Freeman*, 29 June 1900, 518.
[23] "Lord Roberts," *Baptist Times and Freeman*, 12 January 1900, 21; "The Happy Warrior," *Baptist Times and Freeman*, 15 June 1900, 473; "Lord Roberts and His Detractors," *Baptist Times and Freeman*, 24 August 1900, 678; "Our Happy Warrior," *Baptist Times and Freeman*, 14 December 1900, 998; "The Grant to Lord Roberts," *Baptist Times and Freeman*, 9 August 1901, 529; "Reputations Made and Lost," *Baptist Times and Freeman*, 6 June 1902, 418; "Lord Kitchener," *Baptist Times and Freeman*, 13 June 1902, 440.
[24] "Sir Redvers Buller," *Baptist Times and Freeman*, 16 November 1900, 918; "Sir Redvers Buller," *Baptist Times and Freeman*, 1 November 1901, 733-734; "Cronje's Surrender," *Baptist Times and Freeman*, 2 March 1900, 161.

age.[25] The relief of Ladysmith and Mafeking, as well as the capture of Bloemfontein, Johannesburg and Pretoria were noted and celebrated.[26]

Baptist patriotism can also be been seen in support for the monarchy. Like other BACSANZ Baptists, loyalty to the monarchy was widespread. The *Baptist Times and Freeman* followed the itinerary of Queen Victoria, with Victoria's visit to Ireland and an attack on the Prince of Wales in Copenhagen receiving attention in 1900.[27] The life and character of the Queen and her family were discussed, and critics of the Queen were condemned.[28] Her death in 1901 was lamented, with news reports, sermons and eulogies providing coverage of her passing.[29] Loyalty was expressed to her son and heir, Edward VII, and the

---

[25] "Unmanly Fears," *Baptist Times and Freeman*, 5 January 1900, 9; "Lord Wolseley's Prediction," *Baptist Times and Freeman*, 23 March 1900, 225; "Mafeking," *Baptist Times and Freeman*, 23 March 1900, 225; "The War," *Baptist Times and Freeman*, 30 March 1900, 249; "The War," *Baptist Times and Freeman*, 13 April 1900, 293-294; "The War," *Baptist Times and Freeman*, 13 April 1900, 293; "The War," *Baptist Times and Freeman*, 20 April 1900, 313; "Startling Dispatches," *Baptist Times and Freeman*, 20 April 1900, 313; "Sir Wm. Gatacre," *Baptist Times and Freeman*, 20 April 1900, 313; "In the Dark," *Baptist Times and Freeman*, 20 April 1900, 323; "The War," *Baptist Times and Freeman*, 27 April 1900, 334; "The War," *Baptist Times and Freeman*, 4 May 1900, 353; "The War," *Baptist Times and Freeman*, 11 May 1900, 373; "Further Progress," *Baptist Times and Freeman*, 11 May 1900, 373; "The War," *Baptist Times and Freeman*, 18 May 1900, 393; "The War," *Baptist Times and Freeman*, 433; "War Incidents," *Baptist Times and Freeman*, 15 June 1900, 473; "Further War News," *Baptist Times and Freeman*, 15 June 1900, 473; "The War in South Africa," *Baptist Times and Freeman*, 20 July 1900, 577-578; "South Africa," *Baptist Times and Freeman*, 17 August 1900, 657; "When Will the War End?" *Baptist Times and Freeman*, 30 November 1900, 960; "South Africa," *Baptist Times and Freeman*, 12 April 1901, 229.

[26] "Ladysmith Relieved," *Baptist Times and Freeman*, 9 March 1900, 181; "Mafeking," *Baptist Times and Freeman*, 25 May 1900, 413. See also "The Empire's Relief," *Baptist Times and Freeman*, 25 May 1900, 413; "Bloemfontein," *Baptist Times and Freeman*, 23 March 1900, 225; "Johannesburg Surrenders," *Baptist Times and Freeman*, 8 June 1900, 453; "At Pretoria," *Baptist Times and Freeman*, 8 June 1900, 453; "Pretoria and Afterwards," *Baptist Times and Freeman*, 15 June 1900, 473.

[27] "The Queen," *Baptist Times and Freeman*, 6 April 1900, 273; "The Queen in Ireland," *Baptist Times and Freeman*, 13 April 1900, 293; "The Queen and the Prince," *Baptist Times and Freeman*, 27 April 1900, 334; "The Attack on the Prince of Wales," *Baptist Times and Freeman*, 13 April 1900, 293.

[28] "The Royal Family," *Baptist Times and Freeman*, 26 January 1900, 61; "The Queen," *Baptist Times and Freeman*, 9 March 1900, 181; "The Queen," *Baptist Times and Freeman*, 29 June 1900, 518; "Aged 82," *Baptist Times and Freeman*, 1 June 1900, 433; "The Queen," *Baptist Times and Freeman*, 16 February 1900, 122.

[29] "The Queen Gone Home," *Baptist Times and Freeman*, 25 January 1901, 53-55; "The Death of the Queen," *Baptist Times and Freeman*, 25 January 1901, 57; "The Illness of the Queen," *Baptist Times and Freeman*, 25 January 1901, 57; "Prayer for the Queen," *Baptist Times and Freeman*, 25 January 1901, 57; "Our Beloved Queen Is Dead," *Baptist Times and Freeman*, 25 January 1901, 60-61; "Death of the Queen," *Baptist Times and Freeman*, 1 February 1901, 69-70; Rev. Alexander Maclaren, "Christ's Ideal of a Monarch," *Baptist Times and Freeman*, 1 February 1901, 71; "Our New Sovereign,"

events surrounding his coronation were covered in the following months.[30] Like other BACSANZ Baptists, British Baptists wanted to make sure that the anti-Catholic components of the coronation oath remained the same.[31]

Domestic war-related matters worked their way into the everyday affairs of the churches beyond calling people to repentance. For instance, on a Wednesday evening service at Leighton Buzzard, Hockliffe-Street Baptist Church, Rev. H.J. Batts visiting from South Africa gave an evening lecture entitled "What I Saw in Pretoria, during and after the Siege."[32] After the relief of Ladysmith there was a special thanksgiving service at Grantown-On-Spey Baptist. Troops paraded to church and attended a special service.[33] And at the end of the war some churches had special thanksgiving services.[34] Support was evident for the collection of funds for orphans and widows, and a request from the Queen for the churches to take up an offering for the sick and wounded was circulated.[35] One letter to the editor declared that such support should be provided despite what one felt about the war: "Whatever we may think of the present war, none of us but deeply sympathise with the orphans and widows of the gallant soldiers who have just been killed in South Africa....Might not every well-to-do child resign *one* Christmas present to some little orphan, either the present itself or its

---

Baptist Times and Freeman, 1 February 1901, 77; "Our Late Beloved Queen," *Baptist Times and Freeman*, 8 February 1901, 85-86; Rev. Alexander Maclaren, "In Memoriam: Queen Victoria," *Baptist Times and Freeman*, 8 February 1901, 87; "The Funeral of the Late Queen," *Baptist Times and Freeman*, 8 February 1901, 92-93; "Patriotic Declaration," *Baptist Handbook 1902*, 110; "The King," *Baptist Times and Freeman*, 22 March 1901, 181; "Nonconformists and the King," *Baptist Times and Freeman*, 22 March 1901, 181.

[30] R. Howard Henson, "A Suggestion for Coronation Sunday," *Baptist Times and Freeman*, 13 June 1902, 438; "King Edward VII," *Baptist Times and Freeman*, 27 June 1902, 480; "The King's Illness," *Baptist Times and Freeman*, 4 July 1902, 493; "The Coronation: Dislocation of Trade," *Baptist Times and Freeman*, 4 July 1902, 493; "Coronation Honours," *Baptist Times and Freeman*, 4 July 1902, 493-494; Rev. Alexander Maclaren, "The Finger of God ," *Baptist Times and Freeman*, 4 July 1902, 495; T.H., "England's Prayer Today," *Baptist Times and Freeman*, 4 July 1902, 495; Rev. Charles Williams, "The Coronation Postponed," *Baptist Times and Freeman*, 4 July 1902, 496; Rev. Charles Williams, "The Divine Message - What?" *Baptist Times and Freeman*, 4 July 1902, 496; "The King's Convalescence," *Baptist Times and Freeman*, 11 July 1902, 51; "The Coronation," *Baptist Times and Freeman*, 8 August 1902, 592-593; "The King's Letter," *Baptist Times and Freeman*, 15 August 1902, 601; "The Coronation," *Baptist Times and Freeman*, 15 August 1902, 601; Rev. J.R. Wood, "The Coronation of Edward VII," *Baptist Times and Freeman*, 15 August 1902, 608-609.

[31] "The Oath of Supremacy," *Baptist Times and Freeman*, 22 March 1901, 182.

[32] "News of the Churches," *Baptist Times and Freeman*, 22 February 1901, 130. As noted in Chapter Six, Batts wrote a book based on his experience. See H.J. Batts, *Pretoria from Within During the War, 1899-1900* (London: John F. Shaw, 1901).

[33] "News of the Churches," *Baptist Times and Freeman*, 9 March 1900, 197.

[34] Rev. Charles Williams, "Thanksgiving Sunday," *Baptist Times and Freeman*, 13 June 1902.

[35] "Queen's Sunday," *Baptist Times and Freeman*, 12 January 1900, 22.

value?"[36] This sentiment to support the needy despite one's attitude to the war was echoed elsewhere.[37]

Unlike the Baptist press in Canada, Australia and New Zealand, the *Baptist Times and Freeman* spent relatively little attention on the departure and return of troops. As will be seen below, most Canadians, Australians, and New Zealanders were thrilled with the opportunity to send troops to fight in defense of the empire, and followed their soldiers activities with pride. British Baptists, however, were not imbued with the same zeal for their contingents primarily because their troops sent to South Africa were not the nation's first contingents. More specifically, throughout the nineteenth century British Baptists were used to seeing troops be sent to imperial conflicts, whereas it was a novelty for Canadians, Australians, and New Zealanders and a great opportunity to demonstrate to the rest of empire their colonial martial prowess.

Despite lacking the enthusiasm of Baptists in the peripheries, the *Baptist Times and Freeman* did deal with troop-related matters. The paper published a letter written by a soldier in South Africa,[38] reported on notices of troops being sent to South Africa,[39] noted the presentation of medals to soldiers,[40] and printed stories of soldiers around the empire.[41] During the first wartime Christmas "thoughts and sympathies" were sent to the soldiers, along with the hope that they knew Christ's peace.[42] It printed a letter to the editor that encouraged the Baptist Union to petition the government to allow for Baptist chaplains.[43] The reactions to the letter were both positive and negative.[44] It also highlighted casualties and the bungling leadership that led to such deaths.[45]

---

[36] "G.G. Bagster, "Christmas and the War," *Baptist Times and Freeman*, 15 December, 865.

[37] "Help for Soldiers' Families," *Baptist Times and Freeman*, 24 November 1899, 802.

[38] "What the Boers Left Behind," *Baptist Times and Freeman*, 2 November 1900, 894.

[39] "Army Increase," *Baptist Times and Freeman*, 16 February 1900, 122; "Conscription," *Baptist Times and Freeman*, 23 February 1900, 142; "More Troops for Africa," *Baptist Times and Freeman*, 28 December 1901, 1037.

[40] "The Presentation of Medals by the King," *Baptist Times and Freeman*, 21 June 1901, 405.

[41] "A Soldier's History," *Baptist Times and Freeman*, 3 November 1899, 768; "One from the War," *Baptist Times and Freeman*, 23 February 1900, 158.

[42] "Christmas in South Africa," *Baptist Times and Freeman*, 22 December 1899, 869.

[43] T. Turney Chambers, "Baptist Chaplaincies in the Army," *Baptist Times and Freeman*, 23 November 1900, 944;

[44] H. Hardin, "Baptist Chaplaincies in the Army," *Baptist Times and Freeman*, 30 November 1900, 962; W.E. Wells, "Baptist Chaplaincies in the Army," *Baptist Times and Freeman*, 30 November 1900, 962; W.L.T. Foord, "Baptist Chaplaincies in the Army," *Baptist Times and Freeman*, 30 November 1900, 962.

[45] "The War," *Baptist Times and Freeman*, 6 April 1900, 273; "News from South Africa," *Baptist Times and Freeman*, 6 July 1900, 537; "The War," *Baptist Times and Freeman*, 21 December 1901, 1017.

Canada

In Canada, the war led to serious domestic debates and even violence. As Morton has noted, the war may have been a relatively small one but the debate and controversy it engendered was not.[46] Not all Canadians were convinced that Canada should send a contingent to fight against the Boers in South Africa. In the days before, during, and after the First Contingent was sent there was an "acrimonious political debate" over the issue, and no aspect of the South African War has received more attention from Canadian historians than this debate.[47] Some have seen the controversy as a political watershed issue, one that "'split open the cleft' between English and French Canadians, launched the twentieth-century French-Canadian nationalist movement, broke Laurier's power in Quebec, and served as a dress rehearsal for the First World War."[48] As Miller notes, the debate was not solely between English and French Canada. Although the majority of English Canadians were supportive of the war and the sending of Canadian troops, there were a minority of English Canadians who opposed the war.[49]

The attitude to the war's opponents was, at times, quite belligerent. Goldwin Smith, one of the war's most outspoken Canadian English-speaking critics,[50] was often singled out for his opposition to the war.[51] MP Henri Bourassa was taken to task for his anti-war and seemingly anti-British sentiments.[52] Local politicians also faced censure. The *Religious Intelligencer* addressed charges that the governor of Prince Edward Island was a "sympathizer with the Boers" who never allowed an opportunity to pass without "showing his predilections" in the matter.[53] Noting that he was a Roman Catholic, the article concluded that if he truly was pro-Boer he should be removed from office for the good of the country. The Baptist press also identified publications with anti-war attitudes.[54] In a remarkable display of fairness, however, publications were also criticized for certain pro-war attitudes. Many pro-war proponents had feared that the war would be used for partisan gain. Their fears were justified, for the Conservative

---

[46] Morton, *A Military History of Canada*, 70.

[47] Miller, *Painting the Map Red*, 16.

[48] Miller, *Painting the Map Red*, 16.

[49] Miller, *Painting the Map Red*, 16.

[50] See R. Craig Brown, "Goldwin Smith and Anti-Imperialism," *Canadian Historical Review* 43 (June 1962): 93-105.

[51] The range of opposition within the press. Criticisms included *Canadian Baptist*, 26 April 1900, 1. Apparently not all Baptists were opposed to the message of Smith, for he delivered an address before the Young Men's Class of the Beverley Street Baptist Church. See Goldwin Smith, "War," *Canadian Baptist*, 12 December 1901, 5.

[52] "This is a free country, and great freedom of speech is permitted, but men of the Bourassa tribe are dangerous, and it may be necessary, in some form, to let them know it." See "Anti-British," *Religious Intelligencer*, 30 October 1901, 4.

[53] *Religious Intelligencer*, 31 January 1900, 4.

[54] "What A French Paper Says," *Religious Intelligencer*, 4 December 1901, 1.

Party sought to turn discontent over the Liberal's handling of the war into support for their party during the federal election in 1900. The religious press, in general, sought to take a higher road.[55]

While many secular newspapers and politicians demonstrated restraint when it came to criticizing the French for their alleged lack of patriotism during the war, some acted irresponsibly.[56] Such behavior led to growing hostility between English and French Canadians, hostility that eventually erupted into violence. The violence erupted in Montreal on 1 March 1900 when McGill University students celebrated the relief of Ladysmith and the victory at Paardeberg.[57] The parade had traveled through the streets, attacking the offices of *La Presse, La Patrie*, and *Le Journal*, and causing damage at Laval University. The next day Laval students peacefully marched to McGill University, where they were stopped by the archbishop of Montreal and the principal of McGill. The next evening was marked by more violence that necessitated calling the militia to assist the police. This riot was widely reported in Canada and around the world. For some, it was a simple prank gone bad. For others, it was the beginning of the end of French-English relationships in the young nation.

Without exception the Baptist press sought to ensure that the "race question" was not a part of the debate over the war. The loyalty of French Canadians as a people was defended,[58] those who sought to make political capital out of the controversy were roundly criticized, and the actions of the English students during the Montreal riots were condemned.[59] The events in South Africa were considered a chilling reminder of what could happen in Canada if such radicals continued to propound their message of hatred and division. The similarity between South African and Canadian racial problems were highlighted, and the *Messenger and Visitor* stressed how Canada was a model to the world of how two diverse peoples could live together.

> Here in Canada we have doubtless the most favourable illustration which the world affords of diverse and unamalgamated racial elements working together under one government. Here are two races, each preserving and cherishing its own language, literature and traditions, educating its children apart and worshipping apart each from the other, and yet living together under one one flag and one government, with a good degree of harmony, happiness and material prosperity. We heartily rejoice that this can be said of Canada, and we most sincerely hope and pray that there may never come a time when the relations of the two races in this

---

[55] This moderate and conciliatory approach in the press was rooted in a commitment to nation-building. See Heath, "Forming Sound Public Opinion."

[56] Miller, *Painting the Map Red*, 20.

[57] The following description of the riots is taken from Miller, *Painting the Map Red*, 443-444.

[58] "The Sovereignty of Parliament," *Messenger and Visitor*, 21 March 1900, 1; *Canadian Baptist*, 9 November 1899, 1; *Canadian Baptist*, 1 March 1900, 1; *Canadian Baptist*, 8 March 1900, 8.

[59] *Canadian Baptist*, 8 March 1900, 1; "At Ottawa," *Messenger and Visitor*, 14 March 1900, 1.

country shall be less harmonious, and their feeling for the common flag less patriotic than they are today.[60]

The threat of discord, however, was an ever-present danger. The fear was that
politicians and radicals would exacerbate tensions to the point where violence
would break out in Canada. The hope was that the war in South Africa, and
more specifically, the death of French and English Canadian soldiers, would
actually serve as a catalyst for the two races in Canada to unite further.

> Today French and British Canadians are fighting side by side in South Africa, and
> some of them have found a common grave there where they have fought for the
> Queen and the Empire. This patriotic blood, shed in a common cause, should
> prove a potent thing for the healing of racial differences and for cementing the
> bonds of nationality.

Despite such optimistic hopes and fervent exhortations, the war actually had the
reverse effect. The tensions between French and English Canadians left lasting
scars, and set a pattern that would be followed in the next century's even more
tragic wars.[61] Taking its nation-building role seriously, the religious press recognized the threat to the young nation and sought to unite both English and
French. While they may have been guilty of accepting an idealized view of
Canadian unity, Baptist papers can be credited with trying to unite the nation
when there were many forces at work that could have divided Canada in even
more tragic ways.[62]

The sending of Canada's first contingent was marked by public enthusiasm
in English Canada, and the progress of the troops was followed in the secular
and religious papers from the moment they boarded the troopship *Sardinian*. As
Miller and others have noted, the war generated a great deal of interest among
English Canadians. For close to three years "the conflict in South Africa had
defined the lives of many Canadians at home and in South Africa. During this
time books, newspapers, and periodicals informed and poets, artists, musicians,
politicians, preachers, and publicists entertained and inspired a seemingly insatiable public."[63] Often the war's events were chronicled in special sections devoted exclusively to coverage of the war.[64] Editorials, testimonials, essays, pictures and maps also provided much sought after information about the conflict.

---

[60] "The Racial Problem in South Africa and in Canada," *Messenger and Visitor*, 28
March 1900, 4. For similar sentiment, see *Canadian Baptist*, 9 November 1899, 1.
[61] See Miller, *Painting the Map Red*, 444; Page, *The Boer War and Canadian
Imperialism*, 22; Gordon L. Heath, "Canadian Churches and the South African War:
Prelude to the Great War," in *Canadian Churches and the First World War*, ed., Gordon
L. Heath (Eugene: Pickwick Publications, 2014), 15-33.
[62] For an example of the response of the press in the First World War, see Gordon L.
Heath, "The Canadian Protestant Press and the Conscription Crisis, 1917-1918,"
Historical Studies 78 (2012): 27-46.
[63] Miller, *Painting the Map Red*, 424.
[64] For example, from the first month to the last month of the war, the *Canadian Baptist*
had a war column reporting on battlefield events.

While the coverage of the war diminished after the summer of 1900, due in part to an apparent victory, and in part to other events like prohibition or the conflict in China making (or taking) the headlines, the religious press maintained its coverage and war columns until the very end of the conflict. The war and imperial themes penetrated into the smallest of the churches' ministries.[65]

On the domestic front, the sending of the contingents was followed in the press with pride. The First Contingent's organization, departure, performance, and return to Canada garnered the most coverage.[66] Calls for a second contingent were made even before the first had left Quebec. In early November, Laurier and his cabinet decided to make the offer of a second contingent, which was declined by the British authorities. However, after the dismal performance of the British Army in South Africa, and especially after the events of Black Week, on 16 December 1899 Chamberlain informed Laurier that the British would accept another Canadian contingent. Without calling for a parliamentary debate, Laurier and his cabinet promised that another contingent would leave in January 1900.

Local celebrations after victories also made the news. Commenting on the British victories after Paardeberg, the Toronto-based *Canadian Baptist* enthused that "Toronto [had] not witnessed an outburst of loyal patriotism" like that for "many a year."[67] There was no sympathy for those opposed to the war, for as the *Canadian Baptist* went on to say, if "there was a Boer sympathizer in the land that was a day for him to keep indoors, and be indoors, and be quiet as a spy in the enemy's camp or the traitor at home, for loyalty ruled in every British home and hearth in the land."[68] News related to the Canadian troops overseas generated a great deal of coverage and drew reader response. Letters from overseas were reprinted for popular consumption.[69] Special attention was given to local soldiers who had fallen. For instance, the *Religious Intelligencer* reported on the death of Russel C. Hubly, the son of Rev. A. M. Hubly, the pastor of the Reformed Episcopal Church, Sussex, New Brunswick.[70]

---

[65] For instance, see "Prayer Topic," *W.B.M.U. Tidings*, February 1901, 1.
[66] "The War in South Africa," *Canadian Baptist*, 4 January 1900, 16; "The War in South Africa," *Canadian Baptist*, 15 February 1900, 16; *Canadian Baptist*, 22 February 1900, 8; "The War in South Africa," *Canadian Baptist*, 22 February 1900, 16; *Canadian Baptist*, 1 March 1900, 1; "The Canadian Contingent," *Canadian Baptist*, 1 March 1900, 8; *Canadian Baptist*, 22 March 1900, 1; *Canadian Baptist*, 26 July 1900, 1; *Canadian Baptist*, 30 August 1900, 1; *Canadian Baptist*, 8 November 1900, 1. For a poem extolling Canada's soldiers in the contingents, see Mrs. J.J. Baker, "Canadian Heroes," *Canadian Baptist*, 25 October 1900, 12.
[67] *Canadian Baptist*, 8 March 1900, 160.
[68] *Canadian Baptist*, 8 March 1900, 160.
[69] For example, the *Religious Intelligencer* printed the letters of Norman P. McLeod of E Battery, Royal Canadian Artillery on 16 May 1900, 13 June 1900, 25 July 1900 and 2 January 1901. See also F. Leonard Vaux, "Letter From S.A.," *Canadian Baptist*, 30 August 1900, 5.
[70] "For His Country," *Religious Intelligencer*, 18 September 1901, 4.

One of the most public ways in which the churches could declare their support for the war effort to the politicians as well as to the troops themselves was during the troop send-off services. The first contingent's departure from Quebec City was a grand opportunity for the churches to show their loyalty, and they gave their stamp of approval on the Sunday before the troops departed.[71] The second contingent was to depart from Halifax in January 1900. On Thursday, 18 January 1900, Brunswick Street Methodist Church in New Brunswick held a reception and farewell for the contingent sponsored by the Evangelical Alliance and the Women's Christian Temperance Union (WCTU.).[72] The event, unlike most previous sendoffs, was an interdenominational affair. Clergy from the Methodist, Presbyterian, Baptist, and Anglican churches all gave speeches. WCTU and YMCA leaders joined denominational leaders in addressing the audience. The reception was attended by an impressive roster of politicians: B. Russell, MP, Frederick Borden, Minister of Militia, and William Mulock, Post-master General.

There were a number of organizations that provided assistance to the soldiers, as well as to their wives and dependents back in Canada. The Canadian Red Cross, the National Council of Women, the YMCA, the Soldiers' Wives, as well as the Canadian government, all provided assistance.[73] A report in the *Religious Intelligencer* in January 1900 provides an example of support for the Patriotic Fund. Rev. Dr. McLeod created a controversy at a prayer meeting for "Nations and Their Rulers" when he criticized the Fredericton Town Council for not contributing to the Patriotic Fund. He complained of the "Fenian Controls" in the government by which he "meant that the spirit which controlled the action of the Council is not essentially different from the anti-British feeling which the Fenians everywhere are showing."[74] (McLeod's anger needs to be understood in the context of having his own son as a member of a contingent in South Africa.) A month later, the *Religious Intelligencer* approvingly noted the establishment of Patriotic Funds for soldiers and their families. At the same time it lamented that the New Brunswick contingent of soldiers still needed funding. The proposed solution reveals how the pulpit was used to raise money for the war effort: pastors and congregations were expected to come up with ways to raise the necessary funds. In doing so, they would "express practically their sympathy with the souls of Canada who represent them at the front, and by the same act declare their loyalty to the great Empire of which [they were] all proud."[75]

---

[71] Miller, *Painting the Map Red*, 62.

[72] "A Farewell to the Contingent," *Wesleyan*, 17 January 1900, 5; "The Churches and the Contingent," *Wesleyan*, 24 January 1900, 4.

[73] Miller outlines the contributions of these organizations. See Miller, *Painting the Map Red*, 429-432.

[74] "Civic Patriotism: A Prayer Meeting Incident," *Religious Intelligencer*, 17 January 1900, 1.

[75] "Patriotic Funds," *Religious Intelligencer*, 7 March 1900, 4.

Loyalty to the empire and monarchy was on display during the events surrounding Queen Victoria's death on 22 January 1901. Paper coverage indicates the depth of Baptist devotion to the Queen, the royal family, and Great Britain. For instance, it was reported that the war in South Africa had caused her great grief,[76] and that she was one who "reigned in righteousness" and was "ever for peace."[77] The *Canadian Baptist* printed an account of the memorial services held in Toronto,[78] along with the text of a tribute delivered at Jarvis Street Baptist Church.[79] It also reprinted the BCOQ's executive resolution expressing Baptist sorrow and sympathy over the loss of the queen, and loyalty to the new king.[80] A message by Alexander Maclaren in Manchester was printed.[81] Dr. Thomas' tribute to Queen Victoria captured the essence of all of these tributes to the Queen when he proclaimed that the "name of Queen Victoria will go down the ages with a fragrance that no precious ointment could produce."[82] While these tributes to the monarchy may seem to indicate otherwise, the war did engender a growing national sentiment in Canada. One contemporary historian describes Canada's participation in the struggle as an "initiation rite" that gave Canada an increased role in the empire's councils.[83] By participating Canadians felt that they had proven that they belonged to the grown up family of nations. This sentiment was expressed in the *Canadian Baptist*: Canada had taken its first steps towards adulthood and that the "part taken by Canada in the war has certainly made a new and proud name for Canadians."[84] However, that new nation was still considered to be an integral part of the empire.

Australia

Much like Baptists in Canada, Australian Baptists were engrossed with the domestic events initiated or exacerbated by the conflict in South Africa.[85] They also assumed a nation-building role in the budding Federation, supported the

---

[76] "The Death of Queen Victoria," *Canadian Baptist*, 24 January, 1900, 8.

[77] "God Save the King," *Canadian Baptist*, 31 January 1901, 1.

[78] The three churches were College Street, Jarvis Street, and Dovercourt Road. See "The Queen's Funeral," *Canadian Baptist*, 7 February 1901, 8.

[79] "Dr. Thomas' Tribute to the Queen," *Canadian Baptist*, 14 February 1901, 2.

[80] *Canadian Baptist*, 28 February 1901, 1.

[81] Alexander MacLaren, "In Memoriam: Queen Victoria," *Canadian Baptist*, 28 February 1901, 15.

[82] "Dr. Thomas' Tribute to the Queen," *Canadian Baptist*, 14 February 1901, 2.

[83] Berger, *The Sense of Power*, 19. George Stanley makes a similar argument when he writes that Canada's participation in the war was a "step towards independence and self-respect and the recognition of Canadian nationality by the world at large." See George F. G. Stanley, *Canada's Soldiers, 1604-1954: The Military History of an Unmilitary People* (Toronto: MacMillan Company, 1954), 289.

[84] *Canadian Baptist*, 22 March 1900, 177.

[85] Penny notes that, in general, the fusion of nationalism and imperialism in both Canada and Australia were quite similar. See Penny, "Australia's Reactions to the Boer War," 129.

war effort, encouraged political participation, and called the nation to repent-ance for its sins. Regional State distinctions, with their concomitant resent-ments and jealousies towards other States, can be seen in some commentary in the various Baptist papers, but the overall impression is of widespread support for the new Federation and the embracing of a united Australian identity.

While there has been brief attention paid to the development of churches and national sentiment in Australia,[86] there was considerable commentary in the Baptist press on the development of the new nation. Public apathy around vot-ing was noted and lamented,[87] and Baptists were encouraged to get involved in politics and vote in the referendums determining Australian federation as well in the elections after the Commonwealth had been formed.[88] The prompting of Baptists into civic responsibility was encouraged not only through essays in the various denominational papers,[89] but also through Baptist participation in or-ganizations such as the Christian Citizen's League for Queensland.[90] One arti-cle noted that women would someday get the vote, but the time was not yet right.[91] However, the same article indicated that women voting could not do worse than the men, since so many men were uninvolved in the political pro-cess. One bright light for Baptist men, and cause for pride among all Baptists, however, was the selection of a Baptist Member of Parliament in the new Fed-eral Parliament.[92]

A united Australia became a reality on 1 January 1900, and the papers car-ried extensive commentary on all things related to the new Commonwealth.[93]

---

[86] Fletcher, "Anglicanism and Nationalism in Australia"; Withycombe, "Australian An-glicans and Imperial Identity"; McMinn, *Nationalism and Federalism in Australia*.
[87] "Public Apathy," *Queensland Baptist*, 1 April 1902, 43.
[88] "The Council of Churches," *Southern Baptist*, 15 February 1900, 37; "There Are So Many Questions," *Southern Baptist*, 15 February 1900, 38; "We are on the Eve of Gen-eral Elections," *Southern Baptist*, 1 March 1900, 50; W. Whale, "Commonwealth Elec-tions," *Queensland Baptist*, 1 April 1901, 48-49; "Vote as You Pray," *Queensland Bap-tist*, 2 December 1901, 159; "Value of Votes," *Queensland Baptist*, 1 March 1902, 29; "True Idea of Patriotism," *Queensland Baptist*, 1 April 1902, 44; "Coming Events," *Queensland Baptist*, 1 September 1899, 118-119.
[89] "Christian Citizenship," *Queensland Baptist*, November 1899, 154-155; Arthur Mursell, "Christian Citizenship," *Queensland Baptist*, 1 February 1901, 23-24.
[90] "Christian Citizenship," *Queensland Baptist*, 1 June 1902, 72. For other meetings, see "Half-Yearly Meetings at Ipswich," *Queensland Baptist*, 2 June 1902, 77-79.
[91] "Would Women Do Worse?" *Queensland Baptist*, 1 April 1902, 44.
[92] "A Baptist M.P.," *Queensland Baptist*, 1 May 1901, 57-58.
[93] "Federation," *Southern Baptist*, 15 February 1900, 37; "The Commonwealth Bill," *Southern Baptist*, 31 May 1900, 122; "The Commonwealth of Australia," *Southern Bap-tist*, 28 June 1900, 146; "The Proposed Names," *Southern Baptist*, 16 August 1900, 192; "One Most Pleasing," *Southern Baptist*, 17 January 1901, 14; "That Mr. Edmund Bar-ton," *Southern Baptist*, 17 January 1901, 14; "Great Wisdom," *Southern Baptist*, 17 January 1901, 13; "The Commonwealth," *Southern Baptist*, 31 January 1901, 26; "Our Future Capital," *Southern Baptist*, 31 January 1901, 26; "It Is Quite Possible," *Southern Baptist*, 31 January 1901, 26; "The Governor-General," *Southern Baptist*, 17 April 1901,

The reaction to the formation of the new nation was uniformly positive, and, as the following quote illustrates, Baptists celebrated the birth of an Australian national identity:

> The good ship, the Commonwealth of Australia, has at length been fairly launched upon the sea of national destiny, amidst every possible manifestation of enthusiastic loyalty and every honour which could be bestowed. May the God of Nations graciously give to those who hold the helm and trim the sails, the wisdom which is profitable to direct.[94]

There was anticipation for the time when saying "I am an Australian shall bring a flush of pride to the cheeks of all our sons and daughters."[95] Reports on the festivities and functions noted with pleasure the large crowds that celebrated the union.[96] Baptist leaders took part in services in churches and at official government functions, and various Baptist Unions made special addresses to the government expressing their loyalty and devotion.[97]

As for regional differences and State loyalties, it was mentioned that they would have to be abandoned if the new nation was to survive and thrive. For instance, it was noted that mutual suspicion and jealousy needed to stop between Sydney and Melbourne,[98] and the building of a capital somewhere other than those two cities was considered to be wise.[99] Not all tensions were between Melbourne and Sydney, however, for there was some concern expressed in the *Queensland Baptist* over the alleged ignoring of Brisbane and Queensland in the new Federation.[100]

86; "The Federal Elections," *Southern Baptist*, 17 April 1901, 86; "Federation," *Queensland Baptist*, 2 June 1902, 71-72; "A Retrospect," *Queensland Baptist*, 1 December 1899, 168; "Federation," *Queensland Baptist*, 1 August 1900, 100; "Topics of the Month," *Baptist*, 1 January 1901, 1-2; "20th Century Greetings," *Baptist*, 1 January 1901, 2-3; "A Prayer for the State," *Baptist*, 1 January 1901, 3; "Religious Services," *Queensland Baptist*, 1 February 1901, 16; "Paragraphs on Patriotism," *Baptist*, 1 January 1901, 3; "Young People," *Southern Baptist*, 3 January 1901, 4; "The Opening of Parliament," *Southern Baptist*, 29 May 1901, 122.

[94] "The Good Ship, the Commonwealth of Australia," *Southern Baptist*, 15 May 1901, 110.

[95] "The Commonwealth Bill," *Southern Baptist*, 17 May 1900, 110.

[96] "The Corporation and Citizens of Melbourne," *Southern Baptist*, 15 May 1901, 110; "That Such Immense Crowds," *Southern Baptist*, 15 May 1901, 110; "The People," *Southern Baptist*, 15 May 1901, 110;

[97] "The New Commonwealth," *Southern Baptist*, 17 January 1901, 21; "The Commonwealth of Australia," *Southern Baptist*, 17 January 1901, 24; "Annual Report of the Executive," *Baptist Yearbook, 1901-1902*, 15; "Address to the Governor-General," *Baptist*, 1 January 1901, 3; "Our President," *Queensland Baptist*, 1 February 1901, 17.

[98] "Australia Is Now One," *Southern Baptist*, 3 January 1901, 2.

[99] "The Federal Capital," *Southern Baptist*, 12 March 1902, 61; "The Mutual Jealousy," *Southern Baptist*, 12 March 1902, 61.

[100] "Federation Fussiness," *Queensland Baptist*, 1 November 1901, 146; "Commonwealth Celebration," *Queensland Baptist*, 1 February 1901, 16; "The Proclamation,"

The reality of a united Australia quite naturally led to questions being raised about the possibility of Baptists forming a national Baptist Union.[101] The movement of other denominations in that very direction placed additional pressure on Baptists to shift from their many unions based on State identity to a single national Baptist Union that represented all Baptists and provided them with a unified voice and more significant presence in the nation's affairs. Another practical reality was that if they did not unite they would lose even more ground to denominations that did.[102] One proposal was to build a Baptist church in the capital, making the project a work of Baptist congregations across Australia.[103] Such action was deemed to be a positive step towards actual Baptist union and would solidify the Baptist presence in the heart of the new nation, giving it an opportunity to have a godly influence on the affairs of state.

The formation of the new nation also gave added impetus to calls for Christian citizenship, for the success of the new nation depended on its Christian character and God's blessing as he answered the prayers of his people:

> God speed Australia on her new path of progress. The old world and the new will meet on 1st January 1901. The heart of the empire will centre in Sydney for the time being, and the voice of gladness will echo around the world. It is a great occasion, calling for great thanksgiving to God and a new consecration to a life of righteousness. We may say advance Australia but remember it is on your knees.[104]

Leading up to the Federation there was fear expressed that God would be left out of the celebrations. But after the festivities were over the general consensus was that the Christian character of the new nation had been affirmed. Sabbath celebrations should have been avoided,[105] but otherwise the public prayers,

---

Queensland Baptist, 1 February 1901, 16; "Swearing-In," *Queensland Baptist*, 1 February 1901, 16; "Ashamed," *Queensland Baptist*, 1 February 1901, 16.

[101] "Presbyterian Federation," *Southern Baptist*, 28 August 1901, 194; "Baptist Federation," *Southern Baptist*, 28 August 1901, 194; "Baptist Union of South Australia," *Southern Baptist*, 16 April 1902, 89; "Topics of the Month," *Baptist*, 2 June 1901, 1; "Other Federations," *Queensland Baptist*, 1 September 1900, 114; "Baptists and Federation," *Baptist*, 1 February 1902, 7; *Baptist*, 1 June 1902, 2. In regards to the pressure to unite with other denominations, it was deemed to be useless to talk of even further federation of churches until Baptists in Australia had united. See J. Paynter, "Baptist Federation," *Southern Baptist*, 16 October 1901, 235. For a discussion of Australian Baptists and national union, see Manley, *From Woolloomooloo to 'Eternity': Volume 1*, 182-193.
[102] F.J.W., "The Federation of Baptists," *Southern Baptist*, 12 August 1902, 187; Rev. W.J. Eddy, "Australian Baptist Federation," *Southern Baptist*, 12 August 1902, 187; C.W. Walbond, "Federation," *Southern Baptist*, 12 August 1902, 187.
[103] *Baptist*, 1 July 1901, 9.
[104] "God Speed Australia," *Southern Baptist*, 3 January 1901, 2. For the type of prayer coveted by Baptists, see Lord Tennyson's prayer for the new Commonwealth. See Lord Tennyson, "Prayer for the Commonwealth," *Queensland Baptist*, 1 January 1901, 8.
[105] "One Thing Marred," *Southern Baptist*, 15 May 1901, 110. Many months later Baptists were disturbed when Edward VII and his court broke the Sabbath, and declared that

services in churches, and inclusion of God in the preamble to the Constitution boded well for the future.[106] Central to the promotion and preservation of Australia's Christian identity was the need for personal and national righteousness. National greatness, it was believed, would only come about through national righteousness.[107] Consequently, churches needed to pray for godly leaders with Christian character and conviction who were willing, among other things, to fight against social evils in order to make a righteous nation.[108]

While Baptists shared in the surge of Australian nationalism that marked the sending of contingents and the formation of the new nation, their devotion to the monarchy remained steadfast. Like other BACSANZ Baptists, they had a number of loyalties that were not mutually exclusive. In fact, for many Baptists, to be Australian was also to be British. This loyalty to Britain can be seen in the domestic reactions to the death of Queen Victoria, the accession of her son Edward VII, and the royal visit of the Duke of York. In all three cases, Australian Baptists were ardent supporters of the monarchy and the imperial virtues which they allegedly embodied. Queen Victoria was considered to be the ideal monarch and worthy of emulation. As in other parts of the empire, her death led to outpourings of sadness as well as memorial church services among Australian Baptists.[109] Statements of loyalty were expressed to her son Edward VII, and

---

no nation can "be truly religious in which the day of rest is profaned." "The King," *Southern Baptist*, 26 March 1902, 73.

[106] "God Recognised," *Queensland Baptist*, 1 August 1901, 99; "The Commonwealth Celebrations," *Southern Baptist*, 17 January 1901, 15; "Watch Night Services," *Southern Baptist*, 17 January 1901, 15.

[107] A.W.W., "The Birth of a Nation," *Southern Baptist*, 3 January 1901, 7.

[108] "The Baptist Union of Victoria," *Southern Baptist*, 29 November 1900, 267; "The Commonwealth," *Baptist*, 3 September 1900, 1-2; "Christ for the New Century and the New Nation," *Baptist*, 1 November 1900, 4-5; "Changing the Program," *Southern Baptist*, 17 January 1901, 13; "An Open Parliament," *Southern Baptist*, 17 January 1901, 14; "The Opinion of Our Constituents," *Southern Baptist*, 17 January 1901, 14. It was for that reason that Baptists were concerned about a "convicted adulterer" running for office. See "Commonwealth Parliament," *Queensland Baptist*, 1 April 1901, 44.

[109] "The Death of the Queen," *Southern Baptist*, 31 January 1901, 25; "Our Beloved Queen," *Southern Baptist*, 31 January 1901, 25; "Queen Victoria," *Southern Baptist*, 31 January 1901, 26; "And Yet We Cannot," *Southern Baptist*, 31 January 1901, 26; "One Painful Factor," *Southern Baptist*, 31 January 1901, 26; "Young People," *Southern Baptist*, 31 January 1901, 29; J.B., "The Death of Our Great and Good Queen," *Southern Baptist*, 31 January 1901, 31; "The People's Lament," *Southern Baptist*, 14 February 1901, 37; "The Remains of Our Late Beloved Queen," *Southern Baptist*, 14 February 1901, 38; "The Memorial Service," *Southern Baptist*, 14 February 1901, 38; "The Memorial Services," *Southern Baptist*, 14 February 1901, 38; "The Queen's Statue," *Southern Baptist*, 14 February 1901, 39; "The Queen," *Southern Baptist*, 14 March 1901, 64-65; "Her Majesty Led in Prayer," *Southern Baptist*, 17 April 1901, 88; "Our Late Kind Queen," *Southern Baptist*, 17 April 1901, 88; "Our Gracious Queen," *Queensland Baptist*, 1 February 1901, 15; "United Service," *Queensland Baptist*, 1 March 1901, 29; "The Children's Service," *Queensland Baptist*, 1 March 1901, 29; "All Denominations," *Queensland Baptist*, 1 March 1901, 29; "Was Queen Victoria a Roman Catholic?"

prayers were offered for him as he prepared for his accession.[110] Echoing the concerns of Baptists in other colonies, there was apprehension over making any changes to the coronation oath that would open the possibility for a Catholic to be monarch.[111] The royal visit in 1901 of the Duke and Duchess of Cornwall and York (later King George V and Queen Mary) was also a time when Baptist loyalty to the crown was apparent. Statements of loyalty were issued, official welcomes were provided, and even a children's church picnic was rescheduled around the visit.[112]

Besides paying attention to domestic issues such as the birth of the new nation or reactions to issues related to royalty, the three Australian Baptist papers followed war-related matters. International events such as the US control of Panama, German-British relations, the Anglo-Japanese Treaty, the ongoing famine in India, or partition of other parts of Africa and the blessings of European rule were mentioned.[113] The Boxer Rebellion in China drew significant attention as well.[114] However, in regards to the war in South Africa, the bi-

---

Queensland Baptist, 1 March 1901, 37; "Topics of the Month," *Baptist*, 1 February 1901, 1-2; "The Queen's Religion," *Baptist*, 1 February 1901, 2-3; "Memorial Sunday," *Baptist*, 1 February 1901, 3; "Queen Victoria and the Second Advent," *Baptist*, 2 June 1901, 12; "Annual Report of the Executive," *Baptist Yearbook, 1901-1902*, 16; "City Tabernacle," *Queensland Baptist*, 1 March 1901, 40; "Charters Towers," *Queensland Baptist*, 1 March 1901, 40; "Petrie Terrace," *Queensland Baptist*, 1 March 1901, 41; "Toowong," *Queensland Baptist*, 1 March 1901, 41.

[110] "God Save the King," *Southern Baptist*, 31 January 1901, 26; "Our New King," *Southern Baptist*, 31 January 1901, 26; "God Save the King," *Southern Baptist*, 11 June 1902, 133; "An Empire's Prayers," *Southern Baptist*, 2 July 1902, 145; "Annual Report of the Executive," *Baptist Yearbook, 1901-1902*, 16-17; "King Edward VII," *Queensland Baptist*, 2 June 1902, 76-77; Cowper, "Loyalty to a King," *Queensland Baptist*, 2 June 1902, 77; "Coronation Day," *Queensland Baptist*, 1 August 1902, 99.

[111] "The Coronation Oath," *Southern Baptist*, 3 April 1901, 85; "The Coronation Oath," *Southern Baptist*, 29 May 1901, 122; "Topics of the Month," *Baptist*, 2 June 1901, 1.

[112] "The Royal Visit," *Southern Baptist*, 15 May 1901, 110; "Royal Visitors," *Queensland Baptist*, 1 May 1901, 57; "The Royal Visit," *Queensland Baptist*, 1 June 1901, 76-77; "The Melbourne Welcome," *Southern Baptist*, 15 May 1901, 110; "Copy of Address Presented by the Baptist Union of Victoria," *Southern Baptist*, 29 May 1901, 123; "Address to the Duke of York," *Baptist*, 2 June 1901, 14; "Albion," *Queensland Baptist*, 1 April 1901, 54.

[113] "The Partition of Africa," *Baptist*, 4 May 1900, 8; "The Entente Cordiale," *Southern Baptist*, 15 February 1900, 38; "German Feeling Against Britain," *Southern Baptist*, 29 March 1900, 78; "Anglo-Japanese Treaty," *Queensland Baptist*, 1 March 1902, 29-30; "Famine in India," *Queensland Baptist*, 2 July 1900, 86.

[114] "The War in China," *Southern Baptist*, 28 June 1900, 146; "China," *Southern Baptist*, 12 July 1900, 157; "The Chinese Crisis," *Southern Baptist*, 12 July 1900, 158; "Those Events," *Southern Baptist*, 12 July 1900, 158; "We Sympathise," *Southern Baptist*, 2 August 1900, 169; "The Chinese Crisis," *Southern Baptist*, 16 August 1900, 181; "All Eyes," *Southern Baptist*, 16 August 1900, 182; "China," *Southern Baptist*, 16 August 1900, 192; "Chinese Affairs," *Southern Baptist*, 30 August 1900, 193; "China," *Southern Baptist*, 30 August 1900, 194; "Australia," *Southern Baptist*, 18 October 1900,

monthly or monthly nature of the Australian papers meant that detailed chronicles of the war would have been out of date by the time the papers went to press. Subsequently, there were no attempts to provide regular blow-by-blow accounts of the events of the war. That being the case, the *Southern Baptist* (bimonthly) provided substantially more reporting on the events of the conflict than the *Queensland Baptist* and the *Baptist* (both monthly).[115] In fact, the

229; "China," *Southern Baptist*, 1 November 1900, 242; "The Prayers," *Southern Baptist*, 1 November 1900, 242; "We Now Wait Longingly," *Southern Baptist*, 1 November 1900, 242; "What a Spectacle China Presents!" *Southern Baptist*, 15 November 1900, 254; "China," *Southern Baptist*, 3 January 1901, 2; "Some Two Hundred Missionaries," *Southern Baptist*, 17 April 1901, 86; Robert Powell, "Martyrs in China," *Southern Baptist*, 17 April 1901, 90; "Martyred Missionaries," *Southern Baptist*, 15 May 1901, 110; E. Cosslett, "Chinese Christians Abroad," *Southern Baptist*, 15 May 1901, 114; "China," *Southern Baptist*, 29 January 1902, 25; "China in Convulsion," *Southern Baptist*, 30 April 1902, 99; "Dr. Smith Traces," *Southern Baptist*, 30 April 1902, 99; "For the Settlement Arrived At," *Southern Baptist*, 30 April 1902, 99-100; "He Declares that the Attitude," *Southern Baptist*, 30 April 1902, 1000; "China," *Baptist*, 4 August 1900, 2; "The Martyrs' Crown," *Baptist*, 4 August 1900, 2; "Baptist Missions in Asia," *Baptist*, 4 August 1900, 8; "The Massacres in China," *Baptist*, 4 August 1900, 8; "Veteran China Missionary," *Baptist*, 1 September 1902, 1; "China," *Queensland Baptist*, 2 July 1900, 86; Rev. W. Whale, "China," *Queensland Baptist*, 1 August 1900, 101-102; "Pekin," *Queensland Baptist*, 1 September 1900, 114; "Missions in China," *Queensland Baptist*, 1 January 1901, 5; "Our Martyred Missionaries," *Queensland Baptist*, 1 April 1901, 47; "Martyred Missionaries," *Queensland Baptist*, 1 May 1901, 64.

[115] "We Cannot but Thank God," *Southern Baptist*, 2 November 1899, 230; "Prayer Has Been Heard," *Southern Baptist*, 1 March 1900, 49; "The Relief of Kimberley," *Southern Baptist*, 1 March 1900, 50; "Sunday, 11th February," *Southern Baptist*, 1 March 1900, 50; "Joubert," *Southern Baptist*, 12 April 1900, 86; "Kruger," *Southern Baptist*, 12 April 1900, 86; "'Military Critics'," *Southern Baptist*, 15 March 1900, 61; "Recent Cables," *Southern Baptist*, 15 March 1900, 61; "The City of Hobart," *Southern Baptist*, 15 March 1900, 61; "We Hate War," *Southern Baptist*, 15 March 1900, 61; "The Relief of Ladysmith," *Southern Baptist*, 15 March 1900, 62; "The Relief of Mafeking," *Southern Baptist*, 31 May 1900, 121; "The Rejoicing," *Southern Baptist*, 31 May 1900, 121; "Adelaide," *Southern Baptist*, 31 May 1900, 121; "Mafeking Relieved," *Southern Baptist*, 31 May 1900, 121; "Mafeking," *Southern Baptist*, 31 May 1900, 122; "Johannesburg and Pretoria," *Southern Baptist*, 14 June 1900, 133; "Pretoria and Johannesburg," *Southern Baptist*, 14 June 1900, 134; "The War in South Africa," *Southern Baptist*, 26 March 1902, 75; "The Boer War," *Southern Baptist*, 14 June 1900, 134; "Peace Day," *Southern Baptist*, 28 June 1900, 145; "As the War," *Southern Baptist*, 12 July 1900, 157; "The Exodus to South Africa," *Southern Baptist*, 12 July 1900, 158; "The South African War," *Southern Baptist*, 16 August 1900, 181; "There Are Difficulties," *Southern Baptist*, 16 August 1900, 181; "The Boer War," *Southern Baptist*, 30 August 1900, 194; "Peace," *Southern Baptist*, 11 June 1902, 133; "As We Write," *Southern Baptist*, 11 June 1902, 134; "Peace at Last," *Southern Baptist*, 11 June 1902, 135; "The Pacification of South Africa," *Southern Baptist*, 11 June 1902, 135; "A Costly War," *Southern Baptist*, 11 June 1902, 135; "All's Well That Ends Well," *Southern Baptist*, 2 July 1902, 146; "The Aftermath of the Struggle," *Southern Baptist*, 2 July 1902, 146; "Generous Treatment Called For," *Southern Baptist*, 2 July 1902, 146; "The Boer General," *Southern Baptist*, 26 March 1902, 73; "The Prisoners of War," *Southern Baptist*, 28 May

Queensland Baptist let its readers know in advance that it would not be chronicling the war at all, but would occasionally mention items of special interest.[116] However, the lack of reporting on battlefield events did not mean that the editors of the paper were disinterested in what was going on in South Africa. In fact, they were and committed much ink to swaying domestic opinion on war-related issues.[117] Field does note that "beneath all the cheers and patriotic clichés there existed misgiving over the war."[118] Such misgivings can also be seen in the Baptist papers. In fact, as will be seen in Chapter Six, the variety of responses in the Baptist press indicates that there was no homogenous Australian Baptist perspective on the war.

Another cause for alarm was the early defeat of the British on the battlefield. Many Australian Baptists were just as alarmed at such setbacks as other BACSANZ Baptists, and like others they believed that both the nation and empire needed to humble themselves before God for past sins in order to gain the blessing of God for future battles. Chapter Seven examines the day of humiliation in BACSANZ Baptist churches, but suffice it to say here that Australian Baptist assumptions surrounding the need for national repentance were predicated on the assumption that the nation and empire were Christian entities that needed to act as such. While contemporary twenty-first century readers may not take seriously or appreciate the concern for national righteousness, for wartime Baptists this was a critical domestic issue. In fact, by encouraging and exhorting their members and the nation to repent of sins, the churches believed that they were playing a critical role in the enterprise of nation and empire-building.

A third area of concern on the domestic front was that of precedence, and once again this was an issue shared by a number of other BACSANZ Baptists. The fact that this was a pressing issue for the *Queensland Baptist* and not the other two Australian Baptist papers indicates how editorial concerns and/or regional conditions shaped the particular focus of the religious press. The issues related to precedence were vital because of the many functions that necessitated a public presence of denominational authorities. The inauguration of the new Commonwealth raised the question of precedence, and the Executive of the Baptist Union of New South Wales sent to the Premier of New South Wales and the Premier of the Commonwealth its opinion that religious leaders should

---

1902, 123; "A Hopeful Outlook," *Baptist*, 10 March 1900, 2; "The Relief of Mafeking," *Baptist*, 2 June 1900, 1-2.

[116] "Some War Items," *Queensland Baptist*, 2 April 1900, 29-30.

[117] Field notes how the press and public opinion played an important role in pressuring governments to act in support of sending troops. The Baptist press, in its own small way, contributed to this pressure. See Field, *The Forgotten War*, 25.

[118] Field, *The Forgotten War*, 72. See also Penny, "Australia's Reactions to the Boer War," 105-109; Penny, "The Australia Debate on the Boer War"; Connolly, "Class, Birthplace, Loyalty: Australian Attitudes to the Boer War."

participate in the ceremonies according to their numbers in the land.[119] The sendoff of troops was another opportunity for the churches to be involved in formal functions, and Baptists in New South Wales spoke passionately about the exclusion of certain denominations at such functions. For instance, it was felt that there was a "disgraceful case of clerical arrogance" with the dispatch of the second Queensland contingent when an Anglican cleric acted as a "dictator" refusing to allow the Methodists to have a significant role: all in all, the action of the Anglicans was deemed to be "contemptible."[120] Another opportunity for offence was provided by the events related to the death of the Queen and the Coronation of Edward VII. Once again, it was believed that the Anglicans acted arrogantly at such functions.[121] Baptists celebrated amicable relations with other denominations such as the Methodists, but felt that Anglicans were too concerned with ensuring their own power and prestige at such functions to allow for any other denominational presence.[122] For Baptists concerned with religious equality, this was upsetting, but for Baptists trying to gain a national voice and increased national identity, it was also deemed to be potentially crippling.

While considerably less of an issue than the above mentioned items, another domestic concern was that of support for various patriotic funds. One article in the *Southern Baptist* bemoaned the fact that the generosity shown towards war funds was not evident for the Lord's work.[123] The *Baptist*, the paper most critical of the war, echoed similar sentiment when it observed that it was difficult to raise money for God's work, but within days thousands were given to war.[124] Elsewhere, however, the same paper noted with praise the amount of money New South Wales donated to the war effort and to the famine in India.[125] Embedded within a few articles are glimpses of the ways in which raising money for the war effort made its way into the services of the church: part of the church's Day of Prayer on 11 February 1900 was a collection for the Nurses

---

[119] "Annual Report of the Executive," *Baptist Yearbook, 1901-1902*, 15. See also "Religious Services," *Queensland Baptist*, 1 February 1901, 16.

[120] "Clerical Arrogance," *Queensland Baptist*, 1 February 1900, 15. See also "United Services," *Queensland Baptist*, 1 July 1901, 86.

[121] "All Denominations," *Queensland Baptist*, 1 March 1901, 29; "Cathedral Foundation Stone," *Queensland Baptist*, 1 May 1901, 57; "High Churchism," *Queensland Baptist*, 1 August 1902, 104-105; "United Services," *Queensland Baptist*, 2 June 1902, 72. Catholics were also considered to be the problem when it came to precedence. See "Who Shall be First?" *Queensland Baptist*, 1 June 1901, 72.

[122] For instance, a report indicated that Rev. W. Whale spoke at a Methodist meeting, a meeting that was deemed to be a much more amicable event than with Anglicans. See "Conference and the War," *Queensland Baptist*, 2 April 1900, 44.

[123] "Patriotism," *Southern Baptist*, 15 February 1900, 38.

[124] "The War," *Baptist*, 3 February 1899, 3.

[125] "What Has N.S.W. Done!" *Baptist*, 4 August 1900, 2.

Fund, and money was raised for the Patriotic Fund after Rev. Charters Towers lecture entitled "The War: Its Lessons and Our Responsibilities."[126]

As noted above, support for the Australian contingents was widespread, but not unconditional. Various state bodies of Anglicans, Congregationalists, Presbyterians, Roman Catholics and Jews, made it clear that they blessed the efforts of the troops.[127] In most cases, Baptists echoed the same sentiment. The editor of the *Queensland Baptist* made it clear that he did not support the offer of troops before the outbreak of hostilities, for he considered it to be merely an attempt to beat other colonies and an expression of a desire for conflict that was unChristian. However, once war was declared, he endorsed the sending of troops.[128] Support for further contingents was expressed in the months that followed.[129] Notice was made of Baptists in the contingents (and British Army), and pride was exhibited towards Australian soldiers and their martial skills.[130] Coverage of matters related to the contingents was frequent and dealt with a wide range of issues: reports on troop sendoffs,[131] experiences and performance in South Africa, [132] deaths,[133] temperance in the army,[134] leadership (the emphasis being on the godly leadership of Britain's army),[135] evangelism among the troops,[136] and general information.[137] Departures and returns of Baptist soldiers

---

[126] "Flinders Street," *Southern Baptist*, 1 March 1900, 56; "Charters Towers," *Queensland Baptist*, 2 April 1900, 40.

[127] Field, *The Forgotten War*, 45-46.

[128] "Christian Citizenship," *Queensland Baptist*, 1 November 1899, 154.

[129] "We Are Called Upon," *Southern Baptist*, 31 January 1901, 26; "Commonwealth Contingent," *Queensland Baptist*, 1 February 1902, 16; "Sixth Contingent," *Queensland Baptist*, 1 April 1901, 43; "Another Contingent from Queensland," *Queensland Baptist*, 1 January 1900, 2.

[130] "Baptists in the Army," *Queensland Baptist*, 1 February 1901, 17; "Baptist Soldiers," *Southern Baptist*, 27 February 1901, 49; "Our Soldiers," *Queensland Baptist*, 1 May 1901, 58. One commentator claimed that "The Australian Bushman is a match for the South African Boer." See "The Services," *Southern Baptist*, 15 March 1900, 62. Such attitudes contributed to the development of the "Bushman" folk hero. See Barbara Penny, "Australia's Reactions to the Boer War," 119. For a brief statistical analysis of the religious composition of the Australian contingents, see W.M. Chamberlain, "The Characteristics of Australia's Boer War Volunteers," *Historical Studies* 20, no. 78 (1982): 48-52.

[131] "The Military Procession of Last Saturday," *Southern Baptist*, 2 November 1899, 230.

[132] "Minor Miseries of the War," *Southern Baptist*, 1 March 1900, 55.

[133] "The Boer War," *Southern Baptist*, 16 August 1900, 192.

[134] "These Times of Tempestuous Joy," *Southern Baptist*, 15 March 1900, 61; "Beer for Our Boys of the Contingent," *Southern Baptist*, 3 May 1900, 97.

[135] "Lord Roberts," *Southern Baptist*, 3 May 1900, 98-99; "Lord Roberts," *Southern Baptist*, 14 June 1900, 134; "Lord Roberts," *Southern Baptist*, 28 June 1900, 146; "Lord Roberts," *Southern Baptist*, 3 January 1901, 3; "Lord Roberts," *Southern Baptist*, 31 January 1901, 26.

[136] "'The Sons of the Sea'," *Southern Baptist*, 12 July 1900, 158.

were a part of the life of the local churches, with special services and home-comings provided when necessary.[138] One pastor from City Tabernacle was called upon to give three addresses to departing contingents.[139] The appointment of a Methodist chaplain for non-Anglicans was praised, and an article on the work of the army chaplain (written by the Special Correspondent with Australian Troops in South Africa for the *Daily Telegraph*) spoke positively of their contribution and reputation.[140] Soldiers were even used for illustrating spiritual warfare.[141] The sending of troops had united Australia to the empire,[142] and Australia's soldiers had "earned a nation's gratitude, and won for themselves new renown."[143] But not all was rosy when it came to the conduct of Australian's contingents, for there was the infamous situation with Harry "Breaker" Morant. While in following decades the execution of Morant led to indignation among Australians for the perceived mistreatment of one of their own, as well as to the publication of numerous books, plays and even a full length movie, in 1902 the Baptist press mentioned only Lieutenants Witton (Australian) and Picton (English).[144] In the war years, all conduct deemed dishonorable – even and especially that of Australians – was condemned.

---

[137] "A Retrospect," *Queensland Baptist*, 1 December 1899, 168; "Our Second Contingent," *Southern Baptist*, 1 February 1900, 25; "The Federation of Australia," *Southern Baptist*, 1 February 1900, 26; "Our Contingents," *Southern Baptist*, 15 February 1900, 38; "Home Comforts for the Bushmen and Soldiers," *Southern Baptist*, 1 March 1900, 50; "The Boer War," *Southern Baptist*, 1 March 1900, 50; "What the Y.M.C.A. is Doing for the Soldiers," *Baptist*, 1 February 1902, 7..

[138] "Laura," *Southern Baptist*, 1 March 1900, 56; "Mr. William Lucas, F.R.G.S.," *Southern Baptist*, 13 December 1900, 278; "Back from the War," *Southern Baptist*, 3 January 1901, 1; "Alberton," *South Africa*, 3 January 1901, 8. Field claims that the churches "did not figure prominently in the official farewells to the [first] contingent," but did play a "much bigger part" in the sending of the second contingent. The reason for the change was most likely clergy protests related to their earlier exclusion. See Field, *The Forgotten War*, 69.

[139] "City Tabernacle," *Queensland Baptist*, 2 April 1900, 54.

[140] "Chaplains for South Africa," *Baptist*, 10 March 1900, 4; "A Methodist Chaplain," *Queensland Baptist*, 2 April 1900, 44; Frank Wilkinson, "The Army Chaplain," *Baptist*, 1 March 1901, 9-10. See also "A War Correspondent on the Lost Opportunity of the Church," *Southern Baptist*, 15 November 1900, 253. A number of churches had protested the fact that initially no provision had been made for a chaplain in the first contingent. Pressure from Anglican, Methodist and Presbyterian clergy forced the government to permit an Anglican clergyman to accompany the first contingent. See Field, *The Forgotten War*, 47.

[141] Rev. W. Whale," Our Fighting Forces," *Queensland Baptist*, 1 February 1900, 16-17.

[142] "Australia," *Southern Baptist*, 15 March 1900, 62.

[143] "Australia," *Southern Baptist*, 15 March 1900, 62; "We Hate War," *Southern Baptist*, 15 March 1900, 61.

[144] "The Shadow Cast by War," *Southern Baptist*, 16 April 1902, 86; "Tis a Matter for Painful Reflection," *Southern Baptist*, 16 April 1902, 86; "Still Sadder, in Some Respects," *Southern Baptist*, 16 April 1902, 86.

New Zealand

Due to the monthly nature of the *New Zealand Baptist* there was no war column like that in the *Baptist Times and Freeman* or the *Canadian Baptist* that provided a regular detailed summary of the war's events, battle news or cable messages; it made no point to publish news that in many cases was weeks or perhaps a month old. As in other BACSANZ papers, its coverage waned after it looked like the war was over in the summer of 1900. That being said, along with coverage of the war, the paper provided commentary on international events such as the Boxer Rebellion in China,[145] imperial advances in the Sudan,[146] or the treaty signed between Britain and Japan.[147] It also included particular details related to war such as cost, deaths, conduct of soldiers and battlefield results.[148] The overall tenor of wartime coverage made it clear that the editor and paper supported the war effort; in this very tangible way, it both expressed and contributed to the construction of a distinctly New Zealand national identity.

A brief comment about the editorial policy of the paper during the war is in order. The editor noted in June 1900 that the paper had received "quite a sheaf" of correspondence in regards to the war, and that the letters contained "every conceivable shape of opinion" on the war.[149] The paper had been attacked by some for being too supportive of the war, and by others for not being supportive enough. The editor stated that the paper had tried to be fair to both sides, and that those supportive of the war should have had no complaints about the position of the paper (for overall it was supportive of the war effort). He also let

---

[145] "Wars," *New Zealand Baptist*, August 1900, 120; "And Rumours of Wars," *New Zealand Baptist*, August 1900, 120-121; "The Trouble in China," *New Zealand Baptist*, August 1900, 121; *New Zealand Baptist*, August 1900, 123; "Our Martyred Missionaries," *Missionary Messenger*, February 1901, 2-3 (insert in the *New Zealand Baptist* – this article reprinted from the *B.M.S. Herald*); *Missionary Messenger*, February 1901, 2-3; "Secretarial Jottings," *New Zealand* Baptist, February 1901, 26; Lizzie, "On the Verge of Martyrdom," *New Zealand Baptist*, April 1901, 55;

[146] "Overshadowed," *New Zealand Baptist*, February 1900, 24. In this particular article it was noted that previously Baptists were thrilled with Kitchener's capture of Khartoum. Now, it argued, they had more to be pleased with for enemies of the empire had been annihilated or captured, and the "events finally open the great Soudan to the incoming of civilization and Christianity."

[147] "Orient and Occident," *New Zealand Baptist*, March 1902, 107.

[148] For instance, see "The March to Pretoria," *New Zealand Baptist*, January 1900, 9; "A Graveside Memory at Ladysmith," *New Zealand Baptist*, May 1900, 79; "Christian Work at the Seat of War," *New Zealand Baptist*, May 1900, 79-80; "Some Interesting Figures," *New Zealand Baptist*, July 1900, 111; "Temperance Tid-Bits," *New Zealand Baptist*, July 1900, 111; "Chit Chat," *New Zealand Baptist*, March 1900, 48; "Opening the Last Volume," *New Zealand Baptist*, April 1900, 49; "Chit Chat," *New Zealand Baptist*, June 1900, 96; "Chit Chat," *New Zealand Baptist*, September 1900, 143.

[149] "The War," *New Zealand Baptist*, June 1900, 88. See also Clifford, *A Handful of Grain*, 115.

readers know that despite receiving considerable correspondence, he had decided to not print any of it. Why? Because the letters did not add any new data to the discussion and that there was simply too much to print (and if he could not print all, he would not print any). While one hopes that these unprinted letters to the editor were preserved and will be found someday in an attic or closet, in the meantime contemporary researchers must trust the editor's statement that the majority of the letters were from those who had "faith in the justice of the war."

The sendoff of the first troops in Wellington on 21 October 1899 gives evidence of the strong public support for the imperial effort. With Governor Lord Ranfurly and Premier Richard John Seddon providing speeches on the righteousness of the war, and 40,000 (1/20 of the population of New Zealand) cheering people in attendance, the departing soldiers were assured of widespread political and public backing for their cause.[150] Zeal for the imperial cause was also displayed in other war-related celebrations such as the relief of Mafeking, and while support for or attention to the war may have waned during the guerilla campaign, the exuberant celebrations at the end of the war suggests a deep unwavering endorsement for the conflict that remained constant throughout the conflict.[151]

Quite naturally Baptists who were loyal to the empire were grieved to hear of Queen Victoria's death, and celebrated the accession to the throne of her son Edward VII.[152] Royal matters were of concern for reasons other than fealty to the crown, especially if they intersected with critical Baptist interests. For instance, discussion surrounding the changing of the Coronation Oath for Edward VII provoked fears that Protestantism would lose its ground to Catholicism. Baptists, it was argued, "must do their utmost to prevent the alteration of the

---

[150] Crawford with Ellis, *To Fight for the Empire*, 7-21. See also McGibbon, *The Oxford Companion*, 59.

[151] Crawford with Ellis, *To Fight for the Empire*, 84, 90.

[152] In regards to the death of Victoria, see "In Memoriam," *New Zealand Baptist*, February 1901, 17-19; "Sympathy with the Royal Family," *New Zealand Baptist*, March 1901, 41; "Chit Chat," *New Zealand Baptist*, April 1901, 64; "Royal Funeral Parade at Sea," *New Zealand Baptist*, June 1901, 89. For brief summaries of memorial services in Baptist churches, see "Oamaru," *New Zealand Baptist*, March 1901, 45; "Invercargill," *New Zealand Baptist*, March 1901, 45; "Ponsonby," *New Zealand Baptist*, March 1901, 45. For the coronation of Edward VII, see "Regem Habemus!" *New Zealand Baptist*, June 1902, 81; "Prophesy, Son of Man!" *New Zealand Baptist*, June 1902, 81-82; "And Again," *New Zealand Baptist*, June 1902, 82; John P. Hobson, "For the Coronation and After," *New Zealand Baptist*, June 1902, 82; "A.S. Adams, "The Baptists and the Throne," *New Zealand Baptist*, June 1902, 82-83; Wade Robinson, "The Song of the Flag," *New Zealand Baptist*, June 1902, 83-84; "Wanted – The National Anthem," *New Zealand Baptist*, June 1902, 89; "The Coronation Jingle," *New Zealand Baptist*, June 1902, 89. For a description of popular support for the monarchy during the 1901 royal tour, see Judith Bassett, "'A Thousand Miles of Loyalty': The Royal Tour of 1901," *NZ Journal of History* 21, no. 1 (1987): 125-138.

oath."[153] Of concern as well was the sense that certain Baptists had been shunned in June 1901 during the royal visit of the Duke and Duchess of Cornwall and York. A Baptist delegation had arrived at Government House in Auckland on 11 June 1901 to deliver a brief welcome and statement of fidelity to the crown and empire. The response to Baptists at this particular reception was pleasing to the leaders of the denomination. The *New Zealand Baptist* subsequently printed the welcome in its entirety, as well as the lengthy response from the Duke (which was subsequently read in Baptist churches).[154] What irked some Baptists was that they had been ignored by a local government official at the official functions that followed. More specifically, the Canterbury and Westland Associations wrote to the city council outlining their disappointment regarding being excluded from official public functions when the royal couple had visited Christchurch.[155] This concern echoes resentment among others regarding being overlooked at official wartime ceremonies, and reflect that BACSANZ Baptists in general were striving to ensure that they were recognized as a legitimate participant in the national fabric of their particular nation or colony.

Domestic politics were of concern to New Zealand Baptists, and in this regard had a commitment to nation-building in much the same way as other BACSANZ Baptists. Church members were encouraged in the *New Zealand Baptist* to vote in the December 1899 election (prohibition being a main incentive in that case).[156] Regardless of who won the election, the hope was that the leaders chosen would be "holier [rather than]…than cunning."[157] Their vision for godly leaders was rooted in two convictions. First, the empire and New Zealand was at least nominally Christian. It was claimed that the nation had recognized Jehovah as the true God, opened its parliament with prayer, and that Victoria was Queen "by the grace of God." The Bible was used for oaths in court, and was the standard for the formation of laws. These realities demanded "that the men who shall be sent to Wellington to frame and administer our political measures shall be good and godly citizens." Second, it was God who made

---

[153] "The Coronation Oath," *New Zealand Baptist*, August 1901, 120-121. See also "The Coronation Oath," *New Zealand Baptist*, April 1901, 57; "Roman Catholic Progress," *New Zealand Baptist*, August 1901, 121; "The Accession Oath," *New Zealand Baptist*, September 1901, 136-137; "The Roman Catholic Bishop's Oath," *New Zealand Baptist*, September 1901, 137.

[154] "Baptists Welcome T.R.H." *New Zealand Baptist*, July 1901, 104; "The Royal Reply," *New Zealand Baptist*, July 1901, 104-105. For other commentary on the royal visit, see "Our Royal Guests," *New Zealand Baptist*, June 1901, 89.

[155] "Baptists Ignored," *New Zealand Baptist*, August 1901, 122.

[156] "Local Option, and Yours," *New Zealand Baptist*, November 1899, 170; "December the 6th," *New Zealand Baptist*, December 1899, 184-185.

[157] "A General Election Ideal," *New Zealand Baptist*, October 1899, 145-146. The remainder of this paragraph has been drawn from this article. In regards to the Christian identity of Britain and its colonies, see Rev. F.W. Boreham, "Is Great Britain Christian?" *New Zealand Baptist*, July 1901, 99-101.

laws, and the job of politicians was to recognize such laws and line up the nation's laws with the divine statutes. Only people "who have eyes clear enough and minds clean enough" could discern such laws and properly apply them to the pressing issues of the day. Consequently there was a need for Christian politicians with character, who put "principle before policy."

The Christian identity of New Zealand will be explored in a subsequent chapter, but suffice it to say that its purported Christian identity made it imperative that there be a distinctly Christian element to troop sendoffs, troop conduct, and patriotic zeal. Consequently, there was consternation among Baptists when clergy and churches were excluded from troop departure ceremonies, chaplains excluded from contingents, or Sabbath observance was dispensed with in regards to troop parades.[158] Conversely, the *New Zealand Baptist* was pleased to note the distinctly Christian leadership and conduct of the British Army in South Africa.[159] Even patriotic sentiment was carefully monitored to ensure that it was not corrupted by jingoism or militarism.

With tensions rising in South Africa, various British colonies made offers of troops: 11 July the colony of Queensland, 12 July the colony of Victoria, a few days later Malay States and Lagos, followed by the colony of New South Wales.[160] All were rejected at that time. A few months later, on 28 September 1899, Premier Richard Seddon asked the New Zealand Parliament for troops for a contingent and with war looming London immediately accepted the offer.[161] Popular enthusiasm for the war effort fused with the government's quick and unequivocal response to the war helped secure Seddon's Liberal government's dominating electoral victory in December 1899.[162] Black Week led to Seddon wanting to send another contingent, and he was widely supported in this decision. He made an offer on 20 December 1899, and it too was accepted. Subsequent contingents followed to a total of ten.[163] New Zealand sent approximately 6,500 troops out of a total population of 750,000; casualties were 230 deaths.[164] This was the first time that New Zealand had sent troops to fight

---

[158] "Races, Theatre, Church," *New Zealand Baptist*, April 1900, 56; "A Significant Correspondence," *New Zealand Baptist*, April 1901, 49-50. For commentary on and condemnation of Australian clerics in regards to leadership in public services, see "Heathenising Australia," *New Zealand Baptist*, June 1901, 88.

[159] "By the Help of God," *New Zealand Baptist*, April 1900, 56-57.

[160] Pakenham, "The Contribution of the Colonial Forces," 60.

[161] Hall, *The New Zealanders in South Africa*, 6. New Zealanders had volunteered for the First Boer War in 1881, but were never sent due to the war ending. See Crawford with Ellis, *To Fight for the Empire*, 10; McGibbon, *The Path to Gallipoli*, 106.

[162] McGibbon, *The Path to Gallipoli*, 106, 112.

[163] Crawford with Ellis, *To Fight for the Empire*, 12, 23. For an examination of each contingent's contribution to the war effort, see Hall, *The New Zealanders in South Africa*.

[164] Crawford with Ellis, *To Fight for the Empire*, 108-109.

overseas, and, as in Canada and Australia, it set the pattern for subsequent imperial engagements such as the First World War.[165]

Commentary in the *New Zealand Baptist* supported the sending of New Zealand contingents. In the midst of the hype regarding the sending of the first contingent, the *New Zealand Baptist* noted that it viewed with "no small pleasure" the decision of parliament and the sending of the contingent.[166] In the early months of 1900, the war and the sending of troops continued to engender support in the pages of the *New Zealand Baptist*. The extent of the support for the contingent and the seemingly unifying effect of recent events were deemed to be causes for rejoicing: "[W]e rejoice that, in a moment when the Empire stood upon the threshold of a justifiable and honourable war, her sons in this her most remote colony rallied to her side, and thus exhibited to a watchful world an Empire scattered as widely as the poles, and yet knit together as one heart, one mind, one soul."[167] The deaths of those same soldiers would also unite the empire:

> [They] will have a lasting influence for good. The colony will be bound by additional ties to the Mother Land. We value what costs us most. And the rich offering of the life-blood of our bravest citizens for the defence of the Empire will be a fresh tie – beautiful as silken cords and strong as golden chains – that will bind New Zealand afresh in its allegiance to the Home Land.[168]

The contingents themselves were "doing more than they know" to make the colony "famous and popular," and the praise that they engendered in Britain and around the empire was cause for national pride.[169] Compared to reporting in the other weekly BACSANZ papers, coverage of the New Zealand contingents was limited in the *New Zealand Baptist*.[170] However, reports on war casualties made it into the paper[171] as did a report on the casualties of the Seventh Contingent at Bothasberg, the largest single-battle tragedy of the war for the New Zealand contingents.[172] The paper admitted that details of that particular battle were sketchy, but noted that events were a matter for "mourning and lamentation." It was also hoped that the deaths would "stimulate a still more fervent prayer that an honourable peace may soon be established on the soil that is sodden with the blood of our bravest and best."

---

[165] Hall, *The New Zealanders in South Africa,* 86; Crawford with Ellis, *To Fight for the Empire*, 9, 94; McGibbon, *The Oxford Companion to New Zealand Military History*, 63.

[166] "Our Contingent," *New Zealand Baptist*, November 1899, 169-170.

[167] "Our Contingent," *New Zealand Baptist*, November 1899, 169-170. See also "A Nation of Patriots," *New Zealand Baptist*, February 1900, 17.

[168] "The Warriors Taking Their Rest," *New Zealand Baptist*, February 1900, 24.

[169] "Chit Chat," *New Zealand Baptist*, March 1900, 48.

[170] For general comments on the contingents, see "Transvaal Echoes," *New Zealand Baptist*, September 1900, 135.

[171] "The Warriors Taking Their Rest," *New Zealand Baptist*, February 1900, 24; "Transvaal Echoes," *New Zealand Baptist*, September 1900, 134-135.

[172] "Toll for the Brave!" *New Zealand Baptist*, April 1902, 56-57.

Premier Seddon wanted the New Zealand contingent to be the first to arrive in South Africa, and this pressure was an example of the competition between colonies during the war.[173] Premier Seddon boasted often that New Zealand was the first to offer and the first to arrive in South Africa.[174] The war contributed to a "national image of martial prowess,"[175] and New Zealanders claimed that they were among the best horsemen in the British army.[176] There were also to be no joint contingents, for there was too much competition between Australia and New Zealand and it would have been a blow to national pride.[177]

Keith Sinclair notes that through celebrations, sendoffs, giving and fundraising, the war had "powerful effect in establishing and strengthening social cohesion in many other ways."[178] He makes no mention of church activities, but a number of wartime actions of Baptists contributed to the development of such social cohesion. Two examples will suffice to illustrate this claim. First, in the pages of the *Missionary Messenger* one gets a brief glimpse of the support for the Patriotic Fund among Baptists.[179] For instance, one article dealt with the work of missions in India, and in it the author noted how the Patriotic Funds (and India famine) had "drained away a good deal of the surplus cash" from the work of the New Zealand Baptist Missionary Society.[180] Readers were encouraged to remember that in the midst of many pressing needs the work of the society must not be forgotten. Another destination for Baptist money was South Africa, and a fund established for assisting South African Baptists suffering from the war was established and reported on.[181] The generosity of New Zealanders provided more than a boost of self-congratulation, it also provided them with an affirmation that all was well with the empire: "So long as the strong, stern, stalwart form of British might is accompanied, even in the fierce heat of war, by the gentler, tenderer, kindlier form of British mercy, we shall not lose heart. The wedding of Might with Mercy at the altar of the nation, amidst the plaudits of the people, is a happy omen for the future of our flag."[182] Second, in a number of Baptist churches there were special Sunday services, 8 June 1902, in reaction to the end of the war.[183] A church in Auckland had a thanksgiving

---

[173] Crawford with Ellis, *To Fight for the Empire*, 21.

[174] Sinclair, *A Destiny Apart*, 127.

[175] Crawford, "The Impact of the War," 207.

[176] Crawford, "The Best Mounted Troops in South Africa," 73-99.

[177] Sinclair, *A Destiny Apart*, 129.

[178] Sinclair, *A Destiny Apart*, 140.

[179] The *Missionary Messenger* was an insert in the *New Zealand Baptist*, and a paper of the New Zealand Baptist Missionary Society.

[180] "Official Notes," *The Missionary Messenger*, April 1900, 1.

[181] "South African Fund," *New Zealand Baptist*, February 1901, 27.

[182] Might and Mercy," *New Zealand Baptist*, February 1900, 18.

[183] The *New Zealand Baptist* published a number of items related to peace when it looked like the war would be over in the summer of 1900. See "The Peace Proposals," *New Zealand Baptist*, May 1900, 71; Rev. John Muirhead, "War, Peace and Arbitration," *New Zealand Baptist*, July 1900, 98-101; "Wailing the Word," *New Zealand Bap-*

service that evening.[184] Mount Eden Baptist dedicated its morning service to the declaration of peace.[185] The church was "nicely decorated with the Union Jack and other flags" and for his sermon the pastor co-opted the words of Isaiah 37:35: "For I will defend this city to save it for Mine own sake." The pastor of the Baptist church in Thames preached in the morning from 1 Chronicles:16:8-10 because it was a "fitting parallel" to the occasion. He also declared that "England's place among the nations was due to God's immanence in national affairs."[186] The church in Wanganui also celebrated the arrival of peace that morning.[187] The service was marked by praise for the end of the war. The sermon was taken from Psalm 20:7, with the emphasis being on "Lest we forget" and trusting God instead of human strength. The service was deemed to be a "happy occasion" that would "long linger in the memories" of those present. If Sinclair is correct, what would also linger were the effects of such ceremonies on social cohesion.

South Africa

South African Baptist commentary on the war differed from the other colonies of Canada, Australia or New Zealand in that initially there were limited expressions of a budding or nascent nationalism in the *South African Baptist*. Baptists in Canada were cognizant that they belonged to a very young Dominion, those in Australia looked forward to their brand new Federation, and Baptists in New Zealand displayed what could be described as a nascent national identity. Initially, Baptists in South Africa had no similar political entities in mind or promised to them, and besides, even the future of Natal and Cape Colony was uncertain in light of the war. That being said, once victory seemed assured the discourse shifted to reflect a national dream – one of Briton and Boer united under the Union Jack as a new South African Dominion.

Baptists in South Africa were very much aware that their position was significantly different from fellow BACSANZ Baptists, especially Baptists in Britain. One article a few months before the war spoke of how Baptists in South Africa faced unique challenges that their counterparts back in Britain had overcome long ago. South African Baptists considered themselves to be building a foundation, whereas Baptists in Britain carried out their work upon foundations long established.[188] As will be seen in subsequent chapters, Baptists in

---

tist, July 1900, 105. For items related to the peace in 1902, see "Is It Peace?" *New Zealand Baptist*, June 1902, 89; Alice G. Ford, "Peace," *New Zealand Baptist*, July 1902, 109.

[184] "Auckland," *New Zealand Baptist*, July 1902, 106. The article does not specify which church.

[185] "Mount Eden," *New Zealand Baptist*, July 1902, 106.

[186] "Thames," *New Zealand Baptist*, July 1902, 106.

[187] "Wanganui," *New Zealand Baptist*, July 1902, 106.

[188] "To the Work," *South African Baptist*, June 1899, 173-174.

South Africa were heavily dependant on aid in order to build their foundation, and took great pains to make their plight known to Baptists in Britain. The pages of the *South African Baptist* also contained commentary on the unique domestic issues raised by the war, and, like other BACSANZ Baptist papers, editors recognized the power of the press and made a conscious editorial choice to shape political opinions.[189]

Due to the proximity of the war, it is not surprising that the pages of the paper contained commentary on the war. However, blow-by-blow weekly commentary was not an option due to the monthly format of the paper. The paper also suffered because of the war. In the opening months of the conflict the paper could not get through to subscribers in battle zones,[190] and in January 1900 the editor announced the cessation of production until circumstances improved.[191] The paper started publication again in July 1900, for the early British defeats had been reversed and imperial troops were advancing into the heartland of the Boer republics.

The primary reason for concern about the outbreak of war was the realization that a conflict would mean that their lives, churches and even the future of Natal and Cape Colony were at risk. For South African Baptists, war news was domestic news. Two inter-related issues were at the heart of their concern; first, concern over inflaming racial tensions, and second, the general damage caused by a war.

Unlike British, Australian, and New Zealand Baptists, both South African and Canadian Baptists faced wartime racial tensions. As noted above, French-English differences in Canada led to outbreaks of domestic violence and even fears of a civil war. In South Africa, the racial tensions were even more complex and potentially destructive, for in South Africa there was not only the obviously highly charged black-white division but also a white-white conflict that threatened the future of white supremacy.

Tensions between the Boers and British had a long history, the most recent military clashes being the First Boer War (1880-1881) and the Jameson Raid (1895). Holding the 1899 Baptist Assembly in Pretoria, and having President Kruger address the Assembly, was an attempt to foster cordial relations between the two dominant European peoples in South Africa. However, the outbreak of war shortly thereafter dampened any opportunities for future cross-border relationships. The immediate difficulty for some families after the outbreak was that they had family members on both sides of the conflict. Consequently, the war in its opening weeks had "all the horrible aspect of civil war."[192] Besides the heartbreak of waging war against friends and family, the

---

[189] The press was the "new Caesar" that could "provoke wars" and/or "create or destroy reputations." See "Another Waterloo," *South African Baptist*, July 1899, 189-190.
[190] "On the Editorial Stoep," *South African Baptist*, November 1899, 61.
[191] "On the Editorial Stoep," *South African Baptist*, January 1900, 96.
[192] "A Settlement by Thunderbolts," *South African Baptist*, November 1899, 53-54.

fear was that hostilities would do irreparable harm to future relations. A letter to the editor in February 1901 reveals the concern for amicable relations and the need to avoid spreading hatred towards the Boers.

> Let us refrain from all provoking words, from speaking or hearing or reading them, and let us pray that God will turn the hearts of the peoples towards each other. What awful desolations both peoples are suffering now. No more terrible judgment could be passed upon England than? that she would be doomed to continue this war till the Boer people are utterly destroyed. May God spare our nation this....Never since the Civil Wars, save only in America, have we fought with men so nearly allied to us in blood and in spirit as are the men we are fighting with to-day.[193]

Not only were individuals to refrain from stirring up racial tensions, but the churches were also to stay out of the conflict. In fact, the editor of the *South African Baptist* was convinced that the shutting down of the paper for six months had been a blessing in disguise, for the paper had not been able to say anything in the heat of the moment that it had to regret or retract.[194]

Relief was expressed that Baptists had not been the ones stirring up trouble, and that the denomination had not made official pronouncements on the war, since it was felt that such statements would have jeopardized their chances to be involved in uniting the two races in the postwar period.[195] It is in the matter of postwar reconstruction and reconciliation that one gets a glimpse of the nation-building ethos shared by other BACSANZ Baptist papers. Two exhortations by the editor illustrate this commitment to nation-building.

Most were convinced that the successful British advance into the two Boer republics in mid-1900 meant that the war would soon be over. It was in that spirit of optimism that the editor published an article that looked to the "new era" in South Africa. While "statesmen" would be the ones responsible for the new plans for civil government, it was argued that the churches would take on the "holier" and "nobler task of harmonizing and unifying the various peoples."[196] The editor realized that perhaps this vision was not shared by most readers, but believed nonetheless that it was a necessary and nobler vision. What the churches had to offer in particular to the nation-building enterprise was a faith shared by both Boer and Briton, and that faith would be what united the new union:

> We shall be asked where the harmonizing work is to begin and along what lines it is to run. Our vision of it grows clearer every day. The Queen's subjects in this and adjacent Colonies speaking diverse tongues will find deeper than their loyalty to Her throne, the unifying centre of a common Evangelical faith....if only the

---

[193] G.W. Cross, "Dr. Mr. Editor," *South African Baptist*, February 1901, 19.

[194] "The New Era in S. Africa," *South African Baptist*, July 1900, 101-102.

[195] See "A Settlement by Thunderbolts," *South African Baptist*, November 1899, 53-54; "The New Era in S. Africa," *South African Baptist*, July 1900, 101-102; "The Great War," *South African Baptist*, January 1900, 85-86.

[196] "The New Era in S. Africa," *South African Baptist*, July 1900, 101-102.

> Churches will lead the way, we shall enter upon a new age, in which, as the Saxon and Norman are lost in the Briton at home, so English, Dutch and Colonist shall be lost in the citizen of Empire throughout the South African Dominion....Let there be no feud of clergy and there will be none of peoples. If the great religious assemblies exhibit chivalry, and the local Churches cultivate charity, much may be done in little time.

This portrayal of fellow Christian Boers differed dramatically from the harsh portrayals of the Boers in other papers. It was also a vision of an evangelicalism that could unite the empire. But what about the "blacks" in this vision? Once the white races had united they could then carry out their "great mission of evangelizing and civilizing the natives" – something deemed to be critical for the "permanent well-being" of South Africa.

Peace finally arrived two years later, and once again the editor provided a vision for the churches in the postwar period. The cruel guerilla war that had caused such destruction, death and hatred was over. But there could be no successful future if British and Boer animosity continued, and with that concern in mind the editor exhorted his readers to make a fresh start in the spirit of Christian charity:

> Its inwardness for us in South Africa marks a new chapter of our life....We need not boast of it, but we know how to treat and respect a valiant foe. As we are to live with each other in the country, the sooner we make friends the better. Our overtures may perhaps in some cases meet with distrust and coldness, engendered by the recent strife, but a genial and hearty advance of brotherhood will ultimately break the artificial barriers of reserve, suspicion and prejudice....The salvation of the country is to be worked out in the main by the personal factor.[197]

As in the example above, here was the vision of a new country united under the Union Jack, elements of a nascent national dream. Note also the assumption that the churches had a role to play in the building of a new united South Africa. In both exhortations, through their shared gospel and love, the churches were to be a potent and necessary institution in the uniting of hostile peoples.

Besides the concern over racial tensions was the recognition of the damage caused by the war. While the war may have led the editor to praise the increased imperial unity brought about the war and the arrival of so many Baptists from other parts of the empire,[198] such comments were in the larger context of continual lamentations about the impact of the war in general and on the churches in particular. Imbedded within the pages of the *South African Baptist* were indications that the war caused significant suffering and damage beyond the usual death, dislocation and injury of war. As noted above, race relations were strained. Industry had suffered.[199] Communications were broken with other colonists and with the rest of the world, and as a result accurate and up-to-date war

---

[197] "Peace!," *South African Baptist*, July 1902, 74.
[198] "On the Editorial Stoep," *South African Baptist*, September 1901, 111-112.
[199] "Kept in Peace," *South African Baptist*, September 1899, 21-22; "On the Editorial Stoep," *South African Baptist*, July 1900, 107-108.

news was hard to come by.[200] A war losses fund was established to help alleviate suffering, and Baptist contributions were reported in the paper.[201] However, what received the most attention in the paper was the suffering of the churches and denomination.

South African Baptists experienced considerable disruptions in their ministries, and from the onset of war the *South African Baptist* contained reports on the war's impact on the churches. The churches had been hit hard by the violence that had engulfed their region. As one report stated: "Our congregations have been scattered, our ministers have been driven from their homes, and probably every single Church in the country has suffered great financial loss."[202] However, such sweeping statements were not completely accurate. The impact of the war on the churches depended on the location of the church. Baptist churches within the Boer republics, or in war zones, had very different experiences than churches far from battle. For instance, the church in Krugersdorp reported that its ministry had "suffered little from the ravages of war."[203] The church in Alice had a rise in attendance due to the arrival of soldiers in town.[204] A few other churches also reported that despite the war and various hardships their services and ministries had continued unabated.[205] The church in Kimberly seemed to avoid any casualties during the extended and famous Boer siege.[206] The church in Bloemfontein, deep in the heart of Boer territory, was actually bolstered by the arrival of British troops. In one summary of its ministry it was reported:

> The soldiers at the present moment are the mainstay spirituality of the Church. It is they who supply the pulpit of the Sabbath; lead the Tuesday evening meeting for the spiritual deepening of the Christian life, and the Friday evening prayer meeting. Oh! That our own members would band themselves together for united prayer at these prayer meetings instead of allowing the soldiers to do all the praying then indeed the Lord would shower down blessings upon the church, and His smile would be upon us.[207]

While these churches provided positive reports on the survival of their ministries during the war, other reports were not as rosy.

---

[200] "On the Editorial Stoep," *South African Baptist*, December 1899, 80-81; "On the Editorial Stoep," *South African Baptist*, July 1900, 107-108.

[201] "Our Current Funds," *South African Baptist*, October 1900, 143; "Our Current Funds," *South African Baptist*, February 1901, 15; "Our Current Funds," *South African Baptist*, May 1901, 53.

[202] "A Point of Honour," *South African Baptist*, 1 September 1900, 125.

[203] "Krugersdorp," *South African Baptist*, June 1902, 70-71.

[204] "Alice," *South African Baptist*, May 1901, 60.

[205] "Buffalo Thorns-Glen Grey," *South African Baptist*, September 1901, 105-106; "Johannesburg," *South African Baptist*, February 1901, 24; "Johannesburg," *South African Baptist*, September 1901, 112-113.

[206] "On the Editorial Stoep," *South African Baptist*, July 1900, 107-108.

[207] "Bleomfontein," *South African Baptist*, June 1901, 73-74.

The adverse impact of the war can be categorized into two related spheres: local church and denominational life. First, a number of local churches faced adversity, and concern was expressed "for the scattered congregations and their grief-stricken ministers who have seen the labour of long years reduced to the ashes of an almost irretrievable dissolution."[208] Some Baptists fled from Boer territory or conflict and became refugees, consequently other Baptist churches had to invest resources into taking care of them (as well as refugees in general).[209] Reports from Baptists in war zones painted a grim picture of their mistreatment at the hands of the Boers: homes were burned, possessions destroyed, and people mistreated.[210] Young men were away due to the war.[211] One church lamented that it could not have its annual anniversary service, and other churches simply had to shut down completely.[212] Some pastors experienced reduced pay (or no pay at all), church buildings were damaged, Bible distribution was inhibited, and special mention was made of the plight of pastors in Boer territory.[213] One report leading up to the 1901 Assembly provides a helpful summary of the impact of the war on the churches and their pastors:

> Happily, so far as the *personnel* of our Ministry is concerned we have no losses by death, nor have we heard of any large number of our Church members being slain. Some have been wounded, many have had to endure great hardships, and the discomforts of war-time have been with all....In the northern territories, they are British now, our church property has suffered a good deal.[214]

In many cases, the fear was that Baptist work would suffer irreparable harm.

Second, the conflict impinged on denominational structures. It has already been noted how the war necessitated the shutting down of the *South African Baptist* for the first six months of 1900. The war also exacerbated tensions with Baptists in Britain, and the oft-shrill calls for help and the stern condemnations of their seemingly unresponsive fellow-Baptists provides a glimpse of the just how desperate Baptists felt in South Africa.[215] The most significant indicator of the war's impact on the denomination was the decision to cancel the 1900 Baptist Assembly.

---

[208] "A Settlement by Thunderbolts," *South African Baptist*, November 1899, 53-54.

[209] "On the Editorial Stoep," *South African Baptist*, December 1899, 80-81; "Letter to the Editor," *South African Baptist*, January 1900, 92; "Johannesburg," *South African Baptist*, February 1901, 24; "A Token for Good," *South African Baptist*, March 1901, 25-26.

[210] "Baptists in Peril of Boers," *South African Baptist*, April 1901, 45.

[211] "Queenstown," *South African Baptist*, November 1901, 135

[212] "Wakkerstroom," *South African Baptist*, July 1902, 83-84.

[213] "On the Editorial Stoep," *South African Baptist*, November 1899, 61-62; "The Bible in South Africa," *South African Baptist*, April 1901, 43; G.W. Cross, "Baptist Union Notes," *South African Baptist*, December 1900, 172-173.

[214] "After Two Years," *South African Baptist*, May 1901, 49-50.

[215] These tensions are dealt with in Chapter Five.

The Baptist Union Executive had decided to forgo the 1900 meeting for a variety of reasons: cost, travel difficulties, limited hospitality due to the need to take care of refugees, and the realization that wartime responsibilities would keep most people away.[216] By 1901, the war situation had improved enough that South African Baptists could once again plan for an Assembly. Consequently the *South African Baptist* announced in April that the meeting would be held at Bathurst Street Church, Grahamstown, 16-23 May 1901, and the following month the program was printed.[217] The meeting was deemed a success for it provided an opportunity to fill vacated leadership posts, a chance to carry out pressing church business, and was a much-needed time to reconnect with those whom war had separated for close to two years (although a few churches could still not send reports due to the war).[218] A few months later, in September 1901, a smaller group of Baptist leaders and pastors met for the inaugural meeting of the Baptist South African Colonial and Missionary Society, a significant wartime accomplishment considering the devastation and interrupted caused by the on-going war.[219]

As for issues related to contingents, South African Baptists shared concerns with other BACSANZ Baptists. There was apprehension expressed over the issue of precedence in church parades.[220] Spiritual care for soldiers was a priority.[221] In one instance, the pastor of Johannesburg Baptist was appointed officiating minister to the troops in the city.[222] Other items of concern related to local Baptist men who had enlisted,[223] and the deaths of local Baptist soldiers.[224] However, unlike other BACSANZ Baptists, South African Baptists had no overseas contingents to monitor and watch with pride. Baptists did join the imperial forces, but church matters related to the contingents dealt primarily with the troops pouring into the region and what that meant for the local churches.

As noted above, local Baptist churches often benefited from the attendance of Baptist men from overseas. Overseas soldiers appreciated this home-away-from-home. One illustration of the bonds established between incoming troops and local Baptists was that of the service at Wakkerstroom in May 1902.[225] The

---

[216] G.W. Cross, "Baptist Union Notes," *South African Baptist*, December 1900, 172-173.

[217] G.W. Cross, "Next Assembly," *South African Baptist*, February 1901, 19; "The Union Assembly, 1901," *South African Baptist*, April 1901, 40; "Annual Assembly," *South African Baptist*, May 1901, 53.

[218] "Baptist Union of South Africa," *South African Baptist*, June 1901, 61-69; "Rev. E. Baker, "The Presidential Address," *South African Baptist*, July 1901, 77-83.

[219] "Our Home Auxiliary," *South African Baptist*, December 1901, 145-147.

[220] "On the Editorial Stoep," *South African Baptist*, December 1899, 80-81.

[221] "On the Editorial Stoep," *South African Baptist*, December 1899, 80-81. "Baptist Chaplaincies," *South African Baptist*, May 1901, 50.

[222] "Johannesburg," *South African Baptist*, November 1901, 135.

[223] "Queenstown," *South African Baptist*, November 1901, 135.

[224] "In Memoriam," *South African Baptist*, July 1901, 84.

[225] "Wakkerstroom," *South African Baptist*, July 1902, 83-84.

occasion was a joint anniversary service and soldier's tribute. During a part of the festivities the pastor was presented with two theological books "as a small token of the love and esteem of a few soldier friends of the 2nd Batt. N. Stafford Regiment" stationed in town. Providing a church for fellow Baptists was considered to be important, but so was reaching the numerous incoming contingents with the gospel. The denominational paper was used in order to carry out their evangelistic mission. Over the course of many months the *South African Baptist* was distributed free to the sailors on ships arriving in Algoa Bay.[226] This was a costly venture, considering the fact that the paper was already cash-strapped, but one deemed worthy despite the hardship.

The announcement of Queen Victoria's death was a shock, and the *South African Baptist* let it be known that Baptists in the far flung outpost of empire mourned the loss.

> As those far off from the central seat of power, at the southernmost fringe of Her Majesty's African dominions, it is our sad privilege to pay our last act of homage to Her august personality, and bring our wreath, bedewed with affectionate tears, to her bier. By multitudes of loyal hearts, of exiled home-born sons, of colonial-born brothers and sisters, and of various child-like native peoples, Victoria the Great and Good was loved and revered in this bright, weird land."[227]

Besides the obvious racial overtones that betray problematic assumptions about the "child-like" natives, such language reveals an attachment to the monarchy and British identity that ensured colonial loyalty in the midst of the turmoil of war. However, despite the loyalty rooted in familial and cultural ties, there was a nascent nationalism rooted in a dream of a united South Africa where Briton and Boer forged a new political entity in South Africa, one firmly within the empire.

Conclusion

This chapter reinforces Keith Sinclair's claim that the war was a "major stimulus to nationalism among Canadians and Australians as well as New Zealanders, and – for different reasons – among the Afrikaners."[228] BACSANZ Baptists were loyal citizens of the empire as well as patriotic members of their

---

[226] "Our Current Funds," *South African Baptist*, October 1899, 45; "Our Current Funds," *South African Baptist*, November 1899, 65; "Our Current Funds," *South African Baptist*, October 1900, 143; "Our Current Funds," *South African Baptist*, December 1900, 162; "Our Current Funds," *South African Baptist*, January 1901, 2; "Our Current Funds," *South African Baptist*, February 1901, 15; "Our Current Funds," *South African Baptist*, April 1901, 46; "Our Current Funds," *South African Baptist*, May 1901, 53; "Our Current Funds," *South African Baptist*, August 1901, 93; "Our Current Funds," *South African Baptist*, September 1901, 105.
[227] "V.R.J.," *South African Baptist*, February 1901, 13-14. For the Baptist Union's official expression of loyalty, see "Baptist Union of South Africa," *South African Baptist*, June 1901, 61-62.
[228] Sinclair, *A Destiny Apart*, 125.

nation, dominion, federation or colony. The fusion of nationalism, imperialism and Baptist identity can readily been seen in the various Baptist papers' wartime coverage. Once war had been declared, the papers made it clear that they – and Baptists at large – were patriotic, supported the troops, and identified themselves as imperialists. Even for those papers or individuals that were critical of the war it was made clear that their patriotism and support for imperialism was not in question.

What is apparent during the war years was that BACSANZ Baptists had a clear sense of identity as loyal citizens of the empire as well as patriotic members of their nation, dominion, federation or colony. Baptists were actively involved in politics and various social and moral reforms such as the temperance movement or enactment of Sabbath laws. They also, in varying degrees, were absorbed with domestic politics and budding nationalism, and saw themselves as critical components in the nation-building project. The confluence of national and imperial identities among BACSANZ Baptists will be elaborated upon in the following chapter; suffice to say that loyalty to the empire, the Union Jack, and the monarchy was not necessarily considered by those within the empire to make one disloyal to one's national or regional identity. In fact, the war had engendered a more robust nationalism in the peripheries.

Chapter Four

Global Identity

"It was Maclaren - a greater contributor to the essential homogeneity of the Empire than any other Manchester man you can name....There is not a church building in the English-speaking world that he could not fill....he has become an imperishable asset of the Empire." "Imperial Maclaren," *Baptist Times and Freeman*, 16 May 1902, 365.

"[T]he British nation is our nation; we are a living part of that Empire, and they and we - Britain and New Zealand - must rise *or fall* together." S.R. Ingold, "The War in South Africa: The Christian's Proper Attitude Regarding It," *New Zealand Baptist*, April 1900, 61-62.

"But to think that there is so little Christian Imperialism in the official heads of British Baptists, as that they should leave us to our fate unaided...Do Little Englanders so predominate in Baptist Union Councils at home that political bias strangles piety? It is impiety to deny help to needy brethren." "A Point of Honour," *South African Baptist*, September 1900, 125-126.

BACSANZ Baptists encouraged involvement in politics in order to Christianize their nation, and their identity was fused to their unique national identity: Baptists in Australia were Australian Baptists, Baptists in Canada were Canadian Baptists, and so on. However, while BACSANZ Baptists had particular national identities, they also shared a global identity, both real and imagined. BACSANZ Baptists may have been on the margins in terms of the percentage of population, and even looked upon askance by the larger denominations, but the global Baptist community provided Baptists with a sense of belonging to something grander that transcended their small regional presence. They were loyal to their nation, dominion, federation or colony, but they also believed they belonged to a global community that was distinctly Baptist, British and imperial.

The Baptist press played an important role in constructing, nurturing, and sustaining this Baptist global identity. Brackney notes that while "unique indigenous communities and movements of Baptists grew up" in various parts of the world, there were still "clearly identifiable Baptist principles" that linked the larger Baptist community.[1] Those links were nurtured by, among other things, Baptist publications read on both sides of the Atlantic.[2] However, Baptist pa-

---

[1] Brackney, "Transatlantic Relationships," 60.
[2] Brackney, "Transatlantic Relationships," 68-69.

pers did more than create denominational community. Increasingly, historians are recognizing the important role that newspapers played in the construction and sustaining of a British world among colonists around the globe.[3] Carl Bridge and Kent Fedorowich write of the "plethora of networks" that acted as "cultural glue" which "held together" the British world, including religious publications and networks in their conclusions.[4] By the end of the nineteenth century, the international network of Baptist denominational papers continued to unite the movement and act as "cultural glue" for Baptists empire-wide. With the increase in technology over the century (especially trans-continental ocean cables), communication had multiplied exponentially along with the ability of the press to shape public opinion. Bebbington describes the impact of this technology on evangelical global contacts as revolutionary.[5] Sinclair echoes Bebbington when he claims that "It is difficult to exaggerate the importance of newspapers in stimulating national sentiment. They create a sense of community. They enable us to sense – to feel that we *know* – what other members of our community, quite unknown to us as individuals, are doing."[6] What Sinclair claims papers did for developing national sentiment applies as well to the creation of a global community. The international network of Baptist papers played a role in nurturing not only denominational loyalties but also imperial loyalties, what Simon Potter refers to as "diverse connections" and "complex webs of communication" that "forged links between each of the settler colonies."[7] In a very tangible way, the Baptist press within the empire played an important part in the building of a global denominational, evangelical and imperial identity and bond that transcended regional and national identities; it not only helped to cement bonds between the metropole and periphery, but also between the peripheries themselves. As this chapter demonstrates, this global Baptist identity was based on shared religious convictions, personal contacts, formal denominational structures, and an Anglo-Saxon/British imperial identity.

The following examines the ways in which the BACSANZ Baptist press constructed and consolidated a global identity.[8] The ways were varied, and attention waxed and waned as the situation warranted it. Coverage of events occurred through a number of ways. Reporting on events in editorial or news pages was common, but there was a reprinting of material from other Baptist sources that reveals the interconnectedness of the papers. The publishing of the Baptist Union of Great Britain's annual meetings in Baptist papers in the peripheries is just one example of how attention was drawn to, and loyalty formed

---

[3] For instance, see Potter, "Communication and Integration," 190-206.

[4] Bridge and Fedorowich, "Mapping the British World," 6.

[5] Bebbington, *The Dominance of Evangelicalism*, 78-81.

[6] Sinclair, *A Destiny Apart*, 138.

[7] Although in his analysis Potter did not mention the religious press. See Potter, "Communication and Integration," 191.

[8] This chapter does not examine the extensive reprinting of articles from other denominations, a common practice.

with, Baptists in the metropole. Requests for assistance from other Baptist communities (usually to Baptists in Britain) also indicate the expectation of a Baptist and imperial community that would come to the rescue of more needy family members, and organizations established to maintain those family ties not only strengthened Baptist ties but also cemented imperial bonds. The references to the "homeland" or "old country" nurtured loyalty to Britain and a sense of Britishness. While attention in the periphery was most often in relationship to the metropole, commentary on events and issues in the colonies demonstrated a concern for and identification with other peripheries. Underlying this global Baptist, British, and imperial identity was the assumption of Anglo-Saxon identity and superiority.

Links Between Metropole and Peripheries

There was a web of interconnectedness that characterized the Baptist press, and that international network of Baptist newspapers contributed to the formation of a global community. Highlighting the connections between Baptist papers in four continents, and detailing the travels of pastors and other Baptist figures between metropole and peripheries, demonstrates what Potter calls an "unparalleled level of reciprocity to the imperial connection."[9]

Cable reports from London made for news that was oriented to Britain's domestic and international affairs, and some Baptist papers frequently printed detailed cable reports.[10] It was, of course, also news with a distinctly pro-British bias. Canadian Baptists in particular had to deal with news reports that were not London-based, for French-Canadian opposition to the war was due in part to the Paris-based news reports in the French-Canadian newspapers.[11]

The papers were replete with bits of information on domestic events in Britain, as well as events in other colonies. Regular columns such as "Intercolonial and Other Gleanings,"[12] "British and Foreign,"[13] "News and Notes,"[14] "News

---

[9] Potter, "Communication and Integration," 192.

[10] For instance, the *Canadian Baptist* ran a regular section that reported on war news primarily from newspapers and cable reports. See "The War in South Africa," *Canadian Baptist*, 4 January 1900, 16; "The War in South Africa," *Canadian Baptist*, 11 January 1900, 16; "The War in South Africa," *Canadian Baptist*, 18 January 1900, 16; "The War in South Africa," *Canadian Baptist*, 25 January 1900, 16; "The War in South Africa," *Canadian Baptist*, 1 February 1900, 16; "The War in South Africa," *Canadian Baptist*, 8 February 1900, 16; "The War in South Africa," *Canadian Baptist*, 15 February 1900, 16; "The War in South Africa," *Canadian Baptist*, 22 February 1900, 16; "The War in South Africa," *Canadian Baptist*, 1 March 1900, 16; "The War in South Africa," *Canadian Baptist*, 1 March 1900, 16; "The War in South Africa," *Canadian Baptist*, 8 March 1900, 16; "The Week's War News," *Canadian Baptist*, 15 March 1900, 16; "The Week's War News," *Canadian Baptist*, 22 March 1900, 16; "The Week's War News," *Canadian Baptist*, 29 March 1900, 16.

[11] Page, *The Boer War and Canadian Imperialism*, 17.

[12] "Intercolonial and Other Gleanings," *Baptist*, 4 August 1900, 8.

by Mail,"[15] and "Chit Chat,"[16] provided commentary on a plethora of events that provided glimpses into the day-to-day affairs of life in the metropole and peripheries. Readers not only had those columns to look forward to, but editors provided a regular diet of anecdotes, incidents, and international events to spice up their papers as well as inform their readers as to the goings-on in other parts of the empire. For instance, the *Southern Baptist* pointed out that the low birth rate in Australia and New Zealand was a cause for concern.[17] The *Baptist Times and Freeman* reported on the devastating fire in Ottawa (the capital city of Canada), as well as on Canadian loyalty.[18] The *New Zealand Baptist* printed a brief story of a Canadian bishop who modeled humility in his ministry.[19] The *South African Baptist* provided its readers with accounts of the controversial Father Chiniquy, a minister's wife who died in New Zealand, and a humorous story of a Bible translation on the Canadian prairies.[20]

The sources for editors were diverse, including items from both secular and religious sources, but what is of interest here is how the Baptist papers drew upon one another for their news. The following editorial comment in the *New Zealand Baptist* provides a glimpse into how Baptist editors counted on the worldwide network of Baptist papers for their information:

> It is with considerable pleasure we inform our readers that we have been able to add to the list of our exchanges the organs of the Baptist denominations in Canada, the United States, and South Africa, as well as nearly all the Baptist periodicals published in these colonies and the leading denominational papers at Home. We hope by this means to present to our readers a wider and more comprehensive view of the progress of the Churches all over the planet; and we venture to suggest that our readers might well lend a profitable point to their conversations and correspondence by saying a good word for the BAPTIST to their friends.[21]

---

[13] "British and Foreign," *Southern Baptist*, 15 February 1900, 41; "British and Foreign," *Southern Baptist*, 15 March 1900, 65; "British and Foreign," *Southern Baptist*, 29 March 1900, 76.

[14] "News and Notes," *Queensland Baptist*, 1 January 1902, 1.

[15] "News by Mail," *South African Baptist*, September 1899, 23; "News by Mail," *South African Baptist*, October 1899, 47-48; "News by Mail," *South African Baptist*, November 1899, 62-63; "News by Mail," *South African Baptist*, January 1900, 89; "News by Mail," *South African Baptist*, August 1900, 119; "News by Mail" *South African Baptist*, September 1900, 132; "News by Mail," *South African Baptist*, December 1900, 169-170;

[16] "Chit Chat," *New Zealand Baptist*, November 1899, 164; "Chit Chat," *New Zealand Baptist*, January 1900, 14;

[17] "Our Colonies," *Southern Baptist*, 12 October 1899, 218.

[18] "The Ottawa Fire," *Baptist Times and Freeman*, 4 May 1900, 353; "Canadian Loyalty," *Baptist Times and Freeman*, 15 June 1900, 474.

[19] *New Zealand Baptist*, November 1899, 162.

[20] "On the Editorial Stoep," *South African Baptist*, June 1899, 180; "News by Mail" *South African Baptist*, September 1900, 132; "On the Editorial Stoep," *South African Baptist*, September 1902, 105.

[21] "A Larger Horizon," *New Zealand Baptist*, January 1900, 9.

The brief comment of the editor of the *Canadian Baptist* echoes those of his New Zealand counterpart: "As we go to press the English papers are arriving."[22] Some editors drew on particular papers more than others (or at least cited their sources more than others did). For instance, while the Australian *Southern Baptist* drew upon articles from the *Baptist Times and Freeman*[23] *Baptist Magazine*,[24] and *Baptist Standard* (Chicago),[25] it also made a number of references to reports in the *Canadian Baptist*.[26] The *New Zealand Baptist* relied on reports from the *Baptist Times and Freeman*,[27] *South African Baptist*,[28] *Baptist*,[29] *Southern Baptist*,[30] and the *Canadian Baptist*.[31] The *South African Baptist* made frequent mention of reports in the *New Zealand Baptist*,[32] *Baptist Times and Freeman*,[33] *Canadian Baptist*,[34] as well as the *Baptist Monitor* published in

---

[22] *Canadian Baptist*, 15 May 1902, 1.

[23] "The 'Baptist Times'," *Southern Baptist*, 2 November 1899, 229; "Lord Roberts," *Southern Baptist*, 28 June 1900, 146; "The Union of the Scottish Churches," *Southern Baptist*, 17 January 1901, 21.

[24] "Personal," *Southern Baptist*, 14 June 1900, 133; "David Maclaren," *Southern Baptist*, 26 March 1901, 75.

[25] "The Lack of Conversions," *Southern Baptist*, 18 January 1900, 14.

[26] "The 'Canadian Baptist'," *Southern Baptist*, 30 November 1899, 254; "It Appears," *Southern Baptist*, 30 November 1899, 254; "J.A. Dowie," *Southern Baptist*, 15 March 1900, 62; "The Sympathy of the Pope," *Southern Baptist*, 29 March 1900, 74; "The 'Canadian Baptist'," *Southern Baptist*, 29 March 1900, 74-75; "McMaster University," *Southern Baptist*, 18 October 1900, 230; "The 'Canadian Baptist'," *Southern Baptist*, 31 January 1901, 26; "The 'Canadian Baptist' States," *Southern Baptist*, 17 April 1901, 86; "Baptist Cooperation," *Southern Baptist*, 13 August 1902, 181. It also made mention of the *Southern Baptist's* outspoken position on the war. See "The 'Southern Baptist' on the Boer War," *Queensland Baptist*, 1 January 1899, 2.

[27] "Chit Chat," *New Zealand Baptist*, November 1899, 164; "Chit Chat," *New Zealand Baptist*, January 1900, 14;

[28] "Chit Chat," *New Zealand Baptist*, January 1900, 15; *New Zealand Baptist*, March 1900, 37; "Chit Chat," *New Zealand Baptist*, September 1900, 143; "A Good Word from Overseas," *New Zealand Baptist*, My 1901, 73; "Chit Chat," *New Zealand Baptist*, August 1901, 128.

[29] "Odds and Ends," *New Zealand Baptist*, February 1900, 25.

[30] "Chit Chat," *New Zealand Baptist*, March 1900, 48; "Chit Chat," *New Zealand Baptist*, September 1901, 144; "Severe Critics," *New Zealand Baptist*, April 1902, 57.

[31] "Don't You Know?" *New Zealand Baptist*, November 1900, 165; *New Zealand Baptist*, February 1901, 27; "A Good Word from Overseas," *New Zealand Baptist*, My 1901, 73.

[32] "On the Editorial Stoep," *South African Baptist*, December 1899, 81; *South African Baptist*, March 1901, 29; "On the Editorial Stoep," *South African Baptist*, August 1901, 111.

[33] "On the Editorial Stoep," *South African Baptist*, July 1899, 198; "On the Editorial Stoep," *South African Baptist*, January 1900, 96; "On the Editorial Stoep," *South African Baptist*, September 1900, 132; "On the Editorial Stoep," *South African Baptist*, December 1900, 171; Ernest Baker, "A Presidential Message," *South African Baptist*, January 1901, 5-7; "Rev. Ralph Holme, *South African Baptist*, January 1902, 17; "Corona-

Monrovia, Liberia, West Africa.[35] The *Baptist Times and Freeman* printed a number of letters directly from South Africa.[36] The *Canadian Baptist* drew extensively from American Baptist papers, as well as the *Baptist Times and Freeman*.[37]

While editors provided readers with details regarding events and anecdotes from around the globe, what they paid particular attention to were details of religious life. Although reference was made to religious statistics of other denominations or trends in general,[38] the focus of attention was usually on Baptist statistics. Baptist growth outside the empire was noted, with commentary on Baptists in places such as Cuba, Germany and Italy.[39] Baptists in the empire and Baptists in the United States were paramount in coverage.

Treatment of Baptists in the empire can be broken into articles related to the metropole and the peripheries. In regards to the peripheries, the plight of Baptists in wartime South Africa was a natural source of attention (although, as will

---

tion Lore," *South African Baptist*, January 1902, 18-19; "A Baptist Premier," *South African Baptist*, September 1902, 103-104.

[34] "The Free Church Catechism," *South African Baptist*, September 1899, 36.

[35] "On the Editorial Stoep," *South African Baptist*, October 1901, 124.

[36] "Concerning the Transvaal War," *Baptist Times and Freeman*, 26 January 1900, 72; "Another Letter from a Baptist in the Transvaal," *Baptist Times and Freeman*, 2 February 1900, 89; "A Letter from South Africa," *Baptist Times and Freeman*, 23 February 1900, 153; "Baptists in St. Helena and South Africa," *Baptist Times and Freeman*, 13 April 1900, 300; "An Interesting Letter from South Africa," *Baptist Times and Freeman*, 11 May 1900, 381; "Concerning the Transvaal War," *Baptist Times and Freeman*, 26 January 1900, 72; "Another Letter from a Baptist in the Transvaal," *Baptist Times and Freeman*, 2 February 1900, 89; "A Letter from South Africa," *Baptist Times and Freeman*, 23 February 1900, 153; "Baptists in St. Helena and South Africa," *Baptist Times and Freeman*, 13 April 1900, 300; "An Interesting Letter from South Africa," *Baptist Times and Freeman*, 11 May 1900, 381;W. Payne, "A Sunday in Port Elizabeth, South Africa," *Baptist Times and Freeman*, 31 August 1900, 700.

[37] *Baptist Times and Freeman*, 3 May 1900, 1; *Baptist Times and Freeman*, 7 June 1900, 1; *Baptist Times and Freeman*, 26 July 1900, 1; Rev. Alexander MacLaren, "The Cloud of Witnesses," *Baptist Times and Freeman*, 9 August 1900, 2; Rev. Alexander MacLaren, "Rejoicing in Hope and in Tribulation," *Baptist Times and Freeman*, 13 September 1900, 2; Rev. Alexander MacLaren, "A Soul's Tragedy," *Canadian Baptist*, 5 December 1901, 2. For an example from another British Baptist paper, see Rev. John Clifford, "Secret Prayer," *London Baptist Magazine*, 26 April 1900, 10.

[38] "The British Wesleyan Conference," *Southern Baptist*, 14 September 1899, 194; "Topics of the Month," *Baptist*, 1 November 1900, 2; W. Greenwood, "Church Work in England," *Baptist*, 1 March 1902, 4; "Chit Chat," *New Zealand Baptist*, October 1899, 148; "Chit Chat," *New Zealand Baptist*, November 1899, 164; "Chit Chat," *New Zealand Baptist*, December 1899, 183; "Chit Chat," *New Zealand Baptist*, January 1900, 14-15; "Chit Chat," *New Zealand Baptist*, May 1900, 80; "Some Interesting Figures," *New Zealand Baptist*, July 1900, 111; "Chit Chat," *New Zealand Baptist*, August 1900, 127-128; "Chit Chat," *New Zealand Baptist*, February 1902, 30-31.

[39] "Topics of the Month," *Baptist*, 1 January 1901, 1; "Chit Chat," *New Zealand Baptist*, November 1899, 164.

be shown below, South African Baptists did not feel that their predicament was getting enough attention from fellow Baptists). Australian and New Zealand papers often detailed the condition of Baptists in their own lands as well as in other parts of the empire. For instance, the 1901 census results for Australia and New Zealand were analyzed, with particular attention paid to the growth of Baptists.[40] Canadian Baptist statistics were noted, along with commentary on how they were a model for cooperation and organization.[41] The "Intercolonial" section in the *Queensland Baptist* provided a number of updates on Baptists in New Zealand.[42] Other reports provided sweeping summaries of Baptists in other parts of the empire.[43] The *South African Baptist* reported on decisions made by Australian Baptist Associations and annual reports from New Zealand Baptists.[44] Baptist statistics from Canada were also printed.[45] The *Canadian Baptist* reported on the open communion struggle in Australia, Baptist growth in Australia and New Zealand, as well as noted statistics of Baptist growth around the world.[46] The *Baptist Times and Freeman* also reported on Baptists around the empire, noting the 1901 census results in New Zealand and Australia, as well as other statistics and details of Baptist life.[47]

Of particular interest for Baptists, especially in the colonies, was the successful history of Baptists in America (technically not a part of the periphery of empire, but were deemed to be a part of the Anglo-Saxon world).[48] Resolutions

---

[40] W. Higlett, "The Religious Returns of the Census," *Queensland Baptist*, 1 November 1901, 147; "Percentage," *Queensland Baptist*, 1 January 1902, 2; "New Zealand Figures," *Queensland Baptist*, 1 January 1902, 2. For other summaries of statistics, see "Baptist Statistics," *Queensland Baptist*, 1 March 1900, 31.

[41] "Topics of the Month," *Baptist*, 1 August 1901, 1; "A Case for the Plaintiff," *Baptist*, 1 September 1901, 2-3.

[42] "Baptist News," *Queensland Baptist*, 1 March 1900, 39; "Baptist News," *Queensland Baptist*, 2 April 1900, 53; "Baptist News," *Queensland Baptist*, 1 August 1901, 109.

[43] "Baptist World," *Baptist*, 1 March 1902, 8; "Baptists in the World," *Baptist*, 1 March 1902, 12.

[44] "On the Editorial Stoep," *South African Baptist*, December 1899, 81; *South African Baptist*, March 1901, 29.

[45] "News by Mail," *South African Baptist*, November 1899, 62.

[46] *Canadian Baptist*, 15 November 1900, 1; *Canadian Baptist*, 18 January 1900, 1; *Canadian Baptist*, 4 January 1900, 1; "Statistics of the Denominations," *Canadian Baptist*, 18 January 1900, 8; *Canadian Baptist*, 19 April 1900, 1; *Canadian Baptist*, 26 April 1900, 1; *Canadian Baptist*, 14 June 1900, 1; "Fifty Years of Baptist History," *Canadian Baptist*, 18 October 1900, 8; *Canadian Baptist*, 21 February 1901, 1; *Canadian Baptists*, 21 March 1901, 1; *Canadian Baptists*, 2 May 1901, 1.

[47] "Baptists in St. Helena and South Africa," *Baptist Times and Freeman*, 13 April 1900, 300; "Baptists in Australia," *Baptist Times and Freeman*, 5 October 1900, 800; "New Zealand Census," *Baptist Times and Freeman*, 24 May 1901, 337.

[48] "News by Mail," *South African Baptist*, November 1899, 62; "On the Editorial Stoep," *South African Baptist*, July 1902, 76; "On the Editorial Stoep," *South African Baptist*, July 1902, 91. "Baptist World," *Baptist*, 1 March 1902, 8; "The American Year Book," *Southern Baptist*, 30 November 1899, 254; "Baptist Progress," *Southern Baptist*,

and annual reports of American Baptist organizations made it into the pages of various papers.[49] Frequently noted was the phenomenal growth of U.S. Baptists, and for relatively small and marginalized Baptists in Australia or South Africa, the dominant cultural footprint of American Baptists was a source of pride and even validation of their own faith. One gets a sense of the pride in, and envy of, American Baptists and their amazing growth when the *South African Baptist* declared: "At this side of the world we scarcely realise what a great people are the Baptists of America."[50] There were also lessons to be learned from the American Baptist experience, and a number of articles drew attention to how Baptists in the empire could benefit from modeling their ministry on that of American Baptists. For instance, they needed to watch out for "higher criticism, new theology, and lack of consecration,"[51] as well as learn from American Baptists who had better Sunday Schools, leaders who committed more time and money to church work, gave more emphasis on giving to missions, exhibited more loyalty to denomination, and were not ashamed of the ordinance of baptism.[52] In another article in the Australian *Baptist* it was suggested that "Australian Baptists have many things to learn from American Baptists," such as the building of a beautiful cathedral like Broadway Baptist Tabernacle in New York.[53]

Baptist life in Great Britain was also of particular interest not only because of emotional and familial ties to the homeland, but also because Britain was the main source of ministers and financial assistance for Baptists in Canada, Australia, New Zealand and South Africa. Trends within British society in general and the churches in particular were followed closely, as were statistics detailing the growth of Baptists.[54] Reporting on the annual assembly of the Baptist Union

---

14 March 1901, 63; "Religion in the United States," *Queensland Baptist*, 2 April 1900, 45.

[49] Wm. Hublin, "Baptists in the United States," *Southern Baptist*, 13 July 1899, 147; "Topics of the Month," *Baptist*, 1 January 1902, 1.

[50] "The American Baptists," *New Zealand October*, 1901, 150.

[51] "The Lack of Conversions," *Southern Baptist*, 18 January 1900, 14.

[52] Rev. Chas. Williams, "Some Lessons Learned from American Baptists," *Queensland Baptist*, 1 January 1901, 2-4.

[53] "A Baptist Cathedral," *Baptist*, 1 September 1902, 1.

[54] J.M. Howie,, "Baptist Union and Great Britain," *Southern Baptist*, 15 June 1899, 123; "The Autumnal Session of the Baptist Union of Great Britain," *Southern Baptist*, 16 December 1899, 246; "Topics of the Month," *Baptist*, 1 November 1900, 1; "The English Baptist Union Meetings," *Southern Baptist*, 14 June 1900, 133; "Baptists in the United Kingdom," *Southern Baptist*, 16 April 1902, 94; "From the English Baptist Union," *Southern Baptist*, 30 April 1902, 99; "A Scotch Baptist Hero," *Southern Baptist*, 27 February 1901, 52; "English Baptist News," *Queensland Baptist*, 1 December 1900, 160-161; "Federation of Churches," *Queensland Baptist*, 1 February 1901, 20; "Baptist Union," *Queensland Baptist*, 1 March 1900, 30; "Baptist Statistics," *Queensland Baptist*, 1 March 1901, 34-35; Rev. Charles Williams, "Notes and Comments: Denominational and Ecclesiastical," *Baptist Times and Freeman*, 13 December 1901, 852; "Baptist World," *Baptist*, 1 March 1902, 8; "On the Editorial Stoep," *South African Baptist*,

was frequent, with full reports being printed in some papers.[55] For ministers and members with ties back home, such detailed reporting provided updates on the lives and ministry of distant friends and coworkers.

There were a number of British Baptists who were frequently commented upon, and the activities and especially opinions of those Baptist superstars carried significant weight among Baptists in the colonies. Articles dealing with the great Victorian Baptist preacher Charles H. Spurgeon were common, as were items dealing with his wife or one of his sons, Rev. Thomas Spurgeon. For the churches in Australia and New Zealand, the connection with the Spurgeons went deeper than an appreciation of Charles' famous preaching; the churches in those colonies had received significant support from graduates of Spurgeon's College beginning in 1877, as well as from Thomas himself who arrived in 1881. Thomas had preached throughout Australia and New Zealand in the 1880s, and ultimately became the pastor of Auckland Baptist Tabernacle in New Zealand. After the pastorate he served a few years as New Zealand Baptist's national evangelist. Following his father's death, he returned to London to become the pastor of the Metropolitan Tabernacle. This connection with the famous Spurgeons remained long after the return of Thomas to Britain, and it can be seen in the numerous articles detailing aspects of life in the Spurgeon

---

December 1899, 81; "On the Editorial Stoep," *South African Baptist*, July 1902, 76; "On the Editorial Stoep," *South African Baptist*, December 1900, 172; F.W. Boreham, "Is Great Britain Christian?," *New Zealand Baptist*, July 1901, 99-101; "Chit Chat," *New Zealand Baptist*, December 1899, 183; "The Speech from the Throne," *New Zealand Baptist*, December 1899, 184; "The May Meetings," *New Zealand Baptist*, July 1900, 104; "Some Interesting Figures," *New Zealand Baptist*, July 1900, 111; "Chit Chat," *New Zealand Baptist*, September 1900, 143; Robert F. Elder, "Some Impressions of Religious Life in England," *New Zealand Baptist*, March 1900, 34-36; "Chit Chat," *New Zealand Baptist*, October 1899, 148; "Chit Chat," *New Zealand Baptist*, December 1899, 183; "Chit Chat," *New Zealand Baptist*, April 1900, 63-64; "Some Interesting Figures," *New Zealand Baptist*, July 1900, 111; "Chit Chat," *New Zealand Baptist*, September 1900, 143; "Chit Chat," *New Zealand Baptist*, November 1900, 174; "Forward!" *New Zealand Baptist*, April 1901, 56; "Chit Chat," *New Zealand Baptist*, April 1901, 64; "Chit Chat," *New Zealand Baptist*, August 1901, 128; "Chit Chat," *New Zealand Baptist*, September 1901, 144; "The American Baptists," *New Zealand October*, 1901, 150; "Some Interesting Figures," *New Zealand Baptist*, July 1900, 111; *New Zealand Baptist*, June 1901, 83; *New Zealand October*, 1901, 150; "Chit Chat," *New Zealand Baptist*, May 1902, 80; "Forward!" *New Zealand Baptist*, April 1901, 56; *New Zealand Baptist*, June 1901, 83; *New Zealand October*, 1901, 150; *Canadian Baptists*, 17 May 1900, 1; *Canadian Baptists*, 31 May 1900, 1; *Canadian Baptists*, 31 May 1900, 8; *Canadian Baptists*, 13 September 1900, 1; *Canadian Baptists*, 1 November 1900, 1; *Canadian Baptists*, 6 December 1900, 1; *Canadian Baptist*, 17 January 1901, 8. British Baptists reflected on their own experience in articles such as "A Baptist's Retrospective of the Century," *Baptist Times and Freeman*, 28 December 1900, 1046-1047.

[55] For instance, see *Canadian Baptist*, 19 October 1899, 1; *Canadian Baptist*, 16 May 1901, 1; "English Baptist Union," *Canadian Baptist*, 31 October 1901, 2-3; "Rev. Dr. Culross Called Home," *Canadian Baptist*, 16 November 1899, 9.

family, as well as events related to Spurgeon's Tabernacle.[56] Canadian Baptists were also enamored with Spurgeon,[57] as were South African Baptists.[58] And while Baptists in Africa had not had one of Spurgeon's son's reside and pastor in their midst, they did receive pastors from his college and hoped for wartime financial assistance from the London Tabernacle.[59]

Another British Baptist with a high profile in the colonies was Rev. John Clifford. Like Spurgeon, Clifford was a Baptist with an international reputation. His opposition to the war and position as President of the Stop the War Committee made him an unpopular figure among supporters of the war, including among certain Baptists. Nevertheless, his opinions on all issues mattered, and, for churches in the colonies, to have a visit from Clifford was a much sought after prize.[60]

---

[56] "Topics of the Month," *Baptist*, 1 November 1900, 1; "Mrs. C.H. Spurgeon," *Southern Baptist*, 15 February 1900, 38; "Spurgeon's Wit," *Southern Baptist*, 15 February 1900, 41; "Mr. Spurgeon on the Bible," *Southern Baptist*, 15 March 1900, 65; "How Mr. Spurgeon Spent the Week," *Southern Baptist*, 12 July 1900, 161; "Mrs. C.H. Spurgeon," *Queensland Baptist*, 1 March 1900, 29; "News in Brief," *Queensland Baptist*, 1 May 1901, 65; "Chit Chat," *New Zealand Baptist*, October 1899, 148; "Chit Chat," *New Zealand Baptist*, November 1899, 164; "Chit Chat," *New Zealand Baptist*, December 1899, 183; "Chit Chat," *New Zealand Baptist*, January 1900, 15; "Chit Chat," *New Zealand Baptist*, April 1900, 63; "Chit Chat," *New Zealand Baptist*, August 1900, 128; "Jubilee Greetings," *New Zealand Baptist*, May 1901, 66-67; *New Zealand Baptist*, May 1901, 67; "Chit Chat," *New Zealand Baptist*, August 1901, 128.

[57] For a few examples from Canada, see *Canadian Baptist*, 18 June 1900, 1; C.H. Spurgeon, "Arbitration vs War," *Canadian Baptist*, 1 February 1900, 2; "A Service of the Metropolitan Tabernacle," *Canadian Baptist*, 1 February 1900, 10; *Canadian Baptist*, 15 February 1900, 1; "Spurgeon and Ruskin," *Canadian Baptist*, 22 March 1900, 2; *Canadian Baptist*, 19 April 1900, 1; "The Rebuilding of Spurgeon's Tabernacle," *Canadian Baptist*, 3 May 1900, 15; "This Week at the Tabernacle," *Canadian Baptist*, 18 October 1900, 15; Joshua Roberts, "The Spurgeons," *Canadian Baptist*, 30 November 1899, 10.

[58] "Dr. Spurgeon," *South African Baptist*, May 1899, 149; "The Conflagration of a Year Ago," *South African Baptist*, June 1899, 179; "Spurgeon and Ruskin," *South African Baptist*, August 1899, 14; "News by Mail," *South African Baptist*, October 1899, 47-48; "Rev. Thomas Spurgeon," *South African Baptist*, November 1899, 57;"On the Editorial Stoep," *South African Baptist*, July 1900, 108; "On the Editorial Stoep," *South African Baptist*, August 1900, 120; "The Renovated Tabernacle," *South African Baptist*, September 1900, 130-131; "On the Editorial Stoep," *South African Baptist*, November 1900, 155; "The Outgoing Century, *South African Baptist*, December 1900, 161; "Spurgeon and His Century," *South African Baptist*, April 1901, 44-45; "On the Editorial Stoep," *South African Baptist*, May 1901, 58; "On the Editorial Stoep," *South African Baptist*, May 1902, 55.

[59] "The Renovated Tabernacle," *South African Baptist*, September 1900, 130-131; "Durban," *South African Baptist*, November 1900, 160.

[60] "The Rev. Dr. Clifford," *Queensland Baptist*, June 1897, 77; "Dr. Clifford and 'The Primitive Theology'," *New Zealand Baptist*, December 1899, 184; *New Zealand Baptist*, July 1900, 98; "Chit Chat," *New Zealand Baptist*, August 1900, 127; *New Zealand Bap-*

A third Baptist luminary was the Rev. Dr. Alexander Maclaren, pastor of Union Chapel, Fallowfield, Manchester, as well as president of the Baptist Union of Great Britain. His travels to Australia in 1888 may have endeared him to Baptists in the Antipodes, but it was his teaching and preaching ministry that made him such a well-known figure by the end of the century. The *Baptist Times and Freeman* extolled the virtues of Maclaren and claimed that he was one of the most well-known religious personages in the empire:

> It was Maclaren - a greater contributor to the essential homogeneity of the Empire than any other Manchester man you can name. My New Zealander is a devout Churchman, but he did not know the name of the Archbishop of Canterbury, and had never heard of Dr. Moorhouse. One of the greatest links connecting the old English-speaking world and the new is the International Sunday-school Lesson [Maclaren prepared many of them]....Dr. Maclaren probably has more teachers at his feet than any man living. Literally, visibly, his influence is as wide as the Empire - and wider. For he is read week by week by thousands and thousands of teachers in the United States. There is not a church building in the English-speaking world that he could not fill. Men everywhere confess their indebtedness to him...he has become an imperishable asset of the Empire.[61]

This "asset of the empire" was more than cause for pride among Baptists, he (along with Spurgeon or Clifford) was the glue that kept the Baptists in the periphery connected to their brothers and sisters in the faith in the distant metropole.

Another form of direct connection between Mother England and distant colonies was that of personal visits. The visitation of royalty to the colonies was understood to knit the empire together, in the words of the *New Zealand Baptist* their arrival would "cement more strongly the bond between these colonies and the Mother Country."[62] In like manner, visits to or from England by Baptists created and reaffirmed bonds of affection between the widely scattered communions. The reporting of these visits in the denominational papers further played a role in building a sense of being both Baptist and British.

Visits to Britain by colonial figures were an opportunity for those in England to gain firsthand experience of Baptist life throughout the empire, as well as express solidarity with those overseas. The *Baptist Times and Freeman* noted

---

tist, February 1901, 2; "Jubilee Greetings," *New Zealand Baptist*, May 1901, 66-67; "Dr. Clifford on S.A.," *Canadian Baptist*, 16 August 1900, 517.

[61] "Imperial Maclaren," *Baptist Times and Freeman*, 16 May 1902, 365.

[62] "Our Royal Guests," *New Zealand Baptist*, June 1901, 89. See also "A Royal Visit to Australia," *Baptist Times and Freeman*, 21 September 1900, 757; "The Royal Visit to Australia," *Baptist Times and Freeman*, 1 March 1901, 133; "Australian Loyalty," *Baptist Times and Freeman*, 24 May 1901, 337; A.S. Adams, "The Baptists and the Throne," *New Zealand Baptist*, June 1902, 82-83; "The Royal Visit," *Canadian Baptist*, 17 October 1901, 8. See also poem entitled "The Song of the Land." See Wade Robinson, "The Song of the Land," *New Zealand Baptist*, June 1902, 83-84.

such interactions,[63] and, as elaborated upon later in this chapter, personal contacts with South Africa were of special importance due to the need for British
Baptist support for struggling South African Baptists.[64] Accounts of Baptists
travelling to the Old Country were of interest to those who remained behind,
and articles describing their experience can be found in a number of papers.[65]
Occasionally someone returning to Britain meant a loss for the church, for they
had no intention of returning.[66] Two brief reports in the *New Zealand Baptist* in
May and June 1901 provide an example of this reverse migration and - in this
case - loss of a key leader, a potentially crippling blow for a nascent denomination. The two reports read: "The Rev. John Muirhead, Secretary of the New
Zealand Baptist Union, has resolved to return to the Old Country, and sails,
with his wife and daughter, on the 27th of the present month" and "It was with
very sincere regret that we last month informed our readers that ... Muirhead
had resolved to leave these shores and seek a sphere of service among the
Churches of the Old Land."[67] However, those who had plans to visit Britain
were invited to consider representing their denomination by being a delegate at
the Baptist Union Assembly or other important functions.[68] The account of
Rev. Thomas Chapman is noteworthy in that he left Britain twice for the colo-

---

[63] "Entertaining the Australian Delegates," *Baptist Times and Freeman*, 11 May 1900,
373; "Australian Notes," *Baptist Times and Freeman*, 7 March 1902, 188; "Rev. John
Muirhead," *New Zealand Baptist*, January 1902, 9.
[64] For two examples of reporting on personal visits from South Africa, see "South African Notes," *Baptist Times and Freeman*, 7 February 1902, 100; "Rev. Newton H. Marshall, Rev. Thos. Chapman, of Johannesburg," *Baptist Times and Freeman*, 30 May
1902, 404.
[65] "On the Editorial Stoep," *South African Baptist*, August 1900, 121; "Executive
Notes," *South African Baptist*, October 1901, 122-123; "On the Editorial Stoep," *South
African Baptist*, December 1900, 171; "On the Editorial Stoep," *South African Baptist*,
May 1902, 54; "M.A.P.," *New Zealand Baptist*, March 1900, 41; "Rev. John G. Raws,"
Southern Baptist, 15 March 1900, 61; "A Sunday in London," *New Zealand Baptist*,
October 1900, 146.
[66] This reverse migration was not uncommon, for between 1860 and 1930 around 40
percent of emigrants from England and Wales returned to Britain for a period of time.
See Andrew S. Thompson, *Imperial Britain: The Empire in British Politics, c.1880–
1932* (Harlow: Longman, 2000), 19. Simon Potter notes that the positive effect of such
returns was that those return migrants "ensured sustained contact between those who left
and those who stayed behind." See Potter, "Communication and Integration," 191.
[67] *New Zealand, Baptist*, May 1901, 80; "Bon Voyage," *New Zealand Baptist*, June
1901, 89. For another example, see "Resignation of Rev. A. Gordon M.A.," *New Zealand Baptist*, March 1901, 39; "The Rev. A. Gordon, M.A.," *New Zealand Baptist*,
March 1901, 40; "Farewell!" *New Zealand Baptist*, January 1902, 9.
[68] "Rev. John Muirhead," *New Zealand Baptist*, January 1902, 9; "Australian Notes,"
Baptist Times and Freeman, 7 March 1902, 188; "News and Notes," *Queensland Baptist*, 1 January 1902, 1. There was a need for delegates to attend the Ecumenical Missionary Conference (New York) in May 1900, and the *New Zealand Baptist* asked its
readers if anyone visiting at that time and would like to be a delegate. See "Chit Chat,"
New Zealand Baptist, October 1899, 154.

nies.[69] He first left England to work as a pastor in South Africa. Dislocated by the war, he ended up in Ladysmith just as the siege began. He assisted the authorities in Ladysmith as acting chaplain and assistant medical officer. After the siege, he returned to England to where he lectured and preached, and played a critical role in the formation of the South African Baptist Colonial and Missionary Aid Society. He then returned to South Africa to once again take up church work.

The visits of prominent leaders from Britain to the colonies were a high point in the life of local churches and larger assemblies, and provided much needed moral support for the often struggling work of a small and marginalized denomination. They supplied meaningful and tangible connections with the Old Country as well as an opportunity to show off the work of overseas Baptists. There were a number of articles that reveal how Baptists in the colonies sought after Baptist luminaries for evangelistic preaching tours or for special activities such as yearly assemblies or anniversaries.[70] There was an inter-colonial exchange of ministers in Australia and New Zealand that served the same purpose.[71] Most of these visits seemed to be a boon for the churches and a positive experience for the visiting figure. However, as the visit of Rev. J.G. Greenhough illustrates, visits of British leaders were not without their problems.

Greenhough was a former president of the Baptist Union of Great Britain, president of the National Council of the Evangelical Free Churches, and well-known and respected Baptist leader. In the fall of 1900, the *New Zealand Baptist* reported that the Baptist Union of New Zealand wanted Greenhough to be a special guest at their Jubilee celebration in the coming year.[72] The coming of Greenhough was announced at the November 1900 assembly as well as in the December 1900 issue of the *New Zealand Baptist*. His visit was to be a part of a colony-wide series of Jubilee celebrations and evangelistic services scheduled to begin in May 1901.[73] In May 1901, the *New Zealand Baptist* printed an itinerary of Jubilee events, including comments on Greenhough's coming that provide a glimpse of the expectancy surrounding his visit as well as the work and expense that was required to bring him to New Zealand:

---

[69] Rev. Newton H. Marshall, "Rev. Thos. Chapman, of Johannesburg," *Baptist Times and Freeman*, 30 May 1902, 404.

[70] "The Rev. Dr. Clifford," *Queensland Baptist*, June 1897, 77; "Distinguished Visitors," *Southern Baptist*, 3 January 1901, 1; "Distinguished Visitors," *Queensland Baptist*, 2 September 1901, 118; "Rev. C. Williams," *New Zealand Baptist*, January 1901, 9.

[71] "Rev. W. Whale," *Queensland Baptist*, 1 March 1902, 31; "New Zealand Notes," *Queensland Baptist*, 1 April 1902, 44-45; "Intercolonial Visitor," *Southern Baptist*, 4 October 1900, 217.

[72] "A Distinguished Guest," *New Zealand Baptist*, September 1900, 136.

[73] *Annual report of the New Zealand Baptist Union, 1900*, 10 (special supplement to the January 1901 *New Zealand Baptist*); WROX, "Echoes from Christchurch," *New Zealand Baptist*, December 1900, 187-191. For further announcement, see "Chit Chat," *New Zealand Baptist*, April 1901, 64.

At a very great deal of trouble and expense, the Conference has been able to arrange for a visit from the Rev. J.G. Greenhough, M.A., the distinguished President of the National Free Church Council of Great Britain and Ireland. Mr. Greenhough has a world-wide reputation, and he will be one of the most famous and popular ministers that have ever visited these shores. No pains must be sparred to make the most of his distinguished services during his sojourn in New Zealand. Mr. Greenhough will make a tour of the Colony, preaching and lecturing, and will, we understand, bring his visit to a climax by his presence at, and participation in, the great Jubilee Conference to be held at Nelson in November.[74]

Plans were made in anticipation of his arrival, itineraries were published to update churches on his travels, and more details on his life and ministry were published to build further support for his coming.[75] When he arrived in Auckland on 19 October 1901, he was greeted by a deputation consisting of the Rev. A. H. Collins (President of the Baptist Union of New Zealand), Rev. Joseph Clark (of the Auckland Tabernacle), Rev. W. R. Woolley (Secretary of the Baptist Union), and Mr. Patterson. He was met with a great deal of enthusiasm, and during his time in New Zealand he travelled far and wide, preaching and lecturing in local churches, mission society meetings, and the annual assembly.[76] Commentary on his messages was positive. For instance, his address to the annual assembly on mission was "in every respect, a great and inspiring deliverance on a great theme."[77] Early in 1902, the New Zealand Baptist reported that Greenhough had returned safely to England.[78]

---

[74] "Our Jubilee Guest," *New Zealand Baptist*, May 1901, 66. An article in the June issue introduced Greenhough to readers, and provided glowing praise of his accomplishments and oratory skills. See Rev. J.D. Carnegie, "The Rev. J.G. Greenhough, M.A.," *New Zealand Baptist*, June 1901, 83-84. For further expression of excitement at his coming, see "Still They Come!" *New Zealand Baptist*, July 1901, 105.

[75] "Otago and Southland Auxiliary Annual Meetings," *New Zealand Baptist*, July 1901, 103; "Our Guest and His Movements," *New Zealand Baptist*, July 1901, 105; "Rev. J.G. Greenhough, M.A.," *New Zealand Baptist*, August 1901, 122; "The Rev. J.G. Greenhough's Itinerary," *New Zealand Baptist*, October 1901, 154; "Baptist Union of New Zealand," *New Zealand Baptist*, October 1901, 152-153; "Welcome!" *New Zealand Baptist*, October 1901, 154; "Our Guest," *New Zealand Baptist*, November 1901, 170; "Mr. Greenhough in Auckland," *New Zealand Baptist*, November 1901, 170.

[76] "At Last!," *New Zealand Baptist*, November 1901, 171; "Auckland," *New Zealand Baptist*, November 1901, 174; "Auckland," *New Zealand Baptist*, December 1901, 191; "Ponsonby," *New Zealand Baptist*, December 1901, 191; "Thames," *New Zealand Baptist*, November 1901, 174; "Thames," *New Zealand Baptist*, December 1901, 191; "Mount Eden," *New Zealand Baptist*, December 1901, 191; "Palmerston North," *New Zealand Baptist*, December 1901, 191-192; "Wellington," *New Zealand Baptist*, December 1901, 192; "Nelson," *New Zealand Baptist*, December 1901, 192; "Napier," *New Zealand Baptist*, January 1902, 11; "Spreydon," *New Zealand Baptist*, January 1902, 12; "Mosgiel," *New Zealand Baptist*, January 1902, 13; *Annual Report of the New Zealand Baptist Union, 1901* (special supplement to the January 1902 *New Zealand Baptist*).

[77] WROX, "Echoes from Nelson," *New Zealand Baptist*, December 1901, 185- 191.

[78] "Rev. J.G. Greenhough's Return," *New Zealand Baptist*, April 1902, 53.

Hearing that Baptists in New Zealand were planning to have Greenhough for their Jubilee, Baptists in Australia had begun to wonder if they too could benefit from his visit.[79] He did end up visiting major centers in southeastern Australia, but much to the chagrin of Queensland Baptists, he did not venture far north up the east coast.[80]

While Greenhough's visit was an encouragement to the ministry of the local churches in both New Zealand and Australia, and did help forge links between the metropole and peripheries, its benefits were offset by a number of controversies and difficulties. First, Baptists in Queensland felt that they were "outside the currents of thought and action which move further south," and as a result, they missed out having distinguished visitors like Greenhough pay them a visit.[81] The editor of the *Queensland Baptist* faithfully reported on Greenhough's visit to churches in Southern Australia, but those visits rankled him. The problem was not with Greenhough as one disgruntled Baptist noted: "Some friends feel that Queensland has been quite ignored by distinguished representatives such as ... J. G. Greenhough, but this is because our neighbours [Baptists] monopolised them."[82] Sadly, rather than unite Baptists in Australia, Greenhough's visit exacerbated domestic Baptist relations and highlighted regional disparities. Second, Baptists had expected the expenses of Greenhough's visit to be covered by offerings at the meetings. That was not the case, and Baptists in New Zealand were left with a hefty bill to pay after he left.

> The treasurer regrets to say that, so far as his knowledge carries him, there is a deficit of about £80 on the visit of the Rev. J.G. Greenhough. This is a surprise of a painful sort. But we must be brave. We can triumphantly meet every financial engagement; but not without enthusiasm and self-sacrifice. Many of us received special blessings through Mr. Greenhough's visit. Let us show that their impressions are permanent. We had no guarantee fund when we invited our visitor. We

---

[79] "Distinguished Visitor," *Queensland Baptist*, 1 September 1900, 113; "Distinguished Visitors," *Southern Baptist*, 3 January 1901, 1; "Rev. J.G. Greenhough," *Southern Baptist*, 12 June 1901, 149; "Rev. J.H. Greenhough's Farewell," *Southern Baptist*, 28 August 1901, 194; "Rev. J.G. Greenhough," *Queensland Baptist*, 2 September 1901, 119.

[80] "Victoria," *Queensland Baptist*, November 1901, 154-155; "South Australia," *Queensland Baptist*, November 1901, 155; "New South Wales," *Queensland Baptist*, December 1901, 168; "The Rev. J.G. Greenhough," *Southern Baptist*, 16 October 1901, 230.

[81] "Isolation," *Queensland Baptist*, September 1901, 113. In the same article it was lamented that they were deemed so insignificant by their fellow Baptists in New Zealand that they did not even get invited to send a delegate to the New Zealand Baptist Jubilee. For similar comments on disappointment with being excluded from Baptist life, see also "The Rev. J.G. Greenhough," *Queensland Baptist*, September 1901, 119.

[82] "Twentieth Century Fund," *Queensland Baptist*, April 1902, 44. On a more positive note, appreciation was expressed in this article for Rev. Dr. Alexander Maclaren's visit when he toured Australia.

over-estimated the popularity of the lectures. But we met a great man, and heard a great message. And £80 is a trifle to be considered against the benefit.[83]

This deficit led to some critics questioning the decision to invite Greenhough. The financial dilemma was also a crucial factor in the cancelation of the New Zealand Baptist forward movement. Third, Australian and New Zealand Baptists were hurt and offended by some of Greenhough's comments about the colonies. Upon his return to England, Greenhough published a number of items on his travels throughout the empire. Some of these reflections were quite positive and no cause for concern.[84] However, others were deemed offensive by both New Zealand and Australian Baptists. New Zealand Baptists did not appreciate being told that New Zealanders had a lax attitude to Roman Catholics, and especially resented Greenhough informing readers in England that they, and to a lesser degree Australian Baptists, were "a little out of date."[85] This type of condescension directed to colonists did nothing to endear them to Baptists in England. Baptists in Australia were also upset over what they felt were portrayals of Australians that were too sweeping, dogmatic, and mere caricatures.[86]

Greenhough's comments had touched a nerve. Baptists in the peripheries were sensitive to portrayals of colonial life. The *Baptist Times and Freeman* printed items that included perceptions of the colonies, summaries of visits to the colonies, or even advertising for immigration to the colonies.[87] However, while a colonial paper could print positive reflections on a visit by a visitor from the metropole with a sense of satisfaction,[88] what seemed to be unfair appraisals of the colonies provoked the ire of editors in the peripheries. The editor of the *New Zealand Baptist* was critical of "ridiculous paragraphs concerning

---

[83] "Baptist Union Notes," *New Zealand Baptist*, February 1902, 26. See also Arthur Dewdney, "Is It Worthy?," *New Zealand Baptist*, February 1902, 36; R.S. Gray, "Correspondence," *New Zealand Baptist*, February 1902, 36-37; "Baptist Union Notes," *New Zealand Baptist*, March 1902, 43; "Baptist Union Notes," *New Zealand Baptist*, April 1902, 58-59.

[84] Rev. J.G. Greenhough, "New Zealand," *New Zealand Baptist*, May 1902, 67-68; Rev. J.G. Greenhough, "My Visit to Nelson," *New Zealand Baptist*, September 1902, 134; "Mr. Greenhough Toughed the Right Notes," *Southern Baptist*, 11 June 1902, 135; "Our Baptist People There," *Southern Baptist*, 11 June 1902, 135; "Australian Self-Conceit," *Southern Baptist*, 11 June 1902, 135.

[85] "A Word of Warning," *New Zealand Baptist*, April 1902, 57; "Severe Critics," *New Zealand Baptist*, April 1902, 57. What made it even worse for the editor of the *New Zealand Baptist* was that New Zealand Baptists had also recently faced criticism from the Australian *Southern Baptist* for the lack of growth of Baptists in New Zealand.

[86] "A Caricature of Australians," *Southern Baptist*, 26 March 1902, 75; "In Religious Matters," *Southern Baptist*, 26 March 1902, 75; "'The Australian Christian'," *Southern Baptist*, 26 March 1902, 75; "Impressions of Australia," *Southern Baptist*, 11 June 1902, 135.

[87] "Wanted in Canada," *Baptist Times and Freeman*, 22 February 1901, 123; "Spring Emigration to Canada," *Baptist Times and Freeman*, 4 April 1902, 265.

[88] Chas. Williams, "Impressions of New Zealand," *New Zealand Baptist*, June 1902, 86-87.

New Zealand" that sometimes appeared in English periodicals.[89] The editor of the *Queensland Baptist* spoke of humiliation over the confusion and misunderstanding of the colonies in Great Britain.[90] While such sensitivity to criticism could be dismissed as mere colonial insecurity, the defensiveness of editors should, at least in part, be understood as a concern for recruitment to their colony. As one contributor to the *Queensland* Baptist wrote:

> Queensland is not likely to compete with Canada in securing immigrants to populate and develop the territory. The province of Ontario offers great inducements to form a company which shall enable 'desirable' immigrants from Great Britain to settle in Ontario. Places will be found in advance for those sent out, and the company will be repaid out of the wages. The distance, the expense, the risks are greater for Queensland, and it is not easy to equalise conditions. America, Canada, and South Africa will offer a golden future for the adventurous men who seek wider fields for energy and enterprise.[91]

The need was great among Baptist churches, and it was hard enough to recruit church leaders from Britain without negative perceptions of a particular colony clouding a potential pastor's judgment.

This section summarized the web of interconnectedness that characterized the Baptist press, and demonstrated how the international network of Baptist newspapers contributed to the formation of a global community. The following section highlights the role that Anglo-Saxon identity played in the formation of a global community, for cementing the ties between Baptists in the metropole and peripheries was more than personal contacts and shared commentary in the press; Baptists were convinced that they belonged to a global British world, and were united with their co-religionists and fellow citizens of empire by their Anglo-Saxon identity.

Anglo-Saxon Identity

Duncan Bell notes that the imperial ideal in Britain and the colonies was often a constructed and imagined ideal that served different purposes in different parts of the empire for different reasons, and his observation equally applies to BACSANZ Baptist churches.[92] Baptist denominational ties provided a strong ideological and relational link to Baptists in other parts of the empire, and the imperial and British connection supplied even further impetus for global community through shared racial and ideological assumptions. Edward Kohn's

---

[89] *New Zealand Baptist*, May 1901, 80.

[90] "Great Britain and Her Colonies," *Queensland Baptist*, 1 January 1899, 1.

[91] "Immigration," *Queensland Baptist*, 2 December 1901, 159. It was also hard to compete financially with the metropole. An article in the *Southern Baptist* noted that church needed to make a "handsome offer," one that "would prove attractive" to retain the services of a minister from England. See "The Deacons of Collins-Street," *Southern Baptist*, 2 November 1899, 229.

[92] Bell, *The Idea of Greater Britain*.

work on the growing rapprochement between the United States and Britain (which meant Canada as well) is also important to note, for he identifies how common racial discourse united two once-alienated peoples. An important reason for the growing unity was race, argues Kohn, in particular a conviction that the "Americans stood shoulder-to-shoulder with the British people as upholders of Anglo-Saxon civilization."[93] Race did not cause the hoped for reunion of Anglo-Saxons, but did give it a "device with which to adapt to the changing context of Canadian-American relations" and "helped foster ... [closer relations] by giving North Americans a common lexicon, the rhetoric of Anglo-Saxon kinship and Canadian-American affinity."[94] In like manner, the language of race provided BACSANZ Baptists a common lexicon that helped to unite disparate communities in four different continents. Numerous times heartfelt support was expressed for Britain because it was the "mother" or "home" country, and such ties of blood played an important role in the construction of an imagined community.

What that imperial identity meant, of course, was that Baptist global identity was also fused to Anglo-Saxon pre-eminence. This should not be surprising, for it has become a truism that the assumption of Anglo-Saxon racial superiority was intrinsic to the formation of late nineteenth-century national and imperial identity in the British Empire. Myra Rutherdale declares that the late-nineteenth century was "an age of classification" and that the "discourse of difference" was an everyday occurrence.[95] Terms like "race," "breed," "stock," "native," and the like were quite common and, for most, were considered to be inoffensive. Andrew Ross notes that by the end of the nineteenth century the idea of trusteeship had become very influential and this idea of trusteeship shaped attitudes towards race.[96] What this research indicates is that discourse of superiority and trusteeship was often expressed among BACSANZ Baptists. This section demonstrates how Baptists in the peripheries imagined their own identity in the larger Anglo-Saxon world, as well as how assumptions about Anglo-Saxon superiority were an intrinsic element to BACSANZ Baptist global identity.

One last note about race needs to be made. In the African context, the superiority expressed in Kipling's "White Man's Burden" was most often in relation to indigenous Africans.[97] However, during the South African War, the White Man's Burden was directed to other whites, and the one being constructed as

---

[93] Denis Judd, *Empire*, 145.

[94] Edward P. Kohn, *This Kindred People: Canadian-American Relations and the Anglo-Saxon Idea, 1895-1903* (Montreal: McGill-Queen's University Press, 2004), 4, 8.

[95] Myra Rutherdale, *Women and the White Man's God: Gender and Race in the Canadian Mission Field* (Vancouver: UBC Press, 2002), 152-153.

[96] Ross, "Christian Missions and the Mid-Nineteenth-Century Change in Attitudes to Race," 85-105.

[97] The "White Man's Burden" was originally written to Americans engaged in war with Spain over Cuba and the Philippines.

the "other" was actually the white, European Boer. Despite this strange twist on the White Man's Burden, however, the construction of the Boer often served the same purpose as the construction of other "lesser" peoples: the growth and spread of empire.

The following is a description of attitudes towards race among BACSANZ Baptists, as well as a summary of how views of race constructed and solidified the bonds of a global Baptist community. Nevertheless, depictions of the Boers and Africans were far from homogenous; they reveal disparate attitudes among BACSANZ Baptists. In regards to the Boers, attitudes ranged from harsh Social Darwinian rankings of races to the extolling of the paragon virtues of the Boers. As for the "natives" and other non Anglo-Saxons, commentary was often tempered by domestic considerations.

Commentary on the Boers in the Canadian Baptist press reflected assumptions about Anglo-Saxon supremacy that were often venomous and virulent. The Boers were depicted as "simple in some ways, complex in others ... a study in underdevelopment."[98] Boer culture was considered inferior and would be changed after a British victory to a more "complex civilization."[99] The Boer soldier was "ignorant and bigoted" and, at best, their Christianity was a "tribal" religion.[100] Contributing to the negative images of the Boers were accounts of their alleged atrocities. In the opening months of the war, there were numerous accounts of Boer brutality on the battlefield. These stories were often accepted at face value and spread among its readership.[101] The atrocities described were numerous and varied, and the headlines underscored the brutality. By contrast, the conduct of the British soldier, though not perfect, was considered commendable.[102] What was "disgraceful" and "unChristian," it was claimed, were the actions of Boer troops.[103] Such actions, wrote one Canadian soldier from South Africa, led to feelings of "no compassion for Boers."[104] These accounts of alleged savagery were published throughout the entire course of the war, with the criticisms after

[98] James Barnes, "At Modder River," *Canadian Baptist*, 8 February 1900, 94.
[99] "Home Life Among the Boers," *Canadian Baptist*, 22 March 1900, 186. See also "An English Girl in South Africa," *Canadian Baptist*, 29 March 1900, 199; "Sketches of Boer Life: By One Who Has Lived among Them," *Religious Intelligencer*, 26 March 1902, 1.
[100] *Canadian Baptist*, 8 February 1900, 88; *Religious Intelligencer*, 6 December 1899, 6; B.A. Sherwood, "War - And Some Lessons," *Religious Intelligencer*, 21 February 1900, 4.
[101] "Stories of the Humanity and the Inhumanity of the Boers," *Canadian Baptist*, April 5, 1900, 7; *Canadian Baptist*, August 16, 1900, 1.
[102] *Canadian Baptist*, March 15, 1900, 8; Harris, "The Boer War as Canadians See It," 8.
[103] *Canadian Baptist*, August 16, 1900, 1; "Condemned by Boer Evidence," *Canadian Baptist*, 20 February 1902, 16; "The Battle of the Mudder River," *Canadian Baptist*, December 7, 1899, 16; "Stories of the Humanity and Inhumanity of the Boers," *Canadian Baptist*, April 5, 1900, 7; F. Leonard Vaux, "Letter From South Africa," *Canadian Baptist*, 30 August 1900.
[104] F. Leonard Vaux, "Letter From South Africa," *Canadian Baptist*, 30 August 1900.

1900 noting a shift in Boer tactics to an unorthodox guerrilla campaign against British occupation.[105]

The *Baptist Times and Freeman*, however, included constructions of the Boers that were markedly different from their Canadian Baptist counterparts; a striking example of metropole-periphery tension and diversity. There was criticism of the Boers for their declaration of war and its continuation despite the inevitable British victory.[106] However, both nations were reckoned guilty before God:

> There can be but one issue in such a conflict. We are not forgetting the Lord of hosts. The Boers appeal to Mars, and are far more heathen than Christian in the methods they employ. They are more like Ahab when he went up to Ramothgilead than Jehoshaphat when he was threatened by Moab and Ammon. ... We fear that in this war both Boers and British consult other than the Lord, and are not engaged in carrying out His purpose.[107]

Anglo-Saxons may have been deemed the superior race, but, in the case of the war in South Africa, Britain's conduct was deemed shameful. Criticism was directed to British leaders such as Chamberlain and Cecil Rhodes, or to Britain in general.[108] Along with criticism of British personalities and policies, the paper also provided significant positive commentary on the Boers, reflecting the reality that British Baptists were not as universally enamored with the war like other BACSANZ Baptists. Positive images of Boers were printed, along with praise for Transvaal President Kruger, a modern-day Oliver Cromwell:

> Whatever may be the opinion as to his action during the war, there are no two opinions as to the solid strength of Mr. Kruger's character, and the amazing cleverness with which he has held the post of President. History will accord him perhaps more justice than present-day writers are accustomed to deal out to him, and

---

[105] "Stories of the Humanity and Inhumanity of the Boers," *Canadian Baptist*, 5 April 1900, 215; *Canadian Baptist*, 11 April 1901, 240; "Guerrilla Warfare Unchristian," *Canadian Baptist*, 14 November 1901, 736; "South Africa," *Canadian Baptist*, 6 March 1902, 16.

[106] "Unmanly Fears," *Baptist Times and Freeman*, 5 January 1900, 9; "Africa," *Baptist Times and Freeman*, 4 January 1901, 1. One article was critical of Boer General De Wet, and the paper immediately received three letters to the editor condemning the paper for such criticism. See "South Africa," *Baptist Times and Freeman*, 18 February 1901, 37; Charles Brown, "Correspondence," *Baptist Times and Freeman*, 25 January 1901, 64; George P. McKay, "Correspondence," *Baptist Times and Freeman*, 25 January 1901, 64; J. Edwards Roberts, "Correspondence," *Baptist Times and Freeman*, 25 January 1901, 64; "The War in South Africa," *Baptist Times and Freeman*, 1 February 1901, 73.

[107] "Unmanly Fears," *Baptist Times and Freeman*, 5 January 1900, 9.

[108] "Mr. Robinson's Views," *Baptist Times and Freeman*, 19 January 1900, 42; "Midway through the War," *Baptist Times and Freeman*, 19 January 1900, 50-51; "The Friends and Peace," *Baptist Times and Freeman*, 20 July 1900, 584; "A Baptist Missionary and Mr. Rhodes," *Baptist Times and Freeman*, 19 April 1901, 262; "Wheresoever the Carcase Is," *Baptist Times and Freeman*, 30 March 1900, 260-261.

there may come a day when the harsh opinions of the veteran President will be softened by the flight of time into the high praise which we now give to Oliver Cromwell.[109]

The paper exhorted its readers to use moderate language and avoid racial hatred.[110] It also counselled kindness and understanding for Boers who had to face the humiliation of defeat, and urged generosity for the vanquished.[111]

Baptist papers in Australia and New Zealand also included commentary on the Boers. The Australian *Baptist* praised both the conduct of their own soldiers and the Boer soldiers, and criticized those who denigrated the Boers:

> Our soldiers have displayed – are displaying – that pluck and dogged perserverance (sic) in the face of deadly peril which have ever characterised (sic) them. It must also be admitted that the Dutch have displayed precisely the same great qualities....It is deplorable to hear the brutal references to the Boer, and fierce declarations of a desire to see him humbled and beaten down – and sometimes from the lips of men professing to be followers of the Saviour of us all. This is the worst of all. It is to be ardently hoped that such a conciliatory policy will be pursued as shall lay broad a deep the foundation of a future of mutual respect and true brotherhood.[112]

The *Queensland Baptist* shared the same concern for treating the Boers with fairness and respect, and pointed out examples of both the Boer and British army having pious soldiers (as well as drunken depraved ones). It also declared that "God-fearing people on either side" of the war were not the ones who brought about the conflict.[113] However, the *Southern Baptist* questioned whether the praise of Boers was warranted, especially since many Christians in South Africa testified that the Boers were far from the "saints" that many were making them out to be.[114] Images of the Boers in the *New Zealand Baptist* echoed criticisms found in other papers. For instance, the Boer had just enough religion to make them "blindly superstitious," had rulers who were "equally ignorant and equally superstitious," and needed to be conquered by the British so that they could experience a "temporal, mental, moral and spiritual uplifting."[115] They treated the "natives" in Africa as dogs, and needed to be overthrown so

---

[109] "The Boers," *Baptist Times and Freeman*, 8 December 1899, 837; "South African News," *Baptist Times and Freeman*, 21 September 1900, 757; "The Boer Generals in England," *Baptist Times and Freeman*, 22 August 1902, 617-618. The paper even printed the Boer national anthem. See "The Boer's National Hymn," *Baptist Times and Freeman*, 1 December 1899, 821.

[110] "At Pretoria," *Baptist Times and Freeman*, 8 June 1900, 453.

[111] "A Word for Mr. Kruger," *Baptist Times and Freeman*, 8 June 1900, 453-454; "The Spoilers," *Baptist Times and Freeman*, 8 June 1900, 454; "The Boer Generals in England," *Baptist Times and Freeman*, 22 August 1902, 617-618.

[112] "A Hopeful Outlook," *Baptist*, 10 March 1900, 2.

[113] "Look on this Picture and That," *Queensland Baptist*, 1 March 1900, 30-31.

[114] "The Boers are Protestant," *Southern Baptist*, 2 November 1899, 229.

[115] "We Are Pro-Boers," *New Zealand Baptist*, April 1900, 49.

that British justice and equal treatment could be brought to South Africa.[116] Overall, the papers from both Australia and New Zealand were a mix of views, and certainly less harsh than those in Canada.

While commentary in the papers reveals a spectrum of attitudes towards the Boers, the domestic situations of the various BACSANZ churches shaped the nature of a number of discussions regarding race. The British Baptists discussed race relations not as a domestic concern, but as a problem for distant lands. For instance, an article on the "negro problem" in the United States was about an overseas problem, not a domestic issue.[117] Baptists in the periphery, however, faced domestic racial realities and concomitant tensions that the metropole did not face. In fact, Baptists in Canada and South Africa were aware of the need to tread carefully for the threat of racial tensions and even violence loomed large when it came to race relations.

Unlike the experience of Baptists in other peripheries, relation with the Boers was a domestic situation for South African Baptists. Concern was expressed over the fact that when the war was over Briton and Boer would have to live together, surrounded by a sea of "natives." After a six-month hiatus due to wartime difficulties, the *South African Baptist* noted that one good of being silent for six months was that they had had no opportunity to feed "the unholy fires of racial hatred."[118] The only real future for South Africa was to avoid stoking racial animosities and planning for a peace that included both Briton and Boer. Once united, both races would be able to carry out "their great mission of evangelizing and civilizing the natives."[119] Hope was expressed that over time tensions between Boers and Briton would diminish, and a "commonwealth of two congenial peoples might be established on justice, truth, and liberty."[120] How would the two warring peoples be united? The church was to play a critical role in the postwar union:

> But there is the fact that two races, not unlike in origin and religious faith, the English and the Dutch, have to dwell side by side over vast areas as fellow subjects of the Queen. Who is to harmonize them into a perfect nobleness of loyalty, mutual esteem, and unity? The Church must lead. It is her opportunity. The door is open for her as for none other. By fellowship in worship, cooperation in spiritu-

---

[116] S.R. Ingold, "The War in South Africa," *New Zealand Baptist*, April 1900, 61-62; "Chit Chat," *New Zealand Baptist*, April 1900, 63.

[117] "The Negro Problem in America," *Baptist Times and Freeman*, 6 September 1901, 600-601. However, this article reveals racial assumptions about blacks that are both negative and positive. For instance, on the positive side, American slavery was condemned, and the activities of leaders such a Booker Washington were praised. On the negative side, however, were comments regarding how much of Washington's abilities came from his white man's blood (he was racially mixed) as well as a references to his "native savagery."

[118] "The New Era in S. Africa," *South African Baptist*, July 1900, 101-102.

[119] "The New Era in S. Africa," *South African Baptist*, July 1900, 101-102.

[120] "Hail XXth Century," *South African Baptist*, January 1901, 1.

al movements, and the yoke-service of the great philanthropies, she can do more. To neglect it were a sin.[121]

With postwar reconciliation in mind, there were no constructions of medieval, barbaric, or backwards Boers in the *South African Baptist*. Rather, one letter to the editor noted that not since the Civil Wars and in America had the British fought with people "so nearly allied ... [to them] in blood and spirit as are the men we are fighting today."[122]

While racially the Boers were considered to be equal with the British, language surrounding the "natives" in Africa was not so complimentary. In the Old Testament, God had his chosen people who carried out his "Divine purpose" in Egypt and the Promised Land; at the end of the nineteenth century in Africa, God was deemed to be still at work, but now his chosen people were the British.[123] Commentary on the "natives of Africa was marked by Social Darwinian ranking and the idea of trusteeship. The discourse of "lower races" was embedded within the language of the South African Baptist Union Assembly,[124] as well as in various articles explaining the race situation.[125] The most extensive and detailed elaboration of the race situation was a three-part series by Alfred P. Hillier just before the war.[126] The following is a summary of Hillier's conclusions on the "native races."

The physical features of "negroes" were described, including particular shades of skin colour, common skull bone structure, and hair (according to Hillier, African hair was less like hair and more like sheep's wool). The assumption was that races were ranked (whites at the top, blacks at the bottom, and others in between), and within the more general ranking was a specific ranking among Africans: Bantu or Kafir tribes at the top, followed by the Hottentots, with the Bushmen at the bottom. The characteristics of each were then described in detail. The Bushmen were "a race of pigmies about four feet in height," classed with the "Australian aborigines as the lowest races in the human scale, and the cranial capacity ... is lower than in any others."[127] They were

---

[121] "The Open Door in South Africa," *South African Baptist*, September 1900, 137-139.

[122] G.W. Cross, "Baptist Union Letters," *South African Baptist*, February 1901, 19.

[123] "On the Editorial Stoep," *South African Baptist*, October 1900, 146.

[124] "Baptist Union of South Africa," *South African Baptist*, June 1901, 68.

[125] For instance, see John Robinson, "The Colonies and the Century," *South African Baptist*, October 1900, 140-142. Like other Baptist papers the *South African Baptist* printed "The White Man's Burden." A few months later it published "The Brown Man's Burden." See Rudyard Kipling, "The White Man's Burden," *South African Baptist*, October 1899, 38; "The Brown Man's Burden," *South African Baptist*, December 1900, 170.

[126] Alfred P. Hillier, "The Native Races of South Africa," *South African Baptist*, August 1899, 11-13; Alfred P. Hillier, "The Native Races of South Africa," *South African Baptist*, September 1899, 24-31; Alfred P. Hillier, "The Native Races of South Africa," *South African Baptist*, October 1899, 41-42.

[127] Alfred P. Hillier, "The Native Races of South Africa," *South African Baptist*, September 1899, 25.

to be compared to the cave dwellers of the palaeolithic or early stone age in Europe. The Hottentots were related to the Bushmen, but occupied a "higher position in the scale of humanity" than the Bushmen. The highest ranked group, the Bantu or Kafir, comprised many different groups in South Africa (such as the Zulu), and were a group that should command the respect of the white man. They were portrayed as courageous, intelligent, brave, and physically superior to other Africans. But regardless of ranking, from "time immemorial the negro has remained uncivilized" sums up the view that the blacks of Africa were lower races far below the advanced civilization of Europeans.[128]

Hillier argued that the isolation of "natives" from the civilizing influence of outside cultures partially explained the differences between the white and black races, and that the task for Europeans now in contact with them was to raise them up so that, perhaps, they might attain the level of Europeans: "We English, pre-eminently among European races, have incurred great responsibilities towards these natives, and it is our duty, by the aid of our knowledge of the human race and its possibilities, to endeavour, without bias, to understand them, and honourably to do for them what seems wisest and best both in their interests and ours."[129] The overall impact of Britain on the "natives" was deemed to be positive, despite the introduction by colonists of the destructive and evil liquor traffic. In fact, British rule in South Africa was considered better for the natives than the treatment of natives in America, Australia and New Zealand where the "history of the native races is a sad one."[130] Hillier concluded with an optimistic appraisal of impact of British rule, a negative assessment of the ability of the "natives" to rise to the heights of western civilization, and a caution to white rulers. The danger was the rapid growth of the "natives" along with their history of violence towards one another. Compounding the threat was the inability of blacks to absorb British ideals and civilization:

> Mental development, which is often bright and satisfactory in childhood and youth, seems as a rule to end, or at least become seriously checked, in adult life. The belief that, with the same educational advantages, the native will be found mentally equal to the European is not in accordance with experience, either in America or in South Africa, though it is only fair to say that exceptions do exist. The past history of the negro races does not suggest rapid progress. ... Between the white races of Europe and the black races of Africa a great distinction does exist - I believe will continue to exist. The black man is not simply a morally and in-

---

[128] Alfred P. Hillier, "The Native Races of South Africa," *South African Baptist*, August 1899, 11.

[129] Alfred P. Hillier, "The Native Races of South Africa," *South African Baptist*, August 1899, 11.

[130] Alfred P. Hillier, "The Native Races of South Africa," *South African Baptist*, September 1899, 28. In this edition prohibition was portrayed as the answer to the destruction of natives by liquor.

tellectually undeveloped white man, but something different in the economy of human nature.[131]

While the "natives" may be unable to rise to the heights of British civilization, British rule had been able to raise the "natives" from "actual savagery" to relative "peace and prosperity." The hope and challenge for the future of South Africa was that colonial rule developed a "policy of firmness tempered with justice, moderation, and sympathy" so that the development of the "natives" would be marked by a growth of "progress, happiness and welfare."[132]

Unlike other colonies, Baptists in South Africa faced the threat of racial violence on two different fronts. The British versus Boer conflict pitted whites against whites, but the larger threat was white versus black conflict. The growth of the "natives" was considered "alarming," and the churches had a role to place in ensuring peace: in light of the looming demographic challenge the churches needed to "subdue" [the natives] to Christ" to save both themselves and the land.[133]

The pressing racial issue in Canada was between the English and French, and, as noted in the previous chapter, differing perspectives on the war led to domestic debates and rioting. There was an "acrimonious political debate" over the issue of Canada's participation in the war, and no aspect of the South African War has received more attention from Canadian historians than this debate.[134] Some have seen the controversy as a political watershed issue, one that "split open the cleft between English and French Canadians, launched the twentieth-century French-Canadian nationalist movement, broke Laurier's power in Quebec, and served as a dress rehearsal for the First World War."[135] Despite antipathy towards Roman Catholics, a number of Canadian Baptists were highly critical of actions that exacerbated tensions between the French and English. With its two founding races, French and English, it was believed that Canada had the potential to be a shining example to South Africa (and the world) of how two once hostile races could work together to build a nation. In order to ensure that the new nation did not plant the seeds of future self-destruction, throughout the war the press was pro-active in seeking to shape English attitudes towards French Canadians.[136] However, the tensions between French and

---

[131] Alfred P. Hillier, "The Native Races of South Africa," *South African Baptist*, October 1899, 42.

[132] Alfred P. Hillier, "The Native Races of South Africa," *South African Baptist*, October 1899, 42.

[133] "The Open Door in South Africa," *South African Baptist*, October 1900, 139.

[134] Miller, *Painting the Map Red*, 16

[135] Miller, *Painting the Map Red*, 16. As Miller notes, however, the debate was not just between English and French Canada. Although the majority of English Canadians were supportive of the war and the sending of Canadian troops, there were English Canadians who opposed the war.

[136] Heath, "The Canadian Protestant Press and the Conscription Crisis," 27-46.

English Canadians left lasting scars, and set a pattern that would be followed in the next century's even more tragic wars.[137]

Australian Baptist commentary on domestic race relations dealt chiefly with concerns for a White Australia.[138] Non-British immigration from other European countries was a concern. The growth of German Baptists was celebrated, and the need for German-language Baptist churches was anticipated for the foreseeable future - especially for the evangelization of German settlers.[139] German settlers in general were portrayed in unflattering terms ("obstinate customers"), but the piety of German Baptists was praised. Nevertheless, concern was expressed about the assimilation of the waves of German immigrants into Australian society.

> Immigration is bound to go on. It cannot be stopped. Oceans of waters and walls of steel have never stopped the Teutonic race from covering any part of the globe desirable to its sons, and walls of paper are not going to do it today. As long as immigrants come, the Germans are sure to be among them. ... It is true, they will learn English enough to earn bread and to gossip, but not enough to understand preaching. We must help them to be Christian citizens, and to do it let us apply means that are acceptable. The Germans must have a more important place in our denominational missionary campaign.[140]

Assimilation was the stated outcome for these newcomers, but caution was counselled for those who advocated for a forced or rapid assimilation.

> National assimilation, when it is best, is slow. If the change is made too fast, it is very likely superficial, and may include a dangerous loss in the restraining power of personal relation, and we should regret any change so rapid that it would violently tear asunder the family ties. It is dangerous when the hearts of the children are turned from the parents, and that does happen whenever the children forget the tongue of their fathers. And this would be the case it, today, our German Baptist churches were turned into English. We believe that the German churches are organs for the slow assimilation of the Germans, and we ought to help them in their work.[141]

This hesitancy over forced assimilation of Germans was a concern for a number of Baptists, but the more pressing racial issue was what to do with non-white

---

[137] See Miller, *Painting the Map Red*, 444; Page, *The Boer War and Canadian Imperialism*, 22. For how the war set the pattern for the nation and churches, see Carman Miller, "Framing Canada's Great War: A Case for Including the Boer War," *Journal of Transatlantic Studies* 6, no. 1 (April 2008): 3-21; Heath, "Canadian Churches and the South African War."

[138] The *Queensland Baptist* did express concern over how racial hatred in South Africa would ruin many churches. See W.W., "Baptist Churches in South Africa," *Queensland Baptist*, 2 April 1900, 50.

[139] "German Baptists in Queensland," *Queensland Baptist*, 1 August 1901, 108-109; Watchman, "German Baptists in Australia," *Southern Baptist*, 16 October 1901, 238.

[140] "German Baptists in Queensland," *Queensland Baptist*, 1 August 1901, 108-109.

[141] "German Baptists in Queensland," *Queensland Baptist*, 1 August 1901, 108-109.

immigrants, especially in the years following the implementation of the White Australia Policy in 1901.

Since the middle of the nineteenth century there had been concerns expressed over the arrival of Chinese and other non-European races to Australia, and legislators in various Australian colonies had attempted to stem and even reverse the flow of immigrants.[142] One of the first acts of Parliament in the new Federation was the Immigration Restriction Act 1901, an act that was the beginning of what became known as the White Australia Policy. Among other restrictive elements, the act had a dictation test - the ability to write out a text of fifty words of any European language dictated (not just English) - which provided immigration officials the pretense of excluding people based on language rather than on race. This Act was a prime example of what R.A. Huttenback calls the "xenophobic tendencies of Britain's Australian dependencies."[143]

As Ken Manley has demonstrated, Baptist commentary on the policy was mixed and influence in shaping public policy seemingly nonexistent.[144] Apparently supportive of the policy was William Whale, a Baptist pastor known for his concern for social reform.[145] In 1902, the *Queensland Baptist* published an article from Whale that contained commentary that did not mention the White Australia Policy, but certainly echoed its sentiments.[146] Whale's concern was for "manhood" to build the nascent nation, for without it "all is failure." The nation needed upright men and women to "supplant the inferior types" and the "races of unprogressive aboriginals." For that to occur there needed to be an immigration policy that included only the highest caliber of "physical quality": "Blood tells. The policy which makes the specialist look for stud sheep and cattle of an order to reproduce after their kind should should [sic] not be ignored by those who introduce population." All aspects of Australian public life should make this their goal, but especially the church: "But it must be the duty of all teachers in day schools and Sunday schools, in desk, on platform, and in pulpit, all writers, speakers, patriots in church and State to insist on this, to continuously keep this in view as they love their country, and as they would elevate their race and honour, the One who came to redeem." If the church and nation produce such citizens, the nation would be secure from all threats, and "no foreign foe will dread to tread upon these shores."

Reflecting the diversity of opinion on race among Australian Baptists is commentary in the *Queensland Baptist*. A year before Whale's comments the *Queensland Baptist* had printed a brief excerpt condemning the idea of a White

---

[142] R. A. Huttenback, "The British Empire as a 'White Man's Country' - Racial Attitudes and Immigration Legislation in the Colonies of White Settlement," *Journal of British Studies* 13, no. 1 (November 1973), 108-137.

[143] Huttenback, "The British Empire as a 'White Man's Country,'" 117.

[144] Manley, *From Woolloomooloo to 'Eternity': Volume 1*, 393-396.

[145] P.J. O'Leary, "William Whale: The Making of a Colonial Baptist Preacher, 1842-1903," (BA Thesis, University of Queensland, 1987).

[146] W. Whale, "Wanted-Manhood," *Queensland Baptist*, 1 February 1902, 18.

Australia. The context for its criticism was the federal election and the racial rhetoric associated with the various parties vying for power:

> The catch-cry of the Federal elections... [is A White Australia], but it is full of hypocrisy of uncleanliness. A white skin - not a white heart, a white life, a white reputation. Both parties have those seeking to represent Queensland, who can only convey to the rest of Australia that Queensland is black with the blight of adultery, blasphemy, and irreverence. ... it is needful to say that the first qualification for Parliament is to be a real white man, not in skin but in conduct. A clean, honest, truthful man can alone be a fit representative for a self-respecting people.[147]

This emphasis on the character of the person rather than the color of one's skin was a significant departure from some of the racially charged rhetoric of the day. The *Southern Baptist* printed a poem that also condemned the idea of a White Australia. After lines decrying the government's setting aside of God's requirement for justice and love of one's neighbor by an "unjust, heartless, and oppressive ban," the author warns the rulers:

> Ye who assume t'espouse the people's cause,
> And in high place to formulate the laws,
> Beware lest ye betray your sacred trust -
> Remember, ye are children of the dust;
> Remember, ye must give account to Him
> Before Whose searching Eye e'on seraphim
> Their faces veil![148]

The printing of this poem certainly indicates that politicians could not count on automatic support from Australian Baptists when it came to laws that favoured whites.[149] What makes it more difficult when it comes to uncovering attitudes of Australian Baptists to race is that the same paper printed Kipling's "The White Man's Burden" a few years early, followed almost immediately by "The Brown's Man Burden."[150] The publishing of two poems with opposing messages suggests that the paper was appealing to diverse groups within its constituency, something that Potter notes marked other British papers.[151]

The domestic racial situation in New Zealand was not fraught with tensions like those in Canada or South Africa, but the war did raise questions about the Maori, the indigenous peoples of New Zealand. A significant number of Maori wanted to fight alongside whites in the New Zealand contingents, but London had ordered that the Maori could not participate in the conflict due to its desire

---

[147] "A White Australia," *Queensland Baptist*, 1 April 1901, 44.

[148] George Morison, "A White Australia," *Southern Baptist*, 26 March 1902, 83.

[149] For further criticism of a White Australia policy, see "And Yet, this Colour Question," *Southern Baptist*, 15 January 1902, 14; "The Question Is Also," *Southern Baptist*, 15 January 1902, 14; "A Recent Writer Has Said," *Southern Baptist*, 15 January 1902, 14.

[150] Rudyard Kipling, "The White Man's Burden," *Southern Baptist*, 15 June 1899, 123; "The Brown Man's Burden," *Southern Baptist*, 29 June 1899, 142.

[151] Potter, "Communication and Integration," 202.

to keep "natives" out of the war in South Africa.[152] Premier Richard Seddon had tried to overturn this decision, but had been unsuccessful, much to the pleasure of those whites who did not want non-whites fighting alongside British imperial forces. Nevertheless, some Maori did eventually end up fighting under European names.[153]

The *New Zealand Baptist* made no mention of the Maori fighting in the war, but did print a number of items on the Maori. Rev. T.A. Williams bemoaned the lack of evangelization of the Maori by the Baptists, noting that they had focused on India to the detriment of the Maori in their own nation.[154] The following month the NZBMS missionary secretary wrote a rebuttal to Williams. He chastised Williams for taking so long to pay attention to the Maori, and defended the Baptist concentration on India by claiming that they had left the evangelization of the Maori to other denominations while Baptists focused on India.[155] In the following month a letter to the editor came to the defence of Williams by claiming that once Williams had discovered the plight of the Maori he had immediately sounded the alarm.[156] Imbedded in these retorts were a number of assumptions about race that are worth noting. The Maori were a "pagan" people facing extinction, and white New Zealanders were deemed partly to blame: "We have rudely disturbed and shaken their faith in the old deities and practices; we have revolutionised their outlook; we have emptied their mind of the old ideas; and, in return, what have we given them? Nothing, or little more than nothing."[157] The looming extinction of the Maori was due to a number of interrelated factors, all associated with the arrival of Europeans and the conditions born as a result of colonialization:

> The vices they have learned from base Europeans, the idleness in which money realised by the sale of their lands enables them to live, the superstitious customs to which they still cling, in spite of all the knowledge which has been diffused among them; the steady deterioration of a small nation which is compelled to intermarry - all these causes mitigate against their continuance for any extended period.[158]

Along with a renewed concern for the Maori among churches and government, hope for the Maori was derived from the conviction that no race was considered to be permanently fixed in barbarism. The Maori could, with time, be raised to

---

[152] The fear in South Africa was that the "blacks" would become involved in a war between "whites", and both Briton and Boer knew that if that happened their troubles would be dangerously multiplied.

[153] Material in this paragraph on the Maori and the war taken from McGibbon, *The Path to Gallipoli*, 115-117; Gould, "'Different Race, Same Queen,'" 119-127.

[154] T.A. Williams, "The Pagans of Our Own Land," *New Zealand Baptist*, May 1900, 66-67.

[155] "The Pagans of Our Own Land," *New Zealand Baptist*, June 1900, 82-83.

[156] J.J. North, "The Pagans of Our Own Land," *New Zealand Baptist*, July 1900, 109.

[157] T.A. Williams, "The Pagans of Our Land," *New Zealand Baptist*, May 1900, 66-67.

[158] "The Pagans of Our Own Land," *New Zealand Baptist*, June 1900, 82-83.

(or even surpass) the civilization of the Europeans, as the case of once barbarous Europe illustrated.

> The slow and crooked progress of the Christian faith among the Teutonic and Celtic peoples, who are now its foremost champions, ought to bespeak our patience with the Barbaric Tribes. ... The case of the Celts seems to afford some hope that the fate of our neighbours is not fixed. If an Evolutionist had wandered through the Highlands with Fitz-Jarnes, he might have left us a fresh proof of the impossibility of prophecy. The complete change in the conditions of Highland life in the last two hundred years, and the improving prospects in Ireland, may yet be paralleled in these Southern Seas.[159]

The hope for the Indians in India was that they would become world evangelists when Britain's empire had receded, and perhaps the Maori too could rise to such heights.[160] This ranking of the races mirrors much of the Social Darwinism of the day. These instances of the ranking of races were not based on a strictly biological basis, but rather were rooted primarily in cultural differences (differences that could change with education and the adoption of European civilization). Such ranking was also not supposed to devolve into contempt for races, for it was argued that no Christian should be pleased with the demise of the Maori and their "gloomy and unpromising" future, for they were a "noble" and "splendid" race.[161] If they were to become extinct, the "Great Judge" would not hold white New Zealanders "guiltless" and their "blood" would be on the white man's "head."[162]

While constructions of a British race or Anglo-Saxon civilization varied according to the domestic locale, the universal idea among Baptists was a unifying vision of a global British community. Baptists in Canada may have been Canadian Baptists, or Baptists in Australia may have been Australian Baptists, but such local and national allegiances did not preclude loyalty to a grander vision of belonging to a British community that spanned the globe; their national identities were incorporated and subsumed into the larger imperial context of empire. Evangelical zeal and Baptist identity also united BACSANZ Baptists, as did the conviction that they belonged to the British race. This global community was a fusion of both real and imagined realities. As noted above, the connectedness of the press and the personal relations between Baptist communions created and sustained a real community with practical ties. It was imagined in that its constructions were rooted in myths surrounding the idealized race and role of Anglo-Saxons. The following is a brief summary of this fusion of real and imagined community, particularly as it relates to the language of ties of race, blood and family.

---

[159] J.J. North, "The Pagans of Our Own Land," *New Zealand Baptist*, July 1900, 109.

[160] Charles Williams, "An English Baptist's Impressions of New Zealand," *New Zealand Baptist*, January 1902, 15-16.

[161] T.A. Williams, "The Pagans of Our Own Land," *New Zealand Baptist*, May 1900, 66-67.

[162] T.A. Williams, "The Pagans of Our Land," *New Zealand Baptist*, May 1900, 66-67.

The "rhetoric of Anglo-Saxon kinship and ... affinity"[163] can be found in the discourse of all the Baptist papers. As the following chapter on justice will demonstrate, not all Baptists agreed with Britain's involvement in South Africa. However, what was a common sentiment, even among opponents of the war, was the conviction that the empire was united by blood or race, and that Anglo-Saxons had a grand and glorious mission to fulfill. Whether or not in actuality there was such a thing as an actual British race is not important; what needs to be noted is that BACSANZ Baptists believed there was. The belief in a British "race"[164] or Protestant "race"[165] provided a much-needed sense of identity for colonial Baptists, identity expressed in wistful and romantic notions of the "Old Land," "Old Country," "Homeland," "Old England," and "Mother Country."[166] Baptists were portrayed as "communities of Britishers abroad,"[167] and Tasmanian Baptists were most fortunate to be living on an island "most like the island home of England."[168]

Contemporary events provided ample opportunities for expressions of global Anglo-Saxon kinship, as well acted as stimulus for cementing such sentiments. The war forged bonds between the various parts of the empire, and spilt blood was considered to have united the empire: "By the mingling of the spilt blood of our sons with that of Britain's, on the incarnadined fields of South Africa, our unification with the Empire has become such a reality as can never be annulled."[169] The war had led to "outbursts of generosity, thoughtfulness, self-sacrifice and devotion" which had, in the opinion of one author, "proved that all the Queen's subjects are in a very true sense one family."[170] The *New Zealand Baptist* declared a sentiment shared among a number of colonists: "the British nation is our nation; we are a living part of that Empire, and they and we - Britain and New Zealand - must rise *or fall* together."[171] Federation in Australia led to discussions of further federation of empire (something that not all agreed

---

[163] Kohn, *This Kindred People*, pp. 4,8.

[164] "Just as a common foe had called forth loyalty to the Empire, made all people of the British race forget their little differences." See "Baptist Association of Queensland," *Queensland Baptist*, 1 October 1900, 132.

[165] J.B., "The Mission of the British People," *Southern Baptist*, 15 February 1900, 43.

[166] "Jubilee Greetings," *New Zealand Baptist,* May 1901, 66-67; Rev. F.W. Boreham, *New Zealand Baptist*, July 1901, 99-101; "Mr. and Mrs. G.P. Barber," *Southern Baptist*, 15 February 1900, 38; "God Speed Australia," *Southern Baptist*, 3 January 1901, 2; "Our Royal Guests," *New Zealand Baptist*, June 1901, 89; Emerson, "Old England," *Queensland Baptist*, 1 February 1902, 18; Pastorina, "Through Strange Waters," *South African Baptist*, June 1899, 176-177.

[167] "A British Loss," *South African Baptist*, October 1901, 115.

[168] "The Royal Visit," *Southern Baptist*, 15 May 1901, 110.

[169] "Australia," *Southern Baptist*, 15 March 1900, 62.

[170] "The Great War," *South African Baptist*, January 1900, 85-86. See also "A Hundred Years ago - Abroad," *New Zealand Baptist*, February 1900, 17.

[171] S.R. Ingold, "The War in South Africa: The Christian's Proper Attitude Regarding It," *New Zealand Baptist*, April 1900, 61-62.

on).[172] Even an event such as Federation - a step towards nationhood - was cause to celebrate the Britishness of Australians: "Today we claim as our unifying appellation the euphonious name 'Australians.' We have ceased to be 'Colonials,' and form a part of that empire which wears the title - never more proudly worn before - of British."[173] Quite naturally the death of Queen Victoria led to expressions of grief and of oneness with the empire, and events surrounding the coronation of King Edward VII led to statements of loyalty to empire and crown.[174] Discourse in the New Zealand Jubilee in 1901 provides further examples of how colonial Baptist identity was fused to a sense of Britishness and Anglo-Saxon race.[175] Commentary related to the close of the old century and the beginning of the new also reveals the global Anglo-Saxon identity of Canadian, Australian, South African and New Zealand Baptists, and, in such commentary, one gets a glimpse of the assumptions undergirding the sense of Anglo-Saxon supremacy. Views of providence, mission and the Anglo-Saxons will be explored in a subsequent chapter, suffice it to say here that participation in the perceived mission of the Anglo-Saxon race provided colonial Baptists the opportunity to transcend their regional and nation identity and participate in the activities of a race and empire deemed to be mandated with the trusteeship of "lower races." Indeed, despite the sins of empire, the consensus was that the nineteenth century had been a remarkable century, in no small measure due to the contribution of the global British community.[176]

Baptists in the metropole expressed joy over the loyalty to the empire displayed in the peripheries, and shared in the belief in a global, British-Baptist community. Perhaps rooted in late-Victorian anxiety and insecurity regarding the safety of the empire, British Baptists were pleased to have assistance in the

---

[172] Rev. John Muirhead, "War, Peace and Arbitration," *New Zealand Baptist*, July 1900, 98-101; "New Zealand Outside," *New Zealand Baptist*, August 1900, 113; "Is It Too Late," *New Zealand Baptist*, August 1900, 114; "The Principle of Federation," *New Zealand Baptist*, August 1900, 114; "The Goodly Fellowship of the Prophets," *New Zealand Baptist*, August 1900, 114.

[173] "The Birth of a Nation," *Baptist Times and Freeman*, 3 January 1901, 7.

[174] See Chapter Four.

[175] "New Zealand Jubilee," *Queensland Baptist*, 2 September 1901, 119.

[176] H.H. Driver, "Between the Centuries," *New Zealand Baptist*, December 1899, 177-182; John Robinson, "The Colonies and the Century," *South African Baptist*, July 1900, 103-105; John Robinson, "The Colonies and the Century," *South African Baptist*, August 1900, 115-117; John Robinson, "The Colonies and the Century," *South African Baptist*, September 1900, 127-129; John Robinson, "The Colonies and the Century," *South African Baptist*, October 1900, 140-142; John Robinson, "The Colonies and the Century," *South African Baptist*, November 1900, 152-155; John Robinson, "The Colonies and the Century," *South African Baptist*, December 1900, 168-169; "Christ for the New Century and the New Nation," *Baptist*, 1 November 1900, 4-5; Rev. W. Whale, "Our Third Contingent," *Queensland Baptist*, 1 March 1900, 34-35; J.B., "The Mission of the British People," *Southern Baptist*, 15 February 1900, 43; "A Year and a Century," *Messenger and Visitor*, 26 December 1900, 4.

great task of defending it. No one, it was argued, could ever have imagined the "loyal shout of brotherhood" from overseas colonies,[177] and the Canadian displays of loyalty were deemed to have overshadowed and outdone even the British.[178] Commentary surrounding the end of the war and the coronation of Edward VII reveals the high hopes for this united empire. Noting the blessings that had arisen as a result of the war, one commentator wrote that "Chief among these is, of course, the strengthening of the bonds that unite the Colonies to the Mother Country. ... It is impossible to forecast the result of this drawing together of the English-speaking races."[179] A few months later a similar optimism was expressed:

> Sixty years ago our Colonies had hardly entered upon that path of progress which has led them to the magnificent position which they occupy in the world today. Never before were they bound they closely to the mother country by the ties of mutual love....Their loyalty and their love, displayed in the hour of need, make us welcome them with greater joy as they stand by our side now and unite with us in this great, supreme act of the national life.[180]

No doubt such passionate displays of enthusiasm for imperial unity were what the peripheries enjoyed hearing, especially since it elevated their importance in the affairs of empire (even if only in perception). However, such lofty aspirations were not always lived up to, for during much of the war South African Baptists were convinced that their Baptist coreligionists in Britain had let them down. In fact, because of such a strong sense of global community the South African Baptists were deeply disappointed with British Baptist responses to calls for help. As one commentator decried: "But to think that there is so little Christian Imperialism in the official heads of British Baptists, as that they should leave us to our fate unaided - there is the astonishment."[181]

Calls for Help and Baptist Tensions

While the war in South Africa led to exuberant public displays of imperial loyalty in the colonies, as well as optimistic estimates by commentators on how the war had united the various colonies into one global empire, all was not well in the imperial family. The churches in South Africa had experienced wartime dislocation and devastation, and South African Baptists were initially deeply

---

[177] "In the Dark," *Baptist Times and Freeman*, 20 April 1900, 323
[178] "Now she outdoes ourselves, so that our English expressions of patriotism - our street orgies, our vulgar parades - appear, by comparison, almost barbaric." See "Canadian Loyalty," *Baptist Times and Freeman*, 15 June 1900, 474.
[179] "Peace at Last," *Baptist Times and Freeman*, 6 June 1902, 427.
[180] "The Coronation," *Baptist Times and Freeman*, 8 August 1902, 592. For other displays of enthusiasm over the union of the empire, see "Imperialism," *Baptist Times and Freeman*, 13 April 1900, 303; "A Baptist's Retrospective of the Century," *Baptist Times and Freeman*, 28 December 1900, 1046; "Australian Loyalty," *Baptist Times and Freeman*, 24 May 1901, 337.
[181] "A Point of Honour," *South African Baptist*, September 1900, 125-126.

hurt and angered by the lack of assistance offered by Baptists back in the Old Country. By the end of the war, feelings of animosity seem to have been assuaged, but that happy ending was only due to the hard work of a number of individuals who labored to make the plight of the churches known and who had built an organization dedicated to providing aid to South African Baptists. In so doing, the ties of empire were more firmly established and the periphery could once again look to the metropole with fondness.

The various colonial Baptist papers occasionally reported on the impact of the war on South African Baptists. Concern for the churches in the opening months of the war was expressed, and, as the war developed, ongoing reporting noted the plight of the churches, the shutting down of the *South African Baptist*, the cancellation of the South African Baptist annual assembly in 1900, and statistics related to church growth or decline.[182] Direct appeals from South African Baptists to other colonies were also printed.[183] New Zealand Baptists were moved by reports of Baptist suffering in Africa, and responded in 1900 by creating a South African Fund to which New Zealand Baptists were encouraged to contribute.[184]

However, while support from the colonies was appreciated, what particularly rankled South African Baptists was the lack of support from Baptists in England.[185] South African Baptists published complaints about the lack of funds from English Baptists after only a few months of war.[186] Just before the *South African Baptist* ceased production for six months, an article expressed the hope that Baptists in Britain and America would come to their aid if an appeal was made to them.[187] When the paper resumed production in the summer of 1900, an article made it clear to its hard-pressed readers that English Baptists had not

---

[182] "Some Interesting Figures," *New Zealand Baptist*, July 1900, 111; "Chit Chat," *New Zealand Baptist*, August 1901, 128; "Baptist Churches in South Africa," *Queensland Baptist*, 2 April 1900, 50; "Cape Baptists and the War," *Queensland Baptist*, 2 July 1900, 86; "Our Intense Sympathies," *Southern Baptist*, 12 October 1899, 217; "President Kruger," *Southern Baptist*, 2 November 1899, 230; "The South African 'Baptist'," *Southern Baptist*, 18 January 1900, 14; "Baptist World," *Baptist*, 1 March 1902, 8; "The Baptist Denomination in South Africa," *Canadian Baptist*, 14 December 1899, 14; "The Outlook in South Africa," *Canadian Baptist*, 21 November 1901, 7.

[183] Joseph J. Doke, "An Appeal from South Africa," *New Zealand Baptist*, November 1900, 171.

[184] WROX, "Echoes from Christchurch," *New Zealand Baptist*, December 1900, 187-191. For the wording of the resolution, see the *Annual Report of the New Zealand Baptist Union, 1900*, 9. See also "South African Fund," *New Zealand Baptist*, February 1901, 27.

[185] Earlier in the century Australian Baptists had lamented the lack of support among British Baptists for missions in the colonies. See J.D. Bollen, "English-Baptist Relations, 1830-1860," *Baptist Quarterly* 25, no. 7 (July 1974): 290-305.

[186] A donation by Queen Victoria to the South African Refugee Relief Fund was noted, but, of course, this was not a gift from Baptists to Baptists. See "News by Mail," *South African Baptist*, November 1899, 62.

[187] "On the Editorial Stoep," *South African Baptist*, January 1900, 96.

responded to appeals for aid.[188] The executive of the South African Baptist Union summarized attempts made to elicit funds for support, and noted how Baptists in England had rejected their offer, making what seemed to South Africans a "mockery" of their "dire distress." The executive concluded that appeals would have to be made to Canada and Australia, and that hopefully they would care for their fellow Baptists. Over the next few months, a number of harsh criticisms of English Baptists appeared in the paper revealing the degree of despair and anger at Baptists in England. In September 1900, the fusion of imperial and Baptist loyalties was apparent when a lack of regard for fellow Baptists was deemed to be a striking lack of concern for the empire:

> But to think that there is so little Christian Imperialism in the official heads of British Baptists, as that they should leave us to our fate unaided - there is the astonishment. To whom will they do any service of which the master will say "inasmuch...ye did it unto me? if not to their own baptized brethren? Do Little Englanders so predominate in Baptist Union Councils at home that political bias strangles piety? It is impiety to deny help to needy brethren.[189]

The following month's issue included a short list of ways in which Baptists in England had slighted South African Baptists.[190] In November 1900, the lead article included an extensive summary of how English Baptists had failed South African Baptists.[191] "Surely a more disgusting record can hardly be found in the annals of England" was the response to a summary of English Baptist help thus far. The answer of "windbags" in England was that there was to be no substantial support forthcoming, and disgust was palpable:

> What is the value of Baptist divines stumping the island on "Social Problems," or of programmes ringing with philanthropic gush when "they of their own household" perish for bread, and for a roof to cover them from the dust-storms of a land of drought? This much is clear. That denominational Little-Englandism reigns at Furnival Street. That South African Baptists must abide absolutely self-reliant ... when distinguished Baptists would tour South Africa let them take all risks. As Baptists we have sought to realise brotherhood both in and out of adversity, it has been denied; as we have our feelings still "closer acquaintance after the war" will mean just nothing at all.

Despite the "ironical refusal" of the Baptist Union in Great Britain to help Baptists in South Africa, it was hoped that "some of the ministers who have toured South Africa" would remember them and help provide assistance.[192] Other possible aid could perhaps come from Spurgeon's Tabernacle, especially since it had been so helpful in the past.[193] The account of a South African Presbyterian

---

[188] "Baptist Union of South Africa," *South African Baptist*, July 1900, 105-106.

[189] "A Point of Honour," *South African Baptist*, September 1900, 125-126.

[190] "On the Editorial Stoep," *South African Baptist*, October 1900, 145.

[191] "How English Baptists Have Failed Us," *South African Baptist*, November 1900, 149-150.

[192] "On the Editorial Stoep," *South African Baptist*, August 1900, 120.

[193] "The Renovated Tabernacle," *South African Baptist*, September 1900, 130-131.

minister visiting in England who raised over £200 for the suffering Presbyterian church in South Africa was further cause for irritation - the author also observed that such generosity in other denominations could lead to Baptists breaking the tenth commandment.[194] The year 1900 ended on a sour note, and, in a December summary of the South African Baptist Union executive, one author lamented that "even a little" help from England would have been helpful.[195]

Baptists in South Africa did not know it but help was on the way. A few months into the war, articles on the conflict and its impact on South African Baptists began appearing in the *Baptist Times and Freeman*, and reports from South Africa continued into 1900.[196] The plight of South African Baptists described in such reports eventually pricked the conscience of English Baptists and moved them to act in support of Baptists in the theatre of war.

The acting President of the South African Baptist Union, Rev. Ernest Baker, added his voice to the calls for help in 1900. In a number of direct and personal appeals to his British coreligionists he highlighted the needs of Baptists and requested help. A letter in September 1900 noted the need for Baptists in England to ensure that colonial Baptists in the army received a Baptist chaplain, and included a call for funds to assist in the rebuilding of damaged churches.[197] Another letter a month later listed the needs of the churches, appealed once again to the readers of the *Baptist Times and Freeman* to come to the aid of fellow Baptists, and, as the following comments indicate, expressed surprise that English Baptists had not been more willing to provide assistance: "The members of our churches here cannot understand the apathy of home

---

[194] *South African Baptist*, October 1900, 142.

[195] "Baptist Union Notes," *South African Baptist*, December 1900, 172-173.

[196] "The Baptist Denomination in South Africa," *Baptist Times and Freeman*, 17 November 1899, 793-794; "Concerning the Transvaal War," *Baptist Times and Freeman*, 26 January 1900, 72; "Another Letter from a Baptist in the Transvaal," *Baptist Times and Freeman*, 2 February 1900, 89; "A Letter from South Africa," *Baptist Times and Freeman*, 23 February 1900, 153; "Baptists in St. Helena and South Africa," *Baptist Times and Freeman*, 13 April 1900, 300; "An Interesting Letter from South Africa," *Baptist Times and Freeman*, 11 May 1900, 381; "Concerning the Transvaal War," *Baptist Times and Freeman*, 26 January 1900, 72; "Another Letter from a Baptist in the Transvaal," *Baptist Times and Freeman*, 2 February 1900, 89; "A Letter from South Africa," *Baptist Times and Freeman*, 23 February 1900, 153; "Baptists in St. Helena and South Africa," *Baptist Times and Freeman*, 13 April 1900, 300; "An Interesting Letter from South Africa," *Baptist Times and Freeman*, 11 May 1900, 381; W. Payne, "A Sunday in Port Elizabeth, South Africa," *Baptist Times and Freeman*, 31 August 1900, 700. Reporting on events in South Africa made it to church meetings as well. For instance, Rev. H.J. Batts spoke on a Wednesday evening to church members regarding what he saw during his time in Pretoria. See "News of the Churches," *Baptist Times and Freeman*, 22 February 1901, 130.

[197] Ernest Baker, "An Interesting Letter from Capetown," *Baptist Times and Freeman*, 14 September 1900, 249.

friends....our case is urgent. It is now or never."[198] Baker's petitioning of English Baptists continued into early 1901; at that time, he thanked English Baptists for funds sent but requested more since the war continued and the need was great.[199] Baker could not have known it at the time, but in the very same November 1900 issue of the *Baptist Times and Freeman* where he criticized the lack of responsiveness among English Baptist to South African Baptist needs, a letter to the editor included a proposal that the paper begin a shilling fund for the needs of Baptists in South Africa.[200] The response of the paper to the idea was positive and it immediately encouraged readers to donate to the cause.

While the shilling fund was cause for rejoicing, the establishment of The South African Baptist Colonial and Missionary Aid Society in 1901 was exactly what South African Baptists had been hoping for since the outbreak of war. The *Baptist Times and Freeman* announced in August 1901 plans for the establishment of the aid society, and in the following months a number of articles detailed its intended work.[201] Once it was formally established, the *Baptist Times and Freeman* regularly advertised for the society.[202] As subsequent articles demonstrate, the society not only sought to generate giving to the churches struggling due to the desolation of war,[203] but also support for missionary work among the "natives," a touted war aim.[204] The *Baptist Times and Freeman* con-

---

[198] Ernest Baker, "The South African Churches Baptist Churches," *Baptist Times and Freeman*, 16 November 1900, 928.
[199] Ernest Baker, "The Baptists in South Africa," *Baptist Times and Freeman*, 8 February 1901, 88. For other appeals, see "Baptist in Peril of Boers," *South African Baptist*, April 1901, 45.
[200] Fred A. Jackson, "A Shilling Fund for South African Baptists," *Baptist Times and Freeman*, 16 November 1900, 928.
[201] "South African Baptist Union," *Baptist Times and Freeman*, 23 August 1901, 564; "The Baptist South African Colonial and Missionary Aid Society," *Baptist Times and Freeman*, 27 September 1901, 642; "Baptist World in South Africa," *Baptist Times and Freeman*, 4 October 1901, 668; "A Forward Movement in South Africa," *Baptist Times and Freeman*, 25 October 1901, 714; "The Baptist South African Colonial and Missionary Aid Society," *Baptist Times and Freeman*, 11 April 1902, 282; "The Baptist South African Colonial and Missionary Aid Society," *Baptist Times and Freeman*, 2 May 1902, 348.
[202] "The Baptist South African Colonial and Missionary Aid Society," *Baptist Times and Freeman*, 7 March 1902, 189; "The Baptist South African Colonial and Missionary Aid Society," *Baptist Times and Freeman*, 2 May 1902, 348; "The Baptist South African Colonial and Missionary Aid Society," *Baptist Times and Freeman*, 16 May 1902, 364; "The Baptist South African Colonial and Missionary Aid Society," *Baptist Times and Freeman*, 23 May 1902, 390; "The Baptist South African Colonial and Missionary Aid Society," *Baptist Times and Freeman*, 30 May 1902, 404; "The Baptist South African Colonial and Missionary Aid Society," *Baptist Times and Freeman*, 4 July 1902, 505.
[203] R. Howard Henson, "A Suggestion for Coronation Sunday," *Baptist Times and Freeman*, 13 June 1902, 438.
[204] Rev. J.E. Ennals, "Women's Work in South Africa," *Baptist Times and Freeman*, 8 August 1902, 591.

tinued to cover events related to South Africa through to the end of the war,[205] and following in the wake of the establishment of the aid society, came a new column in the paper entitled "South African News and Notes for Baptists."[206]

Baker heard about the Baptist Union of Great Britain's plans to establish the aid society and quickly informed readers of the *South African Baptist* of the decision. He also apologized to English Baptists for his harsh words: "The first refusal of our friends to help us in our distress pained us; and if in the disappointment of the moment we were betrayed into uncharitable expressions we beg to offer them our sincere regret."[207] Baker's change of attitude was mirrored in the denominational paper, for over the course of 1901 the attitude of the *South African Baptist* towards English Baptists softened as it became apparent that help was actually going to come from the Old Country. In early 1901, the invitation from J.H. Shakespeare (Secretary of the Baptist Union) inviting Baptists from colonies to attend the Autumn Assembly in Edinburgh was not received kindly.[208] By the spring there was resentment mixed with a glimmer of hope:

---

[205] Rev. Thomas Chapman, "Chaplains in the Army," *Baptist Times and Freeman*, 26 July 1901, 503; "The Religious Outlook in South Africa," 1 November 1901, 745; "A New Man for Africa," *Baptist Times and Freeman*, 15 November 1901, 784; "South African Notes," *Baptist Times and Freeman*, 7 February 1902, 100; "Baptist World," *Baptist*, 1 March 1902, 8; "The Baptist Premier of Cape Colony," *Baptist Times and Freeman*, 18 July 1902, 537.

[206] "South African News and Notes for Baptists," *Baptist Times and Freeman*, 7 March 1902, 189; "South African News and Notes for Baptists," *Baptist Times and Freeman*, 21 March 1902, 224; "South African News and Notes for Baptists," *Baptist Times and Freeman*, 28 March 1902, 240; "South African News and Notes for Baptists," *Baptist Times and Freeman*, 4 April 1902, 257; "South African News and Notes for Baptists," *Baptist Times and Freeman*, 11 April 1902, 282; "South African News and Notes for Baptists," *Baptist Times and Freeman*, 25 April 1902, 315; "South African News and Notes for Baptists," *Baptist Times and Freeman*, 2 May 1902, 332; "South African News and Notes for Baptists," *Baptist Times and Freeman*, 16 May 1902, 364; "South African News and Notes for Baptists," *Baptist Times and Freeman*, 23 May 1902, 390; "South African News and Notes for Baptists," *Baptist Times and Freeman*, 30 May 1902, 404; "South African News and Notes for Baptists," *Baptist Times and Freeman*, 13 June 1902, 441; "South African News and Notes for Baptists," *Baptist Times and Freeman*, 20 June 1902, 464; "South African News and Notes for Baptists," *Baptist Times and Freeman*, 27 June 1902, 482-483; "South African News and Notes for Baptists," *Baptist Times and Freeman*, 4 July 1902, 505; "South African News and Notes for Baptists," *Baptist Times and Freeman*, 11 July 1902, 520; "South African News and Notes for Baptists," *Baptist Times and Freeman*, 18 July 1902, 537; "South African News and Notes for Baptists," *Baptist Times and Freeman*, 22 August 1902, 627.

[207] Ernest Baker, "A Presidential Message," *South African Baptist*, January 1901, 5-7.

[208] J.H. Shakespeare, "Baptist Union Letters," *South African Baptist*, February 1901, 19; "On the Editorial Stoep," *South African Baptist*, February 1901, 20. Another article was from an English Baptist lamenting that churches in Great Britain were not helping much. See "On the Editorial Stoep," *South African Baptist*, February 1901, 20.

unless our English brethren abandon their churlishness towards us, we shall have to repair our losses ourselves. There seems however a little softening of feeling and, what is better, a little ready help evidenced by succeeding mails from home. We have been blamed for fulminating against British Baptists and told it only made matters worse. That was impossible. Things could not be worse than they were at the moment our writing in November, 1900.[209]

By the summer, it was clear that the Baptist Union of Great Britain had decided to begin an aid society that would address the needs of the churches in South Africa.[210] Over the course of the following months, the South African Baptist informed its readers of developments in the South African Baptist Colonial and Missionary Aid Society.[211] By 1902, there was still a need to be vigilant about ensuring ongoing support for South African Baptist from sources such as the Century Fund,[212] but criticism of English Baptists had been replaced with optimism over what the aid society would not only do for the churches, but what it also meant for the restoration of Baptist relations.

The English Baptist's eventual response to South African Baptist appeals ameliorated the crisis between the two communities. The role of the Baptist press in the resolution of this dispute should not be underestimated. Baptists in South Africa were able to present their concerns directly to the leaders and laity of the Baptist Union of Great Britain, and incessantly petitioned and pressured them to provide support for their distressed churches. Once the decision had been made to form The Baptist South African Colonial and Missionary Aid Society, the *Baptist Times and Freeman* was able to marshal support for the aid society's ministry through a regular column as well as weekly news items. This healing of Baptist relations and the formation of the aid society did more than just reconcile Baptists; it contributed to the healing and binding of imperial bonds between the metropole and periphery.

---

[209] "After Two Years," *South African Baptist*, May 1901, 49-50

[210] This was announced and discussed at the South African Baptist Union Assembly in Grahamstown, as was the sending of a delegate to the Fall Baptist Union of Great Britain Assembly in Edinburgh. See "Baptist Union of South Africa," *South African Baptist*, June 1901, 65.

[211] "Our Aid Society in Great Britain," *South African Baptist*, July 1901, 83-84; "Executive Notes," *South African Baptist*, September 1901, 110; "Executive Notes," *South African Baptist*, October 1901, 122-123; "British Aid in Our Work," *South African Baptist*, December 1901, 139-140; *South African Baptist*, December 1901, 140; "On the Editorial Stoep," *South African Baptist*, March 1902, 29; "On the Editorial Stoep," *South African Baptist*, October 1902, 119; "Baptist Union of South Africa," *South African Baptist*, November 1902,132-133; "South African Colonial and Missionary Aid Society," *South African Baptist*, November 1902,139. One article mentions a pastor in Britain speaking at a church about the need of South African Baptists. See "On the Editorial Stoep," *South African Baptist*, July 1902, 91. For brief comments of how British Baptists still do not know anything about Baptists in Africa, see "On the Editorial Stoep," *South African Baptist*, February 1902, 22.

[212] "A Baptist Triumph," *South African Baptist*, July 1902, 75-76; "Baptist Union of South Africa," *South African Baptist*, November 1902, 138.

Conclusion

While BACSANZ Baptists had particular national identities, they also shared a global identity, both real and imagined. They may have been on the margins in terms of the percentage of population, but the global Baptist community provided Baptists with a sense of belonging to something grander that transcended their small regional presence. They were loyal to their nation, dominion, federation or colony, but they also believed they belonged to a global community that was distinctly Baptist, British, and imperial. The Baptist press played an important role in the construction of this community, for it was created, nurtured and sustained by that press. In a very tangible way, the Baptist press within the empire played an important part in the building of a global denominational, evangelical and imperial identity and bond that transcended regional and national identities. It not only helped to cement bonds between the metropole and peripheries, but also between the peripheries themselves. This global Baptist identity was based on shared religious convictions, personal contacts, formal denominational structures, and British or Anglo-Saxon identity. Underlying this global Baptist, British, and imperial identity was the assumption of Anglo-Saxon identity, superiority, and mission.

Chapter Five

Justice

"It is war – always horrid, always cruel, and almost always mad. To the dread ar-
bitrament of the sword the South African situation is now referred, and there is
nothing more at present to be said. Whatever we may think of the occasion of the
struggle, there is nothing out of place in a religious organ expressing its repugnance to war as a means of adjustment." "A Settlement by Thunderbolts," *South
African Baptist*, November 1899, 53-54.

"We deplore our country's mistakes, but we love her notwithstanding. It is to be
hoped that the recent decided British victories will lead up to a speedy cessation
of bloodshed, and the establishment of righteous rule in the area over which war
has raged. Detesting jingoism, we believe that the dominancy of Britain in South
Africa will mean security, justice and liberty." "A Hopeful Outlook," *Baptist*, 10
March 1900, 2.

In January 1902, the *Baptist Times and Freeman* published a jingoistic poem by
James Crossby Roberts entitled "Song of the Younger Nations." It was a poem
that extolled the martial virtues of the Anglo-Saxons and the unity of the empire, and a portion of it read:

We will fight for England, and for England die.
Alert, united, back to back we stand,
Children of one Great Mother,
Sons of one Great Land;
Born of one Blood, one common Tongue we speak,
Friends to old foeman, New Fighters for the Weak;
God-watch'd and God-begirt,
God-order'd, God-sustain'd
Swift Envoys of the Purpose,
Grim Ministers restrained,
We breed upon the world's round edge,
We rise, the Lust of race to please,
And pledge ourselves the Lion's whelps-
The Younger Nations of the Further Seas.[1]

While this type of poem expressed sentiments found in colonial Baptist papers,[2]
its publication in Britain provoked a number of angry letters to the editor con-

---

[1] James Crossby Roberts, "Song of the Younger Nations," *Baptist Times and Freeman*,
7 February 1902, 105.
[2] Heath, "Passion for Empire."

demning the poem for its militaristic "clap-trap and pernicious sentences."[3] The editor apologized for its inclusion, claiming that he had not noticed its insertion. Backtracking quickly he declared that he did not "endorse the sentiment [of the poem] nor think the lines suitable for a religious paper."[4] The minor brouhaha caused by this poem is evidence that, despite their close identification with nation and empire, there was a spectrum of support for imperial causes as well as a concern for jingoism among BACSANZ Baptists. Scathing international and domestic criticism of the war was widespread in and outside the empire and claims that the imperial cause was unjust were common. BACSANZ Baptists were united in their support for, and identification with, nation and empire, but there was no consensus as to the justice of the cause in South Africa.

From their genesis, evangelicals displayed a passionate concern for justice, and the connection between Baptists and justice has a considerable history. Walter Rauschenbusch and Martin Luther King, Jr. are perhaps the two most well-known Baptist figures whose lives were marked by a focus on justice, but there were others. For instance, Paul Dekar has proposed that nineteenth-century Baptist missionaries were acting implicitly as peacemakers when they worked as agents of reconciliation and fought against social injustices;[5] Brian Stanley has shown how Baptist missionaries were involved in the struggle against slavery and injustice,[6] and Marvia Lawes has illustrated how Baptists in Jamaica resisted slavery and colonialism.[7]

The identification of the British Empire with liberty predated the late-nineteenth century, and by the late-nineteenth century it was assumed by BACSANZ Baptists that there was no empire as righteous as their empire. Despite its problems and injustices, the empire was considered to be the world's most benevolent empire: where the Union Jack flew, liberty and justice reigned. Quite simply, the best way to spread justice was to expand the empire. Conversely, any contraction of empire was deemed a threat to peace, justice and the advancement of human progress. David Bebbington has noted how in the 1870s most British nonconformists were opposed to imperialism, but by 1900 the majority of nonconformists were supportive of it. The reasons for the shift were manifold, but a critical one was the conviction that imperial

---

[3] "Correspondence," *Baptist Times and Freeman*, 14 February 1902, 134.
[4] "Correspondence," *Baptist Times and Freeman*, 14 February 1902, 134.
[5] Paul Dekar, *For the Healing of the Nations: Baptist Peacemakers* (Macon: Smyth & Helwys Publishing, 1993), ch.11.
[6] Brian Stanley, "Nineteenth-Century Liberation Theology: Nonconformist Missionaries and Imperialism," *Baptist Quarterly* 32 (January 1987): 5-18; Brian Stanley, "Baptists, Anti-Slavery and the Legacy of Imperialism," *Baptist Quarterly* 42 (October 2007): 284-296.
[7] Marvia E. Lawes, "A Historical Evaluation of Jamaica Baptists: A Spirituality of Resistance," *Black Theology* 6, no. 3 (2008): 366-392.

intervention was a way to protect innocents and promote liberty.[8] Likewise for Baptists in the metropole and peripheries, humanitarian concerns - which included the promotion or defense of justice - often involved an imperial solution, even if it meant going to war.

Christians had argued ever since St. Ambrose and St. Augustine that a particular conflict needed to be fought for a just cause (*jus ad bellum*) and with just means (*jus in bello*). In order for a war to be deemed "just" it had to meet those two requirements, and Christians could only participate in a war if both criteria were met. By identifying the cause of war in South Africa as just, and the means by which it was fought as just, BACSANZ Baptists were acting within a long-standing Christian tradition. Conversely, when BACSANZ Baptists opposed the war in general, or some particular aspect of it, they too were operating within the just war tradition that demanded a condemnation of wars that failed to fulfill the requirements of justice. Without the conviction that justice "was on their side," BACSANZ Baptists would have acted against a well-developed tradition about support for the use of force. It is with this background in mind that one begins to understand the efforts in the BACSANZ press in the opening weeks to decipher the justice of the imperial cause.

Before exploring BACSANZ Baptist discourse on the justice of the war, a few brief comments on bias, imperialism, and editors are in order. It is a truism to say that opinions were colored by imperial sentiment, and postcolonial works have demonstrated the imperial bias that shaped perceptions of justice. However, it is also too simplistic to assume that BACSANZ Baptists were uncritical propagandists for the empire. That commitment to imperialism did not preclude censure of the empire, for, as will be shown below, BACSANZ Baptists did at times criticize the empire's conduct. In fact, BACSANZ Baptist identification with the empire meant that the empire must be committed to justice, for an ostensibly Christian empire was obliged to uphold a high standard of justice. In that sense, Baptist imperial bias actually lent itself to being critical of empire. As for interpreting events, the various editors claimed to base their convictions on the evidence. Despite their best-stated intentions, however, it was self-evident to some that a pro-British bias influenced interpretations of the war's events. Sanford W. Evans, wartime author of *The Canadian Contingents and Canadian Imperialism: A Story and a Study*, concluded as much in 1901. He stated that there were not enough "facts" to make a firm decision about the justice of the cause. Instead, he argued that Canadian assurance came from confidence in British statesmen and British policy.[9] The implicit Canadian trust in

---

[8] Bebbington, *The Nonconformist Conscience*, ch.6.
[9] He also argued that the French were not as quick to trust the imperial government without first having some type of inquiry into the evidence. See Sanford W. Evans, *The Canadian Contingents and Canadian Imperialism: A Story and a Study* (Toronto: The Publisher's Syndicate, Ltd., 1901), 11.

the British was shared by a number of Baptists in the peripheries, but less so in the metropole.

There is another element to consider in the formation of the churches' pro-war sentiment. Daniel Francis defines a nation as "a group of people who share the same illusions about themselves."[10] Stated more positively, each nation has its own "civic ideology, a framework of ideas and aspirations that expresses itself in allegiance to certain public policies and institutions," which has to be continually "recreated and reinforced."[11] In the case of the war in South Africa, BACSANZ Baptists were firmly convinced of the superiority of the British race and its institutions. While criticism was leveled at people such as Cecil Rhodes, what was never in doubt was the essential goodness and godly calling of the empire. It seemed to some Baptists in the peripheries that criticisms of the justice of the cause led to questioning the "civic ideology" of Britain and its empire. For instance, since Canadian identity was so closely identified with Britain and the empire, to admit that the war was not just was to raise disturbing questions about the very essence of Canadian identity. This was no small consideration since the nation was still in its infancy, and French-Canadian (and Catholic) opposition to the war divided the nation on ethnic and religious grounds. Perhaps that is why, out of all the BACSANZ Baptists, Canadian Baptists appeared to be the most united in their defense of the justice of the cause. This need to reinforce the civic ideology remained when the focus of the criticisms of Britain shifted from questioning the justice of the cause to a condemnation of Britain's means to win the war.[12]

In many ways, papers reflected the views of their readers. As Wilkinson notes, "images in newspapers had to conform to the perception of war that readers already held. In this regard, newspapers had little or no thought for posterity or future reputations of their creators, and they needed to create and foster an immediate connection with their reader audiences."[13] He goes on to say that "this makes the newspapers a form of two-way communication, with readers more than 'blank slates' awaiting to be etched with how to think about the world by the press."[14] That being the case, editorial decisions still determined how a paper presented the case for - or against - the justice of the imperial cause. Some papers presented both sides so that readers could determine for themselves the case for war. There were also examples of vigorous dialogue in

---

[10] Daniel Francis, *National Dreams: Myth, Memory and Canadian History* (Vancouver: Arsenal Pulp, 1997), 10.

[11] Francis, *National* Dreams, 10.

[12] By arguing so passionately about the goodness of the empire the churches seemed to be involved in what Eric Hobsbawm and Terence Ranger have coined the "invention of tradition." The churches would not have understood it to be such, but they were involved in creating, and perpetuating, certain attitudes and behaviors towards empire and nation. See Hobsbawm and Ranger, *The Invention of Tradition*.

[13] Wilkinson, "'To the Front,'" 203-204.

[14] Wilkinson, "'To the Front,'" 203-204.

letters to the editor, with opposing views being printed. Other papers, such as the Baptist papers in Canada, printed nothing that would erode the position that the war was just and needed to be supported. The editor of the *South African Baptist* intentionally sought to avoid making an official pronouncement on the war due to domestic considerations. The sources that editors used also played a part influencing editorial bias. As has already been noted, papers that relied on London-based cable reports had ready-made arguments in support of the war, whereas papers that relied on news from Paris (or elsewhere) received arguments against the justice of the cause. The opinion of South African churches about the war carried significant weight in Britain, Canada, Australia and New Zealand, for they provided what seemed to be an "independent moral endorsement of the justice of the British cause" as well as eyewitness accounts of a distant and murky conflict.[15] As a result, pro-war statements from South Africa were circulated widely outside of South Africa by apologists for the war, as were anti-war statements by those opposed to the war.

BACSANZ Baptists were committed to the ideal of an empire that promoted righteousness, but as these brief comments on bias indicate, determining what was just was not an easy task. In fact, there was considerable divisions among Baptist over certain aspects of the war. The following examines the spectrum of opinion on the war. The first section will relate to the issue of just cause, the second to that of just means.

Just Cause

After Chamberlain's September ultimatum, the two Boer republics issued their own ultimatum to Britain on 10 October 1899 demanding that it remove its troops from the border region, return any troops in South Africa that had recently arrived, and call back troop transports that were en route to the region.[16] The outbreak of war began the next day on 11 October 1899 with the Boer invasion of British territory; it was a pre-emptive strike into Natal and the Cape Colony that quickly besieged Ladysmith, Mafeking and Kimberley before even more British troops could arrive.

In the opening weeks of the war, well-known Toronto Baptist pastor Elmore Harris published in the *Chicago Standard* an article entitled "The Boer War as Canadians See It." The article was a defense of the British and Canadian imperial cause in the war in South Africa, and the aim of writing in the *Standard* was to address American criticisms of the war.[17] Shortly thereafter the

---

[15] For the following comments on South African Anglicanism, see Blunden, "The Anglican Church during the War."

[16] Farwell, *The Great Anglo-Boer War*, 46-47.

[17] Harris also reminded his American readers of how Britain had stood alongside America during its recent war against Spain. Harris contended it was now America's turn to show its appreciation for such support and reciprocate in kind by supporting Britain's war in South Africa.

article reprinted as an excerpt in the *Canadian Baptist*.[18] Harris indicated that, while Britain was not completely faultless in the months preceding the war, the war had been forced upon Britain and the empire by the Boer declaration of war and subsequent invasion of British territory.

Harris was not alone in his deeming the war just because of Boer perfidy and invasion. Their pre-emptive strike was an important consideration among many Canadians, for a common theme in Canadian papers in the opening weeks of the conflict was the conviction that the war had been forced upon Britain. The *Canadian Baptist* argued that the Boers had "cut short the negotiations for a peaceful settlement" by "an ultimatum flung in the face" of Britain.[19] The *Western Baptist* claimed that the Boer declaration of war forced the issue and because of that there was never "a more righteous cause."[20] Like many other denominational publications in Canada, the Baptist press realized the implied ultimatum in the Boer declarations and found it unacceptable. Britain was a world power and the Boer republics were, by comparison, small and relatively insignificant. It was considered amazing that the Boers would address the mighty British Empire in such a manner, and, in the *Religious Intelligencer's* opinion, there could "be only one reply to such absurd and insolent demands, namely, that Great Britain could not even discuss them."[21] The *Messenger and Visitor*, once somewhat sympathetic to the Boer cause, concluded that no country with "self-respect" could "entertain them for one moment."[22] The Boer invasion only fanned the flames of indignation.

Unlike their coreligionists in Britain and, to a lesser degree, elsewhere, the Canadian Baptist press expressed views that trusted British authorities implicitly: stated motives were taken at face value, and the war was deemed to be just because of perceived imperial motives. When Canada's first contingent of 1,000 troops prepared to board the 425 foot *Sardinian* in Quebec City on Monday, 30 October 1899, Prime Minister Wilfred Laurier declared in the presence of the Governor General, the Premier of the province of Quebec, other civil and religious leaders, as well as 50,000 exuberant spectators:

> the cause for which you men of Canada are going to fight is the cause of justice, the cause of humanity, of civil rights and religious liberty. This is not a war of conquest....The object is not to crush out the Dutch population, but to establish in that land ... British sovereign law, to assure to all men of that country an equal share of liberty.[23]

---

[18] Elmore Harris, "The Boer War as Canadians See It," *Canadian Baptist*, 12 (April 1900), 232.

[19] "War With the Boers," *Canadian Baptist*, 19 October 1899, 662.

[20] "War in Transvaal," *Western Baptist*, November 1899, 1.

[21] "The Transvaal War," *Religious Intelligencer*, 18 October 1899, 4.

[22] "The Boer Ultimatum," *Messenger and Visitor*, 18 October 1899, 1.

[23] Page, *The Boer War and Canadian Imperialism*, 13.

Many Baptists agreed with such lofty rhetoric, and throughout the war that message was repeated countless times. On 5 June 1902, the *Canadian Baptist* proclaimed the end of the war in South Africa by printing a map of the "New British South Africa" on the front page. Planted firmly in Pretoria was a British flag framed by the words "Peace, Liberty, Equality."[24] From beginning to end, the war was deemed to be just that: a war fought for the good of others.[25]

It was during the war in South Africa that imperial sentiment in Canada "was brought to its most excited, feverish pitch....As the Spanish-American War had aroused the United States so the South African War stirred Canadians....The Boer War was the great high-water mark of imperial zeal in Canada."[26] Such excessive displays of imperial passion among English Canadians would not be seen again in Canada until the First World War.[27] Berger understands the imperial impulse in Canada during the war to be one form of Canadian nationalism (of course, French-Canadian attitudes to empire were quite different from English-Canadian attitudes[28]). It was this type of nationalism, he argues, that explains Canada's enthusiastic participation in an imperial war.[29] He also notes that Canadian imperialism had a religious impulse to it, something that can be seen in the Baptist defense of the imperial cause in South Africa.

The Baptist press made it clear that, despite the abuses and various evils of imperialism, it was convinced of the positive effects of the empire and identified the benefits of belonging to the empire.[30] Further justifying support for its expansion was the sense of superiority over against the rule of other colonizing powers.[31] An article in the *Religious Intelligencer* made this quite clear:

> Instead of being tyrannical, the British Empire is an object lesson of rebuke to nations ruled with a rod of iron....Do some of those who allow themselves to be carried away by the racial prejudice realize what the downfall of the British Empire would mean to the world?...Let the British power be shattered and not only would our freedom cease but tyranny would soon place the shackles more heavily on

---

[24] *Canadian Baptist*, 5 June 1902, 1.

[25] That sentiment was shared by Canadian Anglicans, Methodists, and Presbyterians, as well as Baptists. See Heath, *A War with a Silver Lining*, ch.2.

[26] Robert Page, *Imperialism and Canada, 1895-1903* (Toronto: Holt, Rinehart, and Winston), 5, 12.

[27] Page, *Imperialism and Canada*, 12.

[28] Silver, "Some Quebec Attitudes in an Age of Imperialism and Ideological Conflict."

[29] Berger, *The Sense of Power*. See also Miller, *Painting the Map Red*.

[30] "A Fruit of Christian Civilization," *Religious Intelligencer*, 27 March 1901, 1; *Canadian Baptist*, 18 January 1900, 1.

[31] "It cannot be questioned but that the colonial system of our Motherland is much better fitted than that of any other country, to advance the material prosperity as well as the higher interests of those under her sway. For other reasons, therefore, than the merely patriotic, all true men may be glad that she will have so large a part in shaping the future of the Dark Continent." *Canadian Baptist*, 2 January 1902, 1. See also *Canadian Baptist*, 12 June 1902, 1; *Canadian Baptist*, 11 January 1900, 8.

those learning to look for emancipation in every foreign land. The honour, the glory, the power of the Briton means progress, civilization, freedom, to the world. It would be a sad day for humanity if the British Empire should ever fall, an evil hour for the people of this continent if the last vestige of British power should leave it.[32]

Not only was the empire deemed to be a force for good in the world, but abolishing or diminishing it in any way would be a catastrophe to the continent of Africa and the world. The Baptists were just as clear in their literature that the war in South Africa was being fought for the Outlanders and the "natives." They assumed that Britain had a moral and legal duty to act in South Africa; it was an integral part of their "White Man's Burden."[33]

The *Canadian Baptist* echoed the same themes and was convinced that "Britain's title as a world-power" was on trial in South Africa.[34] The strategic situation around the world was also cause for concern. Trouble was brewing in China and in India, and a loss of prestige in Africa would have serious ramifications for the empire.[35] Consequently, the war was worth its expense and challenge.[36] The *Canadian Baptist* also painted a grim picture of what the world would be like if Britain lost: "Our only choice lay between the surrender of South Africa – which would have involved the breakup of our Colonial Empire, the setting of the sun of British rule, and the setting back of the clock of the world's progress for perhaps a century – and the present war."[37] With such high stakes at risk, the choice to support the war was considered to be obvious.

Australia's commitment of over 16,000 men to the war was over twice the size of Canada's (something that vexed many Canadians anxious to gain bragging rights for being the most loyal of the colonies). Field provides a helpful

---

[32] "What British Power Means," *Religious Intelligencer*, 22 August 1900, 6.

[33] For examples, see B. A. Sherwood, "War - and Some Lessons," *Religious Intelligencer*, 21 February 1900, 4; *Canadian Baptist*, 8 March 1900, 1; *Canadian Baptist*, 26 October 1899, 1; "What the Boer War is All About," *Canadian Baptist*, 2 November 1899, 11; "Lord Salisbury on the War," *Canadian Baptist*, 16 November 1899, 7; *Canadian Baptist*, 29 March 1900, 1; "The Boer War as Canadians See It," *Canadian Baptist*, 12 April 1900, 8; Rev. John C. Harris, "The Moral Issues of the War: A Johannesburg Minister to His Scattered Church," *Canadian Baptist*, 12 April 1899, 15; "South Africa Blacks," *Canadian Baptist*, 20 June 1900, 4; Rev. John Moffat, "The Cause of the South African War," *Canadian Baptist*, 23 August 1900, 15; "How the Boers Treat the Natives," *Canadian Baptist*, 9 November 1899, 7; Marshall Maxeke, "The Black Man's Side in the Transvaal War," *Canadian Baptist*, 1 December 1899, 7; *Canadian Baptist*, 22 February 1900, 1; "British and Boers, Again," *Canadian Baptist*, 1 March 1900, 11; "The End of the South African War Draws Rapidly Nearer," *Religious Intelligencer*, 8 August 1900, 5.

[34] "The War in South Africa," *Canadian Baptist*, 11 January 1900, 8.

[35] *Canadian Baptist*, 9 August 1900, 1.

[36] "The Price of South Africa," *Canadian Baptist*, 23 May 1901, 11; "England & America," *Canadian Baptist*, 11 January 1900, 11.

[37] Rev. Charles Phillips, "Was the War Inevitable?" *Canadian Baptist*, 8 February 1900, 7.

summary of Australia's reasons for supporting the far-flung imperial conflict, a number of them remarkably similar to the Canadian experience.[38] In a similar vein, Clarke and Wilcox argue that what was seen in Australia in regards to widespread and exuberant displays of imperialism was similar to what was observed in other parts of the empire: "The view from Wollongong or Wagga Wagga was little different to that from Wellington or Winnipeg."[39] The war also garnered widespread support across Australia, and the sendoff of troops in Sydney on 28 October 1899 is one example of such ardent enthusiasm. For over two miles of stores and offices hanging with bunting, flags and posters, 200,000 zealous spectators lined the sides of the road and sang "Rule Britannia" and "Soldiers of the Queen" while the first contingent marched past to their transport.[40] This zeal for the imperial cause was evident in various churches. Patrick identifies how most Australian Methodists were pro-war, ardent defenders of empire, who believed that God in his providence would ultimately bring victory to the British cause.[41] Both Fletcher and Withycombe make it clear that late nineteenth-century Australian Anglicans were, for the most part, committed to the ideals of the empire and Australia's active engagement and defense of the same.[42] Such wholehearted support can be seen in other denominations as well as in various Baptist papers.[43] However, as Field notes in *The Forgotten War*, "beneath all the cheers and patriotic clichés there existed misgiving over the war."[44] Such misgivings can also be seen in the Baptist papers. In fact, the variety of responses in the Baptist press indicates that there was no homogenous Australian Baptist perspective on the war.

The initial responses of Australian Baptist papers were at odds. The *Queensland Baptist* hoped for a short war, lamented the letting use of the "dogs of war" to settle the issues plaguing Boer-British relations and declared the "resort to force" as deplorable to genuine Christians.[45] It expressed concern over the

---

[38] Field, *The Forgotten War*, 3. For further discussion of strategic similarities between Australia and Canada, see Blaxland, "Strategic Cousins."
[39] Quote from page 151, Wilcox, "The Australian Perspective on the War." See also Clarke, "Desperately Seeking Service, 12-27.
[40] Wallace, *The Australians at the Boer War*, 35. See also Penny, "Australia's Reactions to the Boer War," 99; C.N. Connolly, "Manufacturing 'Spontaneity': The Australian Offers of Troops for the Boer War," *Historical Studies* 18, no. 70 (1978): 106-117.
[41] Patrick, "A Dreadful But Absolute Necessity."
[42] Fletcher, "Anglicanism and Nationalism in Australia"; Withycombe, "Australian Anglicans and Imperial Identity."
[43] For attitudes to the war in the Methodist paper entitled *The Methodist*, see Patrick, "A Dreadful But Absolute Necessity." For brief commentary on other churches, see Penny, "Australia's Reactions to the Boer War," 117; Field, *The Forgotten War*, 46.
[44] Field, *The Forgotten War*, 72. See also Penny, "Australia's Reactions to the Boer War," 105-109; Penny, "The Australia Debate on the Boer War"; Connolly, "Class, Birthplace, Loyalty."
[45] "War!" *Queensland Baptist*, November 1899, 150; W.H., "The Boer War," *Queensland Baptist*, November 1899, 151-152.

early offer of troops, supported parliament for sending them once they were accepted by imperial authorities, and encouraged citizens of Queensland to "uphold and desire the success" of the troops.[46] As for the justice of the cause, the editor confessed "that after much consideration" he felt "unable to decide. If it rested upon the mere question of franchise we should say at once that war is not justifiable. But so many other considerations are involved, and we are so far from the scene that our information is necessarily imperfect."[47] The hope expressed was that in the coming months more details would arrive from Britain that would help make an informed decision on the cause of the war, and perhaps at that time Christians would be able to consider just war criteria for legitimate Christian engagement in war.[48] The rampant jingoistic "war fever" in Australia also needed to be avoided, for it was "demonstrably" unChristian, and the refusal to submit the quarrel to arbitration was shameful.[49]

While the *Southern Baptist* expressed optimism in the summer of 1899 that the issue would be settled peacefully, that optimism shifted in the early fall to hope and prayers for peace as war seemed more and more likely.[50] Once war was declared, the editor of the *Southern Baptist* endorsed the war effort and attempted to bolster domestic support for the war in a number of ways, all the while defending the right of naysayers to voice their dissenting opinion.[51] Disagreeing with Dr. Clifford's criticism of Britain's role in the outbreak of the conflict, one article declared that the "Boers have disclosed their hand, and if ever a war was necessary and justifiable this is. The Boers are the real aggressors, and Britain is only acting on the defensive in her action."[52] Elsewhere, it was claimed "never did Britain send forth her armies on a more righteous errand. Our prayer is for a sharp, short, decisive victory, and then peace."[53] It was claimed a number of times that the Boers had been preparing for war over the past few years, and that Britain had done everything it could to avoid the war.[54]

---

[46] "Christian Citizenship," *Queensland Baptist*, November 1899, 154-155.

[47] W.H., "The Boer War," *Queensland Baptist*, November 1899, 151-152.

[48] "Christian Citizenship," *Queensland Baptist*, November 1899, 154-155.

[49] William Page, "The War Fever," *Queensland Baptist*, November 1899, 155-156. See also "The Higher Patriotism," *Queensland Baptist*, February 1900, 20-21.

[50] "Our Two Eyes and Our Two Ears," *Southern Baptist*, 28 September 1899, 205; "The Transvaal," *Southern Baptist*, 28 September 1899, 206; "War May Have Begun," *Southern Baptist*, 12 October 1899, 217; "Out Intense Sympathies," *Southern Baptist*, 12 October 1899, 217; "As We Write," *Southern Baptist*, 12 October 1899, 218.

[51] "The War," *Southern Baptist*, 2 November 1899, 229.

[52] "Dr. Clifford," *Southern Baptist*, 2 November 1899, 230.

[53] "We Cannot Understand," *Southern Baptist*, 30 November 1899, 264.

[54] "The Justification of the Present War," *Southern Baptist*, 2 November 1899, 230; "The Christian Weekly," *Southern Baptist*, 16 November 1899, 241; "It Goes without Saying," *Southern Baptist*, 16 November 1899, 242; "As to the Justifiable Character," *Southern Baptist*, 16 November 1899, 242; "The Boers," *Southern Baptist*, 30 November 1899, 264.

The alleged religious piety of Kruger and the Boers was questioned,[55] a brief historical sketch was printed that portrayed the Boers as the ones primarily in the wrong,[56] testimony from other denominations about the conduct of the Boers were drawn upon to bolster their case,[57] wartime atrocities were invoked to demonstrate that the Boers were "butchers,"[58] and a clergyman with experience in South Africa was interviewed regarding the justice of the British cause (he heartily endorsed it).[59] It unflinchingly endorsed the imperial cause, in part because it was believed that the Boer ultimatum left them "no choice."[60]

At the other end of the spectrum of opinion was the *Baptist*. The overall trajectory of the *Baptist* was opposed to the war and opinions expressed bemoaned its outbreak from the onset.[61] While the paper wished for a British victory, it argued that the war was madness, destructive and pointless, especially since Britain's opponents were fellow Protestant Christians.[62] Articles did not question the patriotism of the soldiers, but did express the conviction that international arbitration should have been used to settle the dispute.[63] When a letter to the editor presented an argument defending the war, a response was quickly posted that argued against the letter and the war.[64] Like other papers, it too lamented the rising militarism caused by the war, something one author called the "brutalizing of the public mind."[65] It also endorsed the "Stop the War" movement in Great Britain.[66]

The various Baptist papers did briefly acknowledge that they were propagating divergent viewpoints. The *Queensland Baptist* observed that the *Southern Baptist* was "very outspoken" on the war.[67] The *Southern Baptist* noted that the *Baptist* had solicited anti-war views on the war, views that the *Southern Baptist*

---

[55] "The Boers are Protestant," *Southern Baptist*, 2 November 1899, 229.

[56] "The Quarrel," *Southern Baptist*, 2 November 1899, 229; "At Majuba Hill," *Southern Baptist*, 2 November 1899, 229.

[57] "Christian People in the Transvaal," *Southern Baptist*, 16 November 1899, 241.

[58] "The Justification of the Present War," *Southern Baptist*, 2 November 1899, 230.

[59] Rev. Dr. Stewart, "The Transvaal Crisis," *Southern Baptist*, 4 January 1900, 6.

[60] "The Long Anticipated Struggle," *Southern Baptist*, 2 November 1899, 230.

[61] I was unable to find any copies of the *Baptist* dated before December 1899.

[62] "The Dogs of War Let Loose," *Baptist*, 22 December 1899, 2; "Pray!," *Baptist*, 3 February 1899, 3; "When Will It End?," *Baptist*, 10 March 1900, 4.

[63] "Devotion to Duty," *Baptist*, 10 March 1900, 4; "Sad," *Baptist*, 10 March 1900, 4; "In 'Sartor Resartus'," *Baptist*, 10 March 1900, 4.

[64] Gideon, "War!," *Baptist*, 3 April 1900, 6; PAX, "War," *Baptist*, 4 May 1900, 7-8.

[65] "The Relief of Mafeking," *Baptist*, 2 June 1900, 1. See also "The War Spirit - or Jesus, Which?" *Baptist*, 10 March 1900, 2; "An Effect of the War," *Baptist*, 10 March 1900, 4; "The False Glamour of War," *Queensland Baptist*, 1 April 1901, 46; "Militarism," *Queensland Baptist*, 2 June 1902, 77; "War Is a Necessary Evil," *Southern Baptist*, 15 February 1900, 37; "There Is a Recklessness," *Southern Baptist*, 18 January 1900, 13; "Much As We Deplore," *Southern Baptist*, 18 January 1900, 14.

[66] "A 'Stop-the-War' Movement," *Baptist*, 10 March 1900, 2.

[67] "The 'Southern Baptist' on the Boer War," *Queensland Baptist*, 1 January 1900, 2.

found reprehensible.[68] However, the editor of the pro-war *Southern Baptist* declared that those in Australia who disagreed with Britain's cause should be allowed a "respectful hearing" and their patriotism should not be questioned.[69] The *Baptist* was even more outspoken about freedom to dissent, no doubt due to the fact that it was so condemning of the war. It claimed that one could be patriotic and still disagree with government action.[70] It printed an extensive article that defended the patriotism of both sides, and noted that while the majority supported the war, at times the minority had in the past proven to be right.[71] It also provided a brief quote that affirmed that its supposedly pro-Boer conduct was actually a manifestation of its patriotism: "Patriotism is brave enough to condemn her country's mistakes."[72] Those commitments to freedom of dissent helped the Baptist papers avoid the strident denunciations of opponents (and even threats of violence) that marked some of the domestic debates regarding the war in Australia.[73]

As the war progressed, some attitudes in the various Australian papers shifted and evolved whereas other opinions solidified. By December 1899, there were indications in the *Queensland Baptist* that the paper had begun to adjust its view towards blaming the Boers for the conflict:

> Personally, we have the growing conviction that, behind the question of the franchise, was the anticipation on the part of the Boers, of a general uprising of the Dutch population against British rule, and the establishment of a South African Republic, embracing the colonies now owned by Britain. The franchise dispute afforded the opportunity desired to put it to the test, but the result will be far different from the Boer expectations.[74]

However, in March 1900 the paper still presented to its readers a brief synopsis of those who supported as well as opposed the war.[75] Eventually, but reluctantly, after months of deliberating as to the justice of the cause, the *Queensland Baptist* printed an article in April 1900 that expressed unequivocal support for the war effort: "It is too late to discuss the rights and wrongs of the present war. Manifestly the British could not silently endure the invasion of territory, even for strategic defense of the Boer States, nor could they leave beleaguered garrisons to the mercy of the Boers."[76]

---

[68] "'The Baptist'," *Southern Baptist*, 1 February 1900, 26.

[69] "The War," *Southern Baptist*, 2 November 1899, 229.

[70] "The Worst Thing," *Baptist*, 3 February 1899, 3.

[71] "A Plea for Liberty," *Baptist*, 10 March 1900, 1-2.

[72] *Baptist*, 1 January 1902, 7.

[73] For instance, see Field, *The Forgotten War*, 28-30.

[74] "The Boer War," *Queensland Baptist*, December 1899, 168-169.

[75] "Some War Items," *Queensland Baptist*, March 1900, 29-30.

[76] Rev. W. Whale, "A Trinity of Tribulations," *Queensland Baptist*, April 1900, 48-49.

In a generous spirit of fair play, the *Southern Baptist* printed an article that condemned the righteousness of the British cause,[77] and printed a letter to the editor that went against the paper's position,[78] but it was clear that the editorial position of the paper had not changed from its original assessment; the war was just and should be heartily supported. Other papers were criticized for their unwillingness to change their position to reflect the evidence that Britain was in the right:

> Still, in spite of all evidence to the contrary, many of the British Christians and re-ligious papers persist in denouncing the war as unrighteous, and would fain bring it to an abrupt termination, leaving the Republics in possession. Surely it must be that, having at first announced themselves as Boer sympathizers, they lack cour-age to reverse their judgment.[79]

Articles and commentary continually reminded readers that the war was just because the Boers had planned for it and ruthlessly precipitated it,[80] and claims that the Boers started the war continued to the very end of the war.[81] Articles also went on the offensive and attacked pro-Boer positions,[82] and views of oth-ers were printed in Britain and in South Africa that vindicated the British posi-tion.[83] At war's end, the British victory was deemed to be a blessing for the British, Boers, and the welfare of the "natives."[84]

---

[77] J, "Another Voice from South Africa," *Southern Baptist*, 2 August 1900, 178. One poem was printed that portrayed the grim realities of war, but it is difficult to discern if it is a statement against the justice of the cause. See Edgar Wallace, "It Is War," *Southern Baptist*, 31 January 1901, 27.

[78] For the exchange, see "A Voice from South Africa," *Southern Baptist*, 28 June 1900, 150; J, "Another Voice from South Africa," *Southern Baptist*, 2 August 1900, 178. For the editor's introduction of this rebuttal, see "Our Correspondent 'J,'" *Southern Baptist*, 2 August 1900, 170.

[79] "The Boer War," *Southern Baptist*, 12 April 1900, 86. See also "'Military Critics'," *Southern Baptist*, 15 March 1900, 61.

[80] "The War Goes On," *Southern Baptist*, 18 January 1900, 13; "The Boers," *Southern Baptist*, 18 January 1900, 14; "The War," *Southern Baptist*, 1 February 1900, 25; J.B., "The Mission of the British People," *Southern Baptist*, 15 February 1900, 43; "The Boer War," *Southern Baptist*, 2 May 1900, 98.

[81] "Peace," *Southern Baptist*, 11 June 1902, 133.

[82] For criticism of Dr. Clifford, see "Dr. Clifford," *Southern Baptist*, 2 November 1899, 230; "Dr. Clifford," *Southern Baptist*, 1 February 1900, 25. For criticism of Stead, see "'War Against War'," *Southern Baptist*, 29 March 1900, 73. For criticism of Noncon-formists in Britain, see "We Cannot Understand," *Southern Baptist*, 1 February 1900, 26. For criticism of the Pope's view of the Boers, see "The Sympathy of the Pope," *Southern Baptist*, 29 March 1900, 74. For criticism of an Irish MP who laughed at Brit-ish misfortune, see "The Laughter of Fools," *Southern Baptist*, 26 March 1902, 75. For a defense of Rhodes' and Jameson's conduct before the war, see "Was the Hon. Cecil Rhodes," *Southern Baptist*, 12 April 1900, 85.

[83] James Moffatt, "A Johannesburg Minister's View of the War," *Southern Baptist*, 15 February 1900, 47; "One of the Most Damaging Facts," *Southern Baptist*, 3 May 1900,

The war against the Boers was deemed to be more than just a legitimate defensive war to protect Britain's colonies, for there were a number of touted reasons to fight that bolstered the claims of justice. The alleged deplorable condition of the Outlanders, the mistreatment of the "blacks," and the spread of missions were all portrayed to be righteous causes for which the empire was fighting.[85] While war was a heinous evil that should be avoided if at all possible, it was, at times, considered to be a necessary evil - the war in South Africa being one of those times.[86]

Commentary in the *Baptist* on the justice of the war continued into mid-1900, but was virtually nonexistent thereafter. Whether or not the editorial decision was due to the paper's antiwar position is uncertain, but what is known is that an antiwar position could lead to a reduction in circulation.[87] Responses to the change of fortunes on the battlefield revealed subtleties within the paper's position. In March 1900, when British successes on the battlefield became more frequent, the paper expressed a "hopeful outlook" on the war.[88] It still "opposed the war," but believed that the "best thing all around will be for the victory to be with our own side." The underlying conviction was an ardent patriotism fused to a confidence in the blessings of British imperial rule:

> We deplore our country's mistakes, but we love her notwithstanding. It is to be hoped that the recent decided British victories will lead up to a speedy cessation of bloodshed, and the establishment of righteous rule in the area over which war has raged. Detesting jingoism, we believe that the dominancy of Britain in South Africa will mean security, justice and liberty [89]

An article in response to the relief of Mafeking in May 1900 reveals similar nuances; the relief of the besieged town was cause for rejoicing, and the conduct of the defenders to be "universally admired."[90] Nevertheless, the impact of the war on attitudes to violence, especially the "flippant record of slaughter," was "debasing" and corrosive of Christian virtues. As will be noted in the following chapter, support for a British victory (whether or not Britain was to blame for the outbreak of war) was also rooted in the conviction that a British

---

98; "The Conflicting Statements," *Southern Baptist*, 2 August 1900, 170; "Vindicating British Honour," *Southern Baptist*, 26 March 1902, 75.

[84] "Peace," *Southern Baptist*, 11 June 1902, 133.

[85] For instance, see "The Outlander's Grievances," *Southern Baptist*, 1 February 1900, 25; "What the Boer War Is All About," *Southern Baptist*, 18 January 1900, 75; James Moffatt, "A Johannesburg Minister's View of the War," *Southern Baptist*, 15 February 1900, 47.

[86] "War Is a Necessary Evil," *Southern Baptist*, 15 February 1900, 37; "We Hate War," *Southern Baptist*, 15 March 1900, 61.

[87] Penny, "Australia's Reactions to the Boer War," 115; Judd and Surridge, *The Boer War*, 252.

[88] "A Hopeful Outlook," *Baptist*, 10 March 1900, 2.

[89] "A Hopeful Outlook," *Baptist*, 10 March 1900, 2.

[90] "The Relief of Mafeking," *Baptist*, 2 June 1900, 1.

victory would be good for the advancement of missions - something that even the *Baptist* endorsed.[91]

Morrison maintains that "theological and philosophical thinking about missions in late-nineteenth and early-twentieth century New Zealand were not easily disentangled from language extolling the virtues of Western civilization, and more particularly those of the British Empire." Central ideas among supporters of empire in the churches were that empire was a means to international unity, the empire was providentially established, the empire exhibited superior moral qualities, and the notion of trusteeship of "lesser" races. Those imperial sentiments were bolstered by the shared British cultural and familial roots of New Zealanders, including New Zealand Baptists. Sinclair argues that both New Zealand and Canada shared a commitment to the empire out of a fear of a larger and looming neighbor; for Canada it was the United States and for New Zealanders it was Australia. He asserts there was a New Zealand nationalism, but it was slow to develop independent of imperial identity.[92] Belich claims that the late-nineteenth century waves of British immigrants made for a colony that was "Better British" – an ideology that stressed the British identity of New Zealanders, and even their superiority over other colonies and even Britain itself.[93] The manifestations of imperial zeal during the war, he argues, need to be seen as manifestations of this British identity, and that "Better Britonism" lasted well into the twentieth century. As others have noted, however, the war did begin a trajectory towards the development of a New Zealand national identity.[94] These imperial commitments, trajectories, and ambiguities can be seen in the Zealand Baptist responses to the war.

Constitutionally, New Zealand was involved in the war "whether it liked it or not," although it was under no obligation to send troops.[95] Just as in Canada and Australia, the sendoff of the first contingent in Wellington on 21 October 1899 indicated strong public support for the imperial effort. Across New Zealand, there was widespread support for the war and the sending of contingents, with no significant domestic debate on, or opposition to, the war.[96] With Governor Lord Ranfurly and Premier Richard John Seddon providing speeches on the righteousness of the war, and 40,000 (1/20 of the population of New Zealand) cheering people in attendance, the departing troops were assured of wide-

---

[91] "The Partition of Africa," *Baptist*, 4 May 1900, 8.

[92] Sinclair, *A Destiny Apart*, 108.

[93] Belich, *Paradise Reforged*, 78.

[94] Crawford with Ellis, *To Fight for the Empire*, 93.

[95] McGibbon, "The Origins of New Zealand's South African War Contribution," 2.

[96] Crawford with Ellis, *To Fight for the Empire*, 25-29. See also McGibbon, *The Oxford Companion to New Zealand Military History*, 59; McGibbon, *The Path to Gallipoli*, 106, 108-109, 112; McKinnon, "Opposition to the War in New Zealand"; Hutching, "New Zealand Women's Opposition to the South African War"; Ellis, "New Zealand Women and the War"; McGibbon, "The Origins of New Zealand's South African War Contribution," 10; Hall, *The New Zealanders in South Africa*.

spread political and public backing for their cause.[97] Zeal for the imperial cause was also displayed in other war-related celebrations such as the relief of Mafeking. While support for, or attention to, the war may have waned during the guerilla campaign, the exuberant celebrations at the end of the war suggests a deep unwavering endorsement for the conflict that remained constant throughout the war.[98] Ellen Ellis' work reveals that even the majority of New Zealand women were "an active force" supporting the war effort.[99]

Both Malcolm McKinnon and Megan Hutching have shown that not all New Zealanders were supporters of the war.[100] McKinnon notes that opposition to the war was based on a number of factors, such as pacifism, anti-capitalism, Gladstonian liberalism, Irish nationalism (a link was seen between the struggle for rights of Boers and the Irish in Ireland), and war weariness. Hutching demonstrates how the National Council of Women (NCW) opposed the war due to a commitment to international arbitration as a way to settle disputes and the natural concern mothers had for their sons. There was limited criticism and opposition from members of parliament, and, while there may have been undercurrents of concern for New Zealand and the empire,[101] public opinion seemed "overwhelmingly in favour" of the government's pro-British response.[102] Those few who did go public with their criticism of the war sometimes faced a strong "backlash" for their seemingly disloyal statements.[103] The position of the *New Zealand Baptist* was that war was evil, but a dishonorable peace was worse.[104]

Such widespread popular support for the imperial cause was mirrored in the pages of the *New Zealand Baptist*, with only one or two "heroic souls" who spoke out against the war.[105] Baptist responses to victories such as the relief of Mafeking demonstrated that – at least in the minds of some – they were "se-

---

[97] Crawford with Ellis, *To Fight for the Empire*. 7-21.

[98] Crawford with Ellis, *To Fight for the Empire*. 84, 90.

[99] Ellis, "New Zealand Women and the War."

[100] McKinnon, "Opposition to the War in New Zealand"; Hutching, "New Zealand Women's Opposition to the South African War," 46-57.

[101] "Nevertheless, it would be a mistake to dismiss New Zealand's action as purely the result of imperial patriotism. As on similar later occasions, imperial sentiment masked an apprehension of the problem at the centre of conflict and a concern for New Zealand's long-term interests." McGibbon, "The Origins of New Zealand's South African War Contribution," 10.

[102] Politician's criticism revolved around British statesmanship leading up to the war. Hall claims that there were "hysterical forms" of public and popular support for the war. See Hall, *The New Zealanders in South Africa*, 3, 87.

[103] Sinclair, *A Destiny Apart*, 126.

[104] "From War," *New Zealand Baptist*, May 1900, 65.

[105] Guy, "Baptist Pacifists in New Zealand," 491. See also Guy, *Shaping Godzone*, 241-242.

cond to none" in their patriotic zeal.[106] The *New Zealand Baptist's* commentary in the opening weeks of the war was limited due to the paper being published once a month. In the first issue published since the war's commencement, the paper made it clear that blind jingoism was not Christian patriotism, nor was revenge for Majuba Hill a valid reason to go to war.[107] The actual cause of the war in South Africa, however, was deemed to be "justifiable and honoura- ble,"[108] and as a result the paper supported the sending of New Zealand troops to the conflict. As for the Boers and their intentions, President Kruger was por- trayed as one who did not actually want war, but due to his miscalculation in pushing Britain to the brink he lost control of the situation and his army forced his hand.[109] But rest assured, the paper encouraged, Britain was not in danger: "[I]t is dangerous at any lime (sic) to play with edged weapons, but when those weapons are British swords, the danger is intense. The die is cast. We can only watch the sorrowful progress of events. Don Quixote has, with many a Puritan- ical prayer, charged the windmill;- (sic) we are not much concerned for the windmill."[110]

The antiwar position of certain English Baptists and their paper the *Baptist Times and Freeman* was perplexing for New Zealand supporters of the war.[111] Frank W. Boreham, editor of the *New Zealand Baptist*, popular and prolific writer, as well as president of the Baptist Union (1900), was "much in demand for patriotic meetings in support of Britain."[112] He too was perplexed with John Clifford, Thomas Spurgeon and Archibald B. Brown's attitudes towards the war.[113] Boreham made it clear to the readers of the *New Zealand Baptist* why he supported the war effort. He also braved criticism by printing an antiwar article. The April 1900 issue of the *New Zealand Baptist* included a substantial article by S.R. Ingold, secretary of Oxford Terrace Baptist Church, Christ- church, on the appropriate Christian attitude towards the war.[114] Ingold claimed that the war was a just one and that a British defeat would be a catastrophe. In response, an anti-war article appeared the following month, authored by Rev. J.J. Doke of the same church in Christchurch. The paper did not endorse Doke's position, but nonetheless it was considered to be important to present

---

[106] "Chit Chat," *New Zealand Baptist*, June 1900, 96. See also "A Nation of Patriots," *New Zealand Baptist*, February 1900, 17-18; "NZBMS," *New Zealand Baptist*, February 1900, 25-26.

[107] "Our Contingent," *New Zealand Baptist*, November 1899, 170.

[108] "Our Contingent," *New Zealand Baptist*, November 1899, 170.

[109] "The Die Is Cast," *New Zealand Baptist*, November 1899, 169.

[110] "The Die Is Cast," *New Zealand Baptist*, November 1899, 169.

[111] "English Baptists and the War," *New Zealand Baptist*, March 1900, 40; "Why This Thusness?," *New Zealand Baptist*, March 1900, 40-41.

[112] Clifford, *A Handful of Grain*, 68.

[113] Clifford, *A Handful of Grain*, 68, 114.

[114] S.R. Ingold, "The War in South Africa: The Christian's Proper Attitude Regarding It," *New Zealand Baptist*, April 1900, 61-62.

the opposite case to readers.[115] This display of fairness was a significant departure from the conduct of more jingoistic papers, as well as a contribution to domestic civility – something lacking among those ardent supporters of nation and empire. It was also a dangerous move in regards to job security, for as the *New Zealand Baptist* noted, a number of newspaper editors had been fired due to their pro-Boer position.[116] Related to the issue of job security, Rev. Doke ended up resigning from his position sixteen months later primarily due to the tensions with congregants over his view of the war. He also had stones thrown through his parsonage window by irked supporters of the war.[117]

Britain was considered to have been forced into war by the Boer preparations and their declaration of war.[118] Although they had not wanted to fight, the paper's conviction was that a British victory would not only advance the cause of peace, civilization, and Christianity, but also that of the "natives."[119] A British loss was simply unfathomable, for the empire itself would begin to unravel. Did New Zealanders want to see India fall to Russia? Did they want to become a French colony? "God forbid," concluded one article.[120] However, with the fall of the empire, the cause of justice around the world would suffer, for the providential blessings of empire upon the world would also come to an end. Of course, the Boers did not see it that way at the moment, but, it was argued, in twenty years or so they would be thankful for British victory.[121] A number of articles used the same type of language: a British victory would bring "lasting influence for good,"[122] a "temporal, mental, moral and spiritual uplifting,"[123] and "peace, and liberty, and justice."[124] At the war's end, the *New Zealand Baptist* reiterated these same sentiments when it published a poem celebrating the end of the war and a British victory:

> Abide with us, sweet Peace! And may no more
> Britain's supremacy depend on war -
> But on her justice, truth and liberty,
> And in the power she holds to make men free![125]

---

[115] "The Rev. J.J. Doke on the War," *New Zealand Baptist*, May 1900, 73. See also Clifford, *A Handful of Grain*, 114.

[116] "Chit Chat," *New Zealand Baptist*, March 1900, 48.

[117] Guy, *Shaping Godzone*, 242. See also Laurie Guy, "Three Countries, Two Conversions, One Man: J. J. Doke: Baptists, Humanity and Justice," in *Interfaces: Baptists and Others*, eds., David Bebbington and Martin Sutherland (Milton Keynes: Paternoster, 2013), 271-273.

[118] S.R. Ingold," *New Zealand Baptist*, April 1900, 61-62.

[119] Forced Against Our Will," *New Zealand Baptist*, April 1900, 49.

[120] S.R. Ingold," *New Zealand Baptist*, April 1900, 61-62.

[121] "The March to Pretoria," *New Zealand Baptist*, January 1900, 9.

[122] "The Warriors Taking Their Rest," *New Zealand Baptist*, February 1900, 24.

[123] "We Are Pro-Boers," *New Zealand Baptist*, April 1900, 49.

[124] "Peace, Liberty, and Justice," *New Zealand Baptist*, April 1900, 49.

[125] Alice G. Ford, "*New Zealand Baptist*, July 1902, 109.

British authorities were initially optimistic that that Cape Colony and Natal colonists would not be needed to crush the Boers. As a result, the war was initially envisioned to be a war fought by the British Army against the two Boer republics. By the end of the war, volunteer South African colonists joined in the fighting and local Africans were issued arms for what was supposed to have been a white man's war. The presence of Boers in British territory (a majority in some places) meant that the British not only had to worry about Boers in the Transvaal and Orange Free State, but also needed to be concerned about a pro-Boer uprising within their own colonies. The successful wartime excursions of Boer commandoes into the Cape Colony and Natal stoked these fears, for if they continued they could have encouraged an uprising. Fortunately for the British, no uprisings occurred. When the war ended, British, Canadian, Australian and New Zealand soldiers returned to lands untouched by war. However, victorious Cape Colony and Natal troops returned home to an uncertain future marked by economic troubles, destroyed property, and racial tensions.

Ian van der Waag notes that the war was a traumatic experience for South Africa. He summarizes how past writing on the war has reflected the shifting loyalties and oft-tortuous history of the racially divided nation, and how there is still today a need for a history that avoids repeating the myths of the past.[126] As for the immediate impact of the war, Britain's stated aim of absorbing the two republics into the empire was achieved with the signing of the Treaty of Vereeniging on 31 May 1902; the two republics were to come under the sovereignty of the British Crown. Less than a decade later, on 31 May 1910, the Union of South Africa was formed, with the key leaders of the new Dominion being Boers. The British had won the war, but in many ways the Boers had won the peace. Despite the war being fought, in part, to alleviate the suffering of the "blacks" under Boer rule, the real losers were the very "blacks" whose plight had quickly been forgotten by the British in their desire for peace and harmony in their new conquest. Apartheid would soon follow.

Many nonconformists in South Africa were distraught by their pro-Boer coreligionists in Britain.[127] Cuthbertson notes that nonconformist support can be seen in the number of ministers that volunteered to be chaplains. He also argues that the majority of nonconformists echoed the sentiments of Bishop Bransby Key of St. John's Kaffraria in the Eastern Cape Colony who believed that a British victory would advance the cause of missions among the "natives." The most significant nonconformist opponents of the war were the Dutch Reformed churches, however, there were a few individual British ministers that openly declared their pro-Boer position, often facing the wrath of colleagues and parishioners for doing so. South African Baptists, as Frederick Hale argues, had a pre-war history of supporting the advancement of the empire if it meant that

---

[126] van der Waag, "War Memories," 180-204.
[127] For the following comments on South African nonconformity, see Cuthbertson, "Pricking the 'Nonconformist Conscience.'"

British mission work could gain a foothold in new lands. Once the war had been declared, only a few Baptists differed from the shrill calls for British victory. In fact, prominent Baptists assumed "pro-war stances which even some Anglican ecclesiastics in southern Africa would have rejected."[128] However, the editor of the *South African Baptist* attempted to ensure that his paper was not the mouthpiece for radical pro-war advocates.

As tensions rose in the summer, the editor of the *South African Baptist* declared that he prayed - unlike other "partisan newspapers" - for peace and against war with all his might.[129] With that hope for peace in mind, the disappointment expressed after war was declared makes more sense:

> It is war – always horrid, always cruel, and almost always mad. To the dread arbitrament of the sword the South African situation is now referred, and there is nothing more at present to be said. Whatever we may think of the occasion of the struggle, there is nothing out of place in a religious organ expressing its repugnance to war as a means of adjustment.[130]

Such repugnance arose from the fact that those in South Africa would have to bear the brunt of the war's trauma and devastation. First, the war was already turning into the nightmare of a civil war, with some congregations having sons on both sides of the conflict. Second, there was fear for the scattered congregations that would be destroyed and the Baptist "labour of long years reduced to the ashes of an almost irretrievable dissolution."[131] Anxiety was heightened all the more because contact had already been lost with a number of churches and pastors. Special concern was also expressed for a number of pastors and churches in the two Boer Republics – what would become of them?[132] Third, the war would "exasperate racial animosities" (mainly Boer and Briton), something that would make for a grim future once the war had ended. With this in mind, even though the paper expressed its patriotism as "strong and unchallengeable," it also exhorted its readers to make sure that they did not display "personal bitterness of vulgar gloating over bloody victories."[133] Rather, what was needed to be done was to pray for those churches in peril as well as the country and the Queen, and to trust in God's sovereignty in the midst of the present upheavals.[134]

Van der Waag claims that the war has "always been controversial" in South Africa, and that the teaching of history was banned in the British occupied new

---

[128] Hale, "Captives of British Imperialism." For a brief discussion of Baptists and the war, as well as the larger context of Baptists and social justice in South Africa, see Hale, "The Baptist Union of South Africa and Apartheid."

[129] "Kept in Pace," *South African Baptist*, September 1899, 21-22.

[130] "A Settlement by Thunderbolts," *South African Baptist*, November 1899, 53-54.

[131] "A Settlement by Thunderbolts," *South African Baptist*, November 1899, 53-54.

[132] "On the Editorial Stoep," *South African Baptist*, November 1899, 61.

[133] "A Settlement by Thunderbolts," *South African Baptist*, November 1899, 53-54.

[134] "A Settlement by Thunderbolts," *South African Baptist*, November 1899, 53-54; "On the Editorial Stoep," *South African Baptist*, November 1899, 61.

republics until a British-colonial view could be taught.[135] Seemingly aware of such tensions in South Africa, the editor of the *South African Baptist* sought to avoid enflaming passions that would make a united future under British rule an impossibility. He stated that the shutting down of the paper in the opening months of 1900 had actually been a blessing in disguise, for its shutting down had kept it from printing material that would only have enflamed enemies of the empire and divided the various races of the land.

> We have been silent for six months. And the wisdom of our suspension of this journal for that period is more manifest to us now than it was at the beginning of it. When feeling is strong it is wise to hold the tongue in firm control, and our silence has at least been a golden preservative against two evils. We have had no controversy amongst ourselves amid the dim of arms, nor have we fed the unholy forces of racial hatred.[136]

While other denominations may have made "verbose resolutions," it was felt that such partisan and jingoistic statements would hinder the true work of the church in the postwar years - the work of uniting, civilizing and Christianizing of the diverse peoples of South Africa.[137]

Despite its claim to be non-partisan,[138] the position of the paper was clearly one of loyalty to the imperial cause. Admiration for the monarchy was sprinkled throughout the paper. Also, articles expressing loyalty to the monarchy increased in number during the months after Queen Victoria's death.[139] In the opening weeks of the war, Baptist patriotism was declared to be "strong and unchallengeable."[140] During the first wartime Christmas, the paper grieved the fact that the angel of death was in the land and that the angels announcing peace were mocked by the war.[141] At the same time, it celebrated the uniting of the empire and prayed for "the speedy and merciful accomplishment of the purposes of her Majesty's Generals and the forces under them."[142] A British

---

[135] van der Waag, "War Memories."

[136] "The New Era in S. Africa," *South Africa*, July 1900, 101-102.

[137] "The New Era in S. Africa," *South Africa*, July 1900, 101-102.

[138] "Kept in Peace," *South African Baptist*, September 1899, 21-22.

[139] "V.R.I," *South African Baptist*, February 1901, 13-14; "On the Editorial Stoep," *South African Baptist*, March 1901, 30-31; "The Queen and Religious Liberty," *South African Baptist*, March 1901, 31; "Catholics and the Late Queen," *South African Baptist*, March 1901, 32-33; "The Queen and the Cadet," *South African Baptist*, March 1901, 33; "Port Elizabeth," *South African Baptist*, March 1901, 36; "Baptist Union of South Africa," *South African Baptist*, June 1901, 61-65; E. Baker, "The Presidential Address," *South African Baptist*, July 1901, 77-83; "To Their Royal Highnesses The Duke and Duchess of Cornwall," *South African Baptist*, August 1901, 91; "God Save the King," *South African Baptist*, May 1902, 50; John P. Hobson, "Coronation Hymn," *South African Baptist*, June 1902, 62; "God Save the King," *South African Baptist*, July 1902, 73; "The King's Coronation," *South African Baptist*, August 1902, 85-86.

[140] "A Settlement by Thunderbolts," *South African Baptist*, November 1899, 53-54.

[141] "Christmas Shadows," *South African Baptist*, December 1899, 69-70.

[142] "Christmas Shadows," *South African Baptist*, December 1899, 69-70.

victory would not only preserve the British presence in Natal and Cape Colony, it would also guarantee a continuation of the blessings of British rule. Like their coreligionists in the other colonies, it was assumed that the extension of British rule in Africa had brought blessing to its subjects and a British defeat would be a disaster.[143] The Baptist minister H.J. Batts experienced the opening months of the war from within Pretoria. After Pretoria's capture by the British he wrote a book recounting his experience, and within its pages he celebrated the liberation of Pretoria. In his view, a British advance and Boer defeat were in the best interests of justice and that in time the Boers would come to appreciate living under the Union Jack since it was "the flag which guarantees freedom and justice and equal rights to all."[144]

While there are a ample examples in the *South African Baptist* that Baptists regarded themselves as loyal citizens of the empire, there were a few items in its pages that indicated both a reserved patriotism and criticism of aspects of imperialism. For instance, in the same article that announced the outbreak of war and declared that Baptist patriotism was "strong and unchallengeable" it was also stated that war was "always horrid, always cruel, and almost always mad. ... Whatever we may think of the occasion of the struggle, there is nothing out of place in a religious organ expressing its repugnance to war as a means of adjustment."[145] Such statements were not exactly a ringing endorsement of a military solution to the problems with the Boers. An even more startling inclusion in its pages is a poem entitled "The Brown Man's Burden" which turns Kipling's "The White Man's Burden" on its head (a poem printed in the *South African Baptist* in the previous year[146]) by revealing the hypocrisy and harm of imperial attitudes towards Africans. A portion of it reads:

Pile on the brown man's burden
To gratify your greed;
Go clear away the "niggers"
Who progress would impede;
Be very stern, for truly
'Tis useless to be mild
With new-caught, sullen peoples,
Half devil and half child./
Pile on the brown man's burden;
And if ye rouse his hate,
Meet his old fashioned reasons
With Maxims up to date.
With shells and dumdum bullets
A hundred times make plain

---

[143] "One thing would stagger humanity more than the price of Britain's victory, that would be her defeat." See "The Great War," *South African Baptist*, January 1900, 85-86.
[144] Batts, *Pretoria from Within During the War*, 231.
[145] "A Settlement by Thunderbolts," *South African Baptist*, November 1899, 53-54.
[146] Rudyard Kipling, "The White Man's Burden," *South African Baptist*, October 1899, 38.

The brown man's loss must ever
Imply the white man's gain./
Pile on the brown man's burden,
Compel him to be free;
Let all your manifestoes
Reek with philanthropy.
And if with heathen folly
He dares your will dispute,
Then in the name of freedom
Don't hesitate to shoot.[147]

Of course the inclusion of one poem does not mean that there was a widespread recognition of the sins of empire, but its inclusion should at least cause one to pause before assuming too much about South African Baptist infatuation with imperialism.[148]

The end of war was announced in the July 1902 issue with a poem and brief article. The poem "Peace!" looked forward to the commerce, farming, and home life that would follow in the wake of the peace settlement. It also expressed the hope of reconciliation between Briton and Boer:

O soul, uplift thyself
To God in song!
O heart, put far from thee
All thought of wrong!
O hand, clasp brother-hand
In union strong!/
Contempt, and bitter hate,
And envy, cease!
Briton and Boer, one brotherhood,
In love increase!
For God has sent to us
His Angel Peace.[149]

The article of the same title expressed the identical hope for reconciliation between the two white races of South Africa, with no mention of the Africans for which the war was purported to have been fought.[150] A brand new era was deemed to be ushered in by the British victory. There was a need to reconcile quickly Boer and Briton for there were deep divisions in the land that needed to be healed: "We need not boast of it, but we know how to treat a valiant foe. As we are to live with each other in the country, the sooner we make friends the better. Our overtures may perhaps in some cases meet with distrust and coldness, engendered by the recent strife, but a genial and hearty advance of broth-

---

[147] "The Brown Man's Burden," *South African Baptist*, December 1900, 170.

[148] For instance, see Hale, "Captives of British Imperialism." For a brief discussion of Baptist and the war, as well as the larger context of Baptists and social justice in South Africa, see Hale, "The Baptist Union of South Africa and Apartheid."

[149] G.W. Cross, "Peace!" *South African Baptist*, July 1902, 73.

[150] "Peace!" *South African Baptist*, July 1902, 74.

erhood will ultimately break the artificial barriers of reserve, suspicion and prejudice."[151] And in the coming years the churches were to have a critical role in the healing and unification of the new country.

The war was initially supported by a majority of Britons. The "Khaki Election" in 1900 was fought primarily over the war: the Conservative government of Prime Minister Lord Salisbury won, his cause bolstered by the recent triumphs of the British on the battlefield. However, from the onset of war start there was a significant pro-Boer element.[152] The churches in Britain were divided over the war. The Church of England was virtually unanimous in its support for the war effort, the conviction being that Britain's cause was righteous and needed to be defended.[153] However, Mark Allen's recent research into the Church of England and the war indicates that the attitudes to the war were complex, nuanced, and, in a certain number of cases, in opposition to the war.[154] While the roots of opposition to the war were not always religious, the nonconformist conscience was "pricked" by the war and there were considerable ruptures among the nonconformists.[155]

Mounting tensions were reported in the *Baptist Times and Freeman* during the summer and early fall, with hope expressed that war could be avoided.[156] Some of the *Baptist Times and Freeman's* early commentary on the outbreak of war was not controversial, such as its concern for soldier's families or the church in South Africa.[157] However, the *Baptist Times and Freeman* quickly admitted that its views on the war would "seem tame and unpopular at such a moment," but that made them "all the more necessary to be expressed."[158] Unlike a number of their Baptist counterparts in other parts of the empire, the *Baptist Times and Freeman* made it clear in the first week of the war that the jingo-

---

[151] "Peace!" *South African Baptist*, July 1902, 74.

[152] For support for the war, see Blanch, "British Society and the War," 210-237. For opposition to the war, see Davey, *The British Pro-Boers*; Laity, "The British Peace Movement and the War"; Jeeves, "Hobson's *the War in South Africa*," 233-246; Nash, "Taming the God of Battles"; Porter, "The Pro-Boers in Britain"; McCracken, *The Irish Pro-Boers*.

[153] Blunden, "The Anglican Church during the War," 279-291; Chapman, "Theological Responses in England to the South African War."

[154] Allen, "Winchester, the Clergy and the Boer War."

[155] Cuthbertson's expression. See Cuthbertson, "Pricking the 'Nonconformist Conscience.'"

[156] "Parliament and the Transvaal Crisis," *Baptist Times and Freeman*, 4 August 1899, 513; "Britishers and Boers," *Baptist Times and Freeman*, 18 August 1899, 558; "The Transvaal Troubles," *Baptist Times and Freeman*, 4 August 1899, 518; "The Transvaal Crisis," *Baptist Times and Freeman*, 1 September 1899, 577; "Peace!" *Baptist Times and Freeman*, 22 September 1899, 637; "Mr. Chamberlain's Defence," *Baptist Times and Freeman*, 27 October 1899, 737.

[157] "Help for Soldier's Families," *Baptist Times and Freeman*, 24 November 1899, 802; "The Baptist Denomination in South Africa," *Baptist Times and Freeman*, 17 November 1899, 793-794.

[158] "Peace in War," *Baptist Times and Freeman*, 20 October 1899, 728.

istic imperialism manifesting itself throughout Britain was unChristian, arbitration not too late, and the outbreak of war a lamentable affair brought about in no small measure due to the mistakes and arrogance of British diplomacy.[159] In the months that followed, the *Baptist Times and Freeman* walked a fine line between criticizing the government for causing the war and supporting the troops in South Africa. The following editorial reveals just how these two arguments were developed in tandem:

> [T]he Boers have had abundant justification of the fear of British designs upon their independence, and upon Boer supremacy within the Transvaal; that Mr. Chamberlain's conduct of negotiations was provocative, while British preparations for war were a menace and a threat which almost warranted the Boers in commencing hostilities before resistance became hopeless. At the same time, it should not be forgotten that there is much to be urged in favour of a South African Federation, inclusive of the Transvaal and the Orange Free State; that equality of rights as between white men throughout and all over South Africa is desirable; and that one supreme authority is far preferable to three co-ordinate and equal authorities in South Africa.[160]

The issue was not that the advancement of British rule would be harmful to the inhabitants of South Africa (British, Boer and "black"). In fact, assuming the moral, temporal and spiritual benefits of British rule, the *Baptist Times and Freeman* made it clear that it hoped Britain would win the war in order to advance the humanitarian benefits of British rule.[161] Although it was noted that there was an element of hypocrisy to Britain's stated aim of freeing the "blacks" due to Britain's past involvement in the slave trade.[162]

There is widespread evidence that Baptist opposition to the war did not indicate a lack of patriotism or support for the empire, although certainly some at that time would have interpreted it to be just that. Despite opposing war as a means to settle the dispute, and a conviction that Britain did not do all that it could do to avoid war (and, in fact, precipitated it), once war was declared the hope expressed was that Britain would win. Baptists were patriotic, and both those who supported the war and those who opposed it wanted Britain to be victorious in battle. Debates over the causes of the war needed to be put aside for energy needed to be invested in winning the war.[163] Humanitarian concerns

---

[159] "The Transvaal War," *Baptist Times and Freeman*, 20 October 1899, 721; "Peace in War," *Baptist Times and Freeman*, 20 October 1899, 728.
[160] "The Transvaal War," *Baptist Times and Freeman*, 10 November 1899, 769.
[161] See also "To-day's Military Situation," *Baptist Times and Freeman*, 10 November 1899, 769; "Lord Loch on the War," *Baptist Times and Freeman*, 15 December 1899, 853.
[162] "The Stain on the British Flag," *Baptist Times and Freeman*, 16 February 1900, 130-131.
[163] "The Transvaal War," *Baptist Times and Freeman*, 22 December 1899, 869; "Midway through the War," *Baptist Times and Freeman*, 19 January 1900, 50-51; "The Jameson Raid," *Baptist Times and Freeman*, 2 March 1900, 161; "The Present War," *Baptist Times and Freeman*, 19 January 1900, 46; "South Africa," *Baptist Times and*

dictated that they hope for a short war and a British victory.[164] Once the war had begun, the argument of many was that the best end to the war would be a victory for the British, "blacks" and even the Boers.[165] Because of the anticipated humanitarian gains of a British victory, support was expressed for annexation and a South African Federation; again, it was lamentable that it had to come through force.[166] There were also examples of Baptist support for the army, navy, defense against foes such as the French, and the learning of lessons so that Britain performed better in its next war.[167] After the new King's speech in February 1901, support was expressed for defending the nation, but not for conquest: "Whether or no, we must resolve that out army shall only be become an engine of defence, and not a weapon for the royal game of war."[168] A resolution to the new King by the Baptist Union of Great Britain and Ireland, in its Spring Assembly, 1901, at Bloomsbury Chapel, affirmed their patriotism.[169] The paper included articles that expressed support for Lord Roberts, hope for victory, pride in the defense of Mafeking, pleasure with ongoing battlefield victories, and even support for a responsible application of the "White Man's Burden" (expressed by none other than the antiwar Dr. Clifford!).[170]

Pro-Boer sentiment, as it was often called, was not appreciated by many in Britain. It was deemed to be unpatriotic and even a dangerous encouragement to the empire's enemies. However, Baptists opposed to the war claimed that they had the right to dissent, and to do so without fear of harm:

> At the bedrock of British liberty is the freedom of speech which is entitled to discuss, within the limits of decency and order, the questions of the day. The men whose speeches have been interrupted by rowdy disturbers, sheltering themselves under the misplaced title of 'patriots,' comprise many who have served their gen-

---

Freeman, 15 February 1901, 101; "South Africa," *Baptist Times and Freeman*, 5 April 1901, 213; "The Transvaal War," *Baptist Times and Freeman*, 20 October 1899, 721; "Better Tidings," *Baptist Times and Freeman*, 12 January 1900, 21; "The War," *Baptist Times and Freeman*, 12 January 1900, 21.

[164] "To-Day's Military Situation," *Baptist Times and Freeman*, 10 November 1899, 769.

[165] "Mr. Chamberlain's Defence," *Baptist Times and Freeman*, 27 October 1899, 737; "Lord Loch on the War," *Baptist Times and Freeman*, 15 December 1899, 853.

[166] "Annexation of the Transvaal," *Baptist Times and Freeman*, 7 September 1900, 717; "The Transvaal War," *Baptist Times and Freeman*, 10 November 1899, 769.

[167] "The New Armada," *Baptist Times and Freeman*, 23 March 1900, 226; "Lessons of the War," *Baptist Times and Freeman*, 13 April 1900, 294; "A Vigilance Committee," *Baptist Times and Freeman*, 6 July 1900, 538; "Lord Roberts and Army Reform," *Baptist Times and Freeman*, 30 May 1902, 397.

[168] "The King's Speech," *Baptist Times and Freeman*, 22 February 1901, 124-125.

[169] *Baptist Times and Freeman*, 26 April 1901, vi-vii (supplement to the *Baptist Times and Freeman*, 26 April 1901)

[170] "Lord Roberts and His Detractors," *Baptist Times and Freeman*, 24 August 1900, 678; "Annexation of the Transvaal," *Baptist Times and Freeman*, 7 September 1900, 717; "Mafeking," *Baptist Times and Freeman*, 25 May 1900, 413; "At Pretoria," *Baptist Times and Freeman*, 8 June 1900, 453; "Dr. Clifford's New Year Address," *Baptist Times and Freeman*, 4 January 1901, 14.

eration in the most distinguished manner....Imperialism is ill served by intemperate and thoughtless rioters.[171]

They urged parliament to defend freedom of speech, especially since those who spoke against the war often faced intimidation and threats of violence.[172]

What was most distressing to the *Baptist Times and Freeman* was that the advances in South Africa would now have to come through war, not peaceful persuasion and dialogue. Blame for the conflict was laid at the feet of Jameson, Rhodes, Chamberlain, the government, and the jingoes, for they had, in varying degrees, brought about the war through their conniving, bungling, deceiving, and manipulating of events.[173] The paper was also critical of Rhodes and the type of peace that he envisioned in South Africa: "Thus it will be if Rhodes and company have their way, for men who school themselves to 'see money' in every movement, and to 'finance' every enterprise, lose the finer instincts of patriotism, and grovel for gold in the graves of their dead heroes."[174] As if damning the motives and actions of Britain's leaders was not controversial enough, the paper printed the lyrics of the Boer national hymn (lyrics that portrayed the British as despots and the Boers as freedom-fighting lovers of liberty), and an article that urged Britons to show "mutual respect and good will" for the Boers.[175] There was even praise for Kruger, portraying him as a modern-day Cromwell.[176] Challenging the simplicity of the jingoists and anti-war advocates, the issues were presented as more complicated than partisans on either side were willing to admit.[177] One article portrayed the Boers and British as both ignoring God: "We fear that in this war both Boers and British consult other than the Lord, and are not engaged in carrying out His purpose."[178] However, the majority of criticism in the *Baptist Times and Freeman* was directed at the British government.

---

[171] "Free Speech," *Baptist Times and Freeman*, 23 March 1900, 225.

[172] "Free Speech," *Baptist Times and Freeman*, 23 March 1900, 225; "Free Speech," *Baptist Times and Freeman*, 13 April 1900, 294.

[173] See also "Mr. Chamberlain's Defence," *Baptist Times and Freeman*, 27 October 1899, 737; "Lord Salisbury on the War," *Baptist Times and Freeman*, 17 November 1899, 785; "Lord Loch on the War," *Baptist Times and Freeman*, 15 December 1899, 853; "Mid-way through the War," *Baptist Times and Freeman*, 19 January 1900, 50-51; "A Baptist Missionary and Mr. Rhodes," *Baptist Times and Freeman*, 19 April 1901, 262; "The Third Year of the War," *Baptist Times and Freeman*, 18 October 1901, 697; "Lord Roseberry - Is It the Last Phase?" *Baptist Times and Freeman*, 26 July 1901, 493.

[174] "Wheresoever the Carcase Is," *Baptist Times and Freeman*, 30 March 1900, 260-261.

[175] "The Boer's National Hymn," *British Baptist Times and Freeman*, 1 December 1899, 821; "The Boers," *Baptist Times and Freeman*, 8 December 1899, 837.

[176] "South African News," *Baptist Times and Freeman*, 21 September 1900, 757.

[177] "The War in South Africa," *Baptist Times and Freeman*, 16 March 1900, 219.

[178] "Unmanly Fears," *Baptist Times and Freeman*, 5 January 1900, 9.

Hopes for peace were frequently reported on in the paper,[179] and key Baptist leaders worked towards ending the conflict. Clifford was instrumental in calling a meeting of nonconformist ministers in London at Memorial Hall in order to work on an agreeable statement regarding the terms of peace.[180] However, the government was accused of bungling attempts at bringing about a much earlier peace. As one author noted, the government's efforts were marked by "incompetence ... appalling ignorance ... [a] lack of energy ... [a] want of foresight."[181] The costs of the war were also chronicled and lamented.[182] Sadly, the paper grieved, the British had not heeded the prophetic call of the Quakers in regards to the present war and instead had become more enamored with war than being prophetic seekers of peace.[183]

But what had happened to the much touted British support for arbitration through the Hague, something that Britain had previously supported?[184] Had Britain's support for arbitration been nothing but a sham? One oft-repeated reason for opposition to the war was the government's refusal to place the dispute before a court of arbitration, especially since Britain had been so supportive of the recent developments in the Hague and the settlement with Venezuela.[185]

> Why not refer the matters in dispute to arbitration? Our representative at the Hague was the most influential of all the advocates of an International Court of Arbitration. Would it not be helpful to the peace of Christendom, and an object lesson for all the great Powers and for the whole world, if Great Britain, conscious of its might, consented to submit its case against the Government of the Transvaal to the judgment of impartial arbitrators?[186]

---

[179] "A Plea for Peace," *Baptist Times and Freeman*, 11 January 1901, 28-29; "General Botha's Refusal," *Baptist Times and* Freeman, 5 April 1901, 216; "South Africa," *Baptist Times and Freeman*, 29 March 1901, 197; "The South African Blue Book," *Baptist Times and Freeman*, 26 April 1901, 269; "The New Policy in South Africa," *Baptist Times and Freeman*, 23 August 1901, 561-562; "Prospects of Peace," *Baptist Times and Freeman*, 28 March 1902, 237; "Hopeful Signs in South Africa," *Baptist Times and Freeman*, 11 April 1902, 269; "The Prospects of Peace," *Baptist Times and Freeman*, 25 April 1902, 309; "The Peace Society and the Peace Negotiations," *Baptist Times and Freeman*, 1 May 1902, 330.

[180] "Conference on the Terms of Peace," *Baptist Times and Freeman*, 19 July 1901, 490.

[181] "The Third Year of the War," *Baptist Times and Freeman*, 18 October 1901, 697.

[182] "War Figures," *Baptist Times and Freeman*, 10 August 1900, 637.

[183] "The Friends and Peace," *Baptists Times and Freeman*, 20 July 1900, 584.

[184] "Intervention Repudiated," *Baptist Times and Freeman*, 17 November 1899, 785.

[185] "Britishers and Boers," *Baptist Times and Freeman*, 18 August 1899, 558; "At the Eleventh Hour," *Baptist Times and Freeman*, 13 October 1899, 705; "Intervention Repudiated," *Baptist Times and Freeman*, 17 November 1899, 785; "Peace and War," *Baptist Times and Freeman*, 22 December 1899, 869; "The King's Speech," *Baptist Times and Freeman*, 22 February 1901, 124-125.

[186] "Why Not Arbitrate?" *Baptist Times and Freeman*, 15 September 1899, 609.

Arbitration was considered to be the more "Christlike method of righting the differences which exist."[187] The Welsh Baptist Union expressed its wish for arbitration at its Annual Meeting at Rhymney, 1899.[188] But it was not to be, and disappointment ran deep for it was felt that an opportunity was lost to show to the world a radically new way to resolve disputes and to demonstrate the Christian character of Britain and its empire.

Key leaders such as Silas Hocking, Ian Maclaren and Clifford were opposed to the war.[189] Clifford was one of the most well-known voices against the war in and out of Baptist circles. Clifford's outspoken attacks on the acquiescence of churches to jingoistic imperialism made him a number of enemies, and, while Baptists *en masse* did not follow his antiwar position, his influence on Baptist opinion remained significant. He spent considerable energy verbalizing and organizing opposition to the conflict as a Baptist minister, executive member of the South Africa Conciliation Committee, and as president of the Stop the War Committee. For instance, the paper reported on a meeting of nonconformist ministers in London who met at Memorial Hall in order to work on an agreeable statement regarding the terms of peace. The meeting was called by, among others, Clifford.[190] He made numerous addresses on the war, including addresses to audiences of young people.[191]

A number of Baptist women were against the war,[192] as were several denominational church bodies. The London Baptist Association was deeply divided over the war, and in 1901 could not agree on a resolution on the war.[193] Baptists at the Welsh Baptist Union meetings at Porth, 1901, declared:

> That this Conference condemns the policy which led up to the present war, and strongly disapproves of the methods of farm burning and concentration camps as causes of unnecessary suffering, and leading to the prolongation of the war. Further, it desires earnestly a speedy termination of hostilities upon the basis of concession at the earliest possible moment, of full rights, citizenship, and self-government as enjoyed in Canada and Australia.[194]

A Free Church Peace Manifesto was freely circulated and found support among Baptists.[195] The *Baptist Times and Freeman* attempted at times to steer a mid-

---

[187] "The Transvaal War," *Baptist Times and Freeman*, 20 October 1899, 721.

[188] "The Transvaal Crisis," *Baptist Times and Freeman*, 8 September 1899, 598.

[189] "Dr. Watson on the War," *Baptist Times and Freeman*, 5 January 1900, 9.

[190] "Conference on the Terms of Peace," *Baptist Times and Freeman*, 19 July 1901, 490.

[191] For instance, see Dr. Clifford, "Brotherhood and the War in the Year 1899," *Baptist Times and Freeman*, 5 January 1900, 8; "Dr. Clifford's New Year's Address," *Baptist Times and Freeman*, 4 January 1900, 14.

[192] "Women and the War," *Baptist Times and Freeman*, 22 June 1900, 497.

[193] "London Baptist Association," *Baptist Times and Freeman*, 27 September 1901, 656.

[194] "Welsh Baptist Union," *Baptist Times and Freeman*, 26 July 1901, 504.

[195] "The Free Church Council and the War," *Baptist Times and Freeman*, 22 March 1901, 191; "Free Church Ministers and the War," *Baptist Times and Freeman*, 26 July

dle course, recognizing that its constituency was divided and the issues complex.[196] Some critics of the war considered the conflict in Africa a "monster evil," yet at the same time there was concern expressed over the antiwar conduct of some: "We regard it as unfortunate that some of those who have depreciated and denounced the South African war, and have pleaded for peace, have been pro-Boer, if not anti-British, in their sympathies."[197] It was claimed the Boers were just as "warlike" as the British, and that there was a "heavy responsibility" for the war that rests on the Boer leadership.

The much anticipated announcement of peace was met with relief and rejoicing.[198] The diversity of Baptist opinions on the war meant that there was no uniform sense that the war had been fought for justice, but imbedded in their commentary was the assumption that the Boers had been treated fairly by the terms of peace. It was also assumed that in the coming years British rule would hasten reconstruction and ultimately lead to the furtherance of justice and equal rights.

Just Means

By the beginning of 1901, it was becoming increasingly obvious that the tactics being used by the Boers had shifted. No longer willing and able to engage the British army in a traditional set-piece battle, the Boers resorted to guerrilla warfare. The British army accordingly changed its tactics. It began to burn the Boers' homes and farms in order to deprive the guerrillas of food, lodging, and support in the countryside. 30,000 homes were destroyed by the end of the war.[199] When the resulting devastation left women, children and the elderly without shelter or food, the British felt obliged to take care of the refuges. The solution that Kitchener devised in December 1900 was to concentrate those people into camps.[200] The supposed benefit of these "concentration camps" was to take care of the refugees, as well as eliminate any possible support for the Boers left in the field from those sympathetic to the Boer cause. The widespread rounding up of Boers into the camps began in earnest after a failed

---

1901, 496; "The Free Church Manifesto," *Baptist Times and Freeman*, 30 August 1901, 577.

[196] "The War in South Africa," *Baptist Times and Freeman*, 16 March 1900, 219.

[197] "A Plea for Peace," *Baptist Times and Freeman*, 11 January 1901, 28-29.

[198] "The Terms of Peace," *Baptist Times and Freeman*, 6 June 1902, 417; "The War - What It Has Cost," *Baptist Times and Freeman*, 6 June 1902, 417; "Peace - How the News was Received," *Baptist Times and Freeman*, 6 June 1902, 417-418; "Peace at last," *Baptist Times and Freeman*, 6 June 1902, 427; Rev. Charles Williams, "Thanksgiving Sunday," *Baptist Times and Freeman*, 13 June 1902, 440; Rev. Charles Williams, "The Work of Peace," *Baptist Times and Freeman*, 13 June 1902, 440.

[199] Martin Marix Evans, "Farm Burning," In *Encyclopedia of the Boer War, 1899-1902* (Santa Barbara: ABC Clio, 2000), 94.

[200] He may have copied this idea from the Spanish in Cuba in 1896. See Farwell, *The Great Anglo-Boer War*, 393.

meeting between Kitchener and Botha to discuss peace terms on 28 February 1901. By the end of the war, around 120,000 Boers, mainly women and children, were inmates of fifty camps.[201] Camps were also created for Bantu and Coloureds, but these camps were not the focus of the opposition's attention.[202]

According to critics, the fact that the British targeted women and children for internment was bad enough, but the treatment of people in the camps made their internment all the more appalling. The death rate was what was most shocking. Farwell estimates that the number of Boer children who died in the camps to be around 20,000 (not including Bantu and Coloured children), and the death rate ranged from a low of 20 per thousand to a high 344 per thousand (for children it was around 300 per thousand).[203] While the British military authorities argued for the necessity of the camps and declared that there was humane treatment of the Boers within the camps, opponents of the camps claimed that they were unjust and barbaric. Through the publicity of published eyewitness accounts such as Emily Hobhouse's, the camps caused a political furor back in Britain and around the Western world.[204] In varying degrees, this controversy was addressed by the Baptist press.

Readers of the *South African Baptist* would never have known of the controversy based on what was in the paper. A two-part article on the Boer prisoners at St. Helena by Rev. T. Aitken, chaplain of British forces in St. Helena, described the treatment of prisoners.[205] It was a generally positive description, noting the conditions of prisoners: "they are well-treated" and having a "re-

---

[201] Farwell, *The Great Anglo-Boer War*, 397.

[202] There were over 115,000 "natives" in camps by the end of the war. At least 14,154 died in the camps, with over 80% of these deaths being children. See Darrell Hall, *The Hall Handbook of the Anglo Boer War, 1899-1902* (Pietermaritzburg: University of Natal Press, 1999), 217. "Incidentally, it went barely noticed at the time [in the secular press] that at least as many blacks also died in their own segregated and even more poorly equipped and managed concentration camps." See Judd and Surridge, *The Boer War*, 196.

[203] He also notes that "As a basis of comparison, the average death rate in England at this time was 19 per thousand and today is less than 11 per thousand." See Farwell, *The Great Anglo-Boer War*, 392. For a different set of figures, see A. C. Martin, *The Concentration Camps, 1900-1902: Facts, Figures, and Fables* (Cape Town: Howard Timmons, 1957).

[204] Farwell, *The Great Anglo-Boer War*, 410. Criticisms of the British actions are still being published. For a contemporary example of such criticism, see Owen Coetzer, *Fire in the Sky: The Destruction of the Orange Free State, 1899-1902* (Weltevreden Park: Covos-Day Books, 2000).

[205] Rev. T. Aitken, "Boer Prisoners at St. Helena," *South African Baptist*, December 1900, 163-164; Rev. T. Aitken, "Boer Prisoners at St. Helena," *South African Baptist*, January 1901, 3.

markable good time."[206] The *New Zealand Baptist* made no mention at all of the controversy.

The Australian Baptist press paid scant attention to questions related to the means by which the war was being fought. There was the recognition that while the Boers could commit crimes in the carrying out of their war aims, so too could the British: there were "good and bad people fighting on both sides."[207] One also needed to exercise caution when reading reports of British misconduct for there was a "good deal of lying" in the newspapers.[208] As for comments directly related to the treatment of the Boers in prison camps, there was no admission or recognition that there had been anything amiss. In fact, the few articles that mentioned the treatment of Boer prisoners painted a fairly benign picture of life in captivity. For instance, articles mentioned that Boer prisoners were allowed special Sabbath Day activities,[209] and Boer prisoners held overseas were detained in model conditions that should be emulated back in South Africa:

> A visitor to the Boer prisoners in Ceylon says the burden of silent drudgery and patience required of those who undertake it here and elsewhere is one that is scarcely recognized by the British public, and is apt to be overlooked in the clash and din of arms. The hope is that when these enemies of our Empire are once more free, that they will carry back to their native land much useful experience, and teach their compatriots improved habits of hygiene and cleanliness, learned from the care bestowed upon them. At all events, they should return to their homes without any feelings of bitterness towards their captors, and moreover prepared to become loyal subjects of the Empire.[210]

Increased opposition to the war in Britain had arisen over reports of British methods, especially the concentration camps.[211] Accounts of British atrocities stirred the nonconformist conscience in Britain,[212] and concern over these reports can be seen in Baptist life.[213] For instance, Baptists at the Welsh Baptist Union summer meetings at Porth, 1901, declared: "That this Conference condemns the policy which led up to the present war, and strongly disapproves of the methods of farm burning and concentration camps as causes of unnecessary suffering, and leading to the prolongation of the war."[214] The *Baptist Times and Freeman* was also concerned about events in South Africa, and informed its readers of

---

[206] Rev. T. Aitken, "Boer Prisoners at St. Helena," *South African Baptist*, January 1901, 3.
[207] "As the War," *Southern Baptist*, 12 July 1900, 157. See also "Our Correspondent 'J'," *Southern Baptist*, 2 August 1900, 170; J, "Another Voice from South Africa," *Southern Baptist*, 2 August 1900, 178.
[208] "As the War," *Southern Baptist*, 12 July 1900, 157.
[209] "News in Brief," *Queensland Baptist*, July 1900, 94.
[210] "The Prisoners of War," *Southern Baptist*, 28 May 1902, 123.
[211] Blanch, "British Society and the War," 250.
[212] Richards, "Political Nonconformity at the Turn of the Twentieth Century," 256.
[213] Davey, *The British Pro-Boers,* 150-151.
[214] "Welsh Baptist Union," *Baptist Times and Freeman,* 26 July 1901, 504.

the concerns regarding the shift in tactics, treatment of prisoners and life in the concentration camps.

The shift in Boer tactics to a guerilla war was observed, and the brutality associated with that type of warfare lamented. One article regretted the fact that "guerrilla warfare inevitably degenerates into savagery," and that the war in South Africa was no exception to that maxim.[215] It was felt that "all the chivalry and glamour of war" was "vanishing" from the conflict, and what was replacing such romantic notions was "a mere lust of blood and thirst for revenge."[216] The treatment of Boer prisoners was identified in conjunction with an exhortation to treat them well since those very prisoners would be needed to rebuild South Africa after the war.[217] However, there was also criticism directed towards British treatment of their own wounded in South Africa. One article bemoaned, the "capacity of the Government for blundering is extraordinary. Increasingly it is becoming almost impossible to trust it in any manner."[218] Controversy over the conditions in the concentration camps was also bemoaned. The paper reported on Miss Hobhouse's visit to Liverpool and Maclaren's address at a meeting she attended in Manchester.[219] In his address to Hobhouse, Maclaren spoke approvingly of her message and invoked the idea that Britain's army should treat its Boer enemies like Christ said to treat one's enemies: "If thine enemy hunger feed him; If he thirst give him drink, for in doing so thou shalt heap coals of fire on his head."[220] Another article defended the actions of the British government when it came to motives. It declared "We do not for one moment believe that any English statesmen intended, or even contemplated" the disastrous situation in the concentration camps.[221] However, while its motives may have been above reproach, its mobilization in reaction to the disaster was where the British government had failed abysmally: "What we have condemned, and do condemn, is the apathy with which the problem has been faced, and the red tapeism which has so long delayed the needful reforms."[222] At the end of the war, allegations of widespread and intentional British crimes were addressed, and dismissed, in an editorial that proclaimed:

---

[215] "Degeneration," *Baptist Times and Freeman*, 6 September 1901, 593.
[216] "Degeneration," *Baptist Times and Freeman*, 6 September 1901, 593.
[217] "Prisoners of War," *Baptist Times and Freeman*, 21 September 1900, 758; "Our Boer Prisoners," *Baptist Times and Freeman*, 3 May 1901, 286.
[218] "The Hospital Scandal," *Baptist Times and Freeman*, 20 July 1900, 578; "In the Train of the War," *Baptist Times and Freeman*, 6 July 1900, 537-538; "The South African Scourge," *Baptist Times and Freeman*, 13 July 1900, 557.
[219] "Miss Hobhouse at Liverpool," *Baptist Times and Freeman*, 12 July 1901, 467; "Dr. Maclaren and the Concentration Camps," *Baptist Times and Freeman*, 19 July 1901, 479.
[220] "Dr. Maclaren and the Concentration Camps," *Baptist Times and Freeman*, 19 July 1901, 479.
[221] "The Concentration Camps," *Baptist Times and Freeman*, 27 December 1901, 870.
[222] "The Concentration Camps," *Baptist Times and Freeman*, 27 December 1901, 870.

By the testimony of friends and foes alike our men have exercised a moderation and self-restraint without parallel in the annals of war. It seems a contradiction in terms to speak of humanity in connection with war, but making due allowance for the stern necessities of the case, we believe that the struggle in South Africa has been conducted on our side with a humanity such as has never before been witnessed.[223]

Such optimism regarding British conduct was supported by the Canadian Baptists as well.

Having condemned guerrilla warfare as early as June, 1900, the *Canadian Baptist* continued to claim that it was "unChristian."[224] It was argued that Britain's "exceptional measures" in response to the shift in Boer tactics, were nothing more than what any other civilized nation would do when faced with guerrilla warfare.[225] Guerrilla warfare was considered murder, and "all who partake in it must expect to be treated as men guilty of that crime."[226] "Pity would be wasted" on the Boers, it was claimed, for all British methods were necessary and deserving.[227] Even the forcing of Boer woman into the camps was deemed a military necessity due to "every" Boer woman being "an intelligence agent."[228]

Not only were the British tactics totally justified in light of the ongoing guerrilla war, but the British soldiers' conduct was also regarded to be exemplary. Stories of atrocities by British soldiers were denied,[229] and it was argued that the British soldiers "had set up a standard of conduct during the war incomparably higher than that ever required before"[230] and that the war had been waged "on more humane principles than have ever ruled in the wars of Continental nations."[231] Continuing to be sensitive to American criticisms of British methods, the *Canadian Baptist* dismissed American concerns by pointing out what it considered to be American hypocrisies in their own history of warfare.[232] In order to support such a portrayal of the soldiers, the *Canadian Baptist* printed a variety of testimonials. The honour and common decency of British officers was portrayed in a story told by a war correspondent[233] and a Belgian lady's account of the "admirable" behav-

---

[223] "Peace at Last," *Baptist Times and Freeman*, 6 June 1902, 427.

[224] "Guerrilla Warfare Unchristian," *Canadian Baptist*, 14 November 1901, 16.

[225] *Canadian Baptist*, 4 July 1901, 16.

[226] "Closing Events in South Africa," *Canadian Baptist*, 7 June 1900, 8.

[227] See *Canadian Baptist*, 6 December 1900, 1. See also "Kitchener's Proposals For Peace," *Canadian Baptist*, 10 January 1901, 16.

[228] "British Victims of the War," *Canadian Baptist*, 19 September 1901, 11.

[229] *Canadian Baptist*, 14 February 1901, 16; "Another Pro-Boer Story Denied," *Canadian Baptist*, 28 November 1901, 16; "The Slanders Against England: Dr. Conan Doyle's Refutation," *Canadian Baptist*, 30 January 1902, 16; "British Slanderers Challenged," *Canadian Baptist*, 30 January 1902, 16.

[230] "British Treatment of the Boers," *Canadian Baptist*, 14 March 1901, 16.

[231] "The Old Year," *Canadian Baptist*, 26 December 1901, 8.

[232] *Canadian Baptist*, 6 December 1900, 1; "The Continental Press on BBitish Methods [sic]," 16; "Cannot Meddle," *Canadian Baptist*, 24 October 1901, 16.

[233] James Barnes, "Orders Are Orders," *Canadian Baptist*, 28 February 1901, 14.

iour of English officers and soldiers.[234] Positive references in the British, continental, and Canadian press as to the conduct of the British army were sought after and reproduced.[235] A report that even the Boers were defending the conduct of the British soldiers was tracked down and printed.[236] The *Religious Intelligencer* found compelling evidence of Britain's innocence in the *London Times*, which had printed letters from two anti-British women claiming how well off the Boers were in the camps. If these anti-British women could hold to such a view, the *Intelligencer* concluded, the American criticisms of the camps must be unfounded.[237]

To the very end of the war, the *Canadian Baptist* defended the camps, calling any stories of atrocities "absurd."[238] In fact, it was argued, British "magnanimity" as evidenced by such good camps actually prolonged the war.[239] "Hardships," it was acknowledged, were "endured" in the camps, but such hardships were dismissed because they "were similar to those of ordinary Boer life."[240] Ignoring any sense of British responsibility for the Boer's situation, the camps were considered essential and "humane" due to the Boer's desperate state.[241] Like some others,[242] the *Canadian Baptist* argued that the camps were "model" institutions and the Boers were as well looked after as if they were in "their own homes."[243] What did bother the *Canadian Baptist*, however, was the neglect of attention towards the suffering of the loyal British subjects in South Africa.[244]

Conclusion

By the late-nineteenth century it was clear to BACSANZ Baptists that there was no empire as righteous as theirs. There was the recognition that it had its share of injustices, but the empire was still considered to be the most benevolent empire on the face of the earth: where the Union Jack flew, liberty and justice reigned. Consequently, for Baptists concerned with the advancement of justice, there was no moral crisis in supporting the empire for the best way to

---

[234] *Canadian Baptist*, 1 August 1901, 1.
[235]"British Treatment of the Boers," *Canadian Baptist*, 14 March 1901, 16; "The Continental Press on BBitish [sic] Methods," *Canadian Baptist*, 5 September 1901, 16; "A Foreign Tribute to the British Army in Africa," *Canadian Baptist*, 24 October 1901, 16; "Called Down," *Canadian Baptist*, 19 December 1901, 16.
[236] "Even Boers Protest," *Canadian Baptist*, 1 May 1902, 16.
[237] "How Well Are They Treated," *Religious Intelligencer*, 27 November 1901, 2.
[238] "South Africa: Those British Camps," *Canadian Baptist*, 24 April 1902, 16.
[239] *Canadian Baptist*, 16 May 1901, 16.
[240] "The Refugee Camps," *Canadian Baptist*, 8 August 1901, 15.
[241] "The Refugee Camps," *Canadian Baptist*, 8 August 1901, 15.
[242] H.S. Caldecott, "A Boer Refugee Camp in Natal," *The Empire Review* 1 (July 1901): 623-626.
[243] "The Refugee Camps," *Canadian Baptist*, 29 August 1901, 16.
[244] "British Victims of the War," *Canadian Baptist*, 19 September 1901, 11. See also "The Refugee Camps," 15.

spread justice was to expand the empire. Conversely, any contraction of empire was deemed a threat to peace, justice and the advancement of human progress. In other words, for many Baptists in the metropole and peripheries, humanitarian concerns - which included the promotion or defense of justice - often had an imperial solution, even if it meant going to war.

While BACSANZ Baptists were committed to the ideal of an empire that promoted righteousness, determining what was righteous was not easy. As this chapter indicates, Baptist conceptions of justice were shaped by their particular realities and perspectives from the metropole or periphery. One does not have to read the *Baptist Times and Freeman* for long to see how British Baptists were divided over the war. The Canadian Baptist press, on the other hand, was uniform in its defense of both the justice of the cause and means in South Africa especially in light of the domestic tensions in the newly-minted nation. The *New Zealand Baptist* supported the war effort, but did allow for a dissenting voice in its pages. The *South African Baptist* supported the war effort, but was muted in its proclaiming the justice of the cause due to fear of inciting further racial tensions. The Australian Baptist press was divided, with one paper opposed to the war, one passionately supportive of the justice of the cause, and one more subdued in its support for the war. In all these cases, BACSANZ Baptists were imbued with a concern for justice, but domestic considerations and perspectives shaped their often varied conceptions of justice.

That being the case, a common thread running through the varied commentary on the justice of the war was a conviction that a victory would be best for all. Even if the war was unjust in its origins, the best outcome for all would be a British victory. As will be demonstrated in the following chapter, the empire's victory would also lead to the advancement of the gospel, another concern at the heart of Baptist identity.

Chapter Six

Missions and Providence

"[I]rrespective of the merits of the war now raging in that country, we believe that the result will be favorable to missionary and religious enterprise." "The Outlook for Missions in Africa," *Religious Intelligencer*, 28 February 1900, 1.

"And if a revival of godliness is what is needed to cause the Lord to turn His face towards us, there is then no greater service we can render to our country than to give ourselves whole-heartedly to seeking first His kingdom and righteousness. The best patriotism is to follow the Lord and to win others to the same." Ernest Baker, "A Presidential Message," *South African Baptist*, January 1901, 6.

"Let our people learn that in supporting Foreign Missions they are acting the part of empire-builders, and their horizon will broaden, and the cause of missions will lift, and the heart of the Church will beat with a stronger and nobler throb." C.S. Mead, "The True Missionary Motive," *Queensland Baptist*, July 1901, 87-89.

The history of Christianity is replete with accounts of missionaries who endeavored to spread the Christian gospel. The early apostles' travel throughout the Roman Empire is recounted in the New Testament book of Acts, and, in subsequent centuries, well-known missionaries such as St. Augustine of Canterbury, St. Patrick and St. Francis Xavier followed in their footsteps. One factor that made the nineteenth-century missionary movement unique was that it corresponded to the rapid spread of European power and race for empire. Since the breakup of European empires after the Second World War, there have been numerous and passionate denunciations of the missionary movement throughout former colonial territories as well as in the West.[1] Andrew Porter's recent work on the history of British Protestant missionaries demonstrates that the relationship between British missionaries and empire was more complex and ambiguous than many postcolonial studies assumed.[2] BACSANZ Baptist attitudes towards missions and empire reflect some of that complexity and ambiguity. Baptists were often openly critical of the abuses of empire, yet concomitantly they supported the view that the British Empire was God's benevolent and providential tool for spreading civilization and Christianity. Without such an empire, they believed, the world would be a more dangerous place,

---

[1] Brian Stanley, *The Bible and the Flag: Protestant Missions and British Imperialism in the Nineteenth and Twentieth Centuries* (Leicester: Apollos, 1990), ch.1.
[2] Andrew Porter, *Religion versus Empire? British Protestant Missionaries and Overseas Expansion, 1700-1914* (Manchester: Manchester University Press, 2004).

metropole and peripheries would be threatened, and the "natives" of such places as South Africa would suffer. Consequently, it was assumed that a British victory would be a boon for the empire, the Boers, the world, and the spread of the gospel. What follows is an exploration of the assumptions that undergirded such a position as well as an analysis of the relationship between British rule and God's providential role for the empire in spreading Christianity.

BACSANZ Baptist piety was marked by a passionate commitment to the spread of the gospel. British Baptists such as William Carey were at the forefront of the development of the nineteenth-century Protestant missionary movement, a century referred to as the "great century of Protestant missions."[3] Over the course of the nineteenth century, Protestant missions and mission societies grew from relative obscurity to a position of prominence within the church. British Protestant denominations were at the vanguard of this missionary movement, sending 9,014 missionaries out of a total of 17,254 Protestant missionaries from all countries.[4] In fact, "by the middle of the nineteenth century, the 'missionary spirit' was being hailed by contemporaries ... as the 'characteristic feature' of the religious piety for which the Victorians were rightly renowned."[5] As the nineteenth century progressed, missionary societies were formed, funds were raised, and an increasing number of missionaries sent. The heroic exploits of foreign missionaries and the clarion call to missionary work were repeatedly presented to the churches. Baptist life was marked by a vigorous commitment to personal conversion and evangelical missions, and the events of the late-nineteenth century fuelled that passion. It seemed as if God had providentially established an empire that aided the growth of the church, and Baptists were not ones to argue with God. While domestic missions played a prominent role in the peripheries in regards to local indigenous peoples,[6] the impulse to send missionaries overseas to those deemed heathens was a central element to Baptist life. Brian Stanley claims "If you wish to mobilize Baptists (and evangelicals as a whole) on an issue that divides the nation down the middle politically, the way to

---

[3] Kenneth Scott Latourette, *The Great Century, A.D. 1800-A.D.1914* (New York: Harper and Brothers Publishing, 1941), 1. As Brian Stanley argues, however, numbers alone would make the twentieth century an even greater century for Protestant missions. See Stanley, *The Bible and the Flag*, 83-84.

[4] The next closest Protestant missionary-sending nation was the United States. Out of those 17,245 Protestant missionaries, the U.S. sent 4,159. See Stanley, *The Bible and the Flag*, 83.

[5] Susan Thorne, *Congregational Missions and the Making of an Imperial Culture in Nineteenth-Century England* (Stanford: Stanford University Press, 1999), 5.

[6] For examples of commentary on home missions in periphery papers, see Rev. T.A. Williams, "The Pagans of Our Own Land," *New Zealand Baptist*, May 1900, 66; "The Pagans of Our Own Land," *New Zealand Baptist*, June 1900, 82-83; "Our Home Auxiliary," *South African Baptist*, November 1901, 145-147; [6] "Our First Native Missionary in South Africa," *South African Baptist*, July 1901, 95-97; "A Dutch-Speaking Mission," *South African Baptist*, May 1902, 51-52; "Baptist Union of South Africa," *South African Baptist*, November 1901, 127-133.

do it is to persuade them that liberty to preach the gospel is at stake."[7] In regards to the crisis in South Africa, BACSANZ Baptists were convinced that what was at stake was the delivery of the gospel to the Africans and that objective could best be accomplished if the British won the war. Consequently, even for many who opposed the war, the ideal outcome in South Africa was a British victory. As one article in the *Religious Intelligencer* stated, "irrespective of the merits of the war now raging in that country, we believe that the result will be favorable to missionary and religious enterprise."[8]

Expressions of BACSANZ Baptist support for the missionary enterprise were ubiquitous. Besides the abundant mission societies and their frequent meetings and reports, there were numerous missionary publications committed exclusively to providing information and inspiration in order to spur Baptists on in their support for the overseas missionary enterprise. BACSANZ Baptist newspapers also included a great deal of missionary information. Rarely did an issue not include some exhortation to support missions, or report on an aspect of mission trials or triumphs. Special columns were committed to the work of the various missionary societies, and inserts were occasionally included that were devoted exclusively to missionary concerns.[9] For instance, the *Baptist* included poetry and various articles to inform readers of the missionary work among Indian women and missions in Africa.[10] It also provided a summary of nineteenth-century missions in the Pacific, with an exhortation to continue the work:

> Let the Churches of this Commonwealth be faithful to the responsibilities which God has imposed upon them for the evangelisation of the thousands of heathens in these seas who are yet without the Gospel of Christ, and, with the cooperation of the island churches, obedient to the same command and impelled by the same love, the issue is certain.[11]

End of the century reflections often waxed eloquently about the advances of western civilization, the British Empire, as well as missionary societies. For instance, the *New Zealand Baptist* printed the presidential address at the annual Baptist Union of New Zealand meeting which included the statement: "the crowning glory of the century has been the Foreign Missionary enterprise."[12] The fixation on the trials and triumphs of mission societies permeated the pages

---

[7] Brian Stanley, "Baptists, Antislavery and the Legacy of Imperialism," *Baptist Quarterly* 42 (October 2007): 289.
[8] "The Outlook for Missions in Africa," *Religious Intelligencer*, 28 February 1900, 1.
[9] The *Missionary Messenger* was an insert in the *New Zealand Baptist*.
[10] Isaac A. Ward, "Our Indian Women," *Baptist*, 1 January 1901, 4-5; "Baptist Missions in Africa," *Baptist*, 4 May 1900, 6; "Missions Work in the Transvaal." *Baptist*, 1 February 1902, 3; Rev. James Green, "Mission Work in the Transvaal," *Baptist*, 1 February 1902, 3.
[11] Rev. Dr. George Brown, "Mission Work in the Pacific," *Baptist*, 1 February 1901, 8.
[12] H.H. Driver, "Between the Centuries," *New Zealand Baptist*, December 1899, 179.

of BACSANZ Baptist papers, and late-nineteenth century political events in China and Africa only intensified that focus.

China's relationship with the West throughout the nineteenth century was strained through wars and one-sided treaties. By the end of the century, tensions were high, missionaries were fearful, and it looked to some like China was to be dismembered and divided among the Western powers.[13] There had been isolated anti-western violence in the years leading up to 1900 and a number of missionaries had been killed. However, in the summer of 1900, Chinese frustrations with the West finally reached the boiling point when an organization called the Society of Harmonious Fists took up arms and sought to wipe out any vestiges of Western influence. This rebellion, most commonly referred to as the Boxer Rebellion,[14] had a direct impact on missionaries in China, for the Boxers were determine to purge the land of any foreign presence including missionaries and their converts.

In the opening weeks of June 1900, the Western powers were caught off-guard and remained on the defensive. While the Boxer Rebellion was mainly focused in the northeast, Westerners anywhere in China felt at risk. Consequently, those who could escape fled to the various western-controlled ports for safety. Westerners (including missionaries) in the capital city of what was then called Pekin[15] were besieged in the foreign legations, and for weeks had to fend off Boxer attacks.

The initial uncertainty surrounding the events in China was disconcerting for editors who wanted to provide a clear picture for their readers. As one Baptist editor lamented: "authentic news of the progress of the mighty struggle raging in the vicinity of Pekin comes but slowly and spasmodically to the reader."[16] Another editor echoed the same frustration, and shared his fears: "if the worst that is being reported from Shanghai and other Chinese coast cities is true, the state of affairs is terrible indeed."[17] After the first few months of uncertainty had passed, editors were able to provide their readers with a clearer picture of the events in China.

There were approximately 2,000 Protestant missionaries in China and approximately 1,000 Roman Catholic priests and nuns.[18] The Boxer Rebellion led to the

---

[13] For a summary of the events that led to the Boxer Rebellion, see Joseph Esherick, *The Origins of the Boxer Uprising* (Berkeley: University of California Press, 1987).

[14] For a description of the events in the Boxer Rebellion, see Chester Tan, *The Boxer Catastrophe* (New York: W.W. Norton and Company Ltd., 1967); Henry Keown-Boyd, *The Fists of Righteous Harmony: A History of the Boxer Uprising in China in the Year 1900* (London: Leo Cooper, 1991); Christopher Martin, *The Boxer Rebellion* (London: Abelard-Schuman, 1968); Victor Purcell, *The Boxer Uprising: A Background Study* (Hamden: Archon Books, 1974).

[15] Now Beijing.

[16] "China," *Religious Intelligencer*, 4 July 1900, 4.

[17] "The Situation in China," *Messenger and Visitor*, 11 July 1900, 4.

[18] Alvyn J. Austin, *Saving China: Canadian Missionaries in the Middle Kingdom, 1888-1959* (Toronto: University of Toronto Press, 1986), 65.

death of 243 missionaries and their children, along with the execution of tens of thousands of Chinese converts.[19] The BACSANZ Baptist presence in China was relatively nonexistent, for they had focused their missionary efforts elsewhere in places such as India. However, they were still shocked and outraged by the horrors that they were reading in the papers.

Not everyone in the West supported the work of missionaries, and some critics felt that missionaries directly contributed to rebellions against British rule. The comments made by British Prime Minister Lord Salisbury at the SPG's bicentenary celebration in 1900 in which he appeared to blame missionaries for the troubles in China echoed those of other critics.[20] Most of the literature published by missionaries in the West after the rebellion was written to defend the actions of missionaries against such accusations.[21] There is a need for further analysis of BACSANZ Baptists and the Boxer Rebellion, but suffice it to say here that the BACSANZ Baptist papers reported the events in China, and that much of the coverage related to the impact that the turmoil and violence had on the missionary enterprise.[22] Many British missionaries expected Western governments to intervene on behalf of missionaries in China.[23]

---

[19] 136 Protestant adults, 53 children, and 54 Catholic priests and nuns. See Austin, *Saving China*, 76.

[20] Greenlee and Johnston, *Good Citizens*, 113.

[21] Purcell, *The Boxer Uprising*, 123.

[22] Wars," *New Zealand Baptist*, August 1900, 120; "And Rumours of Wars," *New Zealand Baptist*, August 1900, 120-121; "The Trouble in China," *New Zealand Baptist*, August 1900, 121; *New Zealand Baptist*, August 1900, 123; "Secretarial Jottings," *New Zealand* Baptist, February 1901, 26; Lizzie, "On the Verge of Martyrdom," *New Zealand Baptist*, April 1901, 55; "NZBMS," *New Zealand Baptist*, February 1901, 65; "Our Martyred Missionaries," *New Zealand Baptist*, February 1901, 68; "On the Verge of Martyrdom," *New Zealand Baptist*, April 1901, 55; Rev. Charles Williams, "Letters from China," *Baptist Times and Freeman*, 31 August 1900, 702; Rev. Charles Williams, "Perils By the Way," *Baptist Times and Freeman*, 31 August 1900, 702; Rev. Charles Williams, "The Sheep in the Wilderness," *Baptist Times and Freeman*, 31 August 1900, 702; Rev. Charles Williams, "Missionaries as Politician," *Baptist Times and Freeman*, 31 August 1900, 702; Rev. Charles Williams, "Missionary Secretaries on the Defensive," *Baptist Times and Freeman*, 31 August 1900, 702; "Our Duty in China," *Baptist Times and Freeman*, 31 August 1900, 702; "A Call for Prayer," *Baptist Times and Freeman*, 31 August 1900, 702; "Baptist Association of Queensland," *Queensland Baptist*, October 1900, 131; "Missions in China," *Queensland Baptist*, January 1901, 5; "Our Martyred Missionaries," *Queensland Baptist*, April 1901, 47; "Martyred Missionaries," *Queensland Baptist*, May 1901, 64; "China," *Baptist*, 4 August 1900, 2; "The Martyrs," *Baptist*, 4 August 1900, 2; "The Massacres in China," *Baptist*, 4 August 1900, 8; Rev. G.C. Lorimer, "Dead and Dying Nations," *Southern Baptist*, 15 February 1900, 43; "We Sympathise," *Southern Baptist*, 2 August 1900, 169; "China," *Southern Baptist*, 30 August 1900, 194; "A Christian Martyr," *Southern Baptist*, 18 October 1900, 229; "China," *Southern Baptist*, 1 November 1900, 242; "China," *Southern Baptist*, 3 January 1901, 2; "Some Two Hundred Missionaries," *Southern Baptist*, 17 April 1901, 86; Robert Powell, "Martyrs of China," *Southern Baptist*, 17 April 1901, 90; "Martyred Missionaries," *Southern Baptist*, 15 May 1901, 110; "He Declares That The Attitude,"

The war in South Africa was also a concern for those passionate about the missionary enterprise. For BACSANZ Baptists concerned with missions, it was believed that the spiritual stakes in the conflict in South Africa also loomed large and that imperial intervention in the war with the Boers was needed for the furtherance of the gospel. Such confidence that mission work would be better off under British rather than Boer rule was rooted in a number of convictions related to British and Boer governance, God's providence, and national and imperial destiny.

Stanley details how British missionaries in the late-nineteenth century entered the political arena to protect their interests.[24] Many Anglican and nonconformist missionaries agitated for an imperial solution when political unrest or uncertainty threatened their mission work. It was assumed, Stanley argues, that British imperial control could best bring about the much needed stability, rule of law, commerce, and technology that would aid the work of the missionaries. In the case of the war in South Africa, those concerned for missions believed that "a triumphant Afrikanerdom would spell spiritual and material ruin for the region's natives peoples."[25] The necessity of an imperial solution to missionary problems in South Africa were frequently expressed in the BACSANZ Baptist press, and the assumption that Boer rule in particular was detrimental to the spread of the gospel was evident in wartime commentary.

The conviction that Boer rule was a hindrance to mission work had a long history. Even before David Livingstone's negative appraisal of the Boers and their treatment of the indigenous peoples, British missionaries had experienced tensions with the Boers over such treatment. As far back as the 1820s, British missionaries had advocated for the rights of indigenous peoples of South Africa.[26] One of the basic issues was whether or not slavery was to be allowed under British rule. Whereas Britain was moving towards the emancipation of slaves within its empire, the Boers had no intention of abandoning slavery. Tensions had been so serious between the missionaries and Boers over the treatment of the Africans that many of the Boers fled northward to escape British rule.[27] As noted in Chapter Five, the advancement of justice was a critical component of BACSANZ Baptist support for the war, for they equated the ad-

---

Southern Baptist, 30 April 1902, 100; "All Eyes," *Southern Baptist*, 16 August 1900, 182; "Australia," *Southern Baptist*, 18 October 1900, 229; "The Prayers," *Southern Baptist*, 1 November 1900, 242; "What a Spectacle China Presents," *Southern Baptist*, 15 November 1900, 254.

[23] James G. Greenlee and Charles M. Johnston, *Good Citizens: British Missionaries and Imperial States, 1870-1918* (Montreal: McGill-Queen's University Press, 1999), 108-110.

[24] Stanley, *The Bible and the Flag*, ch. 5.

[25] Greenlee and Johnston, *Good Citizens*, 88.

[26] Neill, *A History of Christian Missions*, 264.

[27] Of course, there were other reasons for the tensions between the British and the Boers. For a helpful summary of these tensions, see Judd and Surridge, *The Boer War*, ch.1.

vancement of justice with the advancement of empire. In regards to missions, the assumption was quite similar, for an imperial solution was posed for what appeared to be Boer mistreatment of the Africans and especially what was deemed to be a complete disregard for their spiritual condition. It was believed that the gospel could not advance under such conditions; Boer rule simply had to be replaced with one was deemed to be congruent with the missionary enterprise.[28]

A number of wartime articles within the BACSANZ Baptist press decried the Boer's treatment of Africans as it related to mission work. While South African Baptists may have had a pre-war history of supporting the advancement of the empire if it meant that British mission work could gain a foothold in new lands,[29] the Canadian Baptist press was the most consistently outspoken in its criticism of the Boer concern for the spiritual condition of the "natives." The *Canadian Baptist* defended the actions of the British and damned those of the Boers. It claimed that they were "the enemies of progress, ignorant, bigoted, cruel without measure. They have even stood in the way of the mission worker. They treat the natives worse than dogs."[30] The *Western Baptist* echoed this view of the Boers and mission work when it pointed back to the days of Livingstone as an example of Boer mistreatment of the "natives" and of the Boer hindrance to mission work.[31] Elsewhere, the Canadian Baptist press painted an unflattering portrait of the Boers. The Boers were a primitive "seventeenth century" people,[32] were "unsophisticated, unkempt, unwashed, surrounded by a crowd of grubby children" with no desire to evangelize the "natives."[33] If there was any doubt about the lack of Boer concern for mission work it was claimed that statistics attested to the Boer disregard for outreach.[34] At the conclusion of the war, the *Canadian Missionary Link*, a Baptist missionary publication, printed an article that rejoiced in the British victory as an opportunity for missionary

---

[28] Richard Elphick argues that, despite inconsistencies and failures in missionary policy, numerous South Africans were right "to discern some deep affinity between Protestant missions...and the struggle for social equality." See Richard Elphick, "Evangelical Missions and Racial 'Equalization' in South Africa, 1890-1914," in *Converting Colonialism: Visions and Realities in Mission History, 1706-1914*, ed., Dana L. Robert (Grand Rapids: William B. Eerdmans, 2008), 133.

[29] Hale, "Captives of British Imperialism."

[30] "A Missionary View of the War," *Canadian Baptist*, 18 April 1901, 12.

[31] "War in the Transvaal," *Western Baptist*, November 1899, 1.

[32] "The Outlook in South Africa," *Canadian Baptist*, 21 November 1901, 7. Also printed in the *Religious Intelligencer*. See "From South Africa," *Religious Intelligencer*, 11 December 1901, 1.

[33] "Sketches of Boer Life: By One Who Has Lived among Them," *Canadian Baptist*, 13 March 1902, 11. This article was printed again in two weeks. See *Canadian Baptist*, 27 March 1902, 7. Also printed in the *Religious Intelligencer*. See "Sketches of Boer Life: By One Who Has Lived among Them," *Religious Intelligencer*, 26 March 1902, 1.

[34] "Sketches of Boer Life: By One Who Has Lived Among Them," *Canadian Baptist*, 13 March 1902, 11.

advance: "How many there are who have thanked God for the peace so long desired. Not for the ending of war's miseries alone, but for the establishment of a better rule, and especially for the opening of a wider and more effectual door for the Gospel."[35] Other BACSANZ papers, while not always as blunt in their negative portrayals of the Boers, printed articles that agreed with the sentiment that a British victory in South Africa would lead to the advancement of the gospel. As one *New Zealand Baptist* article declared, a "British victory will not only make for the spread of peace, civilisation, and Christianity in South Africa, but be a lasting boon and blessing to the native races."[36]

Assumptions regarding Boer rule and its negative impact on the spread of the gospel certainly played a role in the shaping of public opinion regarding the necessity of a British victory. However, it was the fusion of providence and purpose that was central to BACSANZ Baptist convictions regarding imperial involvement and missions in South Africa. The welter of ideas associated with this fusion provided both national and imperial identity and purpose, explained success and defeat on the battlefield, motivated religious and social reforms, comforted the discouraged, and justified support for the war.

The commonly held view of providence was the conviction that God directly intervened in human history to fulfill his purposes; the "finger of God"[37] could be identified in events such as famine, plague, illness, battles, the fall of ancient empires, and the rise of the British Empire. God was understood to intervene in events "more often than we are always prone to admit."[38] His intervention was sought after in a number of crises, and the assumptions surrounding providence were identical whether the beseeching of God was for rain, health or victory on the battlefield. For instance, a severe drought in Australia led to considerable commentary in the Australian Baptist press. People were urged to pray for rain so that it would return.[39] After months of waiting, a day of humiliation was

---

[35] "Africa," *Canadian Missionary Link*, July-August 1902, 167.

[36] "Forced Against Our Will," *New Zealand Baptist*, April 1900, 49. See also "The Partition of Africa," *South African Baptist*, December 1899, 70; Rev. James Green, "Missions Work in the Transvaal," *Baptist*, February 1902, 3; "The Partition of Africa," *Baptist*, 4 May 1900, 8; "The Boers Are Protestant," *Southern Baptist*, 2 November 1899, 229; "Concerning the Transvaal War," *Baptist Times and Freeman*, 26 January 1900, 72.

[37] For use of this expression, see "Our Ships Immaculate," *New Zealand Baptist*, October 1899, 153.

[38] "Chit Chat," *New Zealand Baptist*, April 1900, 63.

[39] Kenoza, "A Prayer for Rain," *Queensland Baptist*, May 1902, 57; W. Whale, "Prayers for Rain," *Queensland Baptist*, 1 May 1902, 62-63; "The Terrible Drought," *Southern Baptist*, 3 September 1902, 193; "God Has Given," *Southern Baptist*, 28 June 1900, 145; "Prayer Answered," *Southern Baptist*, 16 April 1902, 86; "The Drought in Australia," *Southern Baptist*, 11 June 1902, 135; "Rain Showers of Mercy," *Southern Baptist*, 2 July 1902, 146; "The Break-up of the Drought," *Southern Baptist*, 2 July 1902, 143; "Humiliation," *Southern Baptist*, 3 September 1902, 193; "The Terrible Drought," *Southern Baptist*, 3 September 1902, 193; "Prayers for Rain," *Southern Baptist*, 3 September

called for by government to repent of the sins that caused God to withhold rain.[40] The blessing of the drought was that it was deemed to have led people to pray: "Surely God has blessed us even by the drought, when the heart is humbled and the people pray. No better sight have we seen in this country than the earnest crowds who rush to wait on God. Let the waiting continue, there is blessing in it, and the blessing will come after it."[41] However, the lack of response from God must have led to doubts among the faithful, for there was a need to explain why God did not seem to answer the prayers of his people.[42]

The outbreak of plague in Australia in 1900 was also cause for prayer. Concern was expressed over the arrival of the plague in Adelaide and people were reminded that they should not blame God if citizens rejected God's dietary laws and health regimen that were meant to keep his people free from disease.[43] An all day prayer meeting was held in a town hall to petition God's protection during the threat of the plague spreading.[44] Whale referred to the famine in India, the war in Africa, and the plague as a "Trinity of Tribulations."[45] He asserted that Australians had been "highly favoured by Providence" because they did not have many serious outbreaks of disease, and claimed that the fire of London in 1665 was a providential blessing because it was a "disinfecting process" that saved Londoners from even worse disease. He exhorted citizens to be diligent so that the plague did not spread to the populace and to pray so that God did not bring judgment down on them that was due because of their sins.

God's providential care was seen in the protection of the Prince of Wales from assassination in 1900,[46] and, in 1902, intercession to God was offered for the new King Edward VII during his illness that abruptly postponed his coronation service.[47] Addressing the king's illness at Union Chapel in Manchester,

---

1902, 193; "Prayer for Rain," *Southern Baptist*, 17 September 1902, 205; "Volcanoes," *Queensland Baptist*, 2 June 1902, 71; Ella Wheeler Wilcox, "Unanswered Prayers," *Queensland Baptist*, 2 June 1902, 71; Rev. W. Whale, "Prayer and Providence," *Queensland Baptist*, 2 June 1902, 74.

[40] "Day of Prayer," *Queensland Baptist*, 1 May 1902, 57-58; "Meetings," *Queensland Baptist*, 1 May 1902, 58; "Prayer for Rain," *Southern Baptist*, 3 September 1902, 193; "Prayer for Rain," *Southern Baptist*, 17 September 1902, 205.

[41] "The Great Purpose," *Queensland Baptist*, 1 May 1902, 58.

[42] "Prayer and Providence," *Queensland Baptist*, June 1902, 74; Ella Wheeler Wilcox, "Unanswered Prayers," *Queensland Baptist*, June 1902, 71.

[43] "War Is Bad Enough," *Southern Baptist*, 1 February 1900, 26; "The Plague," *Baptist*, 10 March 1900, 2.

[44] "The Plague," *Baptist*, June 1900, 2.

[45] "A Trinity of Tribulations," *Queensland Baptist*, 2 April 1900, 48-49.

[46] "We Do Unfeignedly Rejoice," *New Zealand Baptist*, May 1900, 73.

[47] "The King's Illness," *Baptist Times and Freeman*, 4 July 1902, 493; Rev. Alexander Maclaren, "The Finger of God ," *Baptist Times and Freeman*, 4 July 1902, 495; "T.H., "England's Prayer Today," *Baptist Times and Freeman*, 4 July 1902, 495; Rev. Charles Williams, "The Coronation Postponed," *Baptist Times and Freeman*, 4 July 1902, 496; Rev. Charles Williams, "The Divine Message - What?" *Baptist Times and Freeman*, 4 July 1902, 496.

Maclaren stated that he did not come with a Bible text, for God had provided a text through the events of the last week. Recent events, he argued, humbled England and the king:

What a rebuke to our foolish and insular pride in our own power and resources! How we plume ourselves on England's might, and drop into the vulgarest kind of Imperialism, recognizing no power but the power of force, no gain but the gain of territory, no wealth but the wealth that may be summed and counted. And this sudden calamity comes storming down upon us, and bids us remember that behind all these there lies the great and sovereign Will which 'blew upon' plans and expectations, 'and they were scattered'; that 'righteousness exalteth a nation'; that 'by the soul only are the nations great and free'; and that for the community as for the individual, the true order of objects and pursuit is set forth in the great word, 'Seek ye first the Kingdom of God, and all these things shall be added unto you.' England in its pride, in its triumph over the conclusion of the war, needed the lesson.[48]

Elsewhere, it was stated that the king's illness had a "chastening effect" which led to the nation bowing its head to learn what God wanted it to learn through the illness.[49] The general call was for people to pray, not just for the king's health, but also for the lessons of his illness to be learned by both sovereign and subjects.[50] After his recovery, satisfaction was expressed because it was felt that the king showed signs of having learned humility and responsibility from the illness.[51] Such virtues, it was understood, were important because his coronation was portrayed as religious service of confession and consecration.[52]

Commentary in the press indicated that God's hand could be seen in the events in South Africa and his providential care could be called upon to aid the imperial cause. Previous empires like Greece and Rome had risen and fallen, and, it was asked, why would Britain's empire be any different? As one author noted: "We believe that He treats the nations as a master treats his men, prospering and promoting them so long as, obeying His commandments, their cause is consistently righteous and constantly just; casting them aside - dismissed, discharged, degraded - when they forget."[53] The examples of Rome and Greece

---

[48] Alexander Maclaren, "The Finger of God," *Baptist Times and Freeman*, 4 July 1902, 495.

[49] "The King's Illness," *Baptist Times and Freeman*, 4 July 1902, 493.

[50] "The King's Illness," *New Zealand Baptist*, July 1902, 104; "God Save the King!" *South African Baptist*, July 1902, 73; "The King," *Southern Baptist*, 26 March 1902, 73; "An Empire's Prayers," *Southern Baptist*, 2 July 1902, 143; "The Divine Message - What?" *Baptist Times and Freeman*, 4 July 1902, 496; "The Coronation Postponed," *Baptist Times and Freeman*, 4 July 1902, 496. See also "Baptist Union of Great Britain and Ireland, Spring Assembly 1901," *Supplement to the Baptist Times and Freeman*, 26 April 1901.

[51] "The King's Letter," *Baptist Times and Freeman*, 15 August 1902, 601; "The Coronation," *Baptist Times and Freeman*, 15 August 1902, 601.

[52] "The Coronation," *Baptist Times and Freeman*, 8 August 1902, 592-593.

[53] "The Supreme Test of Nations," *New Zealand Baptist*, February 1900, 18.

were used also on Coronation Sunday at Collins-Street Baptist Church by J.H. Pryce; based on the biblical text 1 Kings 8:57, Pryce proclaimed that both ancient empires fell because they ignored God.[54] Of course, the lesson to be learned was that the same fate would befall Britain if it ignored God. Many Baptists said amen to Rudyard Kipling's poem *Recessional*, a poem that echoed similar sentiments regarding God's providential raising up and bringing down of empires.[55] And it was within this larger providential context that the vicissitudes of the war were interpreted.

The belief in providence imbued Christians with the conviction that God was on their side and that they would ultimately triumph over all tribulations. As tensions rose in South Africa, readers of the *South African Baptist* were encouraged to pray for peace and remember that they were in the hands of God at all times.[56] One article in the *Southern Baptist* declared that no nation or empire that has Christ reigning over it would fall.[57] The *Western Baptist* admitted that it could not "understand all these mysteries" and that there was a need to "put [themselves]...into the hands of the living God."[58] Baptists were reminded that "God moves in a mysterious way His wonders to perform."[59] The implied promise was, of course, that God and his cause will prevail. Another author asserted that while the events of the world (drought in Australia, famine in India, violence in China, and war in South Africa) were "disheartening," God's providence was a comfort: "Let anyone who mourns a murdered missionary in China; and mother who son fills a grave on the South African veldt, and man whose interests have suffered in the waste of war; let these draw near to God through Jesus Christ and say 'This Lord is my trouble, hide me in thy pavilion'."[60]

But for all its purported comfort, the doctrine of providence was also repeatedly invoked to rebuke for sin. It is too simplistic to assume that BACSANZ Baptists were uncritical propagandists for the empire. For those today uncomfortable with the language of providence it needs to be remembered that it was this sense of providence that allowed - in fact, necessitated - a critique of imperialism. The demand for righteousness meant that there was an ever-constant examination as to whether or not the empire was living up to its high calling,

---

[54] Rev. J.H. Pryce, "The Patriot's Prayer," *Southern Baptist*, 17 September 1902, 207.

[55] Rudyard Kipling, "Recessional," *South African Baptist*, July 1899, 190; "The Biogenesis of Kipling's 'Recessional,'" *New Zealand Baptist*, July 1901, 106.

[56] "Kept in Peace," *South African Baptist*, September 1899, 21-22; "We Cannot But Thank God," *Southern Baptist*, 2 November 1899, 230; "Strangely Led," *South African Baptist*, February 1902, 13-14.

[57] Rev. G.C. Lorimer, "Dead and Dying Nations," *Southern Baptist*, 15 February 1900, 43.

[58] Dr. Parker, "The War Prayer," *Western Baptist*, February 1900, 1.

[59] "Baptist Missions in Asia," *Baptist*, 4 August 1900, 8.

[60] "The Pavilion of God," *South African Baptist*, August 1900, 113. See also "The Bright Light in the Clouds," *Baptist Times and Freeman*, 20 July 1900, 586-587; "A Settlement by Thunderbolts," *South African Baptist*, November 1899, 53-54.

and denunciations of sin, jingoism or abuses followed if it was not.[61] A direct correlation was made between sin and success on the battlefield. Victory was evidence of God's blessing, and defeat was an indication that God was judging the empire for its sins. For example, one letter to the editor of the *Baptist Times and Freeman* argued that refusing to call a day of humiliation to invoke God's blessing before the war began, as well as attacking the Boers on the Sabbath to take advantage of their observance of the Sabbath, brought the "displeasure of the Most High."[62] This was not an isolated sentiment, for, especially in the early dark months of the war, a common narrative was that God was punishing or disciplining Britain and its empire for its sins. Both metropole and peripheries were indicted in the judgment. The empire had been too reliant on its military.[63] It had failed to live up to its high calling and responsibilities.[64] Its defeats were due to hubris,[65] and, as one author declared, "her humiliating reverses [were] ... a Divine chastisement for her sins."[66] Another noted the empire needed "sobering, and God is effecting it through the severe processes of this war."[67] The blundering of Britain's leaders and Boer competency aside, the empire's woes were ultimately attributed to its sins.[68] God was chastening the empire, and while it may appear otherwise, the catastrophes were deemed to be an indication of his love for his people.[69] In one instance, parallels were made between the biblical account of the ancient Pharaoh in Egypt and the modern Boer and British in Africa. What was needed in both cases was to hear the voice of God in the midst of trials: "Black and white, Dutch and British, have alike suffered severely as the result of native wars, locusts, drought, rinderpest, and the present strife. If this conclusion be correct then we cannot expect any lengthened

[61] In this regard, Baptist were not alone among evangelical Protestants. For a discussion of the connection between righteousness, sin, and the support for (and criticism of) empire in Britain, see David Bebbington, "Atonement, Sin, and Empire, 1880-1914," in *The Imperial Horizons of British Protestant Missions, 1880-1914*, ed., Andrew Porter (Grand Rapids: Eerdmans, 2003), 14-31. For Canadian Baptist criticisms of imperialism, see Heath, "When Missionaries Were Hated," 261-276.
[62] A. Roger, "Britain's Reverse," *Baptist Times and Freeman*, 22 December 1899, 879.
[63] "Our Ships Immaculate," *New Zealand Baptist*, October 1899, 153.
[64] "The New Idea and Politics," *New Zealand Baptist*, June 1900, 82.
[65] S.R. Ingold, "The War in South Africa: The Christian's Proper Attitude Regarding It," *New Zealand Baptist*, April 1900, 61.
[66] "There Is No Doubt," *Southern Baptist*, 1 February 1900, 26. The *Southern Baptist* printed an article a few months later that declared the war could be seen as a "national chastisement" for its sins. See "The Boer War," *Southern Baptist*, 3 May 1900, 98.
[67] "The Day of National Intercession," *Southern Baptist*, 15 February 1900, 38.
[68] "The New Idea and National Sin," *New Zealand Baptist*, June 1900, 81; "The New Idea and Culture," *New Zealand Baptist*, June 1900, 81-82.
[69] "An Empire's Litany," *New Zealand Baptist*, May 1900, 65; "Jehovah," *New Zealand Baptist*, May 1900, 66.

respite till men have learned to forsake their sins and turn to God."[70] This understanding of providence provides the necessary context for understanding the day of humiliation.

The humiliating defeats of the British forces in the opening months of the war led to anguished soul searching. Why would God allow his chosen people to experience defeat? The answer was obvious - sin. Such imagery called to mind the Old Testament idea of sin in the camp (Joshua 7) and its effects on Israel's battles. In the Old Testament, sin among God's people led to defeat whereas obedience brought victory. The solution for ancient Israel in time of crisis and defeat, and for the modern British Empire, was repentance and humiliation. God's favor was to be sought so that the nation could carry on with its divine mandate. As would be expected, Christians were exhorted to pray for the empire and God's blessing on the enterprise in South Africa.[71] There were also specific calls for a special day of humiliation.

As losses mounted and the Boers appeared to be unbeatable, calls for a day of humiliation increasingly grew common and more shrill.[72] By early 1900, the calls had been answered with the Church of England designating 11 February 1900 as the date for national intercession and humiliation.[73] The calling of the day of humiliation gave "public witness to the conviction that the success of the nation and of the causes for which it stood in the world was only possible with God's assistance," and expressed the "belief that all Christians in the United Kingdom would be more effective than the prayers of the members of each church alone."[74] It also set a pattern that would be copied in subsequent decades (the last national day of prayer in Britain was in 1950[75]).

BACSANZ Baptist press coverage of the day of humiliation varied. For example, the Canadian Baptist papers virtually ignored the it,[76] whereas the *Southern Baptist* in Australia included significant commentary on the day and its alleged impact and claimed that the event was "universally observed" within

---

[70] Ernest Baker, "A Presidential Message," *South African Baptist*, January 1901, 6. For a similar message, see Rev. E. Baker, "The Presidential Address," *South African Baptist*, July 1901, 77-83.

[71] A.T. Brainsby, "The Christian Patriot's Prayer," *Baptist Times and Freeman*, 6 April 1900, 280; "A Prayer for the State," *Baptist*, 1 January 1901, 3; *New Zealand Baptist*, January 1900, 15.

[72] A. Roger, "Britain's Reverse," *Baptist Times and Freeman*, 22 December 1899, 879.

[73] The Church of Scotland date was 21 January 1900.

[74] Philip Williamson, "National Days of Prayer: The Churches, the State and Public Worship in Britain, 1899–1957," *English Historical Review* 128, no. 531 (April 2013): 337.

[75] Williamson, "National Days of Prayer."

[76] Gordon L. Heath, "Sin in the Camp: The Day of Humble Supplication in the Anglican Church in Canada in the Early Months of the South African War," *Journal of the Canadian Church Historical Society* 44 (Fall 2002): 207-226.

the churches.[77] The *Southern Baptist* in Australia printed support for a day of prayer to reverse the disasters in South Africa.[78] In regards to the outcome of such a day, one article expressed the expectation that "the Lord will favourably regard the bitter cry of His children, and stretch forth His mighty arm in the defense of our beleaguered brethren and in upholding the integrity of our Empire."[79] It also provided a description of a service in Flinders Street Baptist:

> Sunday, 11th February, being set apart as a day of special intercession and prayer that the war in South Africa might be brought to a speedy close, special reference was made to this throughout the day, both in the church and school. The pulpit and platform were adorned with flags, and colours of the Empire, and special appropriate hymns were printed and sung for the occasion, the choir being augmented by an orchestra of about a dozen instruments."[80]

An article in the *Baptist Times and Freeman* supported the day of humiliation, especially because the nation had been deemed arrogant and warmongering, even going so far as to invoke God for battle rather than for humility and peace on earth.[81]

When battlefield victories began immediately following the day of prayer, many considered the real reason for the British successes was the providential intervention of God due to the supplication of his people. A letter to the editor in the *Baptist Times and Freeman* declared that "national prayer has been followed by national success" and what needed to occur was thanksgiving to God for his deliverance.[82] However, elsewhere it was noted that one needed to be careful when ascribing to God certain actions out of risk of taking "God's name in vain."[83] The *New Zealand Baptist* acknowledged a recent Anglican thanksgiving church service for recent successes, but made no mention of similar services among Baptists.[84] However, once again it was the *Southern Baptist* that printed extensive commentary related to the day of prayer. In regards to the relief of Kimberley that followed the day of prayer, it was claimed that "Prayer

---

[77] "The Day of National Intercession," *Southern Baptist*, 15 February 1900, 38. See also "Sunday, 11th February," *Southern Baptist*, 1 March 1900, 50; "A Day of Prayer," *Southern Baptist*, 15 February 1900, 37; "The Council of Churches," *Southern Baptist*, 15 February 1900, 37; J.B., "The Mission of the British People," *Southern Baptist*, 15 February 1900, 43.

[78] "A Day of Prayer," *Southern Baptist*, 15 February 1900, 37; "The Council of Churches," *Southern Baptist*, 15 February 1900, 37.

[79] "Launceston," *Southern Baptist*, 1 March 1900, 57.

[80] "Flinders Street," *Southern Baptist*, 1 March 1900, 56. For commentary on other churches, see "Alberton," *Southern Baptist*, 1 March 1900, 56; "Portland," *Southern Baptist*, 1 March 1900, 57; "Warrnambool," *Southern Baptist*, 1 March 1900, 56; "Launceston," *Southern Baptist*, 1 March 1900, 56.

[81] "The Church and the War," *Baptist Times and Freeman*, 16 February 1900, 122.

[82] Agnes E. Weston, "National Thanksgiving," *Baptist Times and Freeman*, 16 March 1900, 217.

[83] "The Name of God," *Baptist Times and Freeman*, 23 March 1900, 226.

[84] "Chit Chat," *New Zealand Baptist*, April 1900, 63.

Has Been Heard."[85] Another reference to the relief of Kimberley declared: "The Relief of Kimberley we trace to Divine intervention. As believers in the God who hears prayer, we cannot forget that since Sunday, 11th February, the tide of fortune has turned. Let us still hold on to God, humbling ourselves before Him, and yet hoping in His merciful aid."[86] The deliverance of Ladysmith was also due to God's "Divine hand."[87] The tide of war, it was argued, turned after the day of humiliation.[88] It also expressed lament that in the joyous celebrations of victory there were no Baptist churches open for those who wanted to pray and give glory to God who brought about the victory.[89] It did mention, with approval, other services held on Sunday to "give thanks to God, who ruleth over all."[90] When the war dragged on into 1901 with no end in sight, both the *Southern Baptist* and *Baptist Times and Freeman* floated the idea that another one was needed in order to bring an end to the guerilla war.[91] Perhaps buoyed by the apparent success of the earlier day of humiliation, the *Canadian Baptist* encouraged the idea of a new day of humiliation and prayer to bring about spiritual renewal for the work of home and foreign missions.[92]

Embedded within the commentary surrounding providence in general and the day of humiliation in particular were a number of interrelated assumptions regarding national and imperial identity as well as the conflation of the expansion of the empire with the spread of Christianity. These assumptions were in a symbiotic relationship with the evangelical commitment to see souls saved, and as a result many BACSANZ Baptists were ardent supporters of what they considered to be a providentially established empire that appeared to help fulfill their ultimate purpose of Christianizing the nation and spreading the gospel to foreign lands. In short, there was no dissonance in commitments to nation, empire, and missions. Rather, all three were deemed to play a part in a providential plan to bless to the world. Below is a summary of two critical components to such a view: the relationship between national destiny and missions, and the identification of the expansion of the empire with the spread of the gospel.

---

[85] "Prayer Has Been Heard," *Southern Baptist*, 1 March 1900, 49.

[86] "The Relief of Kimberley," *Southern Baptist*, 1 March 1900, 50. See also "Sunday, 11th February," *Southern Baptist*, 1 March 1900, 50.

[87] "The Relief of Ladysmith," *Southern Baptist*, 15 March 1900, 62.

[88] "It Will Be Remembered That," *Southern Baptist*, 31 January 1901, 26.

[89] "But Why Was Not," *Southern Baptist*, 31 May 1900, 121.

[90] "No Small Part in the Celebrations," *Southern Baptist*, 31 May 1900, 122.

[91] "It Will Be Remembered," *Southern Baptist*, 31 January 1901, 26; F.B. Meyer, "A Day of Humiliation and Prayer," *Baptist Times and Freeman*, 18 October 1901, 710.

[92] "A Day of Humiliation and Prayer," *Canadian Baptist*, 24 October 1901, 9; James Grant, "The Day of Humiliation and Prayer," *Canadian Baptist*, 31 October 1901, 5; A. Murdoch, "The Day of Humiliation and Prayer," *Canadian Baptist*, 31 October 1901, 5; "A Day of Humiliation and Prayer," *Canadian Baptist*, 31 October 1901, 5; "Humiliation and Prayer," *Canadian Baptist*, 31 October 1901, 8; "After the Day, What?" *Canadian Baptist*, 7 November 1901, 8.

First, the relationship between national destiny and missions. Previous chapters have demonstrated how Baptists had a genuine sense of identity as loyal citizens of the empire as well as patriotic members of their nation, dominion, federation or colony. What needs to be noted at this juncture is how those same Baptists fused national identity with the missionary mandate. With the triumph of Protestantism in Britain developed the view that Britain and its empire were unique Protestant entities with divine blessing.[93] After Waterloo, British national identity was constructed around five interrelated notions: free, civilized, prosperous, Christian and Protestant, and the "linchpin" of those was Protestantism.[94] The link between Protestantism and empire was also significant. The fusion of imperial and anti-Catholic rhetoric was shared in Britain, South Africa, Australia, New Zealand and Canada.[95] That same Protestant identity was related to national destiny. Stewart J. Brown notes how, for many Britons, the British national identity was infused with a divine purpose. The empire's rise to power was due to its religion, and the nation and empire had a providential purpose for spreading the gospel. They were, Brown goes on to say, like the ancient Hebrew people with a sacred responsibility as God's chosen people, and that sacred responsibility meant sending "Christian missionaries, spreading Christian and moral civilisation, and promoting righteousness in international affairs.[96] Commentary in the *Baptist Times and Freeman* indicates that a number of British Baptists resonated with this sense of national destiny. Hymns and prayers reveal a distinctly Christian identity and calling for the nation.[97] Commentary after Queen Victoria's death indicates the higher calling of British imperialism:

> In our midst are a large, and, we believe, growing party, often exposed to ridicule, who are determined that the Empire shall be exalted in righteousness. We believe in Imperialism in a higher sense - not as some Babylonian brute force, but as a free holy union, where the principle at the base of the customs and laws is 'whatsoever ye would that men should do to you do ye even so to them.' The world is ripe for such an Empire. May it be in these latter days the great gift of God to him who is now called in His providence to the most magnificent position and privilege the world has ever known.[98]

For Baptists, that position and privilege was related to the spread of Christian missions, for Britain's national destiny was tied to its providentially ordained

---

[93] John Wolffe, "Anti-Catholicism and the British Empire, 1815-1914," in *Empires of Religion*, ed., Hilary M. Carey (New York: Palgrave Macmillan, 2008), 58.

[94] Hugh McLeod, "Protestantism and British National Identity, 1815-1945," in *National Religion*, eds., P. van der Veer and H. Lehmann (Princeton: Princeton University Press, 1999), 50.

[95] Wolffe, "Anti-Catholicism and the British Empire," 43.

[96] Stewart J. Brown, *Providence and Empire, 1815-1914* (Harlow: Pearson, 2008), 3.

[97] "Coronation Hymn," *Baptist Times and Freeman*, 30 May 1902, 407; T.H., "England's Prayer Today," *Baptist Times and Freeman*, 4 July 1902, 495.

[98] "Our Beloved Queen Is Dead," *Baptist Times and Freeman*, 25 January 1901, 60-61.

role to be a light to the world and a means of spreading the gospel to foreign lands. At an address to the Manchester Auxiliary of the BMS, Maclaren proclaimed:

> We have heard a great deal about the white man's burden. Ah! The true white man's burden is the burden of the Lord! The Christian man's burden is to spread the name of the Master; and that is what is laid upon England's Churches and upon us ... Do we not submit to the will of our dear Lord and Master, when we say that England has been placed where England stands, that English Christians might be God's witnesses to the ends of the earth?[99]

Maclaren's statement makes it clear that he understood Britain's national and imperial destiny to be tied to the missionary enterprise; God had raised up England for that very purpose. Their Protestant Christian identity and destiny also meant that the nation needed to be purged of its sins and its churches revived so that God could once again bless the imperial enterprise; what pleased some was that the war and its difficulties seemed to lead Britons back to their Christian calling:

> This war may prove to be the harrowing which was required before the good seed could find a lodgment in some ground. The revival, for which thousands have prayed and are praying, may be hastened by these months of anxiety and distress. ... Finally, this war has achieved what no success or extension of empire could have - it has solemnized us. Britons have never been as light-hearted as their French neighbours, but they had been growing careless and worldly ... We recognize thankfully that a new spirit is infusing our life. May it disperse and destroy the awful wickedness which was waging such a hostile force against the purity and power of our nation; and may it nerve all Christians to a more consistent and earnest life![100]

In his New Year's address, Clifford echoed this sentiment when he declared that the war had awakened England to its sins, and as a result was "becoming more and more alive to [their] peril" and committed to their divinely ordained White Man's Burden to spread the faith abroad.[101] The same sense of national destiny in the metropole was also an integral element to understandings of national and imperial identity in the peripheries.

There was a particular view of Canadian nationhood that tied missions to the fulfillment of God's purpose for the young Dominion. Many saw Canada as having a divinely appointed duty that must not be neglected. Berger notes how this "realization of Canadian nationhood [was] contingent upon the acceptance

---

[99] "NZBMS," *New Zealand* Baptist, February 1901, 26-27.

[100] "Midway Through the War," *Baptist Times and Freeman*, 19 January 1900, 50-51.

[101] "Dr. Clifford's New Year's Address," *Baptist Times and Freeman*, 4 January 1901, 14. For further commentary on concern over Britain's vices, Christian identity, and providentially established destiny to spread the faith, see "Features of Parliament," *Baptist Times and Freeman*, 21 December 1900, 1026-1027; "Baptist Union of Great Britain and Ireland, Spring Assembly 1901," *Supplement to the Baptist Times and Freeman*, 26 April 1901.

of racial responsibility and fulfillment of the mission."[102] For some, he argues, Canada could only be a nation if it "acted and functioned like one, and, to them, this meant that she must assume her share of the civilizing work within the Empire and be ready to defend that agency of progress."[103] This civilizing and Christianizing mandate applied to both domestic and foreign missions.[104] Consequently, Canadian English Protestant imperialism was "infused" with religious emotion.[105] Two examples from the *Messenger and Visitor* will demonstrate this conviction. First, it was made clear to readers of the *Messenger and Visitor* that the only explanation that made sense of Canada's seemingly implausible existence was the "Divine Hand upon the affairs of this world."[106] The same article also made it clear that Canada's "national destiny" was to be found within the British Empire, an empire purported to be God's "minister for good" in the world. Second, a sermon by John Watson was printed that fused Britain's identity with that of his ancient people the Israelites.[107] Watson identified Britain with the ancient nation of Israel, challenging readers to see that God had providentially raised up Britain to be a modern-day Israel. A review of Britain's history, Watson argued, could lead to only one conclusion – that Britain had a providentially established mission: "You say that Israel had a special mission; and is any man's eye so blind that he cannot see the mission of England?" Among the benefits of the war, Watson concluded, was that the humiliation of defeat had driven the British back to God. While war should always be lamented, he was convinced that it had purified motives, fortified the moral fibre of the race, united the nation, and strengthened the army.

> Some of us were afraid in past years that our people, through their great commercial prosperity and through certain social influences, were growing soft and losing their moral fibre, and some of us considered that nothing would so cleanse the nation as a great war. We dare not pray for such a thing; for, ah me, the widows and the orphans; but we felt if a war should come, it would cleanse England. And the war had come, and now the mass of our people are coming out of the furnace strong and refined. Has our army ever stood higher in bravery, in patience, in confidence, than today?…Did you ever expect to see the day – I did not – when from

---

[102] Berger, *The Sense of Power*, 231.

[103] Berger, *The Sense of Power*, 231.

[104] Home missions was considered to be the first step in global missions: See "Patriotism and Home Missions," *Canadian Baptist*, 21 June 1900, 4. See also Sean Mills, "'Preach the World:' Canadian Imperialism and Missionary Outreach at the Montreal Diocesan Theological College, 1892-1903," *Journal of the Canadian Church Historical Society* 43 (2001): 5-38. French Roman Catholics did not share in the distinctly Protestant interpretation of this mission. See Berger, *The Sense of Power*, 232. See also Jean-Charles Falardeau, "The Role of the Church in French Canada," in *French-Canadian Society*, eds., M. Rioux and Y. Martins (Toronto: McClelland and Stewart, 1964).

[105] Carl Berger, *The Sense of Power*, 217.

[106] "God and the Nation," *Messenger and Visitor*, 31 January 1900, 4.

[107] Rev. John Watson, "Comfort for England," *Messenger and Visitor*, 28 March 1900, 2-3 (reprinted from *British Weekly*).

homes of affluence at the West End and from the humble homes at the East End, from the cities and from country cottages, young men, uncompelled, would arise and go forward, counting all things but loss for their country's sake? ... the princes of Israel and the people therof [sic] have gone willingly to the death for their country's sake.[108]

All in all, he felt the British had "learned humility" through the dark months of the war, and that being the case, could once again carry out God's purposes for the empire.[109]

In regards to New Zealand, Hugh Morrison notes that nationhood was a contested category, and asserts the fact that "New Zealand reflected British attitudes and trends is hardly surprising given its close imperial ties in this period. At the same time New Zealand was not a carbon copy of the metropole."[110] He also claims that "theological and philosophical thinking about missions in late-nineteenth and early-twentieth century New Zealand were not easily disentangled from language extolling the virtues of Western civilization, and more particularly those of the British Empire." Central to New Zealand supporters of empire were the convictions that empire was a means to international unity, the empire was providentially established, the empire exhibited superior moral qualities, and the empire had a trusteeship of "lesser" races. For New Zealand Baptists, the budding national identity was inseparable from the destiny of the empire of which it was a part. While New Zealand national identity and destiny may have been contested, for a number of Baptists it could not be separated from the alleged missionary mandate of the empire.

Unlike the Boers who purportedly commandeered God, the British were deemed to have been commandeered by God.[111] The British mission - and by extension, the mission of New Zealand - was to spread Christianity by means of the empire. Reference was made to Maclaren's recent address at a BMS auxiliary meeting in Manchester regarding the providentially arranged responsibility to spread the faith:

"Who knoweth whether thou art come to the kingdom for such a time as this?" said Mordecai to Esther; and surely we do not presumptuously read the meanings of Providence, when we apply these words to ourselves. And let me put it into a more clear word than that. Do we not submit to the will of our dear Lord and Mas-

---

[108] Rev. John Watson, "Comfort for England," *Messenger and Visitor*, 28 March 1900, 2-3.

[109] For further examples of the connection between national destiny, imperialism and missions, see W.E. Norton, "The Attitude of the Church Towards the Political Life of the Country," *Canadian Baptist*, 20 December 1900, 2; *Canadian Baptist*, 18 January 1900, 1; *Canadian Baptist*, 8 February 1900, 1; *Canadian Baptist*, 29 March 1900, 1.

[110] Hugh Morrison, "'But we are Concerned with a Greater Imperium': The New Zealand Protestant Missionary Movement and the British Empire, 1870-1930," *Social Sciences and Missions* 21, no. 1 (2008): 97-127.

[111] "Commandeering or Commandeered?," *New Zealand Baptist*, February 1900, 18.

ter, when we say that England has been placed where England stands, that English Christians might be God's witnesses to the ends of the earth?[112]

The implication was clear, New Zealand was to participate in that destiny. Elsewhere, the spread of the empire was linked to the spread of God's truth.[113] Perhaps the clearest expression of New Zealand's national destiny being tied to the imperial vision of spreading the faith is the article by S.R. Ingold of Oxford Terrace Baptist Church in Christchurch. He wrote that while there had been much in the history of the empire that had "not been God-honouring," he was convinced that "as a nation, we have been graciously chosen as the means for the accomplishing of the Divine purpose of succouring the oppressed, liberating the enslaved, and illumining the darkness of the heathen world, as has no other nation."[114] God's providential call on the nation came with responsibilities, and Ingold exhorted his readers to "never forget that, if, as a nation, God has favoured us above the other nations of the earth, our responsibilities are proportionately greater than theirs." He considered the recent setbacks in the battlefield to have actually been a blessing, for God had used them to humble them for their hubris and remind them of their God-ordained responsibilities: "But the reverses we have suffered have undoubtedly had a sobering effect upon us. We believe that, as a people, our eyes are now turned Godward as they have not been of late."[115]

Arthur Patrick identifies how most Australian Methodists were pro-war, ardent defenders of empire, who believed that God in his providence would ultimately bring victory to the British cause.[116] The Methodist impulse to Christianize society, he concludes, was one important reason for their support. Their zeal for the imperial cause was rooted in the widespread conviction that the spread of the empire in Africa advanced civilization to the betterment of its subjects, and especially the fact that it helped put an end to the bane of slavery. Both Brian Fletcher and Robert Withycombe make it clear that late nineteenth-century Australian Anglicans were, for the most part, committed to the ideals of the empire and Australia's active engagement and defense of the same.[117] Despite active participation in events that nurtured a nascent and growing distinct-

---

[112] "NZBMS," *New Zealand* Baptist, February 1901, 26-27.

[113] Alice G. Ford, "Peace," *New Zealand Baptist*, July 1902, 109.

[114] S.R. Ingold, "The War in South Africa: The Christian's Proper Attitude Regarding It," *New Zealand Baptist*, April 1900, 61-62.

[115] S.R. Ingold, "The War in South Africa: The Christian's Proper Attitude Regarding It," *New Zealand Baptist*, April 1900, 61-62. Kipling's rebuke of Britain in "The Islanders" was approved. See "The Islanders," *New Zealand Baptist*, March 1902, 41.

[116] Arthur Patrick, "'A Dreadful But Absolute Necessity': The Boer War according to The Methodist," *Church Heritage* 6, no. 4 (1980): 109-121.

[117] Brian Fletcher, "Anglicanism and Nationalism in Australia, 1901-62," *Journal of Religious History* 23 (June 1999): 215-233; Robert S.M. Withycombe, "Australian Anglicans and Imperial Identity, 1900-1914," *Journal of Religious History* 25, no. 3 (October 2001): 286-305.

ly Australian identity, the Britishness and whiteness of Australia was encouraged by church authorities. Withycombe claims that the nationalities expressed and supported by the church were "complex, actively debated, but not clearly defined." What was clear was that there were common elements in the church's attitudes, elements that revolved around the British monarchy, empire, race, and providential national destiny.[118] Like many of their Methodist and Anglican counterparts, a predominant Australian Baptist national vision understood Australia's national identity to be inseparable from British imperial relations. The war highlighted that imperial relationship, and the events surrounding the Federation led to heightened commentary on the new nation's destiny.

It was asserted that Britain's empire was granted by God for the spreading of Christianity. God had made the Teutonic peoples the chief "guardians and expositors" of the Bible, and in his providence had opened doors for mission work throughout the world.[119] Britain had "a most obvious mission" to spread the faith,[120] and cooperation between Anglo-Saxon powers would lead to the evangelization of the world.[121] What the various papers also made clear was that Australia's national destiny was wrapped up in that imperial and evangelical zeal.

While the Australian Federation in 1900 was exhilarating, and "God's hand" had been seen in the formalities,[122] there was concern that the true purpose of the new nation would be eclipsed by the festivities. Consequently, before and after the Federation, a number of articles raised concerns about disturbing non-Christian elements to the celebrations and services, and reminded readers of the solemn obligations associated with nationhood.[123] The new nation needed to remember to advance on its "knees."[124] God worked through individuals as well as nations, and he would judge them accordingly: obedience would bring his

---

[118] Withycombe, "Australian Anglicans and Imperial Identity," 287.

[119] J.B., "The Mission of the British People," *Southern Baptist*, 15 February 1900, 43.

[120] "Our Correspondent 'J'," *Southern Baptist*, 2 August 1900, 170. See also Rudyard Kipling, "White Man's Burden," *Southern Baptist*, 15 June 1899, 123.

[121] "The Entente Cordiale," *Southern Baptist*, 15 February 1900, 38.

[122] "And so those who believe in Him as the sovereign an immediate controller of nature, will not fail to thank Him for the splendid weather which contributed so largely to the pleasure of the people." See "That Such Immense Crowds," *Southern Baptist*, 15 May 1901, 110; "The Commonwealth of Australia," *Southern Baptist*, 17 January 1901, 24.

[123] "Religion and the States," *Queensland Baptist*, August 1901, 99; "God Recognised," *Queensland Baptist*, August 1901, 99; "Address to the Governor-General," *Baptist*, 1 January 1901, 3; "Young People," *Southern Baptist*, 3 January 1901, 4. There was also commentary in the *New Zealand Baptist* on the need for Australia to remember its Christian identity. See "Heathenising Australia," *New Zealand Baptist*, June 1901, 88; Rev. F.W. Boreham, "Is Great Britain Christian?" *New Zealand Baptist*, July 1901, 99-101.

[124] "God Speed Australia," *Southern Baptist*, 3 January 1901, 2.

blessing and sin his judgment.[125] Of utmost concern was that Baptists remember that the nation's destiny was tied to its involvement in the imperial missionary enterprise. God had placed nations such as India under the rule of the empire so that the gospel could go forth,[126] and Australians needed to embrace national responsibilities by continuing to participate in the "spiritual conquests of the Gospel" made possible through the spreading of the empire.[127] The new nation needed to "understand her responsibilities to the great Orient," responsibilities that included being a "great evangelising agent for the nations around her."[128] Coupled to the national dream was the anticipation that "troops of efficiently equipped men and women will yet pour from our shores in to oriental lands to evangelise them."[129]

The churches in South Africa were in a unique position among BACSANZ Baptists since they were in a continent deemed in its entirety to be a missionary field. They believed that their colonial and budding national identity was fused to a providentially established imperial and missionary mandate to spread the faith to the white Boers and especially to the Africans.[130] In reference to a series of articles entitled "The Colonies and the Century," the editor of the *South African Baptist* declared that God had special purposes for extraordinary nations, and that "God is in the making of current history."[131] Of course, in his opinion the British Empire - including the colonies in South Africa - was one of those extraordinary nations that God had given a unique role for the evangelization of Africa, and he made sure that the *South African Baptist* provided ample articles to reinforce such a view.[132] God was deemed to have opened a door for evangelism in South Africa just like God opened a door for the Apostle Paul (1 Corinthians 16:9).[133] The British Empire in general had led to the arrival and advance of the gospel in Africa, but South African destiny was fused to the evangelistic enterprise. Baptists and other evangelicals had a postwar role to play in uniting the British and Boers.[134] The unity of the two warring peoples was important for an even greater task; as one commentator declared, "And then, dwelling together in unity as brethren, both the peoples of European

---

[125] W. Whale, "The Nations that Forget God," *Queensland Baptist*, August 1897, 104-105; Lord Tennyson, "Prayer for the Commonwealth," *Queensland Baptist*, January 1901, 8; "Great Wisdom," *Southern Baptist*, 17 January 1901, 14; "Humiliation," *Southern Baptist*, 3 September 1902, 193; "Watch Night Services," *Southern Baptist*, 17 January 1901, 15; "The Commonwealth," *Baptist*, 3 September 1900, 1-2.
[126] Rev. W. Whale, "Our Third Contingent," *Queensland Baptist*, March 1900, 34-35.
[127] "Christ for the New Century and the New Nation," *Baptist*, November 1900, 4.
[128] A.W.W., "The Birth of a Nation," *Southern Baptist*, 3 January 1901, 7.
[129] A.W.W., "The Birth of a Nation," *Southern Baptist*, 3 January 1901, 7.
[130] Rudyard Kipling, "White Man's Burden," *South African Baptist*, October 1899, 38.
[131] "On the Editorial Stoep," *South African Baptist*, September 1900, 146.
[132] "Hail XXth Century," *South African Baptist*, January 1901, 1; "V.R.J." *South African Baptist*, February 1901, 13-14.
[133] "The Open Door in South Africa," *South African Baptist*, October 1900, 137-139.
[134] "The Outlook," *South African Baptist*, August 1901, 91-92.

origin [Briton and Boer] will be able to address themselves to their great mission of evangelizing and civilizing the natives - a task with the success of which the permanent well-being of South Africa is inextricably bound up."[135] The Christianizing of the "natives" was not only to be part of the national destiny to reach the continent for the gospel, but also a pragmatic necessity at home if the minority whites were to survive in a postwar South Africa dominated by a black majority.

South Africa would have to be a godly nation if it were to live up to its God-given destiny, and calls for religious revival were rooted in the need for individuals to experience personal salvation and for the nation to be purged of its sins; once those were accomplished, the nation could once again advance, confident of God's providential blessing.[136] For instance, E. Baker mentioned in his Baptist Union presidential address that the number of recent military setbacks must be due to God punishing the empire for sin. His conclusion was that what was needed to restore the fortunes on the battlefield was a revival of religion since ancient history and recent experience had shown that when people humbled themselves, God would relent and bring blessing.[137] Elsewhere, he tied good citizenship to a revival of religion: "And if a revival of godliness is what is needed to cause the Lord to turn His face towards us, there is then no greater service we can render to our country than to give ourselves whole-heartedly to seeking first His kingdom and righteousness. The best patriotism is to follow the Lord and to win others to the same."[138] For Baker, South African patriotism needed to be rooted in a revived and vibrant religion that led to the blessing of God for the fulfillment of the national destiny.

A second assumption was the conflation of the expansion of the empire with the spread of the gospel. Undergirding BACSANZ Baptist commentary on providence and empire was the belief that there was a beneficial, and sometimes even necessary, relationship between the extension of the empire and the spread of the gospel. Chapter Five has shown how the war was supported due to correlations between justice and empire. Related to those assumptions was the conviction that the missionary enterprise was best served by the empire's advancement. Reinforcing that view was the striking (and what they deemed to be providentially arranged) advancement of the empire that coincided with a dramatic advance of the gospel.[139]

[135] "The New Era in S. Africa," *South African Baptist*, July 1900, 101-102.
[136] "The King," *Southern Baptist*, 26 March 1902, 73; Rudyard Kipling, "Recessional," *South African Baptist*, July 1899, 190.
[137] Rev. E. Baker, "The Presidential Address," *South African Baptist*, July 1901, 77-83; "A Plea For Revival," *South African Baptist*, September 1902, 97-98.
[138] Ernest Baker, "A Presidential Message," *South African Baptist*, January 1901, 6.
[139] "Forced Against Our Will," *New Zealand Baptist*, April 1900, 49; S.R. Ingold, "The War in South Africa: The Christian's Proper Attitude Regarding It," *New Zealand Baptist*, April 1900, 61-62; H.H. Driver, "Between the Centuries," *New Zealand Baptist*, December 1899, 177-182; John Robinson, "The Colonies and the Century," *South Afri-*

Assumptions implicit in Livingstone's fusion of Christianity and Commerce may have waxed and waned over the nineteenth century,[140] but they certainly resonated with many during the war in South Africa. In this, Baptists were not alone. As Stanley notes, "for most of the nineteenth century, British Christians believed that the missionary was called to propagate the imagined benefits of Western civilization alongside the Christian message."[141] More specifically, underlying the support for missions under the waving Union Jack was that the alleged benefits of the empire, such as British government, education, culture, commerce and technology, would assist the advance of mission work and aid in the Christianizing of various peoples. Evidence for this association can be seen in numerous articles in the press. During his trip to Queensland churches, C.S. Mead encouraged his listeners to recognize and support the conflation of empire and missions:

> The thought of Empire is in the air, men are learning to "think in continents."...Not that every passing idea is to be grasped at, but this conception [the imperium] is a *true* one, it is a *fundamental* one, and it must be an *increasingly dominant* one. Yet this thrill of Christian imperialism is largely waning in our churches. Let our people learn that in supporting Foreign Missions they are acting the part of empire-builders, and their horizon will broaden, and the cause of missions will lift, and the heart of the Church will beat with a stronger and nobler throb.[142]

He went on to say that when people pray "Thy Kingdom Come" they should be thinking not just of a heavenly kingdom but of an earthy one as well. Military metaphors "permeated hymns and promotional literature" at the end of the nineteenth century.[143] While not commonly used in the BACSANZ Baptist press, when they did occur, the use of such military metaphors further complicated the relationship between missions and empire and made it difficult to identify the line between the temporal and spiritual kingdoms. For instance, reference was made to missionary "troops,"[144] "spiritual conquests,"[145] "subdu-

---

can Baptist, July 1900, 103-105; John Robinson, "The Colonies and the Century," *South African Baptist*, August 1900, 115-117; John Robinson, "The Colonies and the Century," *South African Baptist*, September 1900, 127-129; John Robinson, "The Colonies and the Century," *South African Baptist*, October 1900, 140-142; John Robinson, "The Colonies and the Century," *South African Baptist*, November 1900, 152-155; John Robinson, "The Colonies and the Century," *South African Baptist*, December 1900, 168-169; "Christ for the New Century and the New Nation," *Baptist*, 1 November 1900, 4-5; Rev. W. Whale, "Our Third Contingent," *Queensland Baptist*, 1 March 1900, 34-35; J.B., "The Mission of the British People," *Southern Baptist*, 15 February 1900, 43; "A Year and a Century," *Messenger and Visitor*, 26 December 1900, 4.

[140] Andrew Porter, "'Commerce and Christianity': The Rise and Fall of a Nineteenth-Century Missionary Slogan," *The Historical Journal* 28, no. 3 (1985): 597-621.

[141] Stanley, *The Bible and the Flag*, 157.

[142] C.S. Mead, "The True Missionary Motive," *Queensland Baptist*, July 1901, 87-89.

[143] Miller, *Painting the Map Red*, 10.

[144] A.W.W., "The Birth of a Nation," *Southern Baptist*, 3 January 1901, 7.

ing for Christ,"[146] and an analogy was made between good soldiers of Jesus Christ and good soldiers of the Queen.[147] Elsewhere, the Apostle Paul's instruction in his letter to the Philippians took on distinct political overtones: "Let us lay aside every weight and sectionalism that doth so easily beset us, and let us run with earnestness and faithfulness the national race that is set before us."[148] This type of language only strengthened the perceived bond between the work of missionaries and empire.

A recurring motif in the BACSANZ Baptist press was that military force - followed by British rule - was deemed to be God's instrument to prepare a region or people for the gospel message and open the way for mission work.[149] The empire's advance was reckoned to help the spread of the gospel in at least two ways: it both prepared people for the gospel and protected missionaries and their converts. One commentator noted that "the advantages that the civilization of Europe is bringing to Africa through telegram, railway and steamer may become powerful as well as useful agents in the future spread of the Gospel in this continent."[150] Another noted the partition of Africa and the blessings European rule brought, including the opportunities for spreading the gospel.[151] Kitchener's capture of Khartoum was celebrated, for the "events finally open the great Soudan to the incoming of civilization and Christianity."[152] Commentary on the crisis in China further illustrates this conviction that the spread of empire was an oft-necessary precursor to the gospel. The problem of China was understood to be a part of the larger conflict between the old world and the new. China's conservatism had kept it isolated in the past, but that could no longer be the case; the world had advanced and China needed to modernize.

> But it has become impossible for any people or nation to remain unmoved by the tides and currents of the world's life and thought. Even China can no longer maintain her seclusion and continue to dream on through other centuries as in the past.

---

[145] "Christ for the New Century and the New Nation," *Baptist*, November 1900, 4.
[146] "The Open Door in South Africa," *South African Baptist*, October 1900, 139.
[147] J.W. Weeks, "Soldiership," *Canadian Baptist*, 25 January 1900, 14-15.
[148] Norton, "The Attitude of the Church Towards the Political Life of the Century," 2.
[149] For further analysis of nineteenth century views on the necessary advance of imperial rule and commerce as a preparation for the arrival of Christianity, see Porter, "Commerce and Christianity."
[150] "The Partition of Africa," *South African Baptist*, December 1899, 70.
[151] "The Partition of Africa," *Baptist*, 4 May 1900, 8.
[152] "Overshadowed," *New Zealand Baptist*, February 1900, 24. Over a decade earlier Canadian Baptists had made the same point in regards to the annexation of Burma: "But however mixed may be the motives that lead to the invasion, and however doubtful its justification, there can scarcely be a doubt that, like many other extensions of civilized government, will redound to the highest good of the benighted natives. A new door will be opened for missionary enterprise." See "The Annexation of Burmah," *Canadian Baptist*, 5 November 1885, 4. See also Gordon L. Heath, "The Nile Expedition, New Imperialism and Canadian Baptists, 1884-1885," *Baptist Quarterly* 44, no. 3 (July 2011): 171-186.

The rude, bustling modern world, with its steamships and its railways, its steam and its electricity, and all the enginery of modern industry and modern warfare, has been knocking at her gates and making such a hubbub in her ears that poor China's dreams are sadly disturbed, and she moves uneasily upon her couch, with indications of an awakening that may result uncomfortably for her visitors. Not a few of the sons of China have awakened to the fact that, while their country has been dreaming complacent dreams, the world has been moving.[153]

The Boxers were opposed to this modernization and sought to put a stop to it. It was conceded that modernization would bring disturbances to the traditional economy, and people would lose jobs because of the new factories. However, there was no way to stop the progress. Ultimately, the article concluded, the inexorable advance of Western influence and industry would be a blessing to China: "the change will come, and the people of China will yet be blessed with a Christian faith and a Christian civilization."[154] Elsewhere, this necessary advance of civilization was also portrayed a law of history that could be exploited for the advance of the kingdom of God: "History teaches that the lower races must inevitably pass under the dominion of the higher, and we would rather they should pass under the control of men of our own race and our own religion."[155]

There was no necessary dissonance in commitments to nation, empire, and missions. Rather, all three were considered to play a part in a providential plan to bless to the world. National destiny and missions were deemed to be inextricable; the identification of the expansion of the empire with the spread of the gospel was commonplace. However, there were signs of discontent with imperialism and its supposed benefits. The discontent in the press did not seem to match the degree of disillusionment among certain frontline missionaries, suggesting a marked difference between personal and public attitudes to missions and empire. Nonetheless, criticisms were frequent enough to indicate a degree of unease with the partnership of missions and empire.

BACSANZ Baptist attitudes reflect some of the complexity and ambiguity noted by Porter and others.[156] James Greenlee and Charles Johnston have noted that the Boer War and the Boxer Rebellion in China began to unsettle British missionaries who had assumed that the link between missions and empire was beneficial for the church and its missionary work.[157] These conflicts, they ar-

---

[153] "The Problem of China," *Messenger and Visitor*, 1 August 1900, 4.
[154] For examples, see "Editorial Notes," *Canadian Baptist*, 16 August 1900, 1; "Commercial Benefit of Missions," *Canadian Missionary Link*, September 1902, 6; Mabel F. Mode, "Where We Are In Missions," *Canadian Missionary Link*, September 1900, 13-15; "China," *Religious Intelligencer*, 25 July 1900, 4.
[155] "The New Policy of America," *Baptist Times and Freeman*, 7 June 1901, 369.
[156] Porter, *Religion versus Empire ?*
[157] James G. Greenlee and Charles M. Johnston, *Good Citizens: British Missionaries and Imperial States, 1870-1918* (Montreal: McGill-Queen's University Press, 1999), ch.3. Ruth C. Brouwer notes that in the early 1880's there was some recognition among Canadian missionaries in India and East Asia that British imperial policy sometimes

gue, began to reveal that the empire's mandate and means of rule were not always sympathetic to the work of missions and, in the years leading up to the First World War, missionaries became convinced that the empire often hindered the work of missions. Brown claims that along with the events in South Africa undermining confidence in empire, the debacle in the Congo also eroded faith in imperialism.[158] One gets glimpses of this uncertainty in the BACSANZ press, and unease revolved around two related concerns. The first concern was the realization that the empire did not always benefit the work of missions, and the second was the rise of jingoistic imperialism.

In regards to the first, the inclusion of Henry Labouchère's poem "The Brown Man's Burden" (1899) in a few papers indicates that there was some apprehension about the purported beneficial relationship between imperialism and Christian virtues, not to mention the providential mandate implicit in the white man's burden to reach "the heathen" with the gospel.[159] Another intriguing example of reticence over the relationship between empire and missions was a letter to the editor in the *Southern Baptist*. This brief exchange in the *Southern Baptist* reveals a contested interpretation of the conflation of the spread of the gospel with the spread of empire. It began with a letter from a missionary from South Africa who argued in support of the war and how the advance of the empire aided Christian missions:

> And now our God has arisen, now the fearful wrongs of past generations are to be righted; the Lord of Hosts has sent forth our British army to fight the battles, not of British against Boer, not of Uitlanders against Transvaal oppression, as it appears to human sight, but to fight for the God of the Nations on behalf of *the myriad lives, of the numberless nations with which the interior of Africa is teeming, which only by the success of our British arms, can gain through all the future years opportunities to develop as God would have them develop, and grow into free, enlightened peoples*, to His glory and the blessing of the human race, and the heart satisfaction of Him who died that they might live [emphasis in original].[160]

Not long after, a letter was printed that rebutted such claims. In particular, the author identified the many sins of empire in South Africa, noted the mistreatment of the natives by the British, and questioned the simplistic identification of God with the British cause.[161] The article also claimed that rather than assisting the work of the missionaries, the advance of British rule - with its concomitant sins - actually made the task of missionaries more difficult. The editor felt

---

worked against mission work. See Ruth Compton Brouwer, *New Women for God: Canadian Presbyterian Women and India Missions, 1876-1914* (Toronto: University of Toronto Press, 1990), 80.

[158] Brown, *Providence and Empire*, 436-437.

[159] "The Brown Man's Burden," *Southern Baptist*, 29 June 1899, 142; "The Brown Man's Burden," *South African Baptist*, December 1900, 170.

[160] Mrs. Lewis, "A Voice from South Africa," *Southern Baptist*, 28 June 1900, 150. Also mentioned in "Miss Schreiner," *Southern Baptist*, 15 February 1900, 48.

[161] J., "Another Voice from South Africa," *Southern Baptist*, 2 August 1900, 178.

the need to comment on the inclusion of this article critical of the dominant narrative, and reminded readers that he did not approve of its content because he felt that despite the obvious sins of empire Britain's mission was "obvious" and that there was no "better fitted" for the task.[162] This brief exchange is a reminder that a positive correlation between empire and missions was sometimes contested.

Events in China led to considerable Canadian Baptist commentary on the relationship between missions and empire. There was an admission that imperialism had hurt the cause of missions in China.[163] The real cause of the rebellion was identified as the "earth-hunger" that had "taken possession of the nations."[164] The conduct of the Western powers in suppressing the rebellion further illustrated the evils of Western imperialism. The Germans mistreated the Chinese,[165] and the Russians were the worst abusers.[166] One letter to the editor of the *Canadian Baptist* bemoaned the actions of the Western powers in the Opium Wars, arms dealing, liquor trade, and prostitution, and even defended the right of the Chinese to respond to the appalling behavior of the West.[167] Such horrendous behavior, it was argued, made for a dreadful impression of Christianity.

> A correspondent of the *Times* in Japan writes that the Japanese are horrified at the brutality, cruelty, lust and love of plunder of the Russian troops in China. The French are not so cruel but share with the Russians the crimes of looting and outrage. The British are guilty of nothing but petty pilfering, and the Americans are free from all these charges. Christianity is on its trial before these Buddhist Japanese, in the men and the work best fitted to give the worst impression; for war, at

---

[162] "Our Correspondent 'J'," *Southern Baptist*, 2 August 1900, 170.

[163] For an analysis of Canadian Baptists and the Boxer Rebellion, see Gordon L. Heath, "When Missionaries Were Hated: An Examination of the Canadian Baptist Defense of Imperialism and Missions during the Boxer Rebellion, 1900," in *Baptists and Mission*, eds., Ian M. Randall and Anthony R. Cross (Milton Keynes: Paternoster Press, 2007), 261-276. Similar studies need to be made of other BACSANZ Baptists and the Boxer Rebellion.

[164] "Anti-foreign Crusades in China," *Canadian Missionary Link*, March 1901, 103-105. See also William Ashmore, "Conditions and Causes in China," *Canadian Baptist*, 20 September 1900, 11; "Mischievous Missionaries," *Canadian Baptist*, 27 September 1900, 8; A.T. Pierson, "Mysteries of God's Providence in China," *Canadian Missionary Link*, October 1900, 19-21; "Editorial Notes," *Messenger and Visitor*, 12 September 1900, 5; "The Causes of the Crisis in China," *Messenger and Visitor*, 6 February 1901, 7; "Editorial Notes," *Messenger and Visitor*, 20 February 1901, 4.

[165] "Editorial Notes," *Canadian Baptist*, 2 August 1900, 1.

[166] "Russian Barbarism," *Messenger and Visitor*, 21 November 1900, 1; "Editorial Notes," *Messenger and Visitor*, 26 September 1900, 4; "The War in China," *Canadian Baptist*, 6 September 1900, 16; "Editorial Notes," *Canadian Baptist*, 23 August 1900, 1; "Editorial Notes," *Canadian Baptist*, 20 September 1900, 1; "Editorial Notes," *Canadian Baptist*, 15 November 1900, 1.

[167] "What Rights do the Oriental Races Possess?" *Canadian Baptist*, 26 July 1900, 4.

the best, is unchristian if not anti-Christian."[168]

However, there is no indication in the Canadian Baptist press that the catastrophe in China led to a crisis of confidence in British imperialism and its impact on missions. There was the recognition that imperialism had harmed the missionary enterprise in China, but British imperialism was not implicated in the indictment. Imperialist nations such as France, Germany, and especially Russia, had exhibited what was deemed to be the worst abuses of imperialism, further reinforcing assumptions regarding the superiority and distinctiveness of British imperialism.

The second concern was the rise of militarism in society, often manifested in the worst excesses of jingoism or hubris that marred imperial celebrations. The sin of militarism was seen to plague Britain. In fact, the war not only revealed the latent militarism of Britons, it also exacerbated it. Commentary on militarism was frequent in the *Baptist Times and Freeman*, and concern with militarism was shared by other BACSANZ Baptists. Britain had become "passion-blinded"[169] and had a "pagan spirit" in the land,[170] and this was alarming for an allegedly Christian nation and empire.[171] Individuals such as Clifford and others bemoaned the jingoism in the nation. In a portion of a speech to the Spring Assembly of the Baptist Union on the evils of militarism and misguided patriotism, Clifford stated that patriotism needed to be broadened to include all humanity and no longer be selfish in regards to one's own country: "It will condemn the intolerant and aggressive Imperialism that turns the 'Flag' of the Country into a 'Commercial Asset,' provokes a war for filling the purses of the rich, and uses man – black, brown, red, or white – for the sake of satisfying an insatiable greed for power."[172] In a similar fashion, one article in the *Baptist Times and Freeman* declared:

---

[168] *Canadian Baptist*, 27 December 1900, 9.

[169] "The Pendulum," *Baptist Times and Freeman*, 16 November 1900, 918.

[170] "A Lesson of the War," *Baptist Times and Freeman*, 3 August 1900, 626-627. This article led to a number of letters to editor, all opposed to war. See C.T. Johnson, "Correspondence," *Baptist Times and Freeman*, 10 August 1900, 649; W.E. Wells, "Correspondence," *Baptist Times and Freeman*, 10 August 1900, 649; Geo P. McKay, "Baptists and Peace," *Baptist Times and Freeman*, 17 August 1900, 669; T. Witton Davies, "Baptists and Peace," *Baptist Times and Freeman*, 24 August 1900, 682; J. Chappell, "Baptists and Peace," *Baptist Times and Freeman*, 31 August 1900, 704; H.H. "Baptists and Peace," *Baptist Times and Freeman*, 7 September 1900, 725.

[171] See also "Mr. Carvell Williams and Militarism," *Baptist Times and Freeman*, 26 October 1900, 860; Rev. T. Phillips, "Christians and Militarism," *Baptist Times and Freeman*, 30 November 1900, 968; "The King's Speech," *Baptist Times and Freeman*, 22 February 1901, 124-125; "The Growth of Militarism," *Baptist Times and Freeman*, 14 March 1902, 197.

[172] Dr. Clifford, "Address to Spring Assembly," 4 May 1900, xi, supplement to the *Baptist Times and Freeman*.

We have heard quite enough recently of our "mightiest Empire": we are suffi-
ciently conscious of our prowess as a great military nation; what we want just now
is less flag-waving and more sober striving, less glorification of ourselves and our
country and more heartfelt humility. Armies and "the mightiest Empire" do not
make mightiest nations, nor was the Pharisee preferred before the Publican.[173]

Baptist Associations spoke out against the rising militarism.[174] A speech made
in Leicester at the Autumn 1900 assembly of the Baptist Union of Great Britain and Ireland claimed that Christianity was needed to purify the patriotism of
the day from unChristian assumptions, passions, and behaviors.[175] The *Baptist
Times and Freeman* published poetry against the war spirit.[176] A few years later
the paper published a poem entitled "Song of the Younger Nations" that was
deemed to be jingoistic, and there was an immediate response and a retraction
by the paper.[177]

There was nothing intrinsically wrong with patriotism, nor having an empire.
As one article on imperialism indicated, the issue was not empire *per se*, but
rather the nature of that empire.[178] Noting the imperial aspect of the Queen's
rule, it declared that there were "two chief leading spirits" that were a part of
Britain's imperial expansion: one rejoicing and glorifying in the military power
of empire, the other concerned with ensuring the "exaltation" of righteousness
in the empire. One believed in Troy, the other Jerusalem, and both forces were
"operative" in the empire. The danger was that the "powers of brute force, like
the military displays, dazzle the eye and confuse the thought; they pass along
with brilliant banners and flaming trumpet peals. The powers of moral force, on
the other hand, are noiseless as leaven."[179] The need was for a "strong, unwavering assertion of the Gospel of Christ. The Empire needs such men as some
of our Fathers were, and, we may add, such as some of our Brothers are. For
Baptists are still a power for righteousness in the land." The call was for Baptists to be strengthened so that they could be help contribute to a purer imperialism.[180] Ironically, when making claims about Baptists and their nation-building

---

[173] "'Lest We Forget'," *Baptist Times and Freeman*, 26 October 1900, 853.

[174] "Militarism!," *Baptist Times and Freeman*, 15 June 1900, 483.

[175] Rev. J.M. Logan, "Christian Patriotism," *Supplement to the Baptist Times and Freeman*, 12 October 1900, vi-viii.

[176] F.A.J., "Empire and Fame," *Baptist Times and Freeman*, 28 July 1899, 506; Thomas
Comber, "The Transvaal Crisis," *Baptist Times and Freeman*, 1 September 1899, 590.

[177] James Crossby Roberts, "Song of the Younger Nations," *Baptist Times and Freeman*,
7 February 1902, 105; Geo. P. McKay, "The Song of the Younger Nations," *Baptist
Times and Freeman*, 14 February 1902, 134.

[178] "Imperialism," *Baptist Times and Freeman*, 13 April 1900, 303.

[179] "Imperialism," *Baptist Times and Freeman*, 13 April 1900, 303.

[180] "Hence, for the true glory of our Imperialism, at the commencement of the new century, few things, if any, can be of equal service to that of the complete securing and wise
administration of the Baptist Twentieth Century Fund. See "Imperialism," *Baptist Times
and Freeman*, 13 April 1900, 303.

contribution, there was a hint of pride regarding Baptist accomplishments.[181] This was no minor peccadillo, for pride was deemed a deadly threat and caused the downfall of great empires in the past, and, in the minds of many, it would be the reason for Britain's demise if the nation and empire did not repent.

Like other BACSANZ Baptists apprehensive about enthusiastic displays of wartime fervor, Baptists in New Zealand were concerned about the impact of the war on domestic patriotic sentiment. More specifically, their concerns were over rising jingoism and militarism.[182] Embedded within pro-war commentary were disclaimers that they were opposed to any form of jingoism.[183] These statements must not be seen as statements of opposition to the war effort, for they were not. They do, however, indicate the willingness of Baptists to critique the nation and empire for its sins. For instance, Kipling's comments on the sins of Britain and the empire were deemed to be legitimate criticisms from a true and loyal imperialist that needed to be heeded.[184] The criticisms of the Old Testament prophets were also an example of true patriotism.[185] They criticized the nation for its sins, but they in no way could be deemed unpatriotic; in fact, their criticisms were evidence of their patriotism. In the same way, those who criticized the empire and fought against evils were true patriots.[186] The rising militarism of society brought on by the war was also regreted by a number of New Zealanders. In 1901, a resolution against militarism was adopted by the National Council of Women (NCW), an affiliate of the global International Council of Women.[187] The NCW resolution focused on the worldwide growth of militarism and the need for international arbitration. The concerns expressed in the statement of the NCW made it into a resolution shortly thereafter in the November 1901 annual meeting of the New Zealand Baptist Union. It reads: "That, as followers of the Prince of Peace, we place on record our desire that means may be employed, in accordance with the laws of Christ, to discourage

---

[181] "Looking back to the history of our country, during this century (would that it could have closed as it was only two years ago), none can fail to see that our Empire would have been far poorer in that righteousness which exalts a nation had it not been for the Baptists....We are not unconscious of special excellences in other Denominations....Looking with unbiased thought and feeling at the work of each and all for the century, we trust our brethren of other Denominations will pardon us it we say, We thank our God that we are Baptists." See "A Baptist's Retrospect of the Century," *Baptist Times and Freeman*, 28 December 1900, 1046-1047.
[182] Baptists were not the only ones concerned with the rising militarism of New Zealand society. See Crawford, "The Impact of the War on the New Zealand Military Forces and Society," 205.
[183] "Our Contingent," *New Zealand Baptist*, November 1899, 170; "The Supreme Test of Nations," *New Zealand Baptist*, February 1900, 18.
[184] "The Islanders," *New Zealand Baptist*, March 1902, 41.
[185] "The New Idea and National Sin," *New Zealand Baptist*, June 1900, 81; "The New Idea and Humanity," *New Zealand Baptist*, June 1900, 82.
[186] "The New Idea and Politics," *New Zealand Baptist*, June 1900, 82.
[187] Hutching, "New Zealand Women's Opposition to the South African War."

the military spirit and to promote international arbitration, which may make the appeal to arms for the future needless."[188] The conscious avoidance of the twin evils of jingoism and militarism was necessitated by both the recognition that the war had engendered domestic expressions of both evils and the self-identification of Zealand as a Christian nation. The latter ruled out the former.

There were a number of domestic issues related to the war that were cause for concern among Australian Baptists, in no small measure due to the supposed Christian identity of the colony. One cause for alarm was the widespread patriotism displayed during celebrations. Australian Baptists were encouraged by the ardent displays of patriotism in the opening months of the war, but such ardent displays led to fears of increased militarism in Australian life. Barbara Penny has noted how widespread militarism "permeated" the whole community during the outbreak of war.[189] It was because of this militarism that one Baptist commentator declared:

> People are gone mad. The war fever has produced the madness. To venture to call into question the righteousness, or wisdom of the war, is denounced as unpatriotic. Is this not absurd? Surely a man may love his country, and yet not believe in particular lines of policy. But a worse thing than this has resulted from the war, viz." a brutalizing of the public mind. Men can read descriptions, and look on pictorial representations of horrible deeds of cruelty and butchery, and gloat over them. The whole tendency is not to refine, but to render coarse, not to make pitiful and kind, but bitter and blood-thirsty. This is the inevitable outcome of all wars, and it is an effect much to be deplored.[190]

The issue was not patriotism, for true and Christian celebrating and patriotism was praised.[191] The concern was for those who had confused patriotism with militarism,[192] and the desire was that people fight and celebrate for the right reasons.[193] As one letter to the editor made clear, he supported the war but opposed jingoism.[194]

While war was deemed to have a positive effect by helping purge Britons of their sins, it was also considered to be a great corruptor. The spirit of war – killing and maiming – was against the spirit of Jesus.[195] The glamour of war

---

[188] *Annual Report of the New Zealand Baptist Union (1901)*, 12 (supplement to the *New Zealand Baptist*, January 1902).

[189] "Penny," Australia's Reactions to the Boer War," 101.

[190] "The Worst Thing," *Baptist*, 3 February 1899, 3. The *Queensland Baptist* included a report on the Autumn meeting of the Baptist Union of Great Britain which included a report on how Dr. Clifford condemned the war and militarism. See "English Baptist News," *Queensland Baptist*, 1 December 1900, 160-161.

[191] "National Rejoicings," *Southern Baptist*, 14 June 1900, 133.

[192] "The Higher Patriotism," *Queensland Baptist*, 1 February 1900, 20-21.

[193] "There Is Recklessness," *Southern Baptist*, 18 January 1900, 13.

[194] Gideon, "War!" *Baptist*, 3 April 1900, 6.

[195] "The War Spirit – or Jesus, Which?" *Baptist*, 10 March 2.

was false and misleading.[196] War did inspire with examples of heroism, but it also corrupted morals.[197] The celebrations of victory lent themselves to the temptation of drunkenness, no small concern for churches supportive of the temperance movement.[198] War also led to what was deemed to be a brutalizing of the mind.[199] For example, "If the Boers must be shot, it would become us to do it as an unpleasant task, and to feel grieved over it. Instead of this there is a war spirit taking possession of us. We glory in it. Even the small boys are dressed as soldiers by their fine mamas, and play at killing people....the war fever is raging. Good Lord, deliver us!"[200] The practice of military drill for young boys was another example of the spread of militarism, as was the exorbitant sum of money spent on armaments.[201] What was needed was true patriotism, marked by sobriety and Christian virtue. The war could be supported, but jingoism and militarism needed to be shunned. Churches needed to be opened during victory celebrations so that "pious hearts" had a place to go to thank God for the victory.[202] People needed to be made aware of the horror, gore and death of modern battles, and heed the preacher's call to true patriotism.[203] In so doing, they would not only contribute to peace but also bring God's blessing to Australia, for as the response to Britain's early defeats indicates, victory on the battlefield and prosperity at home was directly related to national righteousness.

Key battles and certain holidays led to expressions of patriotism within the Canadian churches, and provided opportunity for commentary on how national sentiment was advantageous for the nation. Expressions of patriotism on Empire Day and Dominion Day were the fruit of successes on the battlefield. While battlefield successes did bring with them a rise in Canadian patriotism (a positive effect of the war), patriotism could easily become a form of jingoism or militarism. In the euphoria of victory in the spring and summer of 1900, when the streets were often filled with people celebrating a victory, periodicals once again cautioned their readers about the danger of a growing militarism in Canada. The *Canadian Baptist* was concerned about the motives of those celebrating the Empire's victories.

> Our pride in the Empire, and our exaltation in the evidences of its majesty and solidarity, have gone up to fever heat, but what is the real motive of our rejoicing?

---

[196] Rev. Geo Jackson, "The False Glamour of War," *Queensland Baptist*, 1 April 1901, 46.
[197] "An Effect of the War," *Baptist*, 10 March 1900, 4.
[198] "These Times of Tempestuous Joy," *Southern Baptist*, 15 March 1900, 61.
[199] "The Relief of Mafeking," *Baptist*, 2 June 1900, 1-2.
[200] "War is a Necessary Evil," *Southern Baptist*, 15 February 1900, 37.
[201] "The Boy's Brigade of Australia," *Queensland Baptist*, 1 March 1902, 31; "Militarism," *Queensland Baptist*, 2 June 1902, 77.
[202] "But Why Was Not," *Southern Baptist*, 31 May 1900, 121; "No Small Part of the Celebrations," *Southern Baptist*, 31 May 1900, 122.
[203] Rev. J.H. Pryce, "The Patriot's Prayer," *Southern Baptist*, 17 September 1902, 157; "The Epistle of Atkins," *Baptist*, 2 August 1902, 2-3.

Are we glad merely because Britain's foes have been crushed, and Britain's territory enlarged by the addition of "another patch of red" to Her Majesty's world-circling domains? If this be all, then let it be borne in mind that our patriotism will surely ebb and flow, according as the nation's sword is sheathed or drawn. Like the tiger of the jungle, who, having once tasted human flesh, forever afterward prefers it above all other food, we shall be content with nothing else but blood and conquest and the annexation of new territory.[204]

If the celebration was merely the rejoicing in another's defeat, it concluded, then the British Empire would rise and eventually fall like all other world empires. One needed not despair, however, for it was believed that the Canadian people's motives were pure.

But we believe better things than this of our people. While no doubt there is among us some jingoism and vain glorious patriotism, yet we believe that deep down in the consciousness of the people there is an honest recognition of the great truth, that the real greatness of the nation does not consist in mere military prestige, but that the entire fighting force of the Empire…are all *means* to the nation's true end, in the attainment of which they shall pass away.[205]

It is clear that the rejection of militarism was important because the character of the nation was important; the nation's character was important because of its unique Christian identity and responsibilities.

In this regard, the churches sought to counter the growing trend towards the militarization of Canadian society and schools.[206] Berger has noted that "imperialism, military preparedness, and militarism, or the admiration and exaltation of the martial virtues, were inextricably bound together."[207] Consequently, there was a strong movement in Canada to increase its military preparedness and responsibilities. Berger notes that the "revival of American expansionism after 1898, the intensification of the European arms race, and especially the German challenge to the primacy of the British navy" lent a sense of urgency to the discussions for Canada to take responsibility for its own defense.[208] Adding a sense of urgency to the calls for a militarized Canada was the conviction that war and soldierly qualities could reverse the corrosive influences of an increasingly materialistic society. Militarism was perceived by many to be "an antidote to the evils of contemporary social life."[209]

---

[204] "Patriotism and Home Missions," *Canadian Baptist*, 21 June 1900, 388.

[205] "Patriotism and Home Missions," *Canadian Baptist*, 21 June 1900, 388. The *Canadian Baptist's* Maritime equivalent, the *Messenger and Visitor*, was also critical of the jingoism of the day. See Barry Moody, "Boers and Baptists: Maritime Canadians View the War in South Africa," unpublished paper.

[206] Gordon L. Heath, "'Prepared to do, prepared to die': Evangelicals, Imperialism and Late-Victorian Canadian Children's Publications," *Perichoresis* 9, no. 1 (2011): 3-27.

[207] Berger, *The Sense of Power*, 233.

[208] Berger, *The Sense of Power*, 234.

[209] Berger, *The Sense of Power*, 253.

The growing militaristic spirit in Canada was far from universal.[210] As one contemporary supporter of an increased Canadian military bemoaned: "No country exhibits a greater corporate indifference to her defence than does Canada."[211] Nevertheless, it was a pressing concern for some. Berger argues that the churches, especially during their "sendoffs" to the troops, furthered the militarism of the age.[212] From the vantage point of a century later, such uncritical support would seem to be the case. However, the churches at that time would not have seen it as such. Certainly they supported the war effort with sermons and services for the departing troops, but they also saw themselves as having an instrumental role in the taming of the militaristic spirit the development of a true imperialism. They distinguished between their support for imperialism and war, and even militarism and war. This is why the churches could support the one and be opposed to the other.

Conclusion

Confident that they could discern God's providential working in history, BACSANZ Baptists believed that the British Empire had been established for the advancement of, among other things, missionary work. In their minds, no dissonance existed between their evangelical mandate to spread the gospel and their support for the empire. The empire not only protected the missionaries but also pried open doors for their arrival by overthrowing unjust rulers and establishing British rule amenable to Christian missions. One of the reasons why BACSANZ Baptists supported the war effort in South Africa came from the understanding that a British victory would oust what they deemed to be the unjust and anti-mission Boers with an enlightened and benevolent British rule favorable to the work of missionaries.

The conflation of the empire and missions meant that Baptists believed that God expected much from his chosen vessel. The demands of righteousness cut both ways; the expectations for a righteous empire also meant that any display of hubris, militarism, injustice, or exploitation were to be roundly condemned. The tacit conviction undergirding the wartime BACSANZ Baptist denunciations of militarism and the evils of empire was that God had weighed the empire and found it wanting; thus, the early defeats. A revived and purified national vision was needed, bereft of jingoistic imperialism and one marked by a sober realization of God's providential destiny for nation and empire. The difficulty lay in maintaining enthusiasm for empire and its God-given role in raising up nations while at the same time avoiding pagan corruptions of said enthusi-

---

[210] For details on the growing militarism in the years preceding the First World War, see Berger, *The Sense of Power*, ch.10; Desmond Morton, "The Cadet Movement in the Moment of Canadian Militarism, 1909-1914," *Journal of Canadian Studies* 13 (Summer 1978): 56-68.

[211] As quoted in Berger, *The Sense of Power*, 239.

[212] Berger, *The Sense of Power*, 249-251.

asm. The task was daunting, but the commentary in the BACSANZ Baptist press indicates that many were up to the challenge. Attempts to extinguish the growing militarism and shape the budding patriotism reflected the churches' self-conscious identity as vital nation-builders in the future development of their nation, dominion, federation or colony. Along with reforms such as the creation of temperance societies and laws related to the Lord's Day, these attempts were to ensure a vibrant, passionate, but also Christian expression of patriotism.

Conclusion

"As a world community of Baptist believers, we remain incomplete until we have vigorously sought to hear, understand, and respect the diverse viewpoints reflected by others, especially those persons from cultures that have been marginalized through material poverty and the legacy of colonialism and imperialism." "Principles and Guidelines for Intra-Baptist Relationships," Baptist World Alliance, 2013.

One would be hard-pressed today to find a Baptist in what at one time were the peripheries who would agree with the statement "[T]he British nation is our nation."[1] The astonishingly rapid decline of the British Empire in the years after the Second World War - something unfathomable to BACSANZ Baptists a mere two generations earlier - meant that postcolonial BACSANZ Baptists would be forced to rethink their identity and purpose devoid of any triumphalistic metanarrative of imperialism. The above Baptist World Alliance statement on the ills of imperialism is indicative of contemporary Baptist views of empire. Yet, as this book demonstrates, in the not-too-distant past Baptist imagination in the metropole and peripheries was captured by an imperialism that significantly shaped their evangelical convictions related to identity and purpose.

The South African War has drawn the attention of historians of various sorts and in varying degrees. What has been lacking, however, are studies concerning churches and the war. Few studies exist of national church bodies, and none have probed wartime international church bonds. The result has been a failure to explore transnational contacts especially as they related to imperial identities. By directing sustained attention to BACSANZ Baptists, this book significantly advances the analysis of the complicity of religion and empire in the heyday of Western imperialism and wild jingoism, and provides a unique global history of Baptists in the metropole and peripheries. There was a remarkable fusion of Baptist evangelical identity and purpose with popular imperialism, and imperial commitments remained a potent factor in the development of BACSANZ Baptist views of national and global identity, history, providence, justice, and missions. Of particular interest for this research is how this shared global imperial identity and purpose was nurtured by an international network of Baptist newspapers. Those papers cultivated not only denominational fidelity but also imperial loyalties. In a very tangible way, the Baptist press within the empire contributed to the building of a global, denominational, evangelical, and imperial identity and bond that transcended regional and national identities. At the same time, various Baptist newspapers were active in a nation-building role that at-

---

[1] S.R. Ingold, "The War in South Africa: The Christian's Proper Attitude Regarding It," *New Zealand Baptist*, April 1900, 61-62.

tempted to form political opinions and forge what was deemed to be an acceptable Christian nation and a patriotic commitment to their particular national or regional identity.

Shaped by over a century of British imperial success, and nurtured by waves of British immigration, British leaders, British financial support and British literature, BACSANZ Baptist identity and purpose had become fused to popular expressions of imperialism. That imperialism was a shared global phenomenon that transcended regional identities, and one which provided a global community and regional identity for nascent, often isolated, Baptist communities in the colonies. Nevertheless, that mutual imperialism was contextualized and shaped by domestic factors so much that imperialism was a particular form of nationalism for Baptists in both the metropole and peripheries.

BACSANZ Baptists were loyal citizens of the empire as well as patriotic members of their nation, dominion, federation or colony. The war engendered a great deal of public interest, and papers in general increased coverage of the war to satisfy reader's demands for war news. The fusion of nationalism, imperialism and Baptist identity can be readily seen in the various Baptist paper's wartime coverage. Once war had been declared, the Baptist editors made it clear that they – and Baptists at large – were patriotic, supported the troops, and identified themselves with the imperial cause. The nature and extent of the wartime coverage bears this out. However, BACSANZ Baptist sentiment was far from uniform, and uniform and virtually universal support for the empire did not always mean support for the war in South Africa. While some editor's frequently provided passionate content in support of the war, other paper's included commentary that openly opposed Britain's war against the Boers. For some the war was a conflict to promote justice, for others the conflict was folly and a travesty of justice.

While their national identity was inextricably tied to their British heritage and imperial connections, they also shared a global identity. BACSANZ Baptists may have been on the margins in terms of percentage of population, and even looked upon askance by the larger denominations, but the global Baptist community provided Baptists with a sense of belonging to something grander that transcended their small regional presence. They were loyal to their nation, dominion, federation, or colony, but they also believed they belonged to a global community that was distinctly Baptist, British and imperial. The Baptist press played an important role in the construction of this real, yet imagined, community, one where Baptists in the peripheries felt that "The British nation is our nation."

From their genesis Baptists displayed a passionate concern for justice, and the connection between Baptists and justice has a considerable history. By the late-nineteenth century, it was clear to BACSANZ Baptists that there was no empire as righteous as their empire. While it had its problems and injustices, the empire was still considered to be the most benevolent and righteous empire on the face of the earth; where the Union Jack flew, liberty and justice reigned.

For Baptists concerned with the advancement of justice, there was no identity crisis in supporting the empire for the best way to spread justice was to expand the empire. Conversely, any contraction of empire was deemed a threat to peace, justice and the advancement of human progress. In other words, for many Baptists in the metropole and peripheries, humanitarian concerns - which included the promotion or defense of justice - often had an imperial solution, even if it meant going to war. Even if the war in South Africa was unjust in its origins (as some Baptists argued), it was believed that the best outcome for all would be a British victory.

Confident that they could discern God's providential working in history, BACSANZ Baptists were convinced that the British Empire had been established for the advancement of, among other things, missionary work. In their minds, there was no dissonance between their evangelical mandate to spread the gospel and their support for the empire. After all, the empire not only protected the missionaries but also pried open doors for their arrival by overthrowing unjust rulers and establishing British rule amenable to Christian missions. One of the reasons for BACSANZ Baptist support for the war effort in South Africa, then, was that a British victory would oust what they deemed to be the unjust and anti-missions Boers with an enlightened and benevolent British rule that favored the work of missionaries.

While the conflation of the empire and missions meant that there were assumptions about the benevolent rule of Britain that those in the twenty-first century find offensive, it also meant that BACSANZ Baptists believed that God expected much from his chosen vessel. Consequently, there was a continuous examination as to whether or not the empire was living up to its high calling. The demands of righteousness cut both ways, and the expectations of righteousness meant that any displays of hubris, militarism, injustice, and exploitation were to be roundly condemned. The tacit conviction undergirding the wartime BACSANZ Baptist prophetic denunciations of militarism and the evils of empire was that God had weighed the empire and found it wanting; thus explaining the early defeats. A revived and purified national vision bereft of a jingoistic imperialism, and one marked by a sober realization of God's providential destiny for nation and empire, was what the churches sought to engender with prophetic denunciations and calls for national prayer and repentance. The difficulty lay in maintaining enthusiasm for empire and its God-given role in raising up nations while at the same time avoiding pagan corruptions of said enthusiasm. The task was daunting, but the commentary in the BACSANZ Baptist press indicates that many believed that they were up to the challenge. Attempts to extinguish the growing militarism and shape the budding patriotism of the new nation, dominion, federation or colony reflected the churches' conviction that they were to play a key role in the formation of the nation, dominion, federation, or colony. Along with reforms such as the development of temperance societies and laws related to the Lord's Day, those efforts were to ensure a vibrant, passionate, but also Christian expression of patriotism and imperial loyalty.

Bibliography

Primary Sources

Denominational Newspapers

Baptist
Baptist Times and Freeman
Canadian Baptist
Canadian Missionary Link
Messenger and Visitor
Missionary Messenger
New Zealand Baptist
Queensland Baptist
Religious Intelligencer
South African Baptist
Southern Baptist
W.B.M.U. Tidings
Wesleyan
Western Baptist

Denominational Reports

Annual Report of the New Zealand Baptist Union, 1900, 1902
Baptist Union of Great Britain and Ireland Handbook, 1901
BCOQ Yearbook, 1900

Books

Batts, H.J. *Pretoria from Within During the War, 1899-1900.* London: John F. Shaw, 1901.
Evans, Sanford W. *The Canadian Contingents and Canadian Imperialism: A Story and a Study.* Toronto: Publisher's Syndicate, 1901.
Hobson, John A. *Imperialism: A Study.* London, 1902.
Kruger, Paul. *The Memoirs of Paul Kruger.* Toronto: George A. Morang, 1902.

Secondary Sources

Books

Airhart, Phyllis D. "Ordering a New Nation and Reordering Protestantism, 1867-1914." In *The Canadian Protestant Experience, 1760-1990*, edited by George A. Rawlyk, 98-138. Burlington: Welch, 1990.

Allen, Mark. "Winchester, the Clergy and the Boer War." In *God and War: The Church of England and Armed Conflict in the Twentieth Century*, edited by Stephen G. Parker and Tom Lawson, 15-31. Surrey: Ashgate, 2012.

Allen, Richard. *Religion and Social Reform in Canada, 1914-1928*. Toronto: University of Toronto Press, 1971.

Alomes, Stephen. *A Nation at Last? The Changing Character of Australian Nationalism, 1880-1988*. Sydney: Angus & Robertson, 1988.

Armitage, David. *The Ideological Origins of the British Empire*. Cambridge: Cambridge University Press, 2000.

Austin, Alvyn J. *Saving China: Canadian Missionaries in the Middle Kingdom, 1888-1959*. Toronto: University of Toronto Press, 1986.

Badsey, Stephen. "War Correspondents in the Boer War." In *The Boer War: Direction, Experience and Image*, edited by John Gooch, 187-202. London: Frank Cass, 2000.

Ballantyne, Tony. *Webs of Empire: Locating New Zealand's Colonial Past*. Wellington: Bridget Williams, 2012.

Batts, H.J. *The History of the Baptist Church in South Africa: The Story of a 100 Years, 1820-1920*. Cape Town: T. Maskew Miller, nd.

Beaumont, Jacqueline. "The Times at War, 1899-1902." In *The South African War Reappraised*, edited by Donal Lowry, 67-83. Manchester: Manchester University Press, 2000.

Bebbington, David. "Atonement, Sin, and Empire, 1880-1914." In *The Imperial Horizons of British Protestant Missions, 1880-1914*, edited by Andrew Porter, 14-31. Grand Rapids: Eerdmans, 2003.

———. *Baptists through the Centuries: A History of a Global People*. Waco: Baylor University Press, 2010.

———. *The Dominance of Evangelicalism: The Age of Spurgeon and Moody*. Downers Grove: InterVarsity Press, 2005.

———. "Evangelicalism and British Culture," *Perichoresis* 6, no. 2 (2008): 131-153

———. *Evangelicalism in Modern Britain: A History from the 1730's to the 1980's*. Grand Rapids: Baker Book House, 1989.

———. *The Nonconformist Conscience: Chapel and Politics, 1870-1914*. London: George Allen and Unwin, 1982.

Belich, James. *Paradise Reforged: A History of the New Zealanders from the 1880s to the Year 2000*. Honolulu: University of Hawai'i Press, 2001.

Bell, Duncan. *The Idea of Greater Britain: Empire and the Future of World Order, 1860-1900*. Princeton: Princeton University Press, 2007.

Berger, Carl. *The Sense of Power: Studies in the Ideas of Canadian Imperialism, 1867-1914*. Toronto: University of Toronto Press, 1970.

Blanch, M.D. "British Society and the War." In *The South African War: The Anglo-Boer War 1899-1902*, edited by Peter Warwick, 210-237. Burnt Mill: Longman, 1980.

Blaxland, John C. "Strategic Cousins: Canada, Australia and their use of Expeditionary Forces from the Boer War to the War on Terror." PhD diss., Royal Military College of Canada, 2003.

Blunden, Margaret. "The Anglican Church during the War." In *The South African War: The Anglo-Boer War, 1899-1902*, edited by Peter Warwick, 279-291. London: Longman Group Limited, 1980.

Bollen, J.D. *Australian Baptists: A Religious Minority*. London: Baptist Historical Society, 1975.

———. "English-Australian Baptist Relations, 1830-1860," *Baptist Quarterly* 27, no. 7 (July 1974): 290-305.

———. "English-Baptist Relations, 1830-1860," *Baptist Quarterly* 25, no. 7 (July 1974): 290-305.

Borrie, W.D. "'British' Immigration to Australia." In *Australia and Britain: Studies in a Changing Relationship*, edited by A.F. Madden and W.H. Morris-Jones, 101-116. Sydney: Sydney University Press, 1908.

Bourinot, John George. *The Intellectual Development of the Canadian People: An Historical Review*. Toronto: Hunter, Rose & Company, 1881.

Brackney, William. *The Baptists*. New York: Greenwood Press, 1988.

———. "Transatlantic Relationships: The Making of an International Baptist Community." In *The Gospel in the World: International Studies, Volume One*, edited by David Bebbington, 59-79. Carlisle: Paternoster Press, 2002.

Bridge, Carl and Kent Fedorowich. "Mapping the British World." In *The British World: Diaspora, Culture and Identity*, edited by Carl Bridge and Kent Fedorowich, 1-15. London: Frank Cass, 2003.

Bridge, Carl and Kent Fedorowich. "Mapping the British World." *Journal of Imperial and Commonwealth History* 31, no. 2 (2003): 1-15.

Brouwer, Ruth Compton. *New Women for God: Canadian Presbyterian Women and India Missions, 1876-1914*. Toronto: University of Toronto Press, 1990.

Brown, Stewart J. *Providence and Empire, 1815-1914*. Harlow: Pearson, 2008.

Buckner, Phillip. "Canada." In *The Impact of the South African War*, edited by David Omissi and Andrew S. Thompson, 233-250. Houndmills: Palgrave: 2002.

Buckner, Phillip, ed. *Canada and the British Empire*. Oxford: Oxford University Press, 2008.

———. ed. *Canada and the End of Empire*. Vancouver: UBC Press, 2005.

———. "Casting Daylight upon Magic: Deconstructing the Royal Tour of 1901 to Canada." *Journal of Imperial and Commonwealth History* 31 (May 2003): 158-189.

———. "Whatever Happened to the British Empire?" *Journal of the Canadian Historical Association* 4 (1993): 3-32.

Caldecott, H.S., "A Boer Refugee Camp in Natal." *The Empire Review* 1 (July 1901): 623-626.

Carey, Hilary M. *Empires of Religion*. Houndmills: Palgrave, 2008.

Chamberlain, W.M. "The Characteristics of Australia's Boer War Volunteers." *Historical Studies* 20, no. 78 (1982): 48-52.

Chapman, Mark D. "Theological Responses in England to the South African War, 1899-1902." *Journal for the History of Modern Theology* 16, no. 2 (December 2009): 181-196.

Christie, Nancy. Introduction to *Transatlantic Subjects: Ideas, Institutions, and Social Experience in Post-Revolutionary British North America.*" Edited by Nancy Christie. Montreal: McGill-Queen's University Press, 2008.

Clarke, Brian. "English-Speaking Canada from 1854." In *A Concise History of Christianity in Canada*, edited by Terrence Murphy and Roberto Perin, 261-360. Oxford: Oxford University Press, 1996.

Clarke, Stephen. "Desperately Seeking Service: The Australasian Commandments and the War." In *One Flag, One Queen, One Tongue: New Zealand, The British Empire and the South African War*, edited by John Crawford and Ian McGibbon, 12-27. Auckland: Auckland University Press, 2003.

Clifford, J. Ayson. *A Handful of Grain: The Centenary History of the Baptist Union of New Zealand, Volume Two – 1882-1914.* Wellington: New Zealand Baptist Historical Society, 1982.

Coetzer, Owen. *Fire in the Sky: The Destruction of the Orange Free State, 1899-1902.* Weltevreden Park: Covos-Day Books, 2000.

Cole, Douglas L. "Canada's 'Nationalistic' Imperialists." *Journal of Canadian Studies* 5 (August 1970): 44-49.

Connolly, C.N. "Class, Birthplace, Loyalty: Australian Attitudes to the Boer War." *Historical Studies*, 18 (1978): 210-232.

Connolly, C.N. "Manufacturing 'Spontaneity': The Australian Offers of Troops for the Boer War." *Historical Studies* 18, no. 70 (1978): 106-117.

Cook, Terry. "George R. Parkin and the Concept of Britannic Idealism." *Journal of Canadian Studies* 10 (August 1975): 15-31.

Crawford, John. "The Best Mounted Troops in South Africa?." In *One Flag, One Queen, One Tongue: New Zealand, The British Empire and the South African War*, edited by John Crawford and Ian McGibbon, 73-99. Auckland: Auckland University Press, 2003.

Crawford, John. "The Impact of the War on the New Zealand Military Forces and Society." In *One Flag, One Queen, One Tongue: New Zealand, The British Empire and the South African War*, edited by John Crawford and Ian McGibbon, 205-214. Auckland: Auckland University Press, 2003.

Crawford, John and Ian McGibbon, eds., *New Zealand's Great War: New Zealand, The Allies, and the First World War.* Auckland: Exisle, 2007.

Crawford, John with Ellen Ellis. *To Fight for the Empire: An Illustrated History of New Zealand and the South African War, 1899-1902.* Auckland: Department of Internal Affairs, 1999.

Cupit, Tony. "Patterns of Development among Baptists in Australia, New Zealand and Papua New Guinea in the First Fifty Years since their Respective Beginnings." In *The Gospel in the World: International Studies, Volume One,* edited by David W. Bebbington, 251-270. Carlisle: Paternoster, 2002.

Currie, Robert, Alan Gilbert, and Lee Horsley. *Church and Churchgoers: Patterns of Church Growth in the British Isles since 1700.* Oxford: Clarendon Press, 1977.

Cuthbertson, Greg C. "The Nonconformist Conscience and the South African War, 1899-1902." DLitt diss., University of South Africa, 1986.

Cuthbertson, Greg C. "Preaching Imperialism: Wesleyan Methodism and the War," in *The Impact of the South African* War, eds., David Omissi and Andrew S. Thompson (Houndmills: Palgrave, 2002), 157-172.

Cuthbertson, Greg C. "Pricking the 'Nonconformist Conscience': Religion against the South African War." In *The South African War Reappraised*, edited by Donal Lowry, 169-187. Manchester: Manchester University Press, 2000.

Cuthbertson, Greg, Albert Grundlingh, and Mary-Lynn Suttie, eds., *Writing a Wider War: Rethinking Gender, Race, and Identity in the South African War, 1899-1902*. Athens: Ohio University Press, 2002.

Davenport, Rodney. "Settlement, Conquest and Theological Controversy: The Churches of Nineteenth-Century European Immigrants." In *Christianity in South Africa: A Political and Cultural History*, edited by Richard Elphick and Rodney Davenport, 51-67. Berkeley: University of California Press, 1997.

Davey, Arthur. *The British Pro-Boers: 1877-1902*. Cape Town: Tafelberg Publishers Limited, 1978.

Dekar, Paul. *For the Healing of the Nations: Baptist Peacemakers*. Macon: Smyth & Helwys Publishing, 1993.

Duxbury, George Reginald. *David and Goliath: The First War of Independence, 1880-1881*. Johannesburg: South African National Museum of Military History, 1981.

Eddy, J. and D. Schreuder, eds. *The Rise of Colonial Nationalism*. Sydney: Allen & Unwin, 1988.

Ellis, Ellen. "New Zealand Women and the War." In *One Flag, One Queen, One Tongue: New Zealand, The British Empire and the South African War*, edited by John Crawford and Ian McGibbon, 128-150. Auckland: Auckland University Press, 2003.

Elphick, Richard. "Evangelical Missions and Racial 'Equalization' in South Africa, 1890-1914." In *Converting Colonialism: Visions and Realities in Mission History, 1706-1914*, edited by Dana L. Robert, 112-133. Grand Rapids: William B. Eerdmans, 2008.

Esherick, Joseph. *The Origins of the Boxer Uprising*. Berkeley: University of California Press, 1987.

Evans, Martin Marix. "Farm Burning." In *Encyclopedia of the Boer War, 1899-1902*. Edited by Evans, Martin Marix. Santa Barbara: ABC Clio, 2000.

Falardeau, Jean-Charles. "The Role of the Church in French Canada." In *French-Canadian Society*, edited by M. Rioux and Y. Martins, 342-357. Toronto: McClelland and Stewart, 1964.

Farwell, Byron. *The Great Anglo-Boer War*. New York: W. W. Norton, 1976.

Field, Laurie. *The Forgotten War: Australian Involvement in the South African Conflict of 1899-1902*. Melbourne: Melbourne University Press, 1979.

Fletcher, Brian. "Anglicanism and Nationalism in Australia, 1901-62." *Journal of Religious History* 23 (June 1999): 215-233.

Francis, Daniel. *National Dreams: Myth, Memory and Canadian History.* Vancouver: Arsenal Pulp, 1997.

Franzosi, Roberto. "The Press as a Source of Socio-Historical Data: Issues in the Methodology of Data Collection from Newspapers." *Historical Methods* 20 (Winter 1987): 5-16.

Gordon, Donald C. *The Dominion Partnership in Imperial Defence, 1870-1914.* Baltimore: The John Hopkins Press, 1965.

Gould, Ashley. "'Different Race, Same Queen': Maori and the War." In *One Flag, One Queen, One Tongue: New Zealand, The British Empire and the South African War*, edited by John Crawford and Ian McGibbon, 119-127. Auckland: Auckland University Press, 2003.

Grant, John Webster. *The Church in the Canadian Era.* McGraw-Hill Ryerson Limited, 1972. Reprint, Vancouver: Regent College Publishing, 1988.

Greenlee, James G. and Charles M. Johnston. *Good Citizens: British Missionaries and Imperial States, 1870-1918.* Montreal: McGill-Queen's University Press, 1999.

Guy, Laurie. "Baptist Pacifists in New Zealand: Creating Divisions in the Fight for Peace." *Baptist Quarterly* 40, no. 8 (October 2004): 487-499.

———. "Three Countries, Two Conversions, One Man: J. J. Doke - Baptists, Humanity and Justice." In *Interfaces: Baptists and Others*, edited by David Bebbington and Martin Sutherland, 265-275. Milton Keynes: Paternoster, 2013.

———. *Shaping Godzone: Public Issues and Church Voices in New Zealand, 1840-2000.* Wellington: Victoria University Press, 2011.

Hale, Frederick. "Captives of British Imperialism? Southern African Baptists and the Second Anglo-Boer War, 1899-1902." *Baptist Quarterly* 34, no.1 (January 2001): 15-26.

———. "The Baptist Union of South Africa and Apartheid." *Journal of Church and State* 48 (Autumn 2006): 753-777.

Hall, Darrell. *The Hall Handbook of the Anglo Boer War, 1899-1902.* Pietermaritzburg: University of Natal Press, 1999.

Hall, D.O.W. *The New Zealanders in South Africa, 1899-1902.* Wellington: Department of Internal Affairs, 1949.

Hampton, Mark. "The Press, Patriotism, and Public Discussion: C.P. Scott, the *Manchester Guardian*, and the Boer War, 1899-1902." *The Historical Journal* 44, no.1 (2001): 177-197.

Harrington, Peter. "Pictorial Journalism and the Boer War: The London Illustrated Weeklies." In *The Boer War: Direction, Experience and Image*, edited by John Gooch, 224-244. London: Frank Cass, 2000.

Hayden, Roger. *English Baptist History and Heritage.* Didcot: Baptist Union, 2005.

Heath, Gordon L. "Canadian Baptists and Late-Victorian Imperial Spirituality." *McMaster Journal of Theology and Ministry* 15 (2013-2014): 165-196.

———. "Canadian Churches and the South African War: Prelude to the Great War." In *Canadian Churches and the First World War*, edited by Gordon L. Heath, 15-33. Eugene: Pickwick Publications, 2014.

————. "The Canadian Protestant Press and the Conscription Crisis, 1917-1918." *Historical Studies* 78 (2012): 27-46.

————. "'Citizens of that Mighty Empire': Imperial Sentiment among Students at Wesley College, 1897-1902." *Manitoba History* (June 2005): 15-25.

————. "'Forming Sound Public Opinion': The Late Victorian Canadian Protestant Press and Nation-Building." *Journal of the Canadian Church Historical Society* 48 (2006): 109-159.

————. "The Nile Expedition, New Imperialism and Canadian Baptists, 1884-1885." *Baptist Quarterly* 44, no. 3 (July 2011): 171-186.

————. "Passion for Empire: War Poetry Published in the Canadian English Protestant Press during the South African War, 1899-1902." *Literature and Theology* 16 (June 2002): 127-147.

————. "'Prepared to Do, Prepared to Die': Evangelicals, Imperialism and Late-Victorian Canadian Children's Publications." *Perichoresis* 9, no. 1 (2011): 3-27.

————. "Sin in the Camp: The Day of Humble Supplication in the Anglican Church in Canada in the Early Months of the South African War." *Journal of the Canadian Church Historical Society* 44 (Fall 2002): 207-226.

————. "Traitor, Half-Breeds, Savages and Heroes: Canadian Baptist Newspapers and Constructions of Riel and the Events of 1885." In *Baptists and Public Life in Canada*, edited by Gordon L. Heath and Paul Wilson, 198-217. Eugene: Pickwick, 2012.

————. *A War with a Silver Lining: Canadian Protestant Churches and the South African War, 1899-1902*. Montreal: McGill-Queen's University Press, 2009.

————. "'Were We in the Habit of Deifying Monarchs': Canadian English Protestants and the Death of Queen Victoria, 1901." *Canadian Evangelical Review* (2006): 72-97.

————. "When Missionaries Were Hated: An Examination of the Canadian Baptist Defense of Imperialism and Missions during the Boxer Rebellion, 1900." In *Baptists and Mission*, edited by Ian M. Randall and Anthony R. Cross, 261-276. Milton Keynes: Paternoster, 2007.

Hennessy, Peter, "The Press and Broadcasting." In *Contemporary History: Practice and Method*. Edited by Anthony Seldon, 17-29. Oxford: Blackwell, 1988.

Hewison, H.H. *Hedge of Wild Almonds: South Africa, the 'Pro-Boers' and the Quaker Conscience, 1890-1910*. London: James Curry, 1989.

Himbury, D. Mervyn "Baptists and their Relations with Other Christians in Australasia." *Foundations* 17 (1974): 36-50.

Hobsbawm, Eric and Terence Ranger, eds. *The Invention of Tradition*. Cambridge: Cambridge University Press, 1983.

Hudson-Reed, Sydney. *Together for a Century: The History of the Baptist View of South Africa, 1877-1977*. Pietermaritzburg: South Africa Baptist Historical Society, 1977.

————. *History of the Baptist Union of South Africa, 1877-1977*. Pietermaritzburg: S.A. Baptist Historical Society, 1977.

————. *By Taking Heed ... The History of Baptists in Southern Africa, 1820-1977*. Roodepoort: Baptist Publishing House, 1983.

Hughes, Philip J. *The Baptists in Australia*. Canberra: Australian Government Publishing Service, 1996.

Hutching, Megan. "New Zealand Women's Opposition to the South African War." In *One Flag, One Queen, One Tongue: New Zealand, The British Empire and the South African War*, edited by John Crawford and Ian McGibbon, 46-57. Auckland: Auckland University Press, 2003.

Hutchinson, Mark and John Wolffe. *A Short History of Global Evangelicalism*. Cambridge: Cambridge University Press, 2012.

Huttenback, R. A. "The British Empire as a 'White Man's Country' - Racial Attitudes and Immigration Legislation in the Colonies of White Settlement." *Journal of British Studies* 13, no. 1 (November 1973), 108-137.

Inglis, K.S. "The Imperial Connection: Telegraphic Communication between England and Australia, 1872-1902." In *Australia and Britain: Studies in a Changing Relationship*, edited by A.F. Madden and W.H. Morris-Jones, 21-38. Sydney: Sydney University Press, 1980.

James, Lawrence. *The Rise and Fall of the British Empire*. New York: St. Martin's, 1994.

Jeeves, Alan. "Hobson's *The War in South Africa: A Reassessment*." In *Writing a Wider War: Rethinking Gender, Race, and Identity in the South African War, 1899-1902*, eds., Greg Cuthbertson, Albert Grundlingh and Mary-Lynn Suttie, 233-246. Athens: Ohio University Press, 2002.

Jones, Preston "'His Dominion'?: Varieties of Protestant Commentary on the Confederation of Canada." *Fides et Historia* 32 (Summer/Fall 2000): 83-88.

Johnson, Robert E. *A Global Introduction to Baptist Churches*. Cambridge: Cambridge University Press, 2010.

Judd, Denis and Keith Surridge. *The Boer War*. London: John Murray, 2002.

Judd, Denis. *The Boer War*. London: Hart-Davis, MacGibbon, 1977.

Judd, Denis. *Empire: The British Imperial Experience from 1765 to the Present*. New York, Basic Books, 1996.

Keown-Boyd, Henry. *The Fists of Righteous Harmony: A History of the Boxer Uprising in China in the Year 1900*. London: Leo Cooper, 1991.

Kohn, Edward P. *This Kindred People: Canadian-American Relations and the Anglo-Saxon Idea, 1895-1903*. Montreal: McGill-Queen's University Press, 2004.

Krebs, Paula. *Gender, Race, and the Writing of Empire: Public Discourse and the Boer War*. Cambridge: Cambridge University Press, 1999.

Laity, Paul. "The British Peace Movement and the War." In *The Impact of the South African War*, edited by David Omissi and Andrew S. Thompson, 138-156. Hounds Mill: Palgrave, 2002.

Laracy, Hugh. "Priests, People and Patriotism: New Zealand Catholics and the War, 1914-1918." *Australian Catholic Record* 70, no. 1 (1993): 14-26.

Latourette, Kenneth Scott. *The Great Century, A.D. 1800-A.D.1914*. New York: Harper and Brothers Publishing, 1941.

Lawes, Marvia E. "A Historical Evaluation of Jamaica Baptists: A Spirituality of Resistance." *Black Theology* 6, no. 3 (2008): 366-392.

Lehmann, Joseph H. *The First Boer War*. London: Jonathan Cape, 1972.

Leonard, Bill J. *Baptist Ways: A History*. Valley Forge: Judson Press, 2003.

Linder, Robert D. *The Long Tragedy: Australian Evangelical Christians and the Great War, 1914-1918*. Adelaide: Openbook Publishers, 2000.

Lineham, Peter. "First World War Religion." In *New Zealand's Great War: New Zealand, The Allies, and the First World War*, edited by John Crawford and Ian McGibbon, 467-492. Auckland: Exisle, 2007.

Longford, Elizabeth. *Jameson's Raid: The Prelude to the Boer War*. London: Grenada, 1982.

MacKenzie, John M. *Propaganda and Empire: The Manipulation of British Public Opinion, 1880-1960*. Manchester: Manchester University Press, 1984.

Magney, William H. "The Methodist Church and the National Gospel, 1884-1914." *The Bulletin* 20 (1968): 3-95.

Mancke, Elizabeth. *The Fault Lines of Empire: Political Differentiation in Massachusetts and Nova Scotia, ca.1760-1830*. New York: Routledge, 2005.

Manley, Ken. "'The Magic Name': Charles Haddon Spurgeon and the Evangelical Ethos of Australian Baptists." *Baptist Quarterly* 40, no. 3 (July 2003): 173-184.

————. "'The Magic Name': Charles Haddon Spurgeon and the Evangelical Ethos of Australian Baptists," *Baptist Quarterly* 40, no. 4 (October 2003): 215-229.

————. "'To the Ends of the Earth': Regent's Park College and Australian Baptists." *Baptist Quarterly* 42 (April 2007): 130-147.

————. *From Woolloomooloo to 'Eternity': A History of Australian Baptists, Vol. 1&2*. Milton Keynes: Paternoster, 2006.

————. "'Our own church in our own land': The Shaping of Baptist Identity in Australia." In *Baptist Identities: International Studies from the Seventeenth to the Twentieth Centuries*, edited by Ian M. Randall, Toivo Pilli and Anthony Cross, 275-298. Milton Keynes: Paternoster, 2006.

Manley, Ken and Michael Petras. *The First Australian Baptists*. Eastwood: Baptist Historical Society of NSW, 1981.

Markovits, Stefanie. "Rushing Into Print: 'Participatory Journalism' during the Crimean War." *Victorian Studies* 50, no. 4 (Summer 2008): 559-586.

Martin, A. C. *The Concentration Camps, 1900-1902: Facts, Figures, and Fables*. Cape Town: Howard Timmons, 1957.

Martin, Christopher. *The Boxer Rebellion*. London: Abelard-Schuman, 1968.

McBeth, H. Leon. *The Baptist Heritage*. Nashville: Broadman Press, 1987.

McCracken, Donal P. *The Irish Pro-Boers, 1877-1902*. Johannesburg: Perskor, 1989.

McGeorge, Colin. "The Social and Geographical Composition of the New Zealand Contingents." In *One Flag, One Queen, One Tongue: New Zealand, The British Empire and the South African War*, edited by John Crawford and Ian McGibbon, 100-118. Auckland: Auckland University Press, 2003.

McGibbon, Ian. "The Origins of New Zealand's South African War Contribution." In *One Flag, One Queen, One Tongue: New Zealand, The British Empire and the South African War*, edited by John Crawford and Ian McGibbon, 1-11. Auckland: Auckland University Press, 2003.

————. ed. *The Oxford Companion to New Zealand Military History* (Auckland, 2000).

————. *The Path to Gallipoli, Defending New Zealand 1840-1915.* Wellington: GP Books, 1991.

McKernan, Michael. *Australian Churches at War: Attitudes and Activities of the Major Churches, 1914-1918.* Sydney: Catholic Theological Faculty and Australian War Memorial, 1980.

McKernan, Michael. *Padre: Australian Chaplains in Gallipoli and France.* Sydney: Allen & Unwin, 1986.

McKim, Denis. "'Righteousness Exalteth a Nation': Providence, Empire, and the Forging of the Early Canadian Presbyterian Identity." *Historical Papers, CSCH,* 2008, 47-66.

McKinnon, Malcolm. "Opposition to the War in New Zealand." In *One Flag, One Queen, One Tongue: New Zealand, The British Empire and the South African War*, edited by John Crawford and Ian McGibbon, 28-45. Auckland: Auckland University Press, 2003.

McLeod, Hugh. "Protestantism and British National Identity, 1815-1945." In *National Religion*, edited by P. van der Veer and H. Lehmann, 44-70. Princeton: Princeton University Press, 1999.

McMinn, W.G. *Nationalism and Federalism in Australia.* Oxford: Oxford University Press, 1994.

Meaney, Neville. "Britishness and Australian Identity: The Problem of Nationalism in Australian History and Historiography." *Australian Historical Studies* 32, (2001): 76–90.

Meaney, Neville. "Britishness and Australia: Some Reflections." In *The British World: Diaspora, Culture and Identity*, edited by Carl Bridge and Kent Fedorowich, 121-135. London: Frank Cass, 2003.

Millar, T.B. *Australia in Peace and War: External Relations 1788-1977.* Canberra: Australian National University Press, 1978.

Miller, Carman. "Research Resources on Canada and the South African War," *Archivaria* 26 (Summer 1988): 116-121.

Miller, Carman. "English-Canadian Opposition to the South African War as Seen through the Press." *Canadian Historical Review* 55 (December 1974): 422-438.

————. "Framing Canada's Great War: A Case for Including the Boer War." *Journal of Transatlantic Studies* 6, no. 1 (April 2008): 3-21.

Mills, Sean. "'Preach the World': Canadian Imperialism and Missionary Outreach at the Montreal Diocesan Theological College, 1892-1903." *Journal of the Canadian Church Historical Society* 43 (2001): 5-38.

Moir, John. *Enduring Witness: The Presbyterian Church in Canada.* 2nd ed. Burlington: Eagle Press Printers, 1987.

Moody, Barry. "Boers and Baptists: Maritime Canadians View the War in South Africa." unpublished paper.

Morrison, Hugh. "'But we are Concerned with a Greater Imperium': The New Zealand Protestant Missionary Movement and the British Empire, 1870-1930." *Social Sciences and Missions* 21, no. 1 (2008): 97-127.

Morton, Desmond. "The Cadet Movement in the Moment of Canadian Militarism, 1909-1914." *Journal of Canadian Studies* 13, (Summer 1978): 56-68.

Moses, John A. "Australian Anglican Leaders and the Great War, 1914-1918: The 'Prussian Menace,' Conscription, and National Solidarity." *Journal of Religious History* 25, no. 3 (October 2001): 306-323.

Nash, David. "Taming the God of Battles: Secular and Moral Critiques of the South African War." In *Writing a Wider War: Rethinking Gender, Race, and Identity in the South African War, 1899-1902*, edited by Greg Cuthbertson, Albert Grundlingh and Mary-Lynn Suttie, 266-286. Athens: Ohio University Press, 2002.

Nasson, Bill. *The South African War, 1899-1902*. Oxford: Oxford University Press, 1999.

Neill, Stephen. *A History of Christian Mission.* Harmondsworth: Penguin, 1964.

Nelles, H.V. *The Art of Nation-Building: Pageantry and Spectacle at Quebec's Tercentenary*. Toronto: University of Toronto Press, 1999.

Noll, Mark. *The Rise of Evangelicalism: The Age of Edward, Whitefield and the Wesleys*. Downers Grove: IVP, 2003.

O'Brien, Susan. "Eighteenth-Century Publishing Networks in the First Years of Transatlantic Evangelicalism." In *Evangelicalism: Comparative Studies of Popular Protestantism in North America, the British Isles, and Beyond, 1700-1990*, edited by Mark Noll, David Bebbington and George Rawlyk, 38-57. Oxford: Oxford University Press, 1994.

O'Leary, P.J. "William Whale: The Making of a Colonial Baptist Preacher, 1842-1903." BA thesis, University of Queensland, 1987.

Omissi, David and Andrew Thompson. Introduction: Investigating the Impact of the War." In *The Impact of the South African War*, edited by David Omissi and Andrew Thompson. Houndsmill: Palgrave, 2002.

Ostergaard, Karen. "Canadian Nationalism and Anti-Imperialism, 1896-1911." PhD diss., Dalhousie University, 1976.

Paddock, Troy R. E., ed., *A Call to Arms: Propaganda, Public Opinion, and Newspapers in the Great War*. Westport: Praeger, 2004.

Page, Robert. *The Boer War and Canadian Imperialism*. Ottawa: The Canadian Historical Association, 1987.

———. "Canada and the Imperial Idea in the Boer War Years." *Journal of Canadian Studies* 5 (February 1970): 33-49.

———. "Carl Berger and the Intellectual Origins of Canadian Imperialist Thought, 1867-1914." *Journal of Canadian Studies* 5 (August 1970): 39-43.

———. *Imperialism and Canada, 1895-1903*. Toronto: Holt, Rinehart, and Winston, 1972.

Pakenham, Thomas. "The Contribution of the Colonial Forces." In *One Flag, One Queen, One Tongue: New Zealand, The British Empire and the South African War*, edited by John Crawford and Ian McGinnon, 58-72. Auckland: Auckland University Press, 2003.

Patrick, Arthur. "'A Dreadful But Absolute Necessity': The Boer War according to The Methodist." *Church Heritage* 6, no. 4 (1980): 109-121.

Pearson, David. "Theorizing Citizenship in British Settler Societies." *Ethnic and Racial Studies* 25, no. 6 (November 2002): 989-1012.

Penlington, Norman. *Canada and Imperialism, 1896*. Toronto: University of Toronto Press, 1965.

Penny, Barbara R. "Australia's Reactions to the Boer War - A Study in Colonial Imperialism." *Journal of British Studies* 7, no. 1 (November 1967): 97-130.

———. "The Australian Debate on the Boer War." *Historical Studies*, 14 (April 1971): 526-545.

Piggin, Stuart. *Evangelical Christianity in Australia: Spirit, Word and World*. Melbourne: Oxford University Press, 1996.

———. "The American and British Contributions to Evangelicalism in Australia." In *Evangelicalism: Comparative Studies of Popular Protestantism in North America, the British Isles, and Beyond, 1700-1990*, edited by Mark Noll, David Bebbington and George Rawlyk, 290-309. Oxford: Oxford University Press, 1994.

Pocock, J.G.A. *The Discovery of Islands: Essays in British History*. Cambridge: Cambridge University Press, 2005.

Porter, A.N. *The Origins of the South African War: Joseph Chamberlain and the Diplomacy of Imperialism, 1895-99*. Manchester: Manchester University Press, 1980.

Porter, Andrew. *Religion versus Empire? British Protestant Missionaries and Overseas Expansion, 1700-1914*. Manchester: Manchester University Press, 2004.

———. "'Commerce and Christianity': The Rise and Fall of a Nineteenth-Century Missionary Slogan." *The Historical Journal* 28, no. 3 (1985): 597-621.

Porter, Bernard. *Critics of Empire: British Radicals and the Imperial Challenge*, 2nd ed. London: I.B. Tauris, 2008.

———. "The Pro-Boers in Britain." In *The South African War: The Anglo-Boer War 1899-1902*, edited by Peter Warwick, 239-257. Burnt Mill: Longman, 1980.

Potter, Simon J. "Communication and Integration: The British and Dominions Press and the British World, c.1876-1914." *Journal of Imperial and Commonwealth History* 31, no. 2 (2003): 190-206

———. "Communication and Integration: The British and Dominions Press and the British World, c.1876-1914." In *The British World: Diaspora, Culture and Identity*, edited by Carl Bridge and Kent Fedorowich, 190-206. London: Frank Cass, 2003.

Preston, R. A. *Canada and "Imperial Defence": A Study of the Origins of the British Commonwealth Defence Organisation, 1867-1919*. Toronto: University of Toronto Press, 1967.

Prior, Alan C. *Some Fell on Good Ground: A History of the Beginnings and Development of the Baptist Church in New South Wales, Australia, 1831-1965*. Sydney: Baptist Union of New South Wales, 1966.

Pugsley, Christopher. *The ANZAC Experience: New Zealand, Australia and Empire in the First World War*. Auckland: Reed, 2004.

Purcell, Victor. *The Boxer Uprising: A Background Study*. Hamden: Archon Books, 1974.

Ransford, Oliver. *The Battle of Majuba Hill: The First Boer War*. London: John Murray, 1967.

Reid, Brian A. *Our Little Army in the Field: The Canadians in South Africa*. St. Catherines: Vanwell Publishing Limited, 1996.

Reimer, Sam. *Evangelicals and the Continental Divide: The Conservative Protestant Subculture in Canada and the United States*. Montreal: McGill-Queen's University Press, 2003.

Renfree, Harry A. *Heritage and Horizon: The Baptist Story in Canada*. Mississauga: Canadian Baptist Federation, 1988.

Richards, Noel J. "Political Nonconformity at the Turn of the Twentieth Century." *Journal of Church and State* 17 (1975): 239-258.

Rutherdale, Myra. *Women and the White Man's God: Gender and Race in the Canadian Mission Field*. Vancouver: UBC Press, 2002.

Rutherford, Paul. *A Victorian Authority: The Daily Press in Late Nineteenth-Century Canada*. Toronto: University of Toronto Press, 1982.

Said, Edward. *Orientalism*. London: Penguin Books, 1978.

Samson, Jane. "The Problem of Colonialism in the Western Historiography of Christian Missions." *Religious Studies and Theology* 23 (2004): 2-26.

Schreuder, D. M. The Scramble for Southern Africa, 1877-1895: The Politics of Partition Reappraised. Cambridge: Cambridge University Press, 1980.

Semple, Neil. *The Lord's Dominion: The History of Canadian Methodism*. Montreal: McGill-Queen's University Press, 1996.

Smith, Iain R. *The Origins of the South African War, 1899-1902*. London: Longman, 1996.

———. "The Boer War," *History Today* 34 (May 1984): 46-49.

Silver, A.I. "Some Quebec Attitudes in an Age of Imperialism and Ideological Conflict." *Canadian Historical Review* 57 (December 1976): 441-460.

Sinclair, Keith. *A Destiny Apart: New Zealand's Search for National Identity*. Wellington: Allen and Unwin, 1986.

Souter, Gavin. *Lion and Kangaroo: The Initiation of Australia 1901-1919*. Sydney: Collins, 1976.

Stacey, C. P. *Canada and the Age of Conflict, 1867-1921*. Vol. 1. Toronto: University of Toronto Press, 1992.

Stanley, Brian. *The Bible and the Flag: Protestant Missions and British Imperialism in the Nineteenth and Twentieth Centuries*. Leicester: Apollos, 1990.

———. "Baptists, Anti-Slavery and the Legacy of Imperialism." *Baptist Quarterly* 42, (October 2007): 284-296.

———. "Nineteenth-Century Liberation Theology: Nonconformist Missionaries and Imperialism." *Baptist Quarterly* 32, (January 1987): 5-18.

Stanley, George F. G. *Canada's Soldiers, 1604-1954: The Military History of an Unmilitary People*. Toronto: MacMillan Company, 1954.

Sutherland, Martin. "Baptist Expansion in Colonial New Zealand." *New Zealand Journal of Baptist Research* 9, (2004): 3-23.

———. "The *NZ Baptist* as an Agent of Denominational Identity, 1874-1960." *Pacific Journal of Baptist Research* 3, no. 1 (April 2007): 23-39.

Tan, Chester. *The Boxer Catastrophe*. New York: W.W. Norton and Company Ltd., 1967.

Thompson, Andrew S. *Imperial Britain: The Empire in British Politics, c.1880–1932*. Harlow: Longman, 2000.

Thorne, Susan. *Congregational Missions and the Making of an Imperial Culture in Nineteenth-Century England*. Stanford: Stanford University Press, 1999.

Tonson, Paul. *A Handful of Grain: The Centenary History of the Baptist Union of New Zealand, Volume One – 1851-1882*. Wellington: New Zealand Baptist Historical Society, 1982.

Trainor, L. *Imperialism and Australian Nationalism: Manipulation, Conflict and Compromise in the Late Nineteenth Century*. Cambridge: Cambridge University Press, 1994.

Trinier, Harold U. *A Century of Service*. Toronto: Board of Publication of the Baptist Convention of Ontario & Quebec, 1958.

Vance, Jonathan. *Death So Noble: Memory, Meaning, and the First World War*. Vancouver: UBC Press, 1997.

Van der Waag, Ian. "War Memories, Historical Consciousness and Nationalism: South African History Writing and the Second Anglo-Boer War, 1899-1999." In *One Flag, One Queen, One Tongue: New Zealand, The British Empire and the South African War*, edited by John Crawford and Ian McGibbon, 180-204. Auckland: Auckland University Press, 2003.

Wallace, R.L. *The Australians at the Boer War*. Canberra: Australian War Memorial and Australian Government Publishing Service, 1976.

Ward, Stuart. *Australia and the British Embrace: The Demise of the Imperial Ideal*. Melbourne: Melbourne University Press, 2001.

Warwick, Peter, ed., *The South African War: The Anglo-Boer War 1899-1902*. Burnt Mill: Longman, 1980.

Webb, Todd. "How the Canadian Methodists became British: Unity, Schism, and Transatlantic Identity, 1827-54." In *Transatlantic Subjects: Ideas, Institutions, and Social Experience in Post-Revolutionary British North America*, edited by Nancy Christie, 159-198. Montreal: McGill-Queen's University Press, 2008.

———. "Making Neo-Britons: The Transatlantic Relationship between Wesleyan Methodists in Britain and the Canadas, 1815-1828." *British Journal of Canadian Studies* 18, no.1 (2005): 1-25.

———. *Transatlantic Methodists: British Wesleyanism and the Formation of an Evangelical Culture in Nineteenth-Century Ontario and Quebec*. Montreal: McGill-Queen's University Press, 2013.

Whitley, W.T. *A History of British Baptists*. London: The Kingsgate Press, 1932.

Wilcox, Craig. *Australia's Boer War: The War in South Africa, 1899–1902*. Oxford: Oxford University Press, 2002.

Wilcox, Craig. "The Australian Perspective on the War." In *One Flag, One Queen, One Tongue: New Zealand, The British Empire and the South African War*, edited by John Crawford and Ian McGibbon. Auckland: Auckland University Press, 2003.

Wilkinson, A. *Dissent or Conform? War, Peace and the English Churches, 1900-1945*. London: SCM, 1986.

Williamson, Philip. "National Days of Prayer: The Churches, the State and Public Worship in Britain, 1899–1957." *English Historical Review* 128, no. 531 (April 2013): 323-366.

Wilson, Robert S. "British Influence in the Nineteenth Century." In *Baptists in Canada: Search for Identity Amidst Diversity*, edited by Jarold K. Zeman, 21-43. Burlington: G.R. Welch, 1980.

———. "A House Divided: British Evangelical Parliamentary Influence in the Latter Nineteenth Century, 1860-1902." PhD dissertation., University of Guelph, 1973.

Wilkinson, Glenn R. *Depictions and Images of War in Edwardian Newspapers, 1899–1914*. New York: Palgrave Macmillan, 2003.

———. "'To the Front': British Newspaper Advertising and the Boer War." In *The Boer War: Direction, Experience and Image*, edited by John Gooch, 203-212. London: Frank Cass, 2000.

Withycombe, Robert S.M. "Australian Anglicans and Imperial Identity, 1900-1914." *Journal of Religious History* 25, no. 3 (October 2001): 286-305.

Wolffe, John. "Anti-Catholicism and the British Empire, 1815-1914." In *Empires of Religion*, edited by Hilary M. Carey, 43-63. New York: Palgrave Macmillan, 2008.

Author Index

Subject Index

Lightning Source UK Ltd.
Milton Keynes UK
UKHW021356240619

344942UK00009B/2447/P